STORMY'S WORLD

STORMY'S WORLD

inside porn

EDWARD SHORTER

BPT Press

First Edition

ISBN: 978-0-9842285-5-3

Also by Edward Shorter

The Madness of Fear: A History of Catatonia
(Oxford University Press)

Written in the Flesh: A History of Desire
(University of Toronto Press)

A Historical Dictionary of Psychiatry
(Oxford University Press)

Shock Therapy (with Dr. David Healy)
(Rutgers University Press)

Before Prozac: The Troubled History of
Mood Disorders in Psychiatry
(Oxford University Press)

How Everyone Became Depressed:
The Rise and Fall of the Nervous Breakdown
(Oxford University Press)

Table of Contents

Preface

Stormy's on the front page now. We know something has changed when comedian Chelsea Handler says of porn star Stormy Daniels, who allegedly had a brief affair with President Trump, "I'm into her big time. She's relentless. She's destigmatizing porn stars in front of the entire world. She's not stupid. She's not an idiot. She's not a bimbo. She's focused and she's relentless and she's honest and you know what? It's great. This is the year of the woman and she is *that*." [1]

The transformation in what used to be called "smut" is astonishing. One moment, it's a "public health crisis" in Nebraska. The next moment, Stormy's bodyguards are fighting off the photogs as she swans into a court hearing that directly affects the president.

This book sets Stormy in context. But it's not just a biopic. I'm trying to figure out the larger forces at play here. Sexuality is of enormous interest to people. They are keen to find out if the world is changing, and if they are changing with it. This is where porn comes in. People use porn to expand their erotic imaginations.

The argument of this book is that porn drives desire. It gives people new tastes, new ideas that they want to act on. We aren't in the 1950s anymore. People, today, are able to enact their fantasies, and if they see something in porn they really like, they want to do it. This is a huge change in sexuality.

So, how do you study recent changes in sexuality in the absence of surveys that touch on such subjects as roleplaying, where the pollsters seem almost too embarrassed to ask? The pornography industry is a premium portal. As one industry source said, "It's still the directors who, more than anyone else in adult, have their finger on the pulse of the industry, keeping track of the changes...since it all means money in their company's pockets—and more importantly in their own pockets! They need to know, or devise, what's popular...and, especially, keep abreast of what sells."[2]

Porn stars are part of the story of changing sexuality. And Stormy has put porn stars in the headlines. But the backstory is that internet porn has actually been changing people's tastes. Inside industry, people know this, because they live this story. But outside industry, this changing role is almost entirely unknown. We tend to dismiss porn as something sleazy, probably anti-female, and produced by scabrous smelly men with crack-addled crones.

It turns out that this stereotype isn't true at all. Stormy is not untypical, and she is, first and foremost, a businesswoman. She is, in a sense, a kind of role model for young women. The youth are huge porn streamers, and if changes in the sexuality of an entire generation may be said to have a single driver, that driver is porn.

Nobody has told this story. This is the first serious history of the adult industry based on industry sources, and of adult's reach into the real world. The account is balanced, not enthusiastic (but not highly negative either, unlike so much academic writing about porn).

Not everybody will be thrilled with the content of the following pages, because some of it is very, very explicit—it is penned by an academic historian writing a "hardcore" book. But for women on the whole, porn has been a plus. It has permitted them to enlarge their sexual imaginations in the same way as for men. Porn is a gender equalizer, in other words. Indeed, more than an equalizer. The theme of "dominance" now looms big on the female side. Women today love porn almost as much as men do, and this seems to be reflected in changes in their sexual behavior.

One of the big new themes in sexuality is the exchange of power, particularly in the direction of women like Stormy finding their place on top. She joked about spanking Donald Trump. This is not by accident. Across many fronts, women have been asserting themselves as the equals of men, and in the sexual area of roleplaying, there are a lot of women who enjoy being "tops," dominating men. In domination-submission relationships, it is increasingly the woman, not the man, who is dominant. This coincides with a new fury of women about sexual harassment in the workplace, a new unwillingness to accept molestation and unwelcome male expressions of desire. The revolt against sexual harassment, the new popularity of women-on-top: these make sense in the context of what is probably the most salient new social trend of the twenty-first century, the demand of women to be treated equally in social relationships.

The sources for this book come heavily from the chatboards and newsletters of the adult industry itself. No historian has ever used these sources before, and they offer a somewhat ribald, but totally fascinating, view of the giant enterprise of adult entertainment. The book is based on many years of research in this field, as well as extensive knowledge of the industry today, and nothing else like it exists.

I offer here a generally positive picture of porn. But it is not advocacy. There are aspects of porn that are socially very problematic. Youngsters under 18 may watch it on their personal devices and derive quite unrealistic ideas about sexuality. There is no child porn in the San Fernando Valley—where most adult porn was filmed— but that doesn't mean that child porn does not exist! It is a serious social problem. But the people I am writing about—in the adult industry—do not produce child porn, and they have formed organizations to combat it. The argument that "porn hurts women" is, I think, incorrect on the whole, given the number of young women, in particular, who view it. But the whole question of porn and female sexuality does not boil down solely to the binary choice of porn-negative feminism versus porn-positive feminism. Rather, it is layered in subtle ways. And people who think seriously about this interaction must untangle these complexities. So I am not a "porn advocate," but a scholar who is trying to tell an important story in a serious way. We will leave the advocacy to others.

Now, finally, I realize that I am not writing a newsletter. But just as I was completing the manuscript in the summer of 2019, the VR (virtual reality) mode of porn delivery started to take off. I asked myself, should I squeeze in something on this, but then I decided that VR is so huge as to warrant another whole book.

This brings us back to Stormy. As recently as a couple of years ago, porn seemed ready to become again a political issue, with the Christian Right against it, and the free-speech advocates in favor. But by the end of 2018, the GOP had given up on porn. With President Trump dating porn stars, right-wing efforts to ban porn seem increasingly hallucinatory. Journalist Tim Alberta describes "the total abandonment of pornography as a battleground in America's culture war." The industry had simply become too big, too widely watched. According to Alberta, "As of late 2018, five of the 50 most trafficked websites in the United States belong to the adult industry. The biggest site, Pornhub, typically ranks around No. 15, in the neighborhood of titans like Netflix and ESPN." In 2017, Pornhub had an average of 81 million visits per day.

But it's not just that the Right has been overwhelmed. The culture is moving on. The kind of small-town Puritanism that led the state of Alabama to ban vibrators is fading. Even politically-conservative young people believe that they have a right to expand the range of their sexual expression, and, quite simply, porn helps them do it.

Stormy and the Playboy models are now on page one. Porn is joining the mainstream.

Chapter 1:
Introduction

This is the world that Stormy Daniels began in. "We would meet at an undisclosed location like a Ralph's parking lot," said producer Roy Karch of shooting porn around 1978. Of course, porn was illegal in Los Angeles. "As the early morning sun opened the day, one by one cars would begin to arrive. The word had spread through the night where we were to meet. All of us, the cast, the crew, the gear, even the film and videotape stock—the bunch of us with our cars left behind—would be loaded into a van or small truck."

The van would pull into another parking lot, offload everything into another truck, then drive off again "into the still morning, like the porn version of the merry pranksters."

They would leave LA County for another jurisdiction less hostile to porn, and quietly unload the gear and the food from the truck. "The location would have no phones."

Why was that important?

"No chance for a rat among us to drop a dime. Like a small self-contained army of filmmakers, actors and actresses all there to do a day's work, we prepped the sets that would be shot and selected the costumes that would be worn." They checked and re-checked the entrances, "to make sure we hadn't been followed. Making sure that we had a safe hiding place for the shot tape, making sure we would remember later where we had hidden it."

They rigged up the lights, applied makeup, and ran their lines. Then shot the scenes. "As day faded into night and moans and groans were replaced by yawns," they hid the tapes, paid everyone in cash, and the director then yelled, "It's a wrap."

Back again they went to the Ralph's parking lot, whence they had set out 14 hours earlier. "Yes," said Karch, "before it was legal—when we were outlaws—man did we have some fun!"[1]

What started out in California in the trunk of somebody's car has become a multi-billion dollar industry. What began as a few simple thrusts on camera has become a great smorgasbord of carnality, featuring every orifice of the body and every font of sensual pleasure conceivable.

The horizon of change in erotic life is vast. "Sex is changing in America," wrote Al Goldstein in an early issue of *Screw*, the sex tabloid that he founded in 1968. "People are swinging, eating pussy, women are fucking more, married men are sucking cocks.... What are we supposed to do—lie?"[2]

No, not lie. The following pages tell the real story of the great changes in American sex life since the 1970s. And they tell it through the eyes of the adult entertainment industry.

This is certainly not the first book about porn, or the history of porn. There is a burgeoning academic industry devoted to the subject—exemplified in the new journal *Porn Studies*—that focuses much more on the uptake of porn and critiques of the images—rather than the basic theme of this book, which is how porn changes desire. Nobody has really written about this, except to noisily assert that porn creates rapists and so forth, which simply isn't true. But now that Stormy Daniels is on the front page of the newspaper every day, these academic *querelles* seem rather marginal. In the real world, readers want to know what is going on!

Porn Is a Story

Porn is a story, and what gives the story its narrative arc is women. They have, on the whole, had positive experiences with adult entertainment. This may seem paradoxical, in a society where it is commonly believed that "porn hurts women." Yet the story of porn may be told as the story of women's encounter with new erotic images. Women first enter in the 1970s, and they often debut as mature actresses in feature-length adult titles shot on 35mm film and possessing aspirations to serious entertainment—yet almost never "art." Porn is for arousal, not for edification.

Then came the gonzo period of shooting genital action with hand-held cameras, an era that many women found distasteful and exploitative. Then finally, in our own time, there is a strong "sex-positive" reaction to gonzo and a new porn re-emerges that is often woman-centered, appealing to women as sexual beings. This is Stormy Daniels' world. She has transitioned from model to producer.

While there has always been pornography, porn as an industry is only about thirty or forty years old. In previous times, most porn took the form of printed dirty stories in brochures and "dime novels." Producing visual porn on an industrial scale—with all the back-office functions this requires—goes back only to about the 1970s and to the move from Mafia-dominated New York to California. It was only in San Francisco, and then in the ranch-like studios of the San Fernando Valley north of Los Angeles, that porn became an industry.

All kinds of activities began that nobody could ever have contemplated in earlier times: women on top, transgendered people, bondage and domination between adults dressed up in the kind of leather and latex outfits previously associated with "Captain Marvel" comic books. Gays and lesbians strode upon the big stage. And, above all, people started to download "smut" in their living rooms and found themselves wildly excited.

This subject is important because, as UCLA psychiatrist Robert Stoller put it in 1991, "The people who create pornography embody the communications systems that make up a culture's avowed erotic desires."[3] This is an elegant thought, and I am delighted to contribute to a better understanding of our erotic messaging systems. But another way to express it is that this book is about the huge industry that has grown up to gratify a modern taste for masturbation—because porn is exactly that, material to get off on. This is not a trivial matter. Montreal domme Starla Sparklefox said in a 2015 interview, "You have the potential to deeply affect people. They're masturbating."[4]

These are solitary fantasies. But there is more than solitary pleasure. Adult entertainment may awaken new desires that people then explore with their partners. The world of porn is about expanding the sense of erotic pleasures, not just recycling images of conventional fantasies. The audience is not dirty old men wearing raincoats in afternoon cinemas, as it once was, but the whole world of women and men alike. The larger significance of the expansion of the erotic imagination is that it grows the sheer scope of what people want to undertake in bed. It is greater today than ever before.

What is pornography? This is fairly simple. What determines whether something is porn is whether it is licit or illicit. Illicit images are porn. But as something moves toward licit, it ceases to be porn. The trilogy novel *Fifty Shades of Grey*, by E.L. James, published in 2011, is a perfect illustration. *Fifty Shades of Grey* is about a sadomasochistic relationship. There is no doubt that a decade earlier, the details of this relationship—the flogging, the restraints, and the special vaginal insertions—would have been considered pornographic. But by 2014, *Fifty Shades of Grey* had sold over a hundred million copies, was translated into over fifty languages, and would produce several blockbuster movies.[5] With such an enthusiastic worldwide uptake, it is difficult to argue that *Fifty Shades of Grey* is pornography. Everything in it has moved mainline. Many of the classic novels of the twentieth century were once considered pornographic and banned in Boston. The idea that James Joyce, author of the once-banned *Ulysses* (1922), was a pornographer brings a smile to postmodern lips; he was one of the great novelists of the twentieth century. So let's not try to define pornography; megastar Gloria Leonard once quipped that, "The only difference between porn and erotica is the lighting."[6] Let's define instead what society hates—this would be the "community standard" of hatred—and then document that those tastes can change dramatically. This is porn.

Historical Perspective

In historical perspective, recent developments are astonishing. For millennia, masturbation was viewed with horror, a source of moral corruption and, in the nineteenth century, a cause of mental disease and bodily decline. The changes of the last thirty years represent the apex of change rather than the beginning. The taboo on masturbation started to end in the 1920s, and that era saw a significant expansion in the erotic imagination from face and genitals—and sex in the missionary position—to encompass deep kissing, oral sex, and even some anal sex.

Now we are in the middle of another historical sex convulsion, and once again, masturbation plays a key role, as the adult industry puts images out there that endorse female dominance, routine anal play, confusion about gender identity, and roleplay. People don't actually have to undertake all these activities in order to fantasize about them, but the conversion from imagination to action will become ever more frequent. Women's revolt against harassment is the public face of femdom roleplaying in private.

As I said in my previous book, *Written in the Flesh*, composing the history of sexuality from the Middle Ages to about the middle of the nineteenth century was like writing the history of a glacier[7]: all frozen in ice, stretching endlessly for centuries and millennia under the tutelage of the Church and the privations of rural life. Then, in the middle of the nineteenth century, a great awakening began, as the sexual palette began to expand from the missionary position to encompass other erotic zones of the body. This trend towards total body sex reached an apparent culmination in the 1960s, and when I wrote *Written in the Flesh* in 2005, I thought there would be little more to say since the Sixties about the history of sexuality in subsequent decades. What else could change?

But I was wrong. The last several decades have seen big changes in sexual behavior and erotic imaging. This will be apparent to anyone who has worked in a place like the Kinsey Institute for Sex Research in Bloomington, Indiana, with its tremendous archive of historical pornography. The images today on the internet simply did not exist, even in concept, in the earlier twentieth century.

Think of the changes of the last thirty years. "I love reverse gangbangs," said male star Mick Blue in 2015, "because everywhere on your body something is going on. It's like a total sexual overload."[8] (In a "reverse gangbang," a single male takes on a number of females simultaneously.) This kind of complete body involvement applies thoroughly, though perhaps a bit less flamboyantly, to the sexual spheres that have been changing. In transgendering, this kind of total body event has occurred; likewise, in fetish/BDSM. This complete body involvement means largely dominance, in that the feeling of domination itself is a psychological one. However, the submissive male or female may be called upon to look the subordinate role; the "top," or dominant partner, should look commanding. As for the acceleration of the anal side, that's a pretty specific body part. But the act of penetrating the anus—as, for example, the woman "pegging" the man—heaves both of their bodies back and forth.

Porn was a rebellion against the devaluation of sex in the 1960s, and before that had prevailed among married couples—not in society as a whole. Having conceived one or two children early in their marriage, married people often lost interest in sex; we are well informed here about the upper middle classes. John Cuber and Peggy Harroff, who interviewed 437 well-situated individuals, almost all of them married, in the 1960s found, "The overriding fact seems to be that for the majority, by the middle years, sex has become almost nonexistent, something to be stifled, or a matter about which they are downright afraid and negative."[9] So the revolution that took place in adult entertainment in the 1970s and after, for both sexes, should be understood as a reaction against this "devaluation of sex." Al Goldstein, publisher of *Screw* magazine, wrote of those years, "The American libido was still firmly chained in the backyard, hidden from company as if it were a cretinous child."[10]

What was resisted by these couples was the notion that sex may be an intensely sensual experience, involving all the orifices, the limbs, and the very totality of the body itself. One thinks of the number of sexual acts previously illegal, especially in the southern states: the use of vibrators, oral and anal sex, homosexuality, and multiple partners. The community is quite right in fearing sensuality, in that it distracts people from social duties, such as churchgoing on Sunday mornings (rather than dressing up in latex and playing). The eroticized couple is a threat to community ties. As New York pornographer Joe Gallant said in 2005, "I really believe that true pornography, particularly amateur pornography, is the last rebel outpost in society."[11]

Porn revalorizes sex by giving people access to images. It may, or may not, revitalize marriages, but it certainly reverses the previous psychological devalorization of sex—which exists within some relationships even today. Gaining access to images awakens intense desires. Perhaps these newly ardent men and women will stifle the desire within them and not act on it. Or, perhaps, the images will spur them to mobilize—to adultery, divorce, ending the flat-lined relationship, or going for the first time to a gay bar.

What adult images today do is to valorize the entire body as an instrument of pleasure. In the 1920s, the great German psychiatrist Kurt Schneider coined a term for this total-body experience that anticipated current developments. He called it "the body's entire feeling of corporization" (*das Gesamtausdehnungscharakter des Leibes*[12]); he wasn't talking about sex, but it can mean, as well, the sexual involvement of the entire body, as opposed to merely the face and genitals. This desire for total body involvement has been latent for a long time. But, recently, what has changed is a desire to image the body visually and make it come alive in the *imagination*. Here is where the internet enters. It is an internet of images. We look at intensely sensual experiences, such as domination-submission or a double- or triple-penetration scene, and feel that the entire body is involved.

I cited psychiatry a moment ago. I have spent many years writing the history of the discipline. Is any of this sexual material grist for psychiatry? The answer is no. Of course, psychiatric disorders can have sexual manifestations, such as in the case of the psychopath who commits rape. But everything in this book is fully consensual, and none of it is pathological. Children are never involved. Transgender, girl/girl, female dominance, all of these new themes remain bands upon the spectrum of non-pathological sexuality. There are no victims, and everybody involved is thrilled. Official psychiatry's attempts to pathologize everything that is not part of the 1950s sex canon evoke ridicule.[13] It is not pathology that is under the microscope here, but the giddiness of liberation.

This is not the first history of pornography, but it is the first history to see pornography as based on desire rather than on "smut." Dirty pictures go back to the cavemen. But pornography, as an industry, dates from the decades after the Second World War. Porn has had its historians, whose approach is a leer and a frown. For example, in 1964, the Englishman H. Montgomery Hyde produced *A History of Pornography* that combines nudge-nudge peeping tomism with the conventional sexual judgments of the day (BDSM is "perversion").[14] Alas, porn has not fared well in the Senior Common Room of the university profs, who see the porners as "sinister, cigar-chewing humanoids."[15] The present account differs from this prim clucking in trying to understand porn on its own terms, and in using industry sources (which few have ever consulted[16]).

What Is Porn Good For?

Is porn all good news? No, it is not. Observers have raised the problem of young men, in particular, learning porn scenarios, then expecting their surprised and dismayed girlfriends to rehearse them. And it is true that, if your view of the sex space is derived mainly from Pornhub, you will make an unsatisfying first date. Yet these fears about young men reducing women to generic porn stars miss an essential point: young women stream porn, too. Yet it is often not the same porn that young men view. There is a huge variety of "sex-positive porn," adult entertainment produced for women that empowers them sexually, rather than simply making of them men's sexual receptacles. Women's sexual agency is the key concept. This rapidly growing market segment gives women agency to fashion their own fantasies about what happens in bed, rather than being just the passive recipients of scripts that males have learned online. So, yes, the prewritten scenarios of young men can be a problem, unless they are matched by the prewritten—but different—scenarios of their female companions.

But here's a moment of reality-testing: Just as people do not usually re-enact the auto chase scenes they see in films, they do not necessarily re-enact the sex images they consume—the three-ways, the extravagant rituals of domination and submission, or the transsexual men who look like women. But these images place the concepts in people's minds. Viewers become aware that such behavior is possible, and they aspire to it in some lesser and modulated manner that is nonetheless real and meaningful for them. So, it is a history of putting new ideas in people's heads in the way that the novel *Fifty Shades of Grey* has done for roleplays of dominance and submission. This goes way beyond changing where the legs go in bed. It changes how people imagine sex—and then giving them guidance when they start imagining it in new ways. BDSM moviemaker Dee Severe said one reaction to *Fifty Shades of Grey* had been, "Hey, that was kind of hot. I'd like to try some of that with my beloved but I don't know what I'm doing so I feel intimidated. Where can I get some instructions?"[17]

In the adult industry, sales of sex toys have gone through the ceiling after the success of *Fifty Shades of Grey*. The novel owed its precedent-shattering triumph to its awakening of the sexual imagination. "We are on the verge of a sexual revolution," said one porn-industry insider in 2012. "Never before has the media and regular people talked about sex like this. Women who have never read erotic fiction before are now reading it on a regular basis. (You can even find these books at Costco and the airport!)."[18]

Pornography is not just seven-minute hardcore film loops for solitary pleasure. It may also deepen relationships. At one point, "porn" meant the brief stroke-loop, aimed almost exclusively at the male masturbatory market. Yet, after that came couples-oriented feature films. To be sure, as pointed out above, there was an intermission in the 1980s and 90s of what was called "gonzo"—hand-held camera-shooting without a plot. But then adult entertainment started, once again, to speak to couples. Accordingly, the industry has pivoted towards the women's market, also called couples' porn, emphasizing plot and character instead of the dubbed-in moans of the classic stroke vid. Couples porn, too, expands the erotic imagination, but in the context of female agency rather than as a solo male experience.

People in adult have always known they were opening doors. In 1972, at the obscenity trial of the movie *Deep Throat*, the defense called to the stand a California professor who said that "*Deep Throat* has redeeming social value because it might encourage people to expand their sexual horizons."[19] That is exactly right. Expanding sexual horizons is called personality development, and entire armies of counselors are devoted it. The premise is that frankness is healthier than repression.

Porn was once in the province of young males and "raincoaters," men wearing raincoats who would furtively visit the adult movie houses of the day (and masturbate under the raincoat). No more. Porn is becoming a marker of the sexual activation of women under 45, married and unmarried. This group was on the receiving end of the sex-negative agitation of the 1970s and after, and it is the group that is now using porn to experience a sexual mobilization. (In 2014, among Canadian women ages 18-24, 1 in 7 downloaded porn within the last month, up from 1 in 50 in 2004—see Chapter 20.) There is a tension between orgiastic sex and domestication, and women today are showing a definite fantasy interest in such experiences as "pegging," where the woman, wearing a dildo harness, penetrates her partner's anus, and "cock cages," devices that women impose on their partners to completely control their sexuality: no masturbation for you without permission! This is so foreign to women's traditional sexual experience that one wonders what deeper vein is being tapped here. Who are the women interested in this wild, wild stuff that is almost off the charts in terms of lived experience and traditional sex roles? Are these the nurturing mothers and retiring wives as we've known them over hundreds of years, or different creatures entirely, equal to men in work—and in play as well?

The Business of Porn

We can view the history of porn as business history, as changes in supply and demand.

The *supply* of adult material began to change in the 1960s with the popularity of "pulp fiction," cheap paperbacks on "lesbianism" (in quotes, because it was written by and for males, not by and for lesbians), or sadomasochism, subjects that previously, as one disapproving editorialist put it, "used to be treated primarily in medical journals."[20] The crucial moment in the history of supply, however, was the shift from prose "smut" in cheap pulp fiction to images, first in movies on cassette players and DVDs, then on the internet. Images grip the sexual imagination far more powerfully than does prose. While dirty pictures have always been available underground, in the United States, they were difficult to obtain, were often illegal to possess (depending on state law), and would be accompanied by social ruin if discovered.

On the demand side, the adult entertainment industry opened up new tastes, and it was these tastes, as much as the technical accessibility of images, that drove adult entertainment to become the multi-billion dollar globe-spanning industry that it is today. In the 1980s, this new availability created, as director and performer Mike South said, "a rapidly growing demand for our product; we raced to fill it, and when we filled it we kept increasing output, to the point that the market split into vertical markets; no longer was generic porn viable, there was so much of it that the consumer could satisfy his fetish by renting titles that were specifically shot for his likes. Those niches further branched into micro niches...."[21] All these micro-niches corresponded to new tastes! The avalanche of porn was shaping the nature of desire itself.

Nature or Nurture?

Many people in industry go on the assumption that there is a latent "twisted fuck gene"—in BDSM producer Colin Rowntree's phrase—that exposure to porn then activates.[22] Once this gene is activated, its clamor would demand porn. That is one approach.

The other approach is to say that, sexually, we are a tabula rasa, a blank slate onto which circumstances write what they will. You may not know that you like something until you've been exposed to it. One female blogger said, "Once women start exploring they may realize they like something they had never thought about before. For example, looking at naked women is something that turns me on, but I think a lot of women don't know they like something until they've seen it."[23] Gay or not? For years, the psychoanalytic view maintained that patterns of toilet training determined around age three whether one would turn out homosexual. Genes and biology, in this view, had nothing to do with it. Born with a taste for BDSM? For years, a social-work approach said that abuse in early childhood gave people a taste for "abusing" others as adults (a view that completely misunderstood what BDSM is all about—but we come to that later). So nurture has had some noisy advocates.

Yet when it comes to the changes of the last thirty years, I am more on the nurture side than nature. I don't think we were born with a taste for bisexuality or for participating in threesomes. These are ideas that the culture—in this case, adult entertainment—implants in our minds. So nurture wins.

But it's more complicated. The relationship probably goes back and forth, or is reciprocal. First, a leading group of sexual innovators develops a taste for something, let's say, giving "facials," men ejaculating on women's faces. Industry, ever sensitive to changes in real-world demand (because this is how they make their money), perceives this new taste and begins to develop material to satisfy it. This material then goes on the net and becomes accessible to everybody, and there is a massive response to what was initially an elite initiative: now everybody wants to see facials. Men and women alike love them, is the view. Industry floods the market with facials so that virtually every porn video finishes with one. So, we are not born with a taste for facials, but they become somehow so gratifying that we feel we were born with it.

Thus, in the case of facials, yes: society has changed our tastes by creating a new demand. And yes again, industry changes society by exposing great numbers of people to the new supply and inculcating in them a taste for it. The relationship between porn and behavior is reciprocal, in other words: each influences the other at some point in the porn "cycle." And it is a cycle, because sooner or later the taste for facials will probably ebb, just as a 1950s Frederick's-of-Hollywood taste for pink undies has now ebbed. (And Frederick's is currently out of the brick-and-mortar retail business.)

Then there is fetish, sexual accelerants that intensify desire. Makeup and tight-lacing have always existed in court circles as sexual accelerants (although most common people used neither). Fetish and BDSM are also sexual accelerants. BDSM is age-old, but fetish as a sexual accelerant only goes back to around 1870. Both BDSM and fetish are *perceived* by players as overwhelmingly biological, yet the former has a deep historic existence, while the latter does not. So here, adult images and biology reinforce each other. An initial demand, let's say for bondage, exists; the adult industry reinforces it by broadcasting bondage images that people greedily seize upon. And the behavior then spreads virally, in the way that BDSM and fetish are spreading today. It is this reciprocal back-and-forth between the supply of images and the demand of viewers that has fueled the growth of the multi-billion dollar adult industry over the past thirty years.

Currently, the industry is working hard to satisfy a mass market for other tastes as well, which an *avant garde* elite may first have explored. We see this in transsexuality, the current passion for anal sex, the concept of the dominant woman, and porous boundaries between heterosexuality and homosexuality. There is virtually no evidence that these have been present historically in any but minuscule manifestations. And then, in the last ten years, all these sixth-graders came to believe that they are transgendered "females born inside a male body." Really? This is a phenomenon of suggestion (that I intend to consider in a separate volume). And a huge amount of suggestion, proposing to us new tastes and behaviors, comes from porn.

There are also societal changes in the background. Expanding the erotic imagination went hand in hand with a general increase in hedonism after the 1970s: fine wines, gourmet dining, the physical pleasures of a workout, the thrill of a trim, lithe body—all were part and parcel of a general surge of interest in sensual pleasure. Hedonism shows up in the sexual realm as well in the sensualization of the sexual experience. Sex may or may not be a sensuous experience. But, since the 1970s, the sensuous side—the emphasis on lingering foreplay, creams and oils, and sex toys—has come increasingly to the fore. (Kama Sutra's Oil of Love debuted in 1969.) Elizabeth Bergland, spokesperson for the fetish manufacturer Spartacus Enterprises, said in 2008, "Sexual pleasure isn't just derived from the basic physical act of intercourse and orgasm. Rather, what we call sex can be a complete, immersive experience, one that engages every mode of human perception."[24]

So what is it that drives the growth of adult entertainment? The answer lies readily at hand. It is the willingness of people to spend hard-earned cash in order to realize the experiences that thrill them, for example in *Fifty Shades of Grey*; or to pay $5 per minute to interact with a cam girl, who will seem to be excited at the prospect of you having an orgasm; or for you, a veritable bear of a man, to discover that you don't look half-bad in hose and heels. People hunger for this, and they are willing to pay for it.

Increasingly, it is the growing female market that is powering porn. Younger women, in particular, are discovering adult entertainment as portals to new kinds of pleasures they would like to experiment with. Older women have constituted an eager market for *Fifty Shades of Grey*, and are now flooding into the toy stores or going online to order contrivances their mothers would have viewed with horror.

This story is kind of dirty, isn't it? No, it's not. With a few exceptions, there is nothing sleazy or scabrous about most corners of the business. The porners are proud of what they do and go to work in light modern offices, not scuzzy basements, with a sense of mission and accomplishment. The morale of the industry verges on the messianic, putting a lie to public assumptions about furtive unshaved brutes exploiting drugged-out dollies. Says Holly Ruprecht, a sales executive with Cybersocket, "I love what I do and I love what our business does! I am proud of the work we all do to bring sexuality and sexual freedom and acceptance to the front lines."[25] The female "talent," the models and performers in front of the camera, usually migrate away in their late twenties, sometimes going from behind the camera to executive functions. But the Holly Ruprechts of porn tend to be enthusiastic lifers.

This is Stormy's world. Many of these people are wonderfully interesting, and their contributions to enlarging the sexual palette are epochal. Yet their achievements tend to be forgotten, because no one has really told the story of adult entertainment and how it has changed over the last thirty years.

So this is the inside story.

Chapter 2
East Coast, West Coast

Porn Valley began in the San Fernando Valley north of Los Angeles around the mid-1970s. The big problem was the continuing harassment that directors endured from the Los Angeles Police Department. Don Fernando, who began acting in 1975 at age 28 (with *Rites of Uranus),* described the porners' routines that were meant to avoid arrest: the Big Boy Hamburger on Van Nuys Boulevard in Sherman Oaks was the hub. "The MUAs [makeup artists]—three on a feature was common back then—the PC [principal cameraman] and talent would arrive at the Big Boy. Most every male stud was local and had a car then, but a lot of the female talent lived in other states and arrived at World Modeling by Greyhound Bus the day before and usually arrived at the Big Boy by taxi from their motel.

"Everybody would grab breakfast to go, the PC would hand the people with cars a slip of paper with the address and tel. number of the location and a designated route to get to the location. So—you would have 10-20 vehicles taking a dozen separate routes (some basically direct but some pretty much in a circle) to get to the same place to throw off the vice cops. Everybody knew what the L.A.P.D.'s undercover Ford sedans looked like from the rear view mirror so we had instructions that if we were tailed to go to wherever we resided and call the location to receive further instructions....

"Us porn talent were rebels then and pretty much anti-establishment and got a hoot whenever we pulled a shoot off confusing L.A.P.D. Vice.... [It was] good times."[1]

But let's not get ahead of our story. There was a time when pornography was concentrated on the East Coast, rather than the West. The industry's early days were set in New York, luxuriating in its huge pool of female talent.

The New York Scene

Where did it all begin? Maybe with this totally forgettable flick, *Lust Weekend*, shot by Kansas City boy Ron Sullivan (later "Henri Pachard") in Manhattan in 1967. It was his first film, hardcore BDSM for the "grindhouse" cinema market. Unlike the many other porn films of the 60s that floated in semi-legal obscurity, this film marked the beginning of a vast industry. Pachard directed 359 more, and acted in 89, until his death in 2008.

There was a whole porn film scene in New York. Among the most prominent figures was director Cecil Howard, later considered "the very top producer/director of adult stuff."[2] Howard entered the industry in 1971 at 39, and in 1975 directed his first film, *Illusion of Love*, starring Jamie Gillis (Jamey Ira Gurman), later a major male talent. Howard remains known even today for *October Silk* (1980), starring Samantha Fox, Gloria Leonard, and Candida Royalle, later huge names. This was an intensely New York scene.

Kathryn Hartman, a pro-domme in New York in the 1970s who gravitated from Mafia-dominated Star Distributors to the toymaker Nasstoys, recalled the scene: "These were the old-school porn days of wine and roses before our industry became more mainstream. There was a rough edge and a decadent flavor...that was exhilarating at that time and Times Square was still a red light district."[3]

Part of this perfervid New York world was Roberta Findlay, who together with her husband Michael Findlay in the 1960s and early 70s, made a series of horror films with a sadomasochistic overlay. She then turned to porn, and with Cecil Howard directed *Fantasex* in 1976. (She often acted under the name Anna Riva.) After the death of her husband Michael in 1977 in a gruesome helicopter accident, Findlay became one of the first female sex-positive directors in 1982 with *The Playgirl*, featuring powerhouse porn stars Veronica Hart and Candida Royalle. (Something of a derogation from this was her 1985 flick *Shauna*, a bathos-filled account of the life of porn star Shauna Grant—see below).

Pachard himself went on to film such early classics as *Babylon Pink* (1979), lensed by Roberta Findlay and starring Vanessa del Rio, Samantha Fox, and Eric Edwards—who all later became mega names. ("A monster, monster hit movie,"

19

Pachard later said. "Money came in so fast we didn't have time to [count] it."[4]) As well, Pachard shot *The Devil in Miss Jones Part II* in 1982. Considerably before fellow New York producer Candida Royalle became the first woman director to film women-friendly porn, Pachard was doing so, depicting female sexual fantasies (in addition to BDSM, which he favored and, later, anal). And in front of Pachard's camera—which, in the days of film, he felt too uncertain to shoot with himself—trooped many of the stars of the golden age, such as Georgina Spelvin and Ron Jeremy. "I wanted to become the next Alex de Renzy," Pachard later said.[5] (De Renzy was the prolific California cinematographer and producer who brought the porn concept back from Denmark.)

Organized Crime

So the New York scene had a distinctive cast of characters that owed nothing to California. But there was a problem. On the East Coast, the involvement with organized crime was heavy. The Mafia's takeover of the distribution of porn goes back at least to the 1960s. Before then, there was probably not enough money involved to justify interest by organized crime. In 1969, *The New York Times* reported, "Organized crime has gained a foothold in the lucrative market of hard-core pornography." A New York prosecutor said that a newly-created joint federal-state-local task force "had uncovered evidence showing the infiltration of organized crime groups into the area of distribution of hardcore obscene material."[6] The pornography of smutty novels, dirty magazines, the first x-rated pictures of the 1970s such as *Deep Throat*, as well as the film loops of the peep shows, were the province of the East Coast, and it is not widely remembered that it was distributed by the Mafia. Between around 1950 and 1980, the Mafia had a virtually monopoly on shipping porn from the wholesalers to the retailers, although organized crime was little involved in making it.

Al Goldstein founded *Screw* in 1968, and Goldstein recalled that it had been Gambino capo Robert ("DiB") DiBernardo who was his principal protector. If local thugs attempted to bully Goldstein, a simple call to DiB would suffice to silence them. At first, the morally conservative Italian gangsters were unhappy with *Screw*'s in-your-face sexuality. Yet, "they were impressed with my public battles, setting legal precedents, the first proud pornographer." Goldstein continued, "As smut became more mainstream in the wake of *Screw*, DiB's Star Distributors became the largest porn film distributor in the country. And the word on the street was nobody fucks with Goldstein."[7] (Astro News distributed *Screw* in New York, Star Distributors in the rest of the country; both companies were Mafia-controlled. DiBernardo also partnered with Times Square "Sultan of Smut" Richard Basciano, owner of porn-palace Show World, among other properties.[8])

An FBI raid on a Brooklyn warehouse in 1969 netted a huge trove, including "24 8-mm films containing heterosexual and homosexual material." Said Judge Jacob Mishler, "If these aren't obscene, I don't know what is." And sure enough, in 1971, four members of the Colombo family and three associates were convicted of "conspiracy and illegal transportation of pornographic movies and other paraphernalia."[9]

It wasn't just a local New York operation. The Mafia was shipping porn all over the country from their Brooklyn warehouse. Howard Levine, later a prominent executive for the studio Vivid (and after 2011 owner of Exile Distribution), recalled the early days of selling video tapes off the back of his truck in San Francisco. Levine was from Cleveland. He had started working on the West Coast for David Sturman, porn boss Reuben Sturman's son, in 1984. "It was very territorial back then. You didn't really fuck with someone else's customer or you would get a visit."[10]

In 1969, a federal grand jury indicted "a multi-million-dollar pornography ring" that was shipping porn to Pittsburgh, Cleveland, Rochester, and Southfield, Minnesota. Ringleaders were Cosmo and Frank Cangiano of Brooklyn. What else did the investigators find? "$26,000 in counterfeit money and a quantity of stolen stock certificates."[11] So these were not just high-spirited porn-connoisseurs.

Although the Mafia generally did not mix in the production of the usually small-scale movies, it does seem to have taken a hand in financing the bigger screen hits, such as *Deep Throat* that streeted in 1972. Veteran porn-producer Gerard Damiano shot the film in Miami in six days on a $25,000 budget. The profits were to be shared three ways, but once the film started making big bucks, Damiano's partners informed him he'd get his $25,000 back and that would be it.

"That sounds like a bad deal," an inquiring *New York Times* reporter told Damiano.

"I can't talk about it," said Damiano.

"Why?"

"Look," he said, "you want me to get both my legs broken?"[12]

(Al Goldstein confirmed that *Throat* was funded by a branch of the Colombo Family, and that a round of oral sex that he later received from Linda Lovelace was intended as a reward to Goldstein from The Family for the favorable review in *Screw*.[13])

An aura of menace thus hung around porn on the East Coast in the 1960s and 70s. Organized crime was heavily involved in the reproduction and distribution of 8mm silent loops for sale, and the summer of 1973 in New York was filled with police raids on Mafia film laboratories.[14] There was a good deal of social interaction in New York between swingers on the porn scene and mobsters such as Lou ("Butchie") Peraino, who financed *Deep Throat*, so it was not as though there were two solitudes. But indeed, the mob was present.[15]

In this connection, the figure bobs up of Reuben Sturman, one of the classic names in the early history of porn, who is credited by some as an early founder— along with Hugh Hefner—of the modern U.S. sex industry.[16] Sturman was "the peep show king," supplying adult shops with 8mm viewing booths and the porn loops that the raincoats watched for a quarter a two-minute pop. He had 200 shops nationwide, making a multi-million dollar income. Sturman had started out in Cleveland, where he ran the distributor and content provider Sovereign News, later establishing the distributor General Video of America. He acquired a second home—in addition to the one in Cleveland—in Van Nuys in the Valley in the 1980s.

A number of other people who later became key industry figures started out working for Sturman, such as Al Bloom. Bloom's father-in-law, a Sturman operative, recommended Bloom to Sturman as a salesman for a distribution company in the Midwest that Sturman had just purchased, Capitol News. Bloom's memories of these years were very positive: "I loved it from the start. So much intrigue, so much danger, and such interesting people back then—real pioneers, willing to risk arrest for doing something they believed in."[17] Bloom was vice-president of Sturman's studio, Vidco, in Canoga Park in the Valley.

Sturman had close ties to the Gambino family. CBC reporter Max Allen recalled having dinner with Sturman in the back room of an Italian Mafia restaurant, with Max at one end of the long table and Reuben at the other, along with ten of his "Mafia thugs" lined up on the side. Allen called Sturman "the boss of porno in the United States."[18] Reuben and his son, David, were both sentenced in 1991 for income tax evasion,[19] and Sturman died in 1997 in a federal prison in Lexington, Kentucky of natural causes. One law enforcement officer estimated that Sturman's adult shops and video companies took in "between $1 million and $2 million a day," and his fortune was said to be "more than $100 million."[20]

The Mafia was always a secondary theme in the history of the industry. At first, said male porn star Eric Edwards, who entered the biz in New York in 1969, "the public thought we were being run by the Mafia. But for the most part, this business has always been run by Jews. Just normal businessmen—smart guys who know how to make a buck."[21]

Then, with the move of the industry to the West Coast, the Mafia involvement became limited to distribution (where, however, it was extensive). By 1981 *The New York Times* could state that organized crime was not involved in making "sex movies,"—most were produced on the West Coast—though, certainly, the Mafia still figured in the distribution of videotapes; blanks could be factory-bought for $15 and sold, after content was added, for $90-100.[22] In 1999, the *Los Angeles Times* quoted an unnamed FBI source as saying, "There is little indication today that pornography is controlled by organized crime."[23] Producer Colin Rowntree, when asked in 2015 about the involvement of organized crime in adult, said, "In my 21 years online, I have never seen a trace of it in the internet sector."[24] (A measure of how disconnected the industry became from its Mafia past was *AVN's [Adult Video News]* celebration in 2004 of Mary Fried, on the occasion of her retirement, as "the office manager for industry pioneers Ted Rothstein and Robert (DB) DiBernardo...."[25])

Porn in the U.S. has always been bicoastal, with New York as the main center of production and distribution until the 1980s. All the while, the West Coast was becoming steadily more influential.

San Francisco

Before the mid-1970s, the Los Angeles Police Department made LA too hot a scene to shoot porn in. On the West Coast, San Francisco, with its "Summer of Love" and Haight-Ashbury district as a beacon of sexual innovation, became the epicenter of porn production. By 1969, San Francisco had become, as historian Jeffry Escoffier puts it, "the first American city where hardcore movies played in theaters throughout the city." The 28 movie houses offered basically hardcore loops, "simple stories of housewives seducing delivery boys or of thieves forcing their victims to perform sex acts."[26]

Film critic Richard Corliss writes, "The San Francisco films have a grainy, cinema-verité style and a behavioral openness that seems a residue of the Summer of Love."[27] No fan of porn, in 1971 Dianne Feinstein, then president of the city's

Board of Supervisors and later U.S. Senator, called San Francisco the "smut capital of the United States."[28] Write authors Eddie Muller and Daniel Faris, "There seemed to be an endless supply of groovy hippy chicks wearing nothing but flowers in their hair, who'd have sex on-camera in exchange for some really good dope."[29] The film *Hot Circuit* (1971) came out of this milieu, featuring "happy hippies from the Bay Area," as film-historian Jim Holliday put it in 1986, "[who] demonstrate an enthusiasm for sex that allows the picture to hold up some sixteen years later."[30]

Porno films in San Francisco seem to have been initiated in the 1960s by California-born Alex de Renzy, who produced a series of porno loops for the coin machines and smokers known as "San Francisco Shorts." After porn was legalized in Denmark in 1967, de Renzy traveled to Copenhagen, filmed Denmark's first sex fair, and released in 1970 what blogger Luke Ford claims is "the first feature film showing sexual intercourse," *Pornography in Denmark.*[31] The point of the Denmark documentary was to show hardcore scenes of people having sex, not to explain to a learned audience why Denmark led the international porn wave. "People stood in line for hours to see it," journalist Joe Kukura reports. "This would effectively legalize the showing of penetration on screen, and San Francisco was off to the races at becoming a porn-making and porn-watching mecca."[32]

Jim and Artie Mitchell, who ran the O'Farrell theater, a strip-joint adult-film house, produced 14 movies in the years 1970 to 1987. Notably, the Mitchells shot *Behind the Green Door* in 1972 and *The Resurrection of Eve* in 1973. Both films became nationally celebrated in those venues where showing them was allowed. (The number of shorts and loops the Mitchells made was actually much greater; one source puts it as 227[33], starting in the late 60s.) Yet the Mitchell story ended in tragedy, as Jim shot Artie to death in 1991.

Meanwhile, de Renzy himself became a kind of cult figure within the biz, directing as "Rex Borsky " from 1990 on for his Rosebud label. Among the last films he made was *Anal Crash Test Dummies* in 1997, which gives one an idea of the humor. (He died in Los Angeles at 65 in 2001.)

Porn Valley

After discounting all the hype about the "summer of love" and the supposedly sex-ready flower children, the real reason that porn had gravitated to the Bay Area was that enforcement of anti-obscenity legislation in LA—where the rest of the movie business was located—had been tight. "You could shoot up there [in San

Francisco] said director Jim Malibu in 2001, "and not in L.A. because it was too hot police-wise."[34]

Then, in the 1970s, things began to loosen and adult entertainment started to migrate from San Francisco down to LA, quite specifically to Porn Valley, in order to draw upon the huge technical resources of Hollywood.

Porn Valley, as stated, was the San Fernando Valley, just north of Hollywood and surrounded on three sides by mountains. Porn was filmed at several locations in the Valley, but above all in Chatsworth, a district of the City of Los Angeles of about 40,000 people (the Valley is in the County of Los Angeles, but only parts of it are in the City.) And the very epicenter of filming not just porn, but a great many of the movies and TV series of Hollywood before the 1980s, was in one of the ranches of Chatsworth known as the Iverson Ranch, a 500-acre spread in the Simi Hills owned by Karl and Augusta Iverson.

Now, Los Angeles had a long tradition of producing adult literature, particularly in the "triangle" bounded by West Hollywood, Silver Lake, and North Hollywood, the latter of which is actually in the Valley.[35] But aside from the dirty bookstores of North Hollywood (which was county land), the Valley as such was less implicated in the tide of printed "smut" that, much to the concern of the Los Angeles Police Department, poured forth from these precincts in the 1960s. (But on novels, see below.)

Instead, the Valley had a lengthy cinematic tradition. Mainstream had gravitated to Chatsworth from the time of the First World War. Shooting movies there went back to the earliest days; in 1914, a short film called *Brute Force* was filmed in Chatsworth Park. The following year, 1915, filming at the Ranch began with *The Slave Girl;* in the 1920s some of the epics of Hollywood saw action at the Ranch— for example, *Tarzan and the Golden Lion* in 1927.

Desire was not lacking from the shooting schedule in Chatsworth, either, and in 1935, Marlene Dietrich starred in Josef von Sternberg's *The Devil Is a Woman*; in 1936, she featured in *Desire,* a Frank Borzage film (and co-starring Gary Cooper).

In the beginning, the San Fernando Valley was also a locus of pulp-novel porn. One of the major porn publishers, the American Art Agency, was founded by illustrator Milton Luros (born Milton Louis Rosenblatt), who in 1958 became art director of two West Coast men's magazines, *Adam* and *Knight*, which were produced in Northridge, in the Valley just adjacent to Chatsworth. He then helmed his own publishing empire, Parliament News Distributors, which started in North Hollywood, then moved to Chatsworth; the firm offered several popular porn imprints to the mass market, including Barclay House. In 1976, Luros founded Publishers' Consultants in Chatsworth, proposing a multitude of imprints including the *Anal Erotic* series. (Note that my policy on revealing the real names of industry figures is that the reader's right to be informed must be balanced against the performer's desire for privacy. If someone's birth name is already a matter of public record, I include it. Otherwise, the people quoted in these pages are entitled to anonymity.)

But after the late 60s, Porn Valley was cranking up to produce porn cinema, after decades of westerns, Superman, and *Lassie Come Home*. The first porn flick from Chatsworth meant for general release was *The Sadistic Hypnotist* in 1969, directed by Greg Corarito. A year later, in 1970, *Mona: The Virgin Nymph* debuted; produced by Bill Osco and directed by Howard Ziehm and Michael Benveniste, it was shot in the Valley. *Mona* was the first explicit porn flick, showcasing oral sex; it had a national release. There followed Larry G. Spangler's *The Life and Times of Xaviera Hollander* (1973), fashioned on the life of the well-known madam, in which "the early LA studs," including the famous John Holmes (John Curtis Estes)—known for having an enormous penis (see Chapter 12)—began to make an appearance.

Some of these earlier films were shot in Van Nuys or Reseda in the Valley. But, said talent agent Jim South (James M. Souter, Jr.), as the Valley's population grew, the studios were forced to reach further afield and began to settle in Chatsworth. The Spahn Ranch, part of the Iverson spread, saw the filming of *Lash of Lust* in 1972, featuring "female nudity and sex."

In the mid-1970s, the industry is said to have reached a truce with the LAPD in which extreme material such as urination and fisting wouldn't be shot at all, and other porn would be shot outside of LA County.[36] That opened the door part way. Then porn in the Valley became legit as the result of a couple of legal decisions. The *Miller v California* case, decided by the Supreme Court in 1973 (see Chapter 4) made it harder to prosecute "obscenity." Then, in 1988, the *People v Freeman* case "put the brakes on local prosecutors trying to get around *Miller* by charging pornographers with pimping and pandering," as one analyst put it.[37] (Hal Freeman had fought on the basis of First Amendment principles, spending almost $400,000 on his defense;[38] he died soon after his victory, but his name remains sainted in the Valley even today.)

By the 1970s, the mainline film industry had already gathered together the camera people, in the days when porn meant 16 and 35mm feature shoots, the make-up artists, the film editors, and the first-amendment lawyers (Hollywood shoots in 35 mm; to be shown in theaters, 16 mm has to be blown up to 35, producing a grainy print). These resources were so plentiful in Southern California, because they were already present for the mainstream film industry. In Chatsworth, unionized Hollywood grips, electricians, and camera operators would moonlight for non-union wages. "We needed everything Hollywood had," said Raymond Pistol, who got his start in the Valley in the 70s before moving to Las Vegas.[39] Diane Duke, executive director of the industry lobby group Free Speech Coalition, said in an interview in 2007, "People who move to Los Angeles because of the mainstream entertainment industry may not be thinking about the adult entertainment industry when they first get here. But after they have been living here, they realize that adult entertainment is available to them as a career path...There is a lot of shared talent."[40]

New Businesses in Porn Valley

"In our business, you have to be strong to prove you are a real business and not just a bunch of porn farmers." [41]

BEN JELLOUN, PRESIDENT OF INTERCLIMAX, 2006

Among the earliest of the big porn studios was Noel C. Bloom's Caballero Control Corporation; Caballero Control, one of the many pies that Reuben Sturman had a finger in, was launched by Bloom in 1974 with funds generated by a company, Swedish Erotica in San Francisco, that he and his father Bernie Bloom ran; the father published a magazine of that title, and Noel, together with Ted Gorley, produced a number of Swedish Erotica silent loops. Bloom astutely saw video coming, and as early as 1975, began transferring 8mm loops to videocassettes.[42] In 1977, Caballero Control became Caballero Home Video (Caballero, known as "the General Motors of Porn," filmed many of the classic 16 and 35mm titles of porn's "golden age" in the 1970s and early 80s, including *Insatiable* (1980), starring the great swordsman John Holmes and mega-star Marilyn Chambers. Mega-star Seka was an early performer, and Annette Haven, herself later a huge success, worked as production manager on some of the company's bigger shoots in the late 1970s. In 1979, Caballero began, with *Swedish Erotica 283,* shooting a long series of Swedish Erotica features that became the company hallmark. (In 1987, Noel Bloom sold Caballero to Al Bloom, not a relation.[43])

A string of New Yorkers began migrating to Porn Valley. Among the earliest was Roy Karch, who had been shooting 8mm loops in New York since 1972 and then produced the first adult talk radio show from 1974 to 1977, "the Underground Tonight Show." After Betty Dodson led a group of women in masturbation on the show, the station pulled the plug and, in 1977, Karch moved to the Valley.[44] He was the production manager for *Dracula Sucks*, shot in nearby Lancaster in 1978 on 35mm film. The *Reincarnation of Serena* followed in 1979 (though not released until 1983). This was the first porn shot on video in the Valley. Because of the enforcement of the California obscenity laws in LA County, some of these films were actually produced in Palm Springs. Karch later said they would "rent a house, party all night and then make a movie when we finally rolled out of bed in the morning or afternoon." His first big features in the Valley were *The Newcomers* (1983) with Peter North, and *The Sex Goddess* (1984) with Traci Lords (Nora Kuzma) and Tom Byron. Although his contributions have been widely overlooked, it was basically Karch who, with video, brought porn-from-Chatsworth into the living room.[45]

It was a year later, in 1985, that Gregory Dark (Gregg Brown, who had been a classics major at Berkeley) directed *New Wave Hookers* for VCA Pictures, starring Traci Lords and thought to have been one of the top porn titles ever made. Dark later said of Lords, "She's a great actress, a very hot girl. I've never seen a more enthusiastic performer. All the scenes in *New Wave Hookers* were very hot. The girls were competing with each other to see who could have the most orgasms.... These girls were completely wild on the set. It was a fantasy environment. I couldn't believe it."[46] *New Wave Hookers* was shot on video in the Valley, and would have been a huge hit had the company not been forced to withdraw it in 1986 following the revelation that Lords was slightly underage when it was filmed. (She was sixteen in 1984 when her career in porn began.)

The first big studio in Chatsworth was VCA, which Russ Hampshire, who had won a Bronze Star in Vietnam and then managed a McDonald's franchise in El Paso, founded in 1978 as a distributor; in 1982, VCA began filming, issuing *New Wave Hookers* in 1985. As the poster-person of the Meese Commission's antiporn prosecutions, Hampshire served a year in prison in 1988, then sold VCA to Hustler Video in 2003. (The Meese Commission was the Star Chamber of the religious right, see below.) The sign outside VCA's huge head office and warehouse said, "Trac Tech" because, as Hampshire told Frank Rich at *The New York Times* in 2001, "he wanted to stay "as innoculous [sic] as possible."[47]

Vivid

VCA's big rival in the Valley was Vivid Video. The story is this: In 1972, Reuben Sturman hired former Cleveland stockbroker Fred Hirsch to move out to California and set up a loop production company, Sunrise Films, to feed the exploding "peep show" market.[48] Sunrise also had a distribution division, and in 1979, changed its name to Adult Video Corporation. In 1981, Fred's son Steven Hirsch, born in Lyndhurst, Ohio, twenty years previously, left the family firm and began working as a sales rep for porn distributor Cal Vista Video. There he got to know another Cal Vista employee, David "Dewi" James, an older British expat. They agreed that the emerging VCR market could be expanded to include women and couples; they both quit Cal Vista, scraped together $45,000, and in 1984, formed Vivid Video in Van Nuys near Chatsworth.

Vivid put some key people behind the camera. In 1990, Howard Levine came down from San Francisco, where for five years he had been sales manager for Reuben Sturman's General Video of America, to become Vivid's national sales manager; he remained at Vivid for several decades as their senior spokesperson. And Sturman's General Video distributed Vivid's movies.[49] Marci, Steve's sister, had worked for her father from age 18 to 24; she then went off to college and returned in 1992 to function with Steve as production manager and general factotum. In 1994, Kelly Holland began directing for Vivid (as "Toni English," debuting with *Bad Girls: Lockdown*, and stayed with the company for eighty titles (before joining Playgirl TV, then founding her own company, Chick Media, then finally coming to *Penthouse*—and, in 2016, becoming owner of *Penthouse*). (On Holland, see Chapter 3.)

In front of the camera, Hirsch and James revived the old Hollywood "contract star" system, seeking out an actress who could embody the hometown girl-glamour look they wanted rather than the more "porn-chick" type actresses of yore. Thus, they came upon Ginger Lynn Allen, from Rockford, Illinois, a rising star who had just started shooting feature films including *Ball Busters* for Cal Vista in 1984. They grabbed her and, in 1985, Ginger Lynn starred in Vivid's first release, the video *Ginger*. Scriptwriter Penny Antine, who used the porn name Raven Touchstone, was keen that the Ginger films for Vivid all had a feminist spin. She later told film-historian Peter Alilunas, "I determined very early on that I was never going to show a woman in a subservient position. I was about showing the strength of women."[50]

The first cassette box cover featured Ginger as a wholesome, glamorous young woman, and such striking photos had, in the aisles of the adult stores, an electric effect. Ginger Lynn became the first Vivid Girl, a contract performer signed exclusively with that company; many more Vivid Girls followed, including Jenna Jameson, Kayden Kross, and Tera Patrick (after 2003), who became famous and went on to found their own companies.[51] (It was actually Digital Playground who first marketed Tera Patrick into stardom.) "Vivid contract girl" was a concept: In journalist Harris Gaffin's view, they all had a certain look, and in the Vivid catalogue they all had the same makeup and the same hairdo, and were shot from the same photo angle with the same lighting—so much so that a veteran photographer with a trained professional eye was unable to tell them apart![52] The point of "big-name contract girls," as they became known, was to shoot features, not loops or gonzo, because the Valley was otherwise so well-equipped to produce feature films. One did not find young women on contract in Vegas or Miami, and the contract system further reinforced the pre-eminence of the Valley in porn. So, this was the first key to Vivid's success: contract models.

The second key was packaging mainstream while shooting porn. As *AVN* staff writer Tim Connelly later put it, "The Vivid Art Department came out of mainstream design and brought a whole new design aesthetic that stunned the adult industry. Their photographers were mainstream fashion shooters, their girls were shot in state-of-the-art studios with $50,000 lighting packages. Their makeup artists were from major agencies along Wilshire Boulevard, and so were their writers, art directors and marketing managers."

"Our stuff never looked adult because no one came from adult," said Lauren Cauley, a Vivid designer.[53]

Third key: Vivid was a story-driven feature company, not a gonzo company. Levine said, "It's always been important to us to make movies that make some sense.... [Our movies] have something to say as opposed to just a number of sex scenes strung together."[54] In the mid-80s, *Playboy* contacted Hirsch and wanted Vivid to produce features for them—on 35mm film. This gave Vivid a large edge over the rest of the industry, which was shooting on video. (Film is a warmer look.) This is how Vivid erupted into the story-driven Golden Age and became the dominant symbol of that age.

Hirsch had been called "the executive most responsible for transforming a disreputable underground industry into a mainstream, multibillion-dollar business." He scored his biggest coup in 1999, when *Playboy* bought the competing

Spice Network, a cable network. But *Playboy* didn't want the hardcore channel of that network, Spice Hot, so Hirsch bought it from Spice, putting Vivid in the cable business. Vivid split Spice Hot into three channels, and turned right around and sold the whole package back to *Playboy* in 2001 for $82 million.[55] In three years, the audience for the three channels had more than quintupled from 7 million to 36 million.[56] By 2005, with such hits as *The New Devil in Miss Jones*, Vivid's revenues were about $100 million a year, and the company was said to produce about a third of all adult videos seen in the United States.[57]

Porn Valley Blossoms

It was in the 1980s that the big migration from New York to Porn Valley took place. The initial migration in the 70s was more to Van Nuys, with the large industrial buildings near the rail lines of Chatsworth becoming the center of gravity in the 80s.[58] Gloria Leonard, one of the stars in the classic *The Opening of Misty Beethoven* (1976), remembers, as a native New Yorker, when she had to start getting on the plane for tickets that cost almost more than her fee for performing. Why the move? "I think the weather started to appeal to a certain age group of guys, and there were a lot of babes out there getting off the bus each day." Another plus: there was also a lot of cocaine in The Valley, and detoxing themselves from cocaine addictions is part of the biography of a number of Valley entrepreneurs.[59]

Paul Thomas (Philip C. Toubus), or PT, one of the giant figures in the history of the industry, had been working in Montreal (acting in *The Autobiography of a Flea* in 1976), and with Pachard in New York; in 1986, Thomas brought Pachard out to Chatsworth to shoot for Vivid.[60] (Thomas stayed with Vivid thereafter as one of their main directors.) Two years later, in 1988, David Sturman, previously based in San Francisco, founded the production company Sin City Entertainment in Chatsworth; Italian porn star Rocco Siffredi made his American landing there.[61] This sealed the end of the Bay Area as a big center for heterosexual porn, although gay porn remained there.

Many felt it was just nicer working in LA than in New York. Barbara Dare (Stacy Mitnick), a later porn-megastar who had grown up in New Jersey and studied in Manhattan at the Fashion Institute of Technology, recalled with disgust shooting in New York: "I was on sets where there were no showers, no make-up artists. I had an orgy scene for an hour and the director didn't cut.... We were sweating, there were 10 people there—it was just horrible." Everybody told her it was different in

California, so she came out in 1986. "It was different. There was make-up, there was wardrobe, and people treated you like you were special."[62]

For models, the entry portal into Porn Valley was the talent agency World Modeling, first in Sherman Oaks then in Chatsworth, established in 1976 by Jim South, whom author Harris Gaffin describes as "a tall, slow-talking Texan with spit-polished black cowboy boots."[63] For a long time, it was the only modeling agency in town. "For years," said journalist Acme Anderson, "the sign hanging outside World Modeling was the Porn Valley equivalent to Sin City's Welcome to Las Vegas sign." Every big name in porn—and countless lesser aspirants—would pass through those doors. "The performers came and went, directors and producers spent hours poring through [South's] talent books...looking at Polaroids. Each week, usually on Thursdays after lunch, the masses would gather for the casting calls, giving producers an opportunity to meet the talent in person." South gave them the phone numbers of the models they were interested in. "It's a system that worked well in an era when only a few hundred titles were shot annually and the talent came from a small, largely local pool." Later, modeling agencies proliferated, and the talent came from all over the country.[64]

After the California Supreme Court legalized shooting porn in the *Freeman* case in 1988, many more videos started to be made in the Valley. Yet all was still not perfect, because LA County required a shooting permit of $100 a day and an annual fee of $1,700 for a million-dollar liability policy. You could dodge the insurance cost by shooting in a studio (which paid the insurance), but then you'd have to build a set. Or you could ignore the law and shoot, as before, on the QT. But the risk here, in addition to a fine, was confiscation of your equipment. Still, the availability of Hollywood talent was a convincing argument on behalf of the Valley, as opposed to Palm Springs or Las Vegas, and studios and directors plunged ahead.[65]

By 1999, porn was blooming in the Valley, with an estimated 200 production companies releasing annually 7,000 adult films, some studios averaging a title per week.[66] According to the *Los Angeles Times*, while Hollywood jobs were down 13 percent by 1999, jobs in porn were up 25 percent, amounting to some 20,000 positions in the local economy. Porn was considered "among the fastest growing areas on the internet," and one of five shoots in Los Angeles was a porn film.[67] At a certain point, the Valley was said to "account for more than 90 percent of the world's professionally produced porn."[68] By 1999, the Valley evidently had "the world's largest community of porn stars (around 1,600) and 50 of the top 85 porn companies. And the home-video revolution of those years accelerated this growth even more. *Adult Video News* said that home video rentals and sales climbed from $1.6 billion in 1992 to $4.1 billion in 1998.[69]

For newcomers to the big anonymous warehouse-like studios of Chatsworth, it was an age of thrills. Richard Pacheco (Howie Gordon) was 30 in 1978 when, fresh from shooting porn flicks in San Francisco (and being a *Playgirl* centerfold), he came down to the Valley. For a young hippie graduate of Antioch College, everything seemed possible: "I wanted some of whatever was out there," he later said. "I wanted a brown one and a yellow one and a red one. If there had been a green woman, I'd have wanted her, too. Sex, drugs and rock and roll. I wanted them two at a time, three at a time, in this hole and that. I wanted the fat ones and the thin ones, the smart ones and the dumb ones, the bossy ones and the slaves. I wanted them inside and outside, upside and downside. I wanted to taste it all...." [70] Appropriately, one of Pacheco's first films in 1978 was *Sensual Encounters of Every Kind*. Two years later, from this tourbillon of excitement, came Anthony Spinelli's big hit, *Talk Dirty to Me*, with Gordon (now porn-named Pacheco) as the star.

The directors felt the same excitement. What attracted Joone (Ali Davoudian), who founded Digital Playground in 1993 while he was still a student at USC School of Cinematic Arts, to porn was not sex but the freedom to shoot whatever you wanted. Independent filmmaking in mainstream went into a tailspin in the early 1990s when the big studios bought up many of the independents, said Joone. But "in adult, you can do whatever you want as long as the movie has sex in it. I always tell people to look at sex as the commercial that pays for the movie."[71]

Later, after the industry became bigger and sprawled across the country and the globe, a nostalgia lingered for "The Valley." Brittany Andrews, who entered the field in 1995 after a few years of dancing, said in 2008, "The industry back when I was in it was a much more family-oriented feeling—100 percent. There wasn't all this gonzo and degradation and anal. It was feature films being shot in 16mm. It was a more clean mentality, where girls could be stars. Everyone kind of took care of each other."[72]

With the adoption of the compulsory condom law in LA County in 2012, filming porn in Chatsworth dropped off 90 percent. Kelly Holland, then managing director for Penthouse Entertainment in Chatsworth, told the *Los Angeles Times* in 2014, "We're not doing any production locally. This month we're shooting 10 movies in Brazil. Last month we shot five movies in Europe. It's just too complex to shoot here."[73] Still, a flavor of the past lingered, with such productions as *Hot Nude Divorcees Gone Lesbo* (2012). The San Fernando Valley retained many of the industry's back-office services, and continued to be a talisman for adult entertainment.

So, these were early days, before the great changes—said Roy Karch, "before there were silicon infused breasts, teeth whiteners for female talent, blue pills [Viagra] for the male talent, hair extensions and shaved pubes... before most of you were born. Before all of that...there was simply the heat. The heat between two people doing the 'ol in-and-out.'"[74]

Chapter 3:
From the Pussycat
to the Living Room

*"In the 1970s we turned the lights on in the bedroom. This country was in
dire need of growing up about sexuality. Everyone wanted to let loose and take off the black
socks [of old-style stag films]. When we became chic and the movies started getting better,
we gave society a reason...to explore sexuality a little better."*[1]

VETERAN MALE ACTOR ERIC EDWARDS, 2006

The scene opens onto a vast Sahara of desire, watered by only the tiniest of
rivulets. There are all these couples whose flat experiences have led them
to devalue sex. But in a life without sex, there remains only the hope of
images. What was available?

Before the 1970s, there was really no pornography "industry," although there
was plenty of pornography. At the beginning, there were many narratives: pulp
novels, "girlie mags," 8mm stags, peep shows, and adult theaters. None existed on
an industrial scale. Rather, they were isolated back-room efforts, often dominated
by criminal elements, to bring some semblance of erotic inspiration to a starving
public.

What happened was that technological change compressed these narratives into
one, and it was really this compression that gave rise to an industry. Feature-length
movies shown in mainline venues began the compression. Videocassettes followed,
making it possible to view porn in one's own home; this was far better than

creeping into some sleazy theater, and far superior to buying a pulp novel that was just prose, no images. DVDs and the internet continued the compression, offering live action that was viewable in private. The journey from the dirty bookstore of the 1950s to gonzo of the late 1980s tells the story of the transformation of porn from isolated sprouts to a multi-billion dollar industry.

Stag Films

The story actually begins much earlier than the 1970s.[2] The earliest rivulet that feeds into what ultimately becomes the great torrent of online adult entertainment is the stag film, beginning in the U.S. around 1915 and generally shot on 16mm stock, not 8mm, except for the "peep" machines of the adult bookstores. Among familiar early stags were *A Free Ride, Casting Couch,* and the *Modern Magician.*[3] After the Second World War, the unknown actress in *The Nun's Story* (late 1940s) and Bettie Page in various specials of the Klaw family carried the day. The subject matter was usually hard-core eroticism, including fisting and even bestiality, and all of it was totally illegal. (Scholar Eric Schaefer situates the move of formerly "amateur-gauge" 16mm to the art theaters in 1967, when several San Francisco movie houses began screening "beaver" films.[4])

In the United States in 1973, there were about 750 theaters that showed sexually explicit films on a year-round basis. One fifth were devoted exclusively to hard-core porn, the others to "less explicit soft-core material," as *The New York Times* reported. As well, there were innumerable storefront shops with coined-operated machines showing feature films as well as loops.[5]

Erotic writer Chrissie Bentley recalled visiting movie houses showing stags in the 1970s with her pals. "Occasionally you'd see an actual customer shuffling in or out of the main door....He really would look furtive, he really would be wearing a raincoat and, nine times out of ten, he really would be wearing a flat cap, which he'd pull down over his eyes the moment he saw someone else on the street outside."

And then Chrissie and company snuck in through the fire escape. "The room seemed darker than the usual theater and the audience more restless. Rustling sounds, mostly, interspersed with heavy breathing. 'Someone,' whispered Lisa in my ear, 'is having a quiet jerkoff.'

"Only it wasn't so quiet. And it wasn't just some*one*. Judging from the rustling sounds, half the men in the room were at it."

On the screen, the plot of the movie seemed to be "how far could a cock slide up a fat woman's asshole before it bumped tips with the one that was sliding down her throat?" Chrissie and her pals were riveted.[6]

Pulp Novels

For decades, "smut" did not mean images at all, which were widely unavailable, but "pulp novels," once the main form of entertainment of adult males. Skirting the obscenity laws, the dime novels would merely suggest torrid scenes for the famous "one-armed reader," but for an audience starved of anything torrid, it was terrific. The market was heavily middle-class, middle-aged men. *The New York Times* described in 1970 the shoppers at Hyman's Book Store in Des Moines, Iowa: "The most consistent customers are the doctors, lawyers and dentists from nearby office buildings...[who] carry out the books in their briefcases." Some couples' interest was expressed: "What can I do? She won't respond to me."[7]

In the early 1950s, Universal Publishing & Distributing Corp. in New York City became a major publisher of what one bibliographer primly refers to as "digest-sized sleaze." The imprint Beacon Books is considered "the first mass-market size pornographic paperback line."[8]

Pulp scaled up. In 1959, writer William Lawrence Hamling started the Greenleaf Publishing Company in Chicago with the initial imprint Nightstand Books (of Greenleaf's Corinth Publications division). Greenleaf was based in San Diego after 1965. A series of Hamling imprints produced a torrent of pulp. Hamling was sentenced to four years in prison in 1971 for re-publishing the *Presidential Report of the Commission on Obscenity and Pornography* (original 1970)—but, this time, with erotic illustrations.

Magazines

The throaty text of the pulp novels began to give way to images, initially in the form of comic books. Pornographic comic strips were sold under the counter in tobacco shops in the 1940s and were called "Tijuana bibles." Then photo porn images began circulating widely. As early as 1955, a Senate subcommittee considering juvenile delinquency unearthed evidence that the main form of pornography was changing from the printed word, as in the pulp novels with their mildly sexy stories, to images of sex. Peter N. Chambris, the associate counsel of the committee, testified that "technology had caused changes in the nature of pornographic material. Now," he said, "color still photographs, stereoscopic photographs, color and sound movies and phonographic recordings have entered the field. Formerly the principal materials were cheaply printed cartoon booklets and photo postcards."[8]

A world of "men's magazines," or "girlie mags," began to unfold. In 1953, Hugh Hefner founded *Playboy*, featuring Marilyn Monroe from her 1949 nude calendar shoot. In January 1955, Bettie Page posed for *Playboy* wearing only a Santa Claus hat. *Playboy* turned into a huge franchise, and in 1988 Christie Hefner, Hugh's daughter, became CEO and chairwoman of Playboy Enterprises; by 2005, she had become 90th on the *Forbes* list of 100 most powerful women, helming the company to global sales of over $500 million.[9]

Bob Guccione founded *Penthouse* in 1965 in the U.K. and in the U.S. in 1969, attempting a more salacious rival to *Playboy*. Yet *Penthouse* was slow to move to the internet and had several bankruptcies. (It was finally bought by FriendFinder Networks, then acquired by veteran editor Kelly Holland in 2016.)

In 1966, Berth Milton began publishing a girlie magazine called *Private* from a bookshop in Stockholm, progressing then to films.[10] *Private* is considered the first full-color hardcore adult magazine, "the first periodical in the world to legally show sexual penetration," as blogger Luke Ford explained. Issue 2 featured a vagina close up; issue 14, in the summer of 1968, a "cum" shot.[11] In 1985, Milton, a sun-seeker, moved *Private* to Spain. In 1990, Berth Milton's son, Milton Jr., took over the company's headquarters in Barcelona; he moved the Private Media Group into video and expanded the brand to everything from Private Vodka to a Private-branded clothing line. (Milton Jr. lost control in 2001 and became CEO again in 2004.) Mara Epstein took *Private*'s U.S. sales from $250,000 in 2001 to plus $5 million two years later.[12]

Larry Flynt founded *Hustler* as *Hustler Newsletter*, bearing news of his Hustler clubs, in 1972. The magazine itself was created in 1974. The first issue announced, "Anybody can be a playboy and have a penthouse, but it takes a man to be a hustler."[13] Flynt turned the book into an enormous empire, the principal video line of which was Barely Legal, begun in 1999 and at its 150th volume by July 2015, a remarkable testimonial to the staying power of "girls who are too young to drink [but who] can have a sex party."[14] The brand went online in 2004 with Hustler TV offering hardcore. *Hustler* was always more hardcore than *Playboy*. When asked, after *Playboy* decided to drop nude photos (they were quickly restored), if he still regarded *Playboy* as a competitor, Flynt responded, "My only competitor is *Gynecological Monthly*."[15]

By 1979, the 10 leading sex magazines were selling more than 16 million copies a month. *Playboy*, the largest, had one-third of that total.[16] Of newsstand sales in 1981, 20-30 percent were said to be for products "that a decade ago would have been regarded as prurient and either barred from sale or sold under the counter."[17]

Pulp novels and magazines were, of course, sold in adult bookstores, and as the nation's appetite for porn quickened in the 1970s, the number of such stores proliferated. "Theater people have expressed dismay," said *The New York Times* in 1972, "at the deepening encroachment of pornography shops in the theater district. There are 17 such places on Eighth Avenue from 42d Street to 48th Street." The article noted that the former Ripley's Wax Museum had been taken over by the "San Francisco Adult Movie With Live Show."[18]

A Golden Age of Porn Films

"From my understanding, the old porn industry in the 70s-80s was a laid-back drug induced party, not a sado-masochistic nightmare, but that's just hearsay...."[19]

MASTER RYAN, *XBIZ* CHATBOARD, 2013

The feature films of the 1970s and 80s represented, in retrospect, a kind of golden age of porn, with plots, well-developed characters, and high production values. It was certainly more female friendly than the titles that came later. Regarded even today as a female-friendly classic is Cecil Howard's *Scoundrels* (1982), written, as were many of his movies, by Anne Wolff ("Anne Randall") and offering sensitive characters with complex motivations.[20] In the context of the coming gonzo era, the 35mm films of this period, with the warmth that film makes possible, constituted an era that many old hands would look back on with fondness and contemplate the coming gonzo with bitter regret.

Now, these porn flicks of the Golden Age had a remote predecessor, a French film, Roger Vadim's *...And God Created Woman* (1956), starring Brigitte Bardot and Curt Jürgens. Released in the U.S. in 1957, the sight of Bardot's bum unleashed a huge sensation that echoed down the decades, making her a symbol of hot nymphet sexuality and turning St. Tropez, where it was filmed, into a tourist mecca. Vadim said in a later memoir, "Something irreversible had happened. Eight million Americans went to see my film, and although it was often mutilated by women's leagues and local censors, Americans still remember it."[21]

The first commercially successful U.S. film featuring female nudity was Russ Meyer's *The Immoral Mr. Teas* in 1959, which cost $24,000 to produce and grossed more than $1.5 million on the adult circuit.[22] Mr. Teas suddenly has x-ray vision, enabling him to see women as they look without their clothes (including his psychoanalyst). There is no sex in the film. Meyer was a seminal figure—probably best known for *Faster Pussycat! Kill! Kill!* in 1966—and was a direct influence upon such later Porn Valley figures as director Ira Levine (Ernest Greene) and photographer Carlos Batts. "*The Immortal Mr. Teas* had opened the floodgates," write film historians Eddie Muller and Daniel Faris. "In the three years following its release, as many as 150 imitations paraded nude cuties across grindhouse [adult theater] screens."[23]

The nudie cuties turned many burlesque houses into adult theaters. The Pussycat Theater chain in California became a byword. Porn entrepreneur Dave Friedman said later, "Now, instead of the voyeurs staring at some tired old burlesque broad up there, live, onstage—they were suddenly looking at gorgeous, young, blond, tan California girls, in all their pristine glory, with their beautiful little breasts, and their pert little nipples, and their dimpled behinds—in Technicolor—on screens forty feet wide and twenty-five feet high."[24] The portal into adult films was opening.

The name most indissolubly linked with this early twilight land between porn loops and feature films is Bob Vosse, who worked briefly in mainstream film, then made the transition, first to soft porn and then to hard, where he spent the rest of his career. In the 1970s, he filmed in Sweden, then returned to San Francisco, his birthplace, where he worked for the Swedish Erotica Studio, introducing sound to porn loops, which hitherto had been silent.[25] Then, in 1979, he directed *Swedish Erotica 283,* the first of the long Swedish Erotica series, produced and distributed by Noel Bloom and Reuben Sturman's Caballero Control Corporation (later Caballero Home Video), founded in 1974. (Caballero introduced the large box for tapes that would stick out on display counters; it became the industry standard and was known as "the Caballero box.") The early titles in the Swedish Erotica line featured the legendary John Holmes, also known as Johnny Wadd (see Chapter 12). Some observers see the Johnny Wadd series, which began in 1971, as "the start of the star system in the adult film industry."[26]

Vosse continued to direct the Swedish Erotica line until his death in 1999 (yet the series, with his name on it as director, continued to street until the final one, number 115, appeared in 2007, including footage from Holmes, who died in 1988!).

But it is the full-length feature movies of the late 1960s and 70s on 16 or 35mm film that are the true cinematic wellspring of the adult industry. The first film to show oral-genital contact—and to be shown in mainstream theaters!—was the 1967 Swedish import *I Am Curious (Yellow)*, directed by Vilgot Sjöman, an Ingmar Bergman protégé, and starring himself and Lena Nyman: the two stage sexual intercourse, and she kisses his (flaccid) penis. It touched off a censorship brouhaha in the U.S., but was ultimately found by the Second Circuit court not to be obscene. The Wikipedia critic notes, "The film ushered in a wave of nudity and sex never before shown to the general public...pushing the limits of films."[27]

Andy Warhol's *Blue Movie,* shot in New York in 1969, was technically the first porn flick for general release, but it was seized by the police immediately and never really saw the light of day. It foreshadowed gonzo. Towards the end of the movie, Viva stares at the camera and asks, "Is it on?"

Mona: The Virgin Nymph (1970), produced by Bill Osco (son of the pharma baron) and directed by two experienced West Coast porners, Howard Ziehm and Michael Benveniste, was the first major U.S. product from Porn Valley. It had a full plot centering on the heroine's interest in oral sex and many authorities consider it the opening tip of the hardcore wedge. (Yet Mike Henderson's *Electrosex 1975,* also released in 1970—"Three female robots exhaust men with sex."—was said to be the first hardcore adult film to be advertised in New York newspapers.)

A number of porn blockbusters then followed that are almost household words even today. *Deep Throat,* directed by New Yorker Gerard Damiano, was financed by Mafia henchman Lou Peraino, filmed in Miami in six days, and starred Linda Lovelace (Linda Susan Boreman), with Harry Reems (Herbert Streicher) as the male lead. The film did not introduce ejaculation on the face, later called "facials," but it did make facials the yardstick of arousing porn. *Deep Throat* was the first porn blockbuster, costing only $25,000 to produce but said to gross $600 million (that figure has proven controversial, some calling it too high; others, based on the overwhelming worldwide uptake, too low[28]). The reception was mixed. Vincent Canby, *The New York Times* film critic, found it "junk," but really interesting junk; he was riveted the first time he saw it.[29] (*The Times* ran these musings on page one!)

Deep Throat had no Porn Valley connection, but the Valley has become indissolubly linked among antiporners to Lovelace's own story, a story that began with shooting bestiality loops.[30] Over a decades-long campaign, Gloria Steinem and other antiporn activists made her a movement figurehead because of the abuse she supposedly endured from industry.[31] But, as sociologist Chauntelle Tibbals points out, "By her own account, Linda was in no way abused or coerced by porn producers." Her husband and manager ("suitcase pimp") Chuck Traynor was clearly the villain of the piece and inflicted real suffering upon Lovelace, who went on to make other porn flicks. Tibbals judges him as "a brutally aggressive man who subjected Linda to years of violent sexual servitude."[32] Harry Reems called Lovelace's 1980 autobiography *Ordeal* "a total lie."[33] In 2013, Conner Habib, who herself had appeared in around 150 adult films, told *Slate* that Lovelace's experience was highly untypical. Most people now aren't led into porn by manipulative spouses or other terrible circumstances." Yet the myth of "falling into porn" persisted, she said. "The hundreds of well-adjusted and happy porn stars I've interacted with and the tens of thousands of porn stars who live less sensationalized lives than Lovelace are testament to the fact that her story is not ours."[34] But the larger story, for our purposes, is that *Throat* became the vehicle that brought porn into the public eye.

Porn Valley was not involved in the next big adult hit, either, *Behind the Green Door* (1972), which the Mitchell brothers filmed in San Francisco. It starred Marilyn Chambers (Marilyn Ann Briggs), whom Lovelace's soon-to-be ex-husband Traynor would marry. The title showed lesbianism, a public orgy, and even the first major depiction of interracial sex. (Johnnie Keyes, a famous black porn actor, portrayed the "African stud.") Marilyn Chambers herself did better from it financially than any previous adult performer. She also appreciated being treated respectfully as an actress by the Mitchells. When it became known that porn Marilyn was the same Marilyn who appeared simultaneously as the "mom" on boxes of Ivory Snow soap, the sensation—"a publicity man's dream," as Chambers later noted[35]—boosted the film into the stratosphere. Chambers became known as the first "porn star." She returned in 1980 with another porn blockbuster, *Insatiable*, with John Holmes; it was the top selling adult video from 1980 to 1982.

The third hit in this porn trilogy, *The Devil in Miss Jones* (1973), was directed by Damiano, and filmed in New York, but featured a cast that would soon arrive in Porn Valley: Georgina Spelvin, a widely shared theater pseudonym that Michelle Graham adopted only after the movie appeared, played the female lead (Jim Holliday called her "an incredibly accomplished sexual being")[36]; Harry Reems was again the "wood." Spelvin and Reems became Valley regulars. For connoisseurs,

Miss Jones acquired classic status, unlike *Throat*. "*Throat* is a joke," said Damiano later. "*Miss Jones* is a film."[37] (The Mafia controlled the distribution of the film.[38])

These three films—*Throat*, *Green Door*, and *Miss Jones*—took porn close to mainline. "By the mid-1970s," write Eddie Muller and Daniel Faris, "X-rated cinema had become ingrained in the culture."[39] The movies were a lighthearted, feature-length take on adult entertainment, lots of plot in between the sex and not ideal for masturbation (though not wholly unsuitable, either). It was the era of Anthony Spinelli, born in Cleveland as Sam Weinstein, who migrated from mainstream, where he played in *One Potato, Two Potato* in 1964, to shoot such porn classics as *The Dancers* in 1982. At this point, nobody had heard of gonzo.

The Golden Age (*bis*)

One other film became a byword for the epoch: *Last Tango in Paris*, shot in Paris in 1972 by Italian director Bernardo Bertolucci and released in the U.S. in 1973. Starring Marlon Brando and the baby-faced Parisian Maria Schneider (Marie Christine Gélin), the uncut version of the film featured a stand-up scene of anal intercourse that horrified—or transfixed—much of the viewing public (and sent Maria Schneider, unwarned about the scene, into a personal crisis). The film, originally titled *Il Ultimo Tango a Parigi*, was produced by a consortium of Italian, French, and U.S. companies and, despite Brando's presence, it does not really belong among the above-mentioned American triad. Yet "passez moi la beurre s'il vous plaît"—please pass the butter (as an anal lubricant)—became a wink-wink line among U.S. hipsters for many years.

There were so many others, such as Radley Metzger's *The Opening of Misty Beethoven*, a porn take-off on *Pygmalion*, in 1976 (starring Constance Money; Luke Ford regards it as the best porn film ever made[40]). Looking back, the most famous woodsman of them all—Ron Jeremy—said, "All the classics of the [golden era] are big budget films....They didn't have video, DVD, VHS, computers or the internet, it was just feature films. That was it. *Bad Girls, Fly Bi Night, Co-Ed Fever, Fascination, Roommates, Sizzle, A Girl's Best Friend*—these are all some of the real big-budget films [of that time]."[41]

These films constituted the "golden age of porn," and many pro-sex feminists regarded the titles with fondness. At Good Vibrations in San Francisco, one of the first women-centered adult stores, Honey Lee Cottrell and Susie Bright pioneered a positive approach to porn analysis. (Good Vibrations later distributed a number of films starring such feminist figures as Nina Hartley, Gloria Leonard, Annie Sprinkle, Veronica Hart, and Vanessa del Rio.)[42]

From Europe came a second stream of "art house" films that aficionados could watch, generally at small cinemas. The European stream began as loops. According to Luke Ford, the seedbed of the short European loops was the London quarter of Soho in the early 1960s. These loops were then massively exported to Europe and the U.S. What gives the story an interesting twist, however, is that in 1966, young Italian pornographer Alberto Ferro discovered these loops during a trip to London. A year later, Ferro persuaded a keen young Danish legislator to sponsor a bill decriminalizing sexually explicit books and pictures; with Denmark as the new world porn epicenter, Ferro started filming in Scandinavia, in 1970 setting up his own company in Stockholm. Here, he borrowed the name of his Swedish carpenter, Lasse Braun. Further according to Ford, in 1970, Ferro received an enthusiastic phone call from Reuben Sturman, the king of American pornography, and Sturman began importing Ferro's loops for his thriving adult-shop viewing booths. "Used in Sturman's peep shows across the United States, the ten-minute loops probably grossed over two billion dollars," writes Ford.[43]

Then we move it up a notch. In 1975, Ferro brought out *Sensations,* filmed in Belgium. It was shown at the Cannes Film Festival and was the first European porn film to succeed in the U.S. (full-page ads in the New York City papers); Sturman financed it after a brief affair with the leading performer, Brigitte Maier.[44] *Sensations* was the beginning of the porn-y European art films in mainline U.S. theaters, followed by Ferro/Braun's *Body Love* in 1978; shot in the Netherlands, it featured intra-familial sex and lots of cool music. Claude Mulot's *Les Petites Écolières,* showing events in a girls' boarding school, debuted in 1980.

Several other art-house films lit up these years as well. In 1999, Catherine Breillat's *Romance X* launched in France, an art house film featuring explicit, real sex. The heroine, Marie, played by Caroline Ducey, has a sexual relationship with Paolo, played by Rocco Siffredi. The film is of interest as an early venture into BDSM, and as a launch vehicle for Siffredi's later career in Porn Valley (see Chapter 12). In Europe, the film was shown in mainstream theaters, and was broadcast on late-night German television.

Then the industry said goodbye to shooting on 35mm film suitable for movie houses. In 1985, videotapes were only 51 percent of the adult market, by 1994, 91 percent. (And adult material had climbed from 17 percent of the total video market to 28 percent.)[45]

Film required a mastery of the cinema arts that was unnecessary in video. The directors who shot film thought that moving up from the earlier peep-show loops was a triumph of artistry. "When we went from loops to features," said veteran producer and director Wesley Emerson in 2005, "we took time and pride in the final product....Now we have DVD and we stay home and are handed hundreds of films a month, mostly gonzo—more aptly described as loops shot on video." Added pioneering African-American Johnnie Keyes, 57 in 2005, looking back with the same nostalgia, "Quite simply, the industry as a whole emphasized making good movies back then. We gave fuck-films respect."[46] (Yet a difference between porn and entertainment remained. As a producer porn-named "Zander" at his own Ground Zero Entertainment said in 2009, "Bottom line, someone is going to be masturbating to it, so if you lose sight of that, look out. It's a problem when you're 28 pages into a script and you're just getting to the first blowjob."[47])

And the sex itself in the 35mm era seemed different. In 2007, Steve Brickman at Cinderella Distributors said of the "classic porn" era, "You get the feeling that they enjoyed doing it, it was a free love type of thing. Now you watch 'em and it feels more like an assembly line. It's a job."[48] Industry gadfly Mike South said wistfully that today, "The result has all the eroticism of two dogs fucking."[49]

The Video Revolution (and DVD)

Robert Rosen, at the time editing pornographic magazines in New York, described how his girlfriend Georgina, an accomplished actress and porn star, decided to get out of 35mm adult features: "Georgina understood better than most people how, by June 1986, video had revolutionized the porn biz. With cameras suddenly affordable and videotape a fraction of the cost of film, it now took only a couple of grand to shoot a 'professional quality' fuck flick. And out there in the great porno universe, enough people had been scraping together enough money to shoot over 2,000 hardcore extravaganzas in the last twelve months—a nearly fifty per cent increase over the previous year."[50]

The background was that, in 1975, Sony introduced its Betamax videocassette recorder (VCR). The following year, 1976, competitor Matsushita brought out its video home system (VHS). It was the VCR that became, by the end of the 1970s, "the primary means for viewing movies."[51] With the VCR, you no longer had to go to the local sex theater to watch porn; you could buy or rent a video at the store and watch it at home.

In 1979, Art Morowitz, who had a background in running adult theaters and producing X-rated feature films, opened Video Shack at 49th Street and Broadway. "It was," said *The Times,* "the first retail establishment devoted entirely to video cassettes." Dave Friedman, a veteran stag producer at Entertainment Ventures, head of the Adult Film Association of America and owner of a number of adult theaters, said that the potential market was huge. About three million people a week, he calculated, visited adult theaters. "But there are still millions of people who have heard about porno films and want to see one but can't bring themselves to walk into a theater. A lot of these people will buy videocassettes."[52]

With a VCR, you didn't have to join a two-block line in the cold to see *Deep Throat.* Wherever the film was shown, lines would instantly form. But then, as legalist Lawrence Walters pointed out, "In the 1980s, people learned that they did not need to stand out on a public street and risk being seen by their neighbors in order to get a glimpse of erotica. They could pop into the television their videocassette rented from the corner video store with no fear of embarrassment and no risk of getting caught up in an obscenity raid." The adult video industry "exploded," said Walters. "The level of explicitness" rose dramatically.[53]

The triumph of videotape over 16 and 35mm film was rapid and overwhelming. According to an *Adult Video News (AVN)* poll of 500 general video stores, the share of new releases shot on video (as opposed to film) soared from 38 percent in 1984 to 97 percent in 1989.[54] Between 1980 and 1986, the number of video stores in the U.S. grew from under 5000 to over 25,000. The outpouring of hardcore tapes in absolute terms was enormous, rising in the *AVN* 500-store sample from 1,250 in 1988 to over 11,000 in 2002.[55]

First to Shoot Video?

According to *AVN* publisher Paul Fishbein, the first feature shot on video was Armand Weston's *Blue Voodoo* for Gold Stripe Video in 1974, released a decade later.[56] Yet the time lapse makes it difficult to claim a first.

The first director in porn to shoot video seems to have been Roy Karch, in New York in 1974, when he and a friend began taping *The Underground Tonight Show,* cable TV's first X-rated talk show, which ran until 1977; then two years later, in 1979, he videotaped the movie *The Reincarnation of Serena,* making him the clear pioneer of porn video. This contribution was acknowledged in the movie *Boogie Nights* (1997), when in the New Year's Eve scene, a producer says there is already a director out there shooting on video: that director was Karch.[57] (*Serena* was not released until 1983.) David Jennings, however, lensing in San Francisco, produced the first full-length feature video to be released. *All the King's Ladies* was directed by Juliet Anderson (Judith Carr, who introduced Nina Hartley to porn) and debuted in 1981.

Ironically, Karch later turned on videotape as having debased the entire adult enterprise. "It wasn't long before direct to tape became a gentler way of saying direct to the [anal sex]." Gonzo porn was born. Porn star Keli Richards used to scream for the camera in the 1980s, "Deeper, harder, faster!" That was exactly what the industry got with gonzo[58] (see Chapter 10).

Onto TV, Into DVD

Sex on TV had begun in the 1970s—to be precise, in 1972 with Toronto entrepreneur Moses Znaimer's Baby Blue late-night broadcasts at his Citytv station on the UHF dial.[59] Demand grew, and by the early 1980s, the longing for sexual material on pay television was becoming "overwhelming," in the words of a *New York Times* writer. Softcore porn was starting to be broadcast on cable TV. New cable channels such as Escapade, founded in 1981, were commissioning original programming, Later that year, Escapade partnered with *Playboy*, and the channel was retitled The Playboy Channel. *Penthouse* announced in 1981 the debut of its own cable network.[60]

There was one more technical move: in the 1980s, tapes began to give way to discs of various kinds, such as laserdisc. But these were expensive and needed costly equipment to run. Laserdiscs, however, laid the foundation of the new disc formats, and what changed the game definitively was the advent in the late 1990s of the DVD (Digital Versatile Disc, Digital Video Disc), which gave a better picture quality than tape (and could be played on a computer, holding more footage). Stores liked DVDs because they were more compact.

In 1996, Private Media made one of the earliest moves into DVD with its classic *Pyramid 1,* which ran more than six hours and was perfect for the new storage device.[61] DVD definitively overtook videotapes in 2003 when, for the first time, more DVDs were rented than videocassettes. Observed Bo Andersen, president of the Video Software Dealers Association, "This is a milestone in the history of home video. Since the advent of video rental 25 years ago, videocassettes have been the dominant format for video rental. Now, just over six years since its launch,

DVD has supplanted that pioneering technology...."[62] And it was Private USA that, in August 2004, became the first big studio to ditch videotapes entirely and go over to DVD.[63] Others quickly followed, and the end fell on that day in March 2007 when director Will Rider shot *Britney Rears 3*. It was "the very last Hustler movie on VHS," Rider said.[64]

Women Join the Porn Scene

"Women didn't discover their power until video came along.
Until then the power belonged to the director."[65]

HENRI PACHARD, 2005

Until video, the male directors lensed what excited males. Kay Parker (Kay Rebecca Taylor), an older English performer who'd been in LA since the late 70s, told psychiatrist Robert Stoller around 1985 why women were so unsatisfied with traditional male porn: The standard scenes would be "a cum shot, preferably in the woman's face or on the chest; one lesbian scene...and an orgy scene. That was the formula. Well, when the women started watching these things, they said, 'What is this crap?'" Women didn't like exterior cum shots. 'We don't do these in our real life.... We don't enjoy orgy scenes for the most part. And one sex scene after the next seems just simply bullshit."[66] So that was ground zero.

It was in the 1980s that video opened the door to women directing porn. They didn't need the backing of a big studio, big crew, or big budget. As stated, Juliet Anderson lensed *All the King's Ladies* in 1981 for David Jennings' production company Superior Video (At Superior, Jennings used the nom de porn J.D. Blackthorne.) In 1981 as well, Anderson stepped before the camera to play in Superior Video's *Physical*, a title that Jennings saw as opening the couples' market. "*Physical* put female protagonists in positions of prestige and power," he later said.[67]

In 1984, Candida Royalle founded Femme Distribution (later Femme Productions). She was not the first female director in adult; Gloria Leonard began directing in 1978, but Royalle founded the first adult entertainment company "owned and operated solely by a woman," as a 2015 obituary pointed out. "Critically acclaimed titles followed soon thereafter."[68] These would have included *Femme* (1984), *Three Daughters* (1986), and *My Surrender* (1996), all directed by Royalle and distributed by Femme Productions. Of *Femme*, the studio later said that it was "the very first ground-breaking video that put Femme Productions on the map and showed the world that women like adult movies too, they just like it done their way."[69]

At first, Royalle had trouble gaining acceptance for this new-style woman-friendly porn. "It was almost like saying, 'I'm making porn for people who live on Mars,'" she later told an interviewer.[70] The male reviewers at first did not take kindly to it and called it "the porn equivalent to Muzak." Yet she acquired a solidly feminist reputation in an industry that was leaning ever more feminist. "She unapologetically put authentic female pleasure on the map," said author Lily Burana.[71]

An interviewer later asked Royalle if Femme Productions created soft porn especially suitable for women. "Not necessarily! Everyone forms this conclusion that women all want romance. Well, that's not even always true." In Royalle's *Urban Heat* (1984), "one of my hottest pieces," an older woman seduces a younger man in a freight elevator. "That's it. There's no romance. They don't live happily ever after. It's just hot and it's a fantasy and is one of the all time favorite scenes for women."[72] (For more on Royalle, see Chapter 6.)

In 1991, Steve Hirsch at Vivid asked Gloria Leonard to take responsibility for a series of videos "directed by women for women."[73] And in 1992, she directed *Two Hearts* for them, starring Ona Zee, Peter North, and Veronica Hart. Two years later, in 1994, Kelly Holland got into directing with the handle Toni English under a contract with Vivid; she became the founder of Chick Media, which produced adult entertainment for women, and in 2009, as stated, she became the executive producer of Penthouse Films. She mentored many younger men and women in the business and, as of 2013, had directed 195 films.

These were the beginnings of the women's movement in porn. They would become much more powerful in the new century.

Jimmyland

In the interval between feature films and gonzo, there is an interlude called, affectionately, "Jimmyland" after porn director and historian Jim Holliday (William Carlson), who often is cited in these pages. Holliday, who entered the industry in 1976 and died prematurely of diabetes in 2004 at 56, had a distinctive directorial style featuring gorgeous young women—his "Angels"— and subtle humor. Holliday shunned raunch but adored enthusiasm. He told psychiatrist Robert Stoller in an interview, "To define what I've always looked for—the normal—in fuck films is pretty people preferably...plot, production values, in a healthy setting, pretty people enjoying themselves." He scorned the "Ice Goddesses," the '10's'," [on a looks scoring system from one to ten] and said, "give me a '6' that enjoys sex and really gets into it, has an enthusiastic smile on her face.... I'll take that anytime."[74]

"The greatest attraction of Holliday's work," said journalist Gram Ponante, "was his ability to bring smiles to the faces of his female talent....Holliday put these women on pedestals and they responded with enchanting performances." And then he threw in lines that went completely over his performers' heads. Asks the villain in *Brown Eyed Blondes* (1999), "Are those twats edible or are they just festering sludge?" In the dialogue with Ponante, journalist Joanne Cachapero added, "A trip to Jimmyland is also a trip back to a time when there was no fish-hooking, not much slapping, nothing too degrading or excessively extreme." Speaking in 2007, she was slaking gonzo. "Just hot sex and girls having fun in the hot sun with any absurd excuse to fuck like bunnies. It works because it's a light-hearted romp." Holliday had a special fondness for model Jill Kelly, and when he stepped in front of the camera, said Cachapero, they "flirt and kiss and tease each other like shy school kids on a prom date."

But older viewers could identify with this, wanting themselves to be Holliday and not some post-adolescent muscle stud. Cachapero: "And you suddenly realize that one of the reasons Holliday is a great pornographer is because he's also the quintessential fan boy....And what porn fan wouldn't want to be in Holliday's position? His world is populated by an endless supply of trashy coeds, naughty nurses, nympho cheerleaders and perky pirates."[75]

Indeed. It was this world that now came to an end. (See Chapter 10 on gonzo.)

Chapter 4:
Is Porn Bad?

*"No one really got hurt from watching pornography,
unless they got too close to the VCR and got electrocuted."*

BILL MARGOLD.[1]

Not everybody likes porn. Jessica Drake, a porn star for Wicked later herself in the news because of an imputed relationship with Donald Trump[2], was at the local grocery store "walking out with my groceries and a man came up to me and said, 'Do you want to protect the poor women who are in porn?'

"I turned my necklace around—I wear a Wicked necklace—and I was like, 'Yes, tell me all about those poor women in porn.' And he proceeded to tell me what grave danger we were all in, and I took in all the information and just shook my head."[3]

"Is porn bad?" is a loaded question, because the excitement of healthy adult sexuality skids off quickly into areas that are socially problematic: child porn, the exploitation of women, unhealthy sexual models for impressionable adolescents. So we must avoid the perils of advocacy.

Yet in the past, we have had a great deal of advocacy, and it was all negative. Porn has always had its enemies. Once, it was the religious right, later the anti-sex feminists. Images with the ability to affect men and women so powerfully have always been seen as a threat to community values and have incited efforts to ban them. In the U.S. after the Second World War, these bans were sweeping, vindictive, and highly successful. But with videotape, DVDs, and the internet, it became impossible to abolish porn, and the antierotic movement has been, for the moment, largely defeated.

Censorship of Porn

Federal censorship of obscenity began in 1873 with the lobbying work of Anthony Comstock, agent for the New York Society for the Suppression of Vice. The new law stipulated, among other things, that sending "obscene, lewd, lascivious, indecent, filthy or vile" articles through the mail was illegal. The Post Office had a long history of barring such works as Ernest Hemingway's *For Whom the Bell Tolls* from the mails.[4] In 1959, a House subcommittee deliberated about tightening postal regulations, and leaders from Nebraska and Iowa shared with this committee their ideas about "stopping New York publishers from sending their filth" to the Midwest.[5] J. Edgar Hoover, director of the FBI, declared that "sex crimes and obscene and vulgar literature often go hand in hand."[6]

Yet contrary to the Zeitgeist in Nebraska and Iowa, in the country as a whole, a libertarian breeze began to blow in the late 1950s, and the rest of the "obscenity" story is really efforts to dismantle the federal censorship apparatus, restore freedom of expression, and end the Mafia's rule over porn. It was these developments that made possible the rise of Porn Valley.[7]

In 1957, the Supreme Court struck the first great breach in the obscenity prohibition in the case of Samuel Roth (*Roth v United States);* Roth was a New Yorker convicted of "mailing obscene, indecent and filthy literature." The Court decided that there was a distinction between sex and obscenity, the latter defined as material "utterly without redeeming social importance." Justice William J. Brennan, who wrote the majority opinion, said that "sex and obscenity are not synonymous," and that sexual material becomes obscene only when it appeals to "prurient interests." Moreover, "the standard for judging obscenity, adequate to withstand the charge of constitutional infirmity, is whether, to the average person, applying contemporary community standards, the dominant theme of the material, taken as a whole, appeals to prurient interest."[8] Brennan's opinion, with all its tut-tutting about obscenity, sounded conservative, yet *Roth* became the breach through which "non-obscene" sexual material could be driven. Observer Alex Henderson later noted, "It is safe to say that without the *Roth* decision, the U.S. probably would not have become the world's biggest erotica-producing country."[9]

Then in *Memoirs v Massachusetts* (1966), the Court held that to define material as obscene, three standards must be met—and all three had to "coalesce." Chief Justice Warren Burger, a generally conservative figure, later summarized the *Memoirs* decision: (1) the dominant theme had to be an appeal to "prurient interest"; (2) the material had to be "patently offensive" because it flew in the face of community standards; and (3) "the material is utterly without redeeming social value." It was this last point that sunk the moralists' ship; if any smidgen of "redeeming value" could be detected, the work was not obscene. Redeeming value became a hook on which to hang an entire industry.

The morality case was further damaged by the report of the President's Commission on Obscenity and Pornography in 1970 that found federal, state, and local antipornography laws should be repealed and that "exposure to pornography was harmless."[10]

Redeeming value became at once a joke. Said director and film critic Jim Holliday of Radley Metzger's *The Private Afternoons of Pamela Mann* (1974), "Throughout the film there is an idiot interviewer asking supposedly significant questions of Pamela, providing 'socially redeeming value.'" From the get-go, "value," of course, was a colossal scam, but it existed to keep the Christian right from running to the rifle racks.[11]

In 1973, in *Miller v California* the Supreme Court abandoned the "utterly without" standard of *Roth* but reaffirmed the three-pronged test of obscenity— prurient interest, "patently offensive," and "lacks serious value."[12] Chief Justice Warren Burger prided the Court on finally having arrived at a standard of obscenity, but it was really a non-standard because all three prongs had to be met, and often the prosecution would fall short on one or the other. First-Amendment lawyer Lawrence Walters later said, "A lot of adult businesses have essentially ducked law enforcement investigations because of the difficulties in applying the *Miller* test and understanding it."[13] In essence, *Miller* had the effect of splitting the country into a patchwork of micro-moral town standards, where what was acceptable in Boston might not fly in small towns in Arkansas. There things rested until the advent of the internet meant that it was no longer possible for moralists anywhere to regulate what people downloaded or streamed in private.

The famous three-pronged test really opened the floodgates. When Al Goldstein was invited to show porn films at the University of Alabama in 1974, he at first thought he was being sent up. "Can you imagine a hairy New York Jewish pornographer walking onto the campus of the University of Alabama with a filthy movie under his arm to show the students—and then give them a lecture? Even my shrink said not to come." But the house was packed. Only the local Baptist ministers were upset.[14]

In the big cities, the battle against porn was largely over by the mid-1970s, killed by the generally hip spirit of the times. Baffled by their continuing inability to define exactly what was obscene, urban police forces and prosecutors were widely deciding they had better things to do. People were lining up to see *Deep Throat* and, as *The New York Times* reported in November 1974, "In most places residents appear to be apathetic." Said a spokesperson for the Denver police, "We feel that pursuing obscenity cases now would be a waste of taxpayers' money."[15]

But it was not entirely over. In 1976, a Cincinnati court condemned Larry Flynt, publisher of *Hustler*, to seven to twenty-five years in prison, a decision that was then overturned on a technicality (Flynt was then shot and paralyzed for life in 1978 by a maddened antiporn advocate). Flynt had ongoing legal battles in the decades ahead. Police harassment continued in Los Angeles right up until the *Freeman* case in 1988 (see below). In 1988 as well, Tracey Adams (Deborah Blaisdell), porn superstar with 265 performer credits to her name, called the police busts "a matter of course...I've had cops bust sets I've been working on and they gave me a list of their favorite films I was in," she said.[16] Evidently, they wanted free copies.

The Los Angeles Police Department continued to hound content providers over "obscenity" and "pandering" until the courts disarmed the vice squad in the *Freeman* decision in 1988.

In smaller communities, it was a very different story. Residents of states in the mid-south and southeast remained highly resistant to adult video stores. While the average number of adult cassettes stocked in 1995 by video stores in the northeast was 549, and the West Coast 608, the number of adult titles stocked in the mid-south was 182, in the southeast, 171.[17] In these communities, "adult" was a swear word, and state legislators and the feds responded to ongoing local outrage about adult video stores, in particular.

The report of the Meese Commission in 1986, a "fervently antiporn" politically-driven panel led by Attorney General Edwin A. Meese and stacked with antiporn advocates, revived obscenity prosecutions.[18] By 1992, censorship groups in such places as Canyon Lake, California, were attempting to zone adult bookstores out of existence; the Committee for Public Decency in Londonderry, New Hampshire, prompted local antiporn regulation; and the city council in Youngstown, Ohio, was on the case about video booths.[19] These initiatives could be multiplied manifold. Happily, almost all of them failed, overturned in court. Yet the intimidation effect was huge. (Many of these efforts reeked of hypocrisy: online porn viewing was highest in such states as Utah, Mississippi, Oklahoma, and Louisiana—precisely where this pious moralizing was most intense.[20])

Phil Harvey, who founded toymaker Adam & Eve in 1970, recalled that "several mail-order companies were forced out of business by the threat of multiple, simultaneous prosecutions—a tactic that was devastating. They would go to the owners of these companies and say, 'We will indict you in Virginia, and we will bring indictments at the same time in Alabama and North Carolina. If we don't get a conviction in the first trial, we will move on to the next trial—or maybe we'll conduct two trials at once to really make your life hell. So you might as well plead guilty and get out of business.'"[21] A number of them did. As late as 1991, Steve Hirsch, the founder of Vivid Video, paid a $500,000 fine in Mississippi.[22]

There was one last federal lunge: under the influence of social conservative groups, in 2005, the Department of Justice formed the Obscenity Prosecution Task Force which did, in fact, bring cases against producers such as Max Hardcore. But the air quickly seeped out of it and, in 2011, Eric Holder, Obama's Attorney General, shut the task force down by folding it into the Child Exploitation and Obscenity Section.

The question of "child pornography"—images of under-eighteen adolescents and children—has confused the discussion. Enemies of adult entertainment have sought to conflate "child pornography" with "pornography," making it sound as though images destined for adults somehow involved children. They do not. In the San Fernando Valley, there is no such thing as child pornography, only the crime of depicting children in sexual situations, which the adult industry vigorously opposes. Adult pornography is a legal form of expression; the imaging of children is profoundly illegal, and this paragraph would not be necessary were it not for the efforts of censors, as First-Amendment lawyer Lawrence G. Walters puts it, "to blur the lines between protected speech, in the form of adult erotica on the one hand, with patently illegal material in the form of child pornography on the other, by mixing the two at every opportunity."[23] Adult entertainment has nothing to do with children, and anyone who suggests otherwise will have a hidden agenda.

Now, in the adult area, there were developments of direct interest to Porn Valley. In 1975, the California legislature repealed the law against "oral copulation" (sodomy), one effect of which was making it legal to shoot oral sex. This considerably diminished the enforcement ardor of the police in the obscenity area. Then in February 1989, the California Supreme Court overturned pornographer Harold Freeman's 1988 "pandering" (prostitution) conviction in *People v Freeman*, effectively legalizing the shooting of porn in California. The Court said that the pandering statute did not cover the hiring of actors who would be engaging in sexually explicit but non-obscene performances."[24] California and New Hampshire became the only two states where making adult entertainment was legal. Yet the adult industry had concentrated in the Valley long before the *Freeman* decision.

By the advent of the Obama Administration, federal prosecutions for porn had virtually come to an end. As First-Amendment specialist Kimberly Harchuck noted, "The adult industry was hopeful that obscenity prosecutions finally were a thing of the past."[25]

The Sex-Negative Attack on Porn

> *"If I'm so exploited, how come it's the only industry in the world where women make double what the men make?"*[26]

STORMY DANIELS, PORN STAR AND DIRECTOR, 2008

In responding to the rapidly growing pornography industry in the 1970s and 80s, women divided into two camps: the sex-negative activists and the sex-positive feminists. For a while, the condescension of the Senior Common Room and the media dominated the airwaves with horrific and entirely untypical examples. In the 1990s, the sex-positive feminists found their voice, and not only welcomed porn but helped shape it.[27] By the new century, the sex-negative attack on the adult industry had come to seem cranky and marginal. Scholar Linda Williams, whose 1989 book *Hard Core* is considered the founding document of pornography studies, writes, "The feminist rhetoric of abhorrence has impeded discussion of almost everything but the question of whether pornography deserves to exist at all."[28] Yet this judgment capped two decades of bitter antiporn advocacy.

Women's organizations that oppose adult entertainment go far back in time. In 1959, Mrs. Charles P. Adams, president of the New York City Federation of Women's Clubs, led the federation in a resolution to "obtain evidence of pornography and report it to the authorities."[29] One of her successors, Mrs. David McInnes, told the Presidential Commission on Obscenity in 1970 that "a Communist conspiracy must be at work, when prayers were prohibited in schools and pornography was permitted in the theaters."[30]

Yet the success of feature-film porn in the 1970s made it hard to ignore that explicit sexual content was gaining a new place in American society. In the late 1970s, opposition to porn shifted from the hands of the anti-obscenity moralists to the burgeoning sex-negative movement. The argument was not that porn damaged morality but that it harmed women.[31] In March 1977, feminist and media-intellectual Nora Ephron argued that *Hustler* was "a truly obscene magazine" and, thus, not protected by the First Amendment.[32] At a conference at New York University in early December 1978, the militant activists confronted the defendants of free speech. Antiporn spokesperson Andrea Dworkin, later author of *Pornography: Men Possessing Women*[33], said, "All over this country a new campaign of terrorism and vilification is being waged against us. Fascist propaganda celebrating sexual violence against women is sweeping this land...inundating cities, college campuses, small towns. Pornography is the propaganda of sexual terrorism." Herald Fahringer, who had defended Al Goldstein of *Screw* and Larry Flynt of *Hustler*, tried to argue against this rhetoric but was hissed into silence, as opposed to the standing ovations that Dworkin received.[34] Antiporn activism had been simmering within the women's movement for some time, but now it reached the public prints.[35]

These were strong accusations, but were they true?

Moral Panic

In the United States—much less in Europe—in the public eye, porn has been lumped together with cyberbullying and teen sexting in a kind of moral panic, a reflexive social alarm, that places *adult* videos on the level of "child exploitation and human trafficking," as Georgina Voss, a British technology researcher, puts it.[36] Sociologist Chauntelle Tibbals sarcastically described the "the polarizing 'porn wars'...which generally broke down to *either* porn is wholly awful *or* porn is just mostly awful."[37]

Porn star Lindsey Lovehands describes a picnic on the beach in Florida with two friends, one who knew she was a performer and one who didn't. Lindsey had a "lengthy and friendly" conversation with the friend not in the know, and the talk came about to a mutual male acquaintance who was married to a porn star.

The friend: "Well, I don't know what she expected...married to that 'porn star' (said with upturned eyes and squinted-up nose as if she had just smelled 100 pounds of fish that had been left out in the sun for a week) with all those tattoos... my GOD, so DISGUSTING."

Lindsey: "I smiled and looked at the ONE friend there who DID know I was Lindsey Lovehands, and with a knowing wink to him said, 'You know you never know what goes on in people's relationships, what kind of people they REALLY are, you can't judge a book by its cover.'"

Lindsey continued the story: "This person of course had no real reply to me, but instead she again made with the gesticulations of a self-righteous know-it-all who had NO idea that me, the woman who had just previously given her the BEST recipe for braised rack of lamb...has also sucked off 16 guys and let them pop on her face. Imagine that."[38]

Appalling indecency? No, in many living rooms, among men and women alike, Lindsey Lovehands is a name to conjure with.

And talk about knee-jerk prissiness! Dee Severe, a producer specializing in kink videos, described the reaction of her fellow filmmakers when it became apparent that she and her husband were shifting gears: "When we started shooting fetish content I was really happy. I thought, hey, here's an opportunity for us to hire our starving filmmaker friends and get them some experience and actual money. Well, they were HORRIFIED that we were doing this....The upside was, they let us use the group's cameras for free for two years when we offered to rent them, because they didn't want our dirty porn money."[39]

By the new millennium, the moral panic over porn was rehearsing several mantras: "Porn means child porn." "Porn hurts women." "Porn is addictive." Heavy accusations, to be sure.

The Bill of Indictment

"I have spoken with people who truly believe adult businesses are run out of darkly lit basements by perverts in devil costumes."[40]

SABRINA MILLER, GAMMA ENTERTAINMENT, 2011

Antiporners laid out a number of reasons for banning the industry, censoring the content, and otherwise driving this menace into the night.

Porn Ruins Sex?

It would be a mistake to dismiss this argument too glibly, because even within the industry, there is an awareness that porn can damage connectivity. "Barefootsies," an industry insider with a foot fetish who is anything but a prude, said on the *XBIZ* board in 2014 that he himself did not watch porn. Yet, "I have conversations with friends who have admitted that porn has made it difficult for them to be fully present with their partner when making love because instead of connecting with their own—as well as their partner's body, energy, sensations and emotions—they were more likely to get stuck in sexuality imagery in their minds. Kind of like if you're having sex with your partner while watching TV."[41]

The philosophical issues at stake here may be subject to a cohort difference: Many older people today still see sexuality as embedded in human relationships, and deplore the absence of feeling in the almost random coupling they perceive in porn. For the younger generation, by contrast, sex is often a form of recreation rather than of human connectivity. Witness the popular hookup sites Tinder for straights and Grindr for gays. Both philosophies represent valid viewpoints; neither is right or wrong.

Yet the "porn-ruins-sex" argument has been politicized. In a Cox Media Group opinion poll in 2014 of people under 40, 33 percent of respondents did believe that porn had a negative effect on sex (48 percent thought not). The profile of the porn-ruins-sex camp was: 63 percent Evangelical Christians (only 27 percent of Roman Catholics believed this); 52 percent were Republicans (only 20 percent of Democrats believed this); and largely undereducated (only 22 percent of those with a graduate degree thought porn ruined sex; 48 percent of those with a condemnatory view of porn had not finished high school).[42] The belief in porn's harmfulness for sex was, thus, heavily identified with the children of the Christian Right.

Porn Objectifies Women?

Another argument is that porn "objectifies" women. What does that mean? Here we might find an unpleasant aspect of porn in which the sex act itself is stripped of meaning; Toby Ross, at the producer-distributor Big Dik Factory, captured this quite well when he talked of turning on Pornhub for lack of anything better to do after they discovered they couldn't get CBS to see the Tonys. "I must say that although the films were full of hard action and squirts like fountains, they made me sick. (I felt it in my stomach) the exaggerated OOHS and AAHS that were on a running loop playing ad nauseum as the actors were obviously not moving their mouths, the emphasis on dehumanized sex and the level of objectification, the bodies, cocks and asses floating aimlessly as if filmed by a serial killer."[43] If this is what we mean by objectification, we can have a discussion—not about banning it, but whether this is what intelligent people should be watching.

But objectification can also mean misogyny. Webmistress Heather Corinna, 30, who ran a female-oriented site, said in 2001, "[In] lots of mainstream male porn sites, the language is really misogynistic, such as 'you want to fuck this pussy.' Not a person—genitals....Aside from being insulting, it's a real turn off. Lots of mainstream porn sites just look like they're pimping their women as objects, meat to be sold, not as people actively participating in what's going on."[44] As a rule of thumb, porn that women find it difficult to relate to could be said to be objectifying them. They can't get into the game as full players.

Yet usually, "objectification" is taken to mean "seeing women as sex objects," rather than denying them sexual agency. Said English journalist and pro-domme Nichi Hodgson in 2014, "Well, of course [porn objectifies women]—and what's wrong with objectification? Contrary to many of my feminist peers, I don't consider it short-hand for dehumanization."[45]

Objectified or no, young women have to earn a living. And porn offers a clear path to survival. Producer Steve Lick knew "a 36-year-old mother who just got a job as a webcam model after she was let go from her office manager job. I also know an elementary school teacher who has done two fetish shoots for Kink to earn some extra money while her husband is trying to find a new job."[46] What are we supposed to say to these people? Don't work in porn because you'll be objectified? Really?

Broken People?

"I think outsiders view us as a bunch of depraved porn freaks, but for the most part this is a family industry and the people are intelligent and professional."

ZACHARY GOODE, ELECTRIC EEL, 2015[47]

Antiporners bring out the argument that porn damages the performers or that only damaged people became performers. This provokes incredulity within the industry. Kayden Kross, at 22 already a super-porn-star, expressed indignation at the notion that she got into porn because she had somehow been "abused" as a child. "I can't buy into this Madonna/Whore complex," she said in 2008.

Kross segued into the economics of being a porn star, which really trump most potential objections. "I got into porn because I like money, and the idea that wealth or success is bad will never resonate with me....Economically the best thing I can do right now is porn, and I'm not ashamed of that. The dollar amount I make in porn is very high compared to the dollar amount one would pull in from an average job with a good education."[48]

In 2004, Canadian painter Denise LaFrance was interviewing porn-megastar Candida Royalle. LaFrance, who had some knowledge of the industry, said, "I've met some of the most humanistic, caring, loving, conscientious people in my entire life [in the industry]."

Royalle then responded, "That's right. If we let our daughters know that these women aren't so troubled and they're having a pretty damned good time and they like the autonomy and the financial independence, then that might dispel the whole myth of disarray that's supposedly necessary to make such a living."[49] Royalle had entered the industry in the 1970s (see Chapters 3 and 5), had a wide circle, and simply did not know any of these broken people—or, at least, too few to mention. (A scholarly study of 177 porn actresses and controls in 2013 found that porn stars did not have higher rates of childhood sexual abuse and had higher levels of self-esteem than controls, refuting the "damaged goods" hypothesis.[50])

Antiporners claimed that the talent hated the conditions in industry and soon quit in demoralization. Porn opponent Luke Ford, in a widely cited statement, declared that "most girls who enter the porn industry do one video and quit. The experience is so painful, horrifying, embarrassing, humiliating for them that they never do it again."[51]

But the statement, however driven its moral fervor, is factually incorrect. In reality, according to Jon Millward's careful 2013 statistical analysis, only 10-30 percent of women porn actresses quit after a single film, and 53 percent do three or more films.[52] Some stay in adult, essentially, for life, first as performers then as directors. Stormy Daniels (Stephanie Clifford) was born in 1979 in Baton Rouge, began stripping at 17; in 2002 she appeared in her first film, *American Girls, #2*, and shortly thereafter was cast as the lead in Wicked's *Heat*. In September 2002, she signed an exclusive contract with Wicked, directing with them starting in

2004. In the next fifteen years of performing, directing, and guest appearances, she made a great deal of money and was in no sense a victim.

Brittany O'Connell entered the industry at 19, and at age 37 was still performing as well as producing videos for her own website. "I really do love this industry," she said in 2009. "Some people were born to be porn stars. I was one of them. I used to feature across the country [in the 1990s]. I love to entertain."[53] There are many actresses like O'Connell and Clifford.

The broken-people argument has specially infected media accounts of the industry, where reporters are repeatedly astonished to discover that porn stars are, in fact, real people. After meeting superstar Keisha, journalist Christine Schoenwald gushed, "She spoke of how she had never been molested, had had a happy childhood, and from very early on enjoyed sex."[54] Astonishing!

Porn Hurts Women?

> *"I have been exploiting this business for 14 years*
> *and will continue to do so for the rest of my life."* [55]
>
> PORN STAR ANNETTE HAVEN, 1987

The argument that porn hurts women surfaced in Judge Joel Tyler's Criminal Court in New York in 1973, as the prosecution strove to prove *Deep Throat* obscene. Judge Tyler found that "this feast of carrion and squalor," this "nadir of decadence," was indeed obscene and dangerous to the commonweal.[56] "Porn hurts women" became a kind of slogan in the Senior Common Room. Porn arouses a priggish distaste in intellectuals such as MIT's Noam Chomsky, who believe that porn "humiliates and degrades women."[57] Their acolytes in the media have produced generally quite biased documentaries in which we are assured that young women in porn will have a horrible experience (as for example the documentary *Hot Girls Wanted*, which is situated in untypical Miami and where the young women live in the agent's home!)[58] Diane Sawyer's moralistic documentary on porn for ABC's Primetime Live in 2003 featured a tearful Belladonna as a hapless porn victim. This would be the same Belladonna who accepted later that year an X-Rated Critics Organization's award, explaining on the podium her success simply: "I love to fuck. Thank you."[59] In 2003 as well, Belladonna became the most recent Evil Angel director with her title *Evil Pink*. Sawyer didn't realize she'd been gamed by a trained actress.

62

As for the attitude of the anti-sex feminists towards BDSM, a kind of fastidious distaste could not have been more marked. The Women Against Pornography group found leather-clad lesbian sadomasochists such as Pat Califia beyond belief. The 1982 antiporn tract *Against Sadomasochism* described lesbian BDSM as "firmly rooted in patriarchal sexual ideology."[60]

The porn-harms-women argument then received a boost in 1986 in the Attorney General's Commission on Pornography, also known as the "Meese Report" after social-conservative Attorney General Edwin Meese.[61] The report maintained, to general incredulity, that "violent pornography," such as found in BDSM, "bears a causal relationship to both sexual violence and sexual discrimination." The commission, headed by Virginia prosecutor Henry E. Hudson, "known for his efforts to banish pornography from Arlington County," was top-heavy with other prosecutors and clerics, several of whose careers ended in disgrace (apropos hypocrisy!)[62] Meese himself resigned in 1998 owing to a questionable role in a scandal. The report had little credibility among academics knowledgeable about the relationship. Its suggestion that the industry was somehow mob-controlled was greeted with disbelief.[63] Yet Evelina Kane, staff coordinator of Women Against Pornography, described the report as "a major breakthrough in raising the consciousness of the country."[64]

The huge body of "effects" research is split about the impact of viewing porn on attitudes, especially of young people. Some studies say it makes adolescents more aggressive, others that it makes no difference. This entire literature is permeated with suspiciousness of sex on the internet.[65]

But if porn hurts women, then gay porn would hurt gay men, right? The sex-negative campaigners are silent on gay porn, which drives Allison Vivas, the president of content-provider Pink Visual, crazy. "There is a huge market for gay pornography, which features only men, and yet this seems to be overlooked in arguments about exploitation of the actors or how the medium might degrade participants."[66] Silence, too, about transgendered porn—and the transgendered are among the most avid of all porn viewers.

Sexual Violence?

Does porn prompt men to go out and commit rape? In fact, there seems to be a negative correlation between porn and rape. When porn is widely diffused, rapes decline. Over the period 1980 to 2000, as Anthony D'Amato, law professor at

Northwestern University in Chicago has demonstrated, "the incidence of rape in the four states having the least access to the internet showed an actual increase in rape" (between 1980 and 2000, national rape levels were going down). And, in three of the four states having the most access to the internet, rape levels declined. (Alaska was the anomaly, where both rape and internet access increased.) D'Amato concluded, "There is a precise negative correlation between the two [porn and rape]."[67] After a careful review of the literature, Rutgers law professor George C. Thomas found in 1993 that "no available scientific evidence establishes a causal relationship between pornography and rape."[68]

Porn Addiction?

"Tiger Woods claims to be addicted to sex. Bullshit! These are hot women he was having sex with. If he was having sex with a dead chicken, I'd say, wow, that guy is addicted to sex." [69]

COMEDIAN GREGG ROGELL, 2011

Is porn "addictive," like narcotics and alcohol? People tend to like things that produce pleasure, that's for sure. Yet the medical term addiction has been widely slung about, as in "Twitter addiction."[70] Porn addiction seems to have been anchored by Christopher Cooper, executive director of the Kansas City chapter of the Coalition Against Pornography, who in 1987 characterized porn use as an addiction.[71] Out of this, an academic cottage industry has grown. [72] There may be people who spend hours a day on the computer, but it's not "porn" they're addicted to but the fetish or niche in which they have an obsessive interest, an interest that may prove destructive to their family lives and relationships. But this capacity for personal havoc is not the fault of "porn." It's the fault of their sexual constitution. After a careful review of the scholarly literature, Barry Reay and co-authors concluded in 2015, "Sex addiction is a label without explanatory force."[73]

An Elle/MSNBC poll in 2004 of 15,246 people involved in internet dating established that the great majority of men, and almost a majority of women, accessed "erotic images" online. Yet only 2 percent of the sample engaged in "sex-seeking" behaviors (more than 11 hours per week), including viewing porn, the survey found.[74]

Within the industry, as one might expect, the concept of porn "addiction" is widely disbelieved, and most think it the result of addictive personalities being steered in the adult direction. "OldJeff" recalled one colleague who'd been working with him at Max Cash. "He was working on content. I called him about something or other and asked how he was doing. Quote: 'If I see one more boob today, I am going to puke.'"[75] So, no addiction there, despite long viewing.

Finally, if there is such a thing as being "addicted" to porn, it's quite unlike other addictions. In 2015, investigators at several institutions, led by Nicole Prause in the department of psychiatry at UCLA, undertook neuropsychological testing and EEG studies of 55 men and women who identified themselves as excessive porn users ("excessive viewing of visual sexual stimuli" was the jargon). How did they differ from controls? For one thing, they did not, in objective testing, seem to have neuropsychological problems. For another, unlike people with other kinds of addictions, "those with higher hypersexuality scores do not appear impaired in their ability to regulate their sexual arousal." This would militate against an argument that porn leads to rape (see above). The probands did not demonstrate an EEG measure called "late positive potentials" while viewing porn, meaning they did not get all that worked up about it (unlike other addictions).[76]

Reality testing: Much of the argument about "porn addiction" fails to differentiate between injudicious use (causing your marriage to break up) and disease ("addiction"). What constitutes "excessive" viewing remains unclear, but unwise viewing, yeah, no problem with that.

Real and Unreal

If there are dangers in adult entertainment, they do not lie, in my view, in the danger that women or men will be objectified or martyred. Any representation of people must necessarily present something less than their full humanity. The real danger is that people will take porn fantasies as a standard they must somehow fulfill in the real world, a standard of swaggering masculinity and of tall, thin busty blondes that exists only in the studios of Porn Valley, and not in the real world. Jessica Drake, who according to one journalist is the very image of the genre—"tall, thin, blond, big boobs"—cautions against taking porn for reality. "People were asking sex questions," she said in an interview, "that made me understand they weren't really able to differentiate between porn for fantasy viewing and a more realistic sex ed. I had a couple tell me there was something wrong with them because they couldn't have anal sex as easily as they saw it portrayed in movies." She continued, "For the person just starting out, if they see a movie where a woman orgasms in 30 seconds, that's not real. If they see a movie with no foreplay, straight to anal, that's not real....These are professional sex actors. Do not try this at home."[77] But much entertainment is fantasy. We do not allow children to watch porn, and part of being an adult is the ability to discern mercantile images from the grit of daily life.

Women in Industry Reject the Antiporn Argument

"It sometimes feels like me, a couple of guys who are porn fans, and a couple of my pro-sex-worker neo-feminist buddies vs a horde of psycho angry prudes."[78]

DEE SEVERE, PRODUCER, 2012

The antiporn view is not widely shared among women within industry.[79] A good deal of the criticism of porn comes from a handful of ex-porn stars who served as bowsprits for the antiporn movement, and from *bien-pensant* liberal intellectuals in the Senior Common Room; both create a sense of unreality. Ex-porn-star Shelley Lubben, for example, called pornography "modern day slavery" for thousands of women.[80]

Many women in porn find these criticisms unjust. Jacklyn Lick confronted Lubben, "I just want to say for the record that not ALL porn stars are addicted to drugs and alcohol." During her own time in industry, "I WAS NEVER ON DRUGS!!!! Guess what, I'M STILL NOT ON DRUGS!!! In fact, I am very strict about nutrition, diet and never even drink alcohol, except for discovering in the last couple of years that I really enjoy red wine, and began making my own." While in industry, Lick also taught "kickboxing, health and fitness [and] personal training.... I come from a very excellent family, and my parents have been married for almost 46 years."[81] Smoke started coming out of a number of porn stars' ears after they read Lubben. The main thrust was that the abusive conditions Lubben supposedly witnessed never really happened to most people.

Diane Duke, 54, a feminist who worked at Planned Parenthood for twelve years before becoming CEO of the Free Speech Coalition, a trade association that fights censorship, told *Cosmo* in 2015, "If a woman is in porn, then our society either believes that she is a victim or she is a slut. Our society cannot wrap their heads around the fact that women are sexual beings....Women can't want sex, and women can't be in these videos without it being something that is coerced or forced upon them." Duke continued, "Women in our industry are powerful.... They are making the decisions that they want to around their bodies. And it's so exciting, it's so empowering. Porn now is so great for women."[82]

A young woman with the handle "Adult Blog Writer" said she entered the industry "out of financial desperation. I was crying before I started. I thought it would be so awful to become a phone sex operator. But I knew it would be McDonald's or Walmart with the no experience I had, so I knew I HAD to make it work, and I have. I quickly learned there was not the horrors I imagined, there's actually a lot of humor to this work....It's actually been the best thing that has happened to me."[83] The many young women who stay in the industry beyond the first film or two almost all endorse this opinion. They tend to find the antiporn arguments bizarre.

Other women have known all along this is really what they wanted to do. Nica Noelle, shooting for Mile High Media as an experienced director with a long list of successes behind her, said some women were simply born to the métier. "Some of us are born courtesans, born entertainers, and sex is the area we feel compelled to explore. I don't know why anyone with an interest in sex or sex work is immediately assumed to be a victim, or it's assumed that they were abused. I think that's just another way to stigmatize us."[84]

Even though many porn stars protest, "Yeah, this is what we want, it feels great!" the voices of condescension insist, as actress Asa Akira, 29, put it in a 2014 interview, "that maybe I'm still hiding things. That I'm not telling myself the truth."

This made Asa furious. "First of all, it's really offensive that they're not even entertaining the idea that a woman like me might exist....What does it say about them that they can't even imagine that a woman might be a sexual human being and an exhibitionist and in porn because she wants to be doing it? They'd rather think of me as a victim or a drug addict."[85]

Still other women had Saul-on-the-road-to-Damascus type conversion experiences. "It started in the 1970s," said Caryn Goldberg, later president of Unzipped Video, "when I marched against pornography as a raging lesbian feminist." But then she discovered, "I actually kind of enjoyed it. I realized I was part of a subculture of lesbians who like gay [male] porn." And then she discovered that the people who produced it were not in fact "sleazy pornographers. I met the most amazing people in the gay adult industry who I really liked.... It was nothing like I expected." And why did she, a lesbian, relish gay male porn? "I'm gonna so lose my lesbian card for this, but I think that the visual of male sexual excitement is more to look at, because there's a hard dick that explodes, as opposed to a woman where it all happens inside." She said lots of lesbians liked gay male porn.[86]

So there were many different roads that led women to porn, none of them passing through the Senior Common Room.

Sex-Positive Feminism

Women in the industry became part of the broader pro-sex feminist pushback against the antiporners that took place in the "porn wars" of the 1980s. The intellectual structure of what became "pro-sex feminism" was laid out by New York journalist Ellen Willis in an article in the *Village Voice* in 1979.[87] Willis introduced the phrase "pro-sex" in 1981.[88] Nina Hartley, for example, was a founding member in 1984 of the Feminist Anti-Censorship Task Force and of the San-Francisco-based group Against Censorship Together.[89] And it was in 1984 that scholar Gayle Rubin penned what has become the intellectual strutwork of the feminist rejection of anti-sex activism.[90]

Outside of industry, about a quarter of those who enjoy online porn are women (see Chapter 20). And witness the great success of the sadomasochistic novel *Fifty Shades of Grey*, one of the most widely read literary works of modern times with over 100 million copies sold, mainly to women. It is difficult to see all these women conspiring in their own "degradation."

Virtue and evil are in the eye of the beholder. The adult content varies, depending on one's viewpoint, from the unspeakably vulgar to the wildly exciting. But subjectivity is driving the train here. The concept of "obscenity" collapsed in court because it depends so much on the esthetic taste and cultural values of the viewer, and community standards here vary considerably.

First-Amendment lawyer Paul Cambria recalled of the Max Hardcore obscenity case he defended in Manassas, Virginia, that there were "all these middle-aged ladies on my jury." The prosecution thought that the case was aced: Surely, they would uphold righteous standards? Cambria said in his summation, "Why wouldn't this material be acceptable if, for example, you and your mate could download one of these adult movies and use that material to strengthen your bond? Maybe you're getting older, maybe it helps you spice up your relationship. Maybe it will help a relationship in the sense that you and your husband will continue to be attracted to each other, and he won't feel he has to take off with the secretary." He struck a chord, he said, with several of the jurors. Max Hardcore was acquitted.[91] Members of the jury saw not horrifying filth but material of practical value. (Paul Cambria, a Buffalo attorney quite close to the industry, is particularly remembered for the Cambria List. He sensed in 2001 that porn was going to have trouble with George W. Bush in the White House and John Ashcroft as attorney general. The list included such no-nos as "blindfolds," "bondage-type toys or gear," "male/male penetration," and "black men-white women" themes.[92] The list soon became a joke, but it scared many people in the industry and made black-white sex appear as something particularly forbidding—see Chapter 19.)

Finally, despite Andrea Dworkin, is there really that much violence in porn? Actually, not. In 2015, U.K. porn entrepreneur Jason Maskell offered a balanced perspective to the *Financial Times*, saying that most viewers' tastes were rather mild. "A lot of them want good-quality product, good sets and good locations, shot well, edited well, good-looking performers. All this stuff about the rough and the horrible, they don't want that. Most times, that's not what sells. There's a small niche that may go to the more extreme, but that's not what people are searching for."[93] In fact, the overwhelming majority of porn is vanilla. It's not about the degradation of anyone. BDSM scenarios involving (consensual) degradation of either men or women are much a minority.

By 2014, the antiporn trend within feminism was much weakened. Many feminists decided that women's freedom to choose outweighed paternalistically "protecting" them, and that the alliance with the Christian Right had been an unholy one. Pro-sex feminist Nadine Strossen called legal efforts against pornography "a fairly dead issue."[94]

Indeed, feminist porn had, by this time, become such a familiar and long-standing phenomenon that media gush about the "reclamation" of porn by women grated on feminists in the industry; this had been going on for decades. Said writer-director Jacky St. James in February 2017, "Do you realize how patronizing it is to women working in the adult industry to hear you [a journalist] say this as if it was somehow a new concept?" Figures such as Angie Rowntree, producer of the feminist porn site Sssh.com, had been around for decades and had little patience for becoming "sensationalized clickbait for mainstream fodder."[95]

Today, people who characterize porn as "smut" are increasingly rare. The term has disappeared from *The New York Times*. Instead, the idea of enlarging one's sexual horizons doesn't appear half-bad. Just ask the transgendered.

Chapter 5:
Porn Stars

"If you suck a cock one time in one obscure movie or web site everyone may call you a 'porn star' regardless of the fact that almost no one has heard of you."[1]

JIM GUNN, PORNOGRAPHER, 2012

In the early days of 16mm porn loops, the models were mainly "lifeless tattooed hookers," as one observer said,[2] and they brought to the screen a characteristic lack of enthusiasm. Thirty years later, they tended to be keen young women from small towns in the South.

This enthusiasm is the story. What greatly adds to the psychological appeal of porn is that many of the models, though professional, seem positively joyous about sex—and this enthusiasm becomes visible in animated performances that have a great erotic impact. So if we want to know why porn has succeeded in reaching out to so many, this is part of the story: the changing nature of the models themselves.[3]

Starting Out

"Finding new talent is not difficult. Every day thousands of new girls turn 18."[4]

KRISTIN, AN EXECUTIVE AT NUBILES

How do you start out? Getting on the bus, of course. But which bus? In the 1990s, when Hollywood was still making "B" movies, some models got on the bus for West Hollywood, then when that didn't pan out, drifted up to Chatsworth. As veteran porner Jimmy Cooper told the *XBIZ* board in 2011, "Many of the girls who would have become B-movie stars in the 90s are becoming porn stars today because those B-movie roles have been squeezed out."[5]

Or the bus might stop in front of Jim South's agency World Modeling on Mason Avenue in Chatsworth. "We used to get 30 or 40 girls a week," said South in 2005, advertising in 15 Southern California newspapers; the internet then thinned that figure to "10 or 15 girls a week."[6] Before the internet, they would turn up Polaroids in hand. (The Polaroid camera of the 1960s produced instant photos.) The photos would then be filed in the agency book, and shooters would leaf through the pages looking for candidates. Or the young women would just be sitting there in South's office and the directors would strike up a conversation, get to know the model a bit, and then decide. The internet changed all this as the directors contacted the models via email. "Running ads is almost useless now," said South in 2005.[7]

Porn was driven by beauty. "You need the hot girl," said veteran director Roy Karch, "and everything else is just you winking at the camera. But the viewer is looking at the hot girl."[8] Mike South (Mike Strothers) added, "You [the girl] must be pretty—this one probably goes without saying but if you want to be a top level girl you have to have top level looks. Period."[9] So this was probably principle number one in recruitment: You had to look hot.

And be shaved! Richard Pacheco encountered a shaved co-star for the first time as he played opposite Brooke West in 1983 in *The Mistress*. "Like kissing Mother Nature right on the lips."[10] Shaving pubic hair was already à la page when Ambassador Video featured *Shave Tail: Discover the Ultimate Lust of a Shaved Lady!* in December 1984. Cinema Tech Studios shrieked "Actual shaving on video" in January 1985.[11] Photographer Earl Miller doubtless accelerated this trend when lensing Melissa Wolf for *Penthouse* in June, 1985.[12] (Yet the trend had not yet overtaken Vidco when, in 1987, they advertised their latest hit, *Furburgers*."[13]) By 2014, the overwhelming majority of models—female and male—were shaved.

The young aspirants had to be over 18, and prove it with a photo ID. The Traci Lords (Nora Kuzma) incident was a colossal embarrassment for the industry when it was discovered, after she shot a hundred-plus tapes, that she was only 16 when in 1984 she made the first, *Breaking It*. And after she turned 18, she only did one more porno, *Traci, I Love You*, a 1987 video, before going mainline. All her previous tapes were removed from the shelves; all her scenes in her previous titles edited out, "resulting in monumental financial loss."[14] To this day, the name Traci Lords evokes a shudder. You could *look* as though you were underage, and that would guarantee sales (*AVN* ran a stocking guide to "selected young girl titles"[15]). But actually being underage virtually never happened.

Pretty early in the game, the beginners would have to look like porn stars, which is to say, according to an analysis of 7,000 female performers in the Internet Adult Film Database (IAFD), thinner than the U.S. average female population (by 48 pounds)[16]. How else do you look like a porn star? According to data on the over 27,000 models in Roald Riepen's site Freeones.com, from the founding of the site in 1998 to 2013, 44 percent were brunettes (only 31 percent blonde). And only 21 percent had "fake boobs."[17] (A mania for breast augmentation began among models around 1993, a result, ironically, of the falling rates for still shoots and the models' need to maintain a competitive edge;[18] of those in the Riepen survey who did have breast augmentation, the mammaries were often truly incongruous. Jenna Jameson was asked (countless times), "Are those real?" She would fire back, "Yeah, right. It's natural to be 110 pounds with double-D's."[19]

The big surprise in the Freeones database was age: the models were not all 18-year-olds, and many had been in the industry for years. The average age at which these models started their careers was 27, their average age at retirement was 38, and the average model age in the database was 34.[20] This goes so much against conventional conceptions of the industry as exploiters of young beauty that one wonders if we haven't been sold a bill of goods (a) by industry ads, which certainly highlight youthfulness, and (b) by antiporn claims that the industry trashes innocent young lives. Both sides of the age coin are erroneous, in other words. When pornographer Paul Markham said in 2012, "Teens are the biggest niche with every major subniche covered except MILF [Mommies I'd Love to Fuck] and Grannies," he was talking about demand.[21] The supply was somewhat older.

In the early days, models were recruited heavily from the ranks of the flower-children in San Francisco or from strippers. Strippers were not an accident. Russ Meyer was among the earliest pornographers, and he said of the many strippers in his films, "The reason I use them...is because they have proper credentials, the right equipment and an awful lot of experience with men. Which is 90% of the so-called acting ability for my films." He added that strippers like to have "some goof hanging around that can pick up their laundry, take orders, etc. And some of them even cuckold the shit out of 'em."[22] With Meyer himself, for example.

Yet with the video revolution, porn models were increasingly found among ambitious young women who did not have a background in stripping. They liked sex, were maybe a touch exhibitionistic, and did not mind beginning careers in the sex industry by doing it on camera. The website Yanks.com, founded in 2002, featured "amateur girls playing, filmed by girls watching." Each model had a separate page on the site for either her video or a series of photos; all were "solo girls," naked or semi-naked, masturbating or otherwise in alluring postures, very soft core but quite popular.[23] The organizers asked the 316 "Yank Girls" to fill out a "Big O" questionnaire, and the responses suggest that, among this population of apprentice models and budding porn stars, a kind of hypersexuality was the rule. A hundred respondents said the most orgasms they had ever experienced in one day was 4-6, and 80 said 10-14. In the absence of data on a control group, it is difficult to say whether this is a lot, but it strikes me as quite high.

Model Eden Marie, 48, was among those who shared her thoughts about orgasm in a questionnaire. She was otherwise an artist who listed her "hobbies" as "reclining" and "being spanked." She identified herself as "pansexual." "Do you squirt?" asked the questionnaire. She responded, "Not every time, but I have and it shocked me and my partner at the time. It feels amazing." The most interesting thing anyone has ever asked you to do in bed? She responded, "A guy asked me to dress up like a guy and peg him while I swore at him. Yes, I did it. I am a very sexually adventurous person." Her favorite fantasy? "I love threesomes so I always think about having no strings sex with two very willing partners. I want the sex to be hot, dirty, and nasty, also preferably in a dangerous spot where we might be seen. I love the idea of people watching us all get off....I am soaking wet right now just thinking about it."

"Do you think women who don't masturbate are missing out on something?" Answer: "Yes, I think they are missing out on knowing their own body and their own limits."[24] At 48, she was considerably older than most of the site's models, yet the responses are insightful, frank, and speak to a very sexual being.

This may be part of the "eroticizing" of younger women that seems to have occurred in our time, reflected in such measures as a falling age at first sexual intercourse, increasing number of sexual partners, and willingness to perform oral sex on similarly eroticized young males. (For example, according to the National Health and Social Life Survey of the National Opinion Research Center in the early 1990s, the percent of women who'd had five or more sex partners before 18 rose from 2.5 percent for the cohort born 1933-42 to 9.6 percent for those born 1963-74.[25]) Saharah Eve, a femdom, said in 2010 of this eroticized cohort of young women, "There is a whole generation of young nubile chicks willing to do porn. They grew up on the residual influence of generation X's stashed DVDs and skin mags, along with an evolving digital technology that has made 'sexting' an everyday affair."[26] An academic study conducted in 2006 of 176 female performers found that 53 percent entered the industry for money, 27 percent for sex, still others for fun, creative expression, and the like, so sex was definitely high on their priorities.[27]

Thus, as the young aspirants got off the Greyhound bus, many of them were dead keen on sex. But there might be surprises here. One was that, despite the universally self-professed enthusiasm for "fucking," it would be nature, or their bodies, or their tolerance of day after day of "pounding," that would pretty well end the performing careers of some after 300 scenes. This figure is widely accepted in industry, and director Vicky Vette said in 2016, "The average performer has 300 scenes in her. And you can do those in the first year, or stretch them out."[28]

Oral sex was self-understood as a fundamental part of every model's life. (As it was a part of sex in general. In a survey by toymaker LELO in 2014, 46 percent of all respondents preferred oral to penetrative sex, and 60 percent "regularly reach orgasm by oral stimulation alone."[29]) There were almost no models who shied away from oral sex and the only twist here is how quickly you could learn to "deep-throat" someone, as Linda Lovelace had done in *Throat*. Danyel Cheeks had learned the skill after some ardor. She said in a 1993 interview, "I learned to deep throat many years ago [as a stripper in Indiana]. I started out like everybody else, choking and hitting teeth. But within a year or so, I learned how to breathe in and breathe out [at the out-thrust] to make everything easier. I was very determined to learn to do it after seeing Linda Lovelace in action."[30]

But the job might require other kinds of sex with which your school chums were less familiar. According to the IAFD data base, 87 percent of models were willing to "take a facial," 62 percent to do anal, and 53 percent interracial. At this point, however, the willingness shades off into unwillingness: only 39 percent agreed to double-penetration (one penis in the vagina, another at the same time in the anus), 31 percent to swallow ejaculate, and 28 percent to do a "cream pie" (oral contact with internal ejaculate).[31]

A Career Path

"The former free-spirited hippies and love children of the seventies
have been replaced by career-oriented performers." [32]

PORN HISTORIAN JIM HOLLIDAY, 1993

In terms of success and failure, there is a gamut of experience. Here, we need a nuanced picture. Some models are porn stars in the making and drive hard towards professional careers. Some are part-time and have lives outside. Others lead marginal existences, become addicted and unreliable, and pass quickly from the scene. Still others are preyed upon, suffer casual violence, and find themselves defenseless.

Becoming a "porn star" passed from an aspiration that no middle-class young woman could conceivably contemplate to a recognized career path. The possibility of making lots of money from the exploding video revolution lured many. "These new stars weren't going to wait for wealth to 'trickle down,'" said pornographer David Jennings of "this new breed of porn queens."[33] British-born Taylor Wane, a *Penthouse* Pet in June 1994 and performer in more than 300 adult films, transitioned easily to a business career in adult, using the skills she had developed. "I always was a businesswoman," she said in 2006. "I knew I had to market myself and push myself in a certain direction that would afford the best way for me to gain the most notoriety. I decided my boobs would be the best vehicle."[34]

Brittany Andrews, who came into the industry in 1995 and had a lot of cinema credits, used filming as a way of keeping her credibility as a porn star. She had little interest in achieving the kind of fame that her former roommate Jenna Jameson had won, and aspired mainly to succeed in business. She created a fetish presence for herself as the "Niche Bitch." Andrews said in an interview, "I'd do 10 movies a year and that enabled me to be able to do what I really wanted to be doing," namely, "overseeing the operation of multiple websites and dozens of employees." And she ended up driving a Mercedes convertible, traveling the world, and buying couture gowns. Said the journalist who interviewed her, "Pretty good for a pink-Mohawked punk rocker who dropped out of school in the 7th grade."[35]

Yet what was in demand was not future executives but fresh, pretty, and apparently inexperienced young women (because, according to the Freeones data base mentioned above, there were relatively few of them). For the *Break My Hymen* series, producer Kelly Madison at Kelly Madison Media "puts out Craigslist ads [that say] if you are 18 and virgin—please apply."[36] Pornographer and blogger Mike South was the H.L. Mencken —the caustic editor of the *Baltimore Sun*—of adult entertainment. He said in 2003 of the impact of the phrase "first timer": "The most powerful thing you can put on a [DVD] boxcover is that a gal is a first timer, or it is the first time she has done a particular sex act on tape. People go nuts over this. And, if the title has the word Teen in it, it is a guaranteed success."[37] This would be comparable to the oomph of "twinks" in the gay world: late adolescent males.

In getting ahead, one issue was reliability. The image of drugged-out, flipped-out crack whores is quite incompatible with the reality of the high levels of professionalism that many models were expected to bring to their work. Said Mike South, "The companies I work with have expectations of the girls I bring to them. I have the highest standards when it comes to presenting you for a contract and you have to conduct yourself accordingly."

Then he said, he wouldn't accept aspiring young women who did drugs, had an eating disorder, or only did "girl/girl." Nor did he want part-time prostitutes, apropos of drifting back and forth between modeling and escorting (see below). "My clients want girls that are representative of their companies and they don't run escort services."

But then South came to the core of what was required for success as a model, and it goes very much against the stereotype. "If you are not smart and dependable, I don't want you. I'm an advisor not a baby sitter....Make sure you dress and act appropriately and get to where you are supposed to be on time, and make sure you don't end up on TMS with your babysitter loading your drunken or drugged ass into a car. I expect you to be where you are supposed to be, when you are supposed to be there, dressed appropriately and with a good attitude. If you are not capable of that every single time, I don't want you."[38]

The problem of no-shows bedeviled industry. How did English-born Francine Amidor, an executive at LA Direct Models, usually begin her day? "Eight a.m. at my desk with a cup of tea, scanning emails and waiting for the early morning phone calls of why a person can't possibly go to work (the range of which can be due to bubonic plague or an alien sighting), looking for replacements, jobs being added onto our schedule as other talent agencies' models are a noshow."[39]

So, babysitters were wanted, as Mike South put it, "people whose job is to keep the girl from getting fucked up, keep her on time for her appearances, keep her from running out and partying, making sure she is dressed appropriately, making sure she doesn't run off with some guy or girl, and making sure she doesn't say something embarrassing. Now just imagine what a girl would be worth if she didn't have to have a babysitter."[40]

How to do well? One way, as Mike South suggested above, was to become a "contract girl," having an exclusive contract with a big studio. Vivid Video had pioneered this in the 1980s (see Chapter 2). The upside for a contract girl was steady income over a long term. To be sure, independent young women not under contract could make a lot of money if they were in demand. Kayden Kross (Jenna Nikol), a university student from Sacramento who at the time was a contract girl for Adam & Eve (previously with Vivid), said in 2008 that contract girls could earn "in excess of 20 grand a month, just from shooting scenes, plus whatever their websites and other streams of income are pulling in. Rolled together, their incomes can rival the payoff of eight years of medical school plus residency." Contract girls, continued Kross, might make less in a given month than freelancers because they shot less. But they didn't risk flooding the market with their image, and if the relationship with the sponsor continued over time, "long-term, our income can exceed that of the independent star."[41]

Stormy Daniels, born Steffanie Clifford in Baton Rouge in 1979, started out as a stripper, then drifted into the industry as a contract girl for Wicked. She became a producer-director for Wicked and by 2010 had directed 65 films, performed in 184. What did she like best about porn? asked an interviewer in 2005. "I like the fact that it allows me to do something both fun (sex) and creative (writing and directing) and make enough money to do the things I love like having horses."[42] So, being a contract girl could be a rocket to the top. (And indeed, she did rocket to the top: following widespread publicity about an alleged affair with President Trump, in May 2018, *Penthouse* made her "Penthouse Pet of the Century," a move that left the industry, more or less, agog.[43])

But there was also a downside to being a contract girl. In addition to a salary and a guarantee of appearing in a certain number of films, you might be expected to have sex with the male staff and clients. Mike South heard of this only in 2003, but he found what reached his ears harrowing: "Porn's dirty little secret, I am learning, is that the contract girls are often required to perform sexual favors." He gave examples, naming names. "A [name redacted] Contract Girl tells me that they are required to 'entertain' at parties for [redacted's] big customers and that the entertainment does NOT mean playing a piano, more like 'tooting a flute.'"[44] The industry, in general, is not abusive of women; everything that happens before the camera is entirely consensual. But is there abuse behind the camera? For sure.

At the end of the day, few porn stars had the acumen of a Stormy Daniels or a Brittany Andrews. And few made lots of money. Having your own website and owning your own content was virtually the only way to earn more than, say, $50,000 a year. As Don Houston at XCritic put it in 2014, "A good nursing degree would net most female performers a better return on investment than the big bucks they make when they are the flavor of the month...."[45]

Failures

Woodsman Ron Jeremy often couldn't remember the names of the young women he had sex with on camera. It didn't matter. "It's impossible to say how much longer any of them will be around. Very few performers stay in the business for longer than a few years.... You almost don't want to remember their names because they might be gone before you get a chance to work with them again."[46]

For many young women, porn was a shattering experience.[47] Veteran porn star Lindsey Lovehands, who had joined the industry later in life, said, "If I had entered this business when I originally wanted to at age 18, I would have probably been chewed up and spit out, penniless I might add, by age 22, which incidentally, is why I believe that the age to enter porn needs to be raised to 21 because an 18-year-old, with rare exceptions, is ill-equipped to fully comprehend ALL the facets of what they are getting into."[48] (The point was timely: a number of directors were distressed at some of the abuse the "extreme porners" had inflicted on young models. See Chapter 7.) For many of these young women, producer David Jennings' dyspeptic assessment would have hit the nail on the head: "Most ladies find X-rated stardom a lonely road, strewn with broken relationships, leering fans, hostile media, angry relatives, menacing cops, back-stabbing competitors and exploitative agents, managers and producers."[49]

Full of dreams, new arrivals were often quite uninformed about actual conditions. In 2007, 24-year-old performer Taryn Thomas from Bloomfield, NJ, who had been in hardcore in LA for about three years and had suffered a major anal tear, said, "There are girls coming into the business left and right who haven't watched gonzo or seen what that first step in the career is probably going to be. And that's why there is such a big turnover. The misconception—you know, that they're going to star in *Pirates* or a Michael Ninn feature right away—really does lead to a lot of girls leaving pretty fast."[50] Kurtis Potec, the accounts manager for Xtube, agreed. By 2008, when he spoke with *XBIZ*, the market for watching solo girls masturbate—the easiest possible work!—had dried up. "Typically, everyone thinks they are the next big porn star, so they come in with really high expectations. When they realize nobody wants to watch them sit in their chair and touch themselves, they leave."[51]

Brooke Tyler, in her forties and a veteran MILF, knew a lot about what happens to young aspirants in the industry, and when she was interviewed in 2014, she thought they had zero chance of stardom. Turning up in Porn Valley, she said, was a recipe for failure. "There is no career in porn for 99.45 percent of these girls." Why no career? Because, said Tyler, everything they shoot ends up on the tubesites, where it is re-run so many times that the girl's image soon reaches "saturation." (Tubesites are free, on the model of YouTube.) The future? "She gets a few scenes here and there, and before you know it she is doing the million man double anal cream pie...The vast majority of Porn Valley performers are destined for the industry standard of an extremely short career.... The good news is that their retirement package ensures that they will always be able to log on to Pornhub and watch their own scenes for free in HD [high definition], for eternity, resting comfortably knowing they will never be paid another dime for any of it." So Tyler didn't really know any porn stars, "just a bunch of talent passing through Porn Valley and landing permanently on Porn Hub."[52] (Observers call this kind of saturation the "retrogressive dynamic": the more familiar your face becomes, the lower your rates, in an industry that clamors for fresh, young faces.[53])

Passing through into what? This is a question all industry aspirants must ask themselves before getting on that Greyhound bus. As one insider put it, "What do they do after the lights go out, when no one's interested in putting them on a [DVD] box cover, and they are 28 and can't strip? What kind of job do you get that's going to carry you through the next 30 or 40 years, when what you put on your resume is: starred in *She Swallows Buckets of Cum, vol. 9?*"[54] And when you do finally go back to that small town in Indiana you came from, as Bree Olson did, you will find that you have become a social outcast and are unemployable as far as the locals go. Olson said, "People look at me as if I am the same as a sex offender... and they assume the absolute worst in every way."[55]

Bree Olson made millions and understood what was required of her. But there were a lot of eighteen-year-olds, thrust into an unfamiliar environment where fame—rather than a lifetime of working at the Seven Eleven—seemed just around the corner, who were simply disoriented. They did not understand what was required for success, and so didn't have it. Susan Yannetti, in charge of publicity at Vivid in 1997, found this hair-tearingly frustrating. "If I tell them I can get them an interview with *Rolling Stone*, it doesn't mean anything to them. If I set them up, I get 'My boyfriend's father is in town,' or 'I can't, I have to go to the mall.' I'm thinking, 'What kind of bitch are you? What the hell do you care about your boyfriend's father? This is your career!'" But many of the models didn't see it that way. "Their ambition is to be a headliner at the Pink Poodle and that's it for them."[56] The problem here was not the tubesites, overexposure, and lack of royalties. It was that the models themselves had little concept of "fame," and what was required to achieve it. Jenna Jameson, Vicky Vette, and Brooke Tyler did get it.

So, many candles went quickly out. The average female porn star left the industry after three years, the average male after four, according to Millward's analysis of the IAFD data base.[57] Mike South, who in Atlanta had seen the candles of many southern belles go out, commented in an email, "In the worst cases they contract an std [sexually transmitted disease] and realize the business isn't as safe as they were led to believe. This happens a LOT more than the industry will admit to. In a lot of cases, they realize that it isn't the fantasy they thought it would be and disappear. Sometimes they had no intention of staying in the biz, they do a few scenes, make a quick payday to get themselves out of whatever situation they were in and they leave."[58] In 2006, guest blogger BL for Mike South lamented, "The young gonzo porn chicks who are around for six months and disappear. [They] just all look alike, act alike, fuck alike. They're animated centerfolds."[59] And soon gone. This was the *lumpenproletariat* of the porn world.

Do the Models Enjoy Sex?

Jim Holliday commented in his review of the porn classic film *Teenage Fantasies (1972)*, *"The performers have great enthusiasm, as if they really are enjoying themselves and sex, which is often a rarity in adult films."* [60]

Mmmmm, sex. But does this sound like fun? Joanna Angel, webmaster of the site Burning Angel, had been shooting porn. Her day had been nonstop. Then, at 7, she went to a shoot she had booked that lasted until 11. When she got home, she decided to do her income tax, but then, "I went upstairs to get a snack because I forgot to eat all day and while I was bending over reaching for a yogurt on the bottom shelf my boyfriend started having sex with me. I really needed this, but right as I was about to come I realized that my website is running low on content so I screamed, 'Wait! Go get the camera.' So we had to ruin the moment, get the camera, prop it up somewhere and pretend that we just started fucking."[61]

So, do the models enjoy sex? This is difficult, because all models in interviews say, "I love to fuck." Samantha38G said on a chatboard in 2012 that when she started thirteen years ago, "We all had to be wanton sluts in interviews or men wouldn't buy the product."[62] So this kind of spin has to be controlled for in evaluating the models' own comments about their sexual responses. Yet industry sources were rarely seen by the surfers and have some credibility.

The models project sensuousness, as we see in Chapter 11. But did they really live it in their bodies? This is an experiential question, not a cinematic one. It is important, because the antiporners so often claim that the models are exploited and only pretend to enjoy the sex. But do they? Porn videos are so filled with fake groaning that one assumes nobody must be enjoying it very much if they have to pipe in all that noise. Yet, by their own testimony, many porn stars really did like to have sex. This did happen and was not just for the consumption of credulous fans.

There seems to be here a gamut of experience. At one end of the gamut, the lusty models relish sex on camera and off, and can scarcely get enough of it. In the middle are the models who distinguish between porn sex and private sex as different experiences. At the other end are models who feel uncomfortable on camera, do not orgasm (unlike many passionate performers who do), and quickly leave the industry.

Here is the negative end. In 1986, director Paul Thomas asked porn star Gina Carrera to think up a really good sex scene.

Gina: "Look, P.T., I just can't think of a scene. Just make one up for me."

Thomas: "I want it to come from you. Are there just so many that you're having trouble choosing?"

Gina: "No, I'm afraid there aren't any at all. I hate sex scenes. I just close my eyes and think about the money."[63]

That was the negative end of the sex spectrum.

At the positive end, how to tell if they like the sex? Do they keep going after "cut"? Said porn star Lisa Ann in 1996, "I did a three-way in *No Tell Motel* with Jenteal and Amanda Addams that we kept going long after they stopped shooting."[64]

In shooting *Las Vegas Maniacs* (also called *Las Vegas Hustle*) with co-star Richard Pacheco in 1984, Annette Haven demanded that the director keep shooting because she hadn't yet climaxed. Said Pacheco, "That day, Annette insisted on doing her own orgasm for real. She refused to simulate it. She argued that it would look better. She DEMANDED that the director shoot it that way."[65]

Kayden Kross, at the positive end, was credible when she said in 2008, "I got into porn because I cannot stand monotony. I do not want to throw my energy into anything that doesn't change day to day and doesn't allow me to build something...I got into porn because I really do like the sex. There is a rush that still hasn't gone away when I have sex on a set. There is a rush in talking about it. There is something very carnal that takes over when I see men like the ones I work with. I'm always asked what my biggest fantasy is in interviews and I have a hard time articulating it. For me, there is nothing like fucking a man for the sheer purpose of fucking him....I will get off on the way his muscles move when he grabs me. I will get off on his jaw line. I will get off on him getting off on me. That is what I fantasize about."[66]

Kross was dumbfounded at the claim of antiporn activist Shelley Lubben "that women do not enjoy making porn movies [and] continue to lie to their fans and proudly insist they enjoy making porn movies." "I love sex," said Kross. "I do. And I'm not just telling myself that....And I can get off in the scenes. She must have been doing it wrong."[67]

Maybe Lubben didn't "pick her talent," select the woodsmen she wanted to perform with. But industry veteran Jesse Jane, a contract girl with Jules Jordan Video, picked male partners. "I don't like to fake it on film. I'm really into my films. You never see me look at the camera ever. I've never cared where it is. I just want to fuck and have a good time fucking."[68]

The directors are constantly yelling "cut," changing positions. Not only do the male actors lose wood, the female actors find it difficult to climax. Many complained, as Dave Cummings put it, "about being left high and wet." Angela Summers said, "The guy's hitting your spot. Then the director calls for another position. You want to tell him where to go, but you can't." So, what to do? Jennings continued, "[Annette] Haven and [Lilly] Marlene recruited crewmen to help them reach a climax; most actresses just live with the frustration."[69] Summoning the hired help to finish one off really does settle the question, Did the models get off?

We truly are in another world here. Lindsey Lovehands, a young woman from Atlanta who had become a veteran performer, was completely sex-positive. "I know there are many people in the industry who...are saying to themselves, 'WTF [what the fuck] is this broad talking about? Porn is replete with scumbags and weirdos, deadbeats and criminals. Every porn chick is a junky who tricks on the side. They have to get coked-up just to take on three guys at once.' I for one consider that a privilege, not a right...three guys I mean."

In the same post, describing a gig as a feature stripper at a club in Tampa, together with porn star Delilah Strong, Lovehands said admiringly of Strong, "She has taken more cocks at once than I can only dream of, but I am hoping to reach her status soon."[70] There is a gleefulness about sex here that is not just put on for fans—because few fans read these industry blogs.

Yes, Atlanta was a happening place. To get true gleefulness, said Mike South, you have to get away from Porn Valley, where the models are filming for a paycheck, and go to a place like, say, Atlanta or Dayton, where the young women on camera are not really models at all but amateurs shooting because they want an unusual sexual experience that they're unlikely to have with their boyfriends. In fact, four of the young women in his shoot *Southern Magnolias #2* (2003) were from Dayton, referred by his friends Tim Case and Felicia Fox. "Most of them are doing it once or twice to have a good time and make a few bucks, and see themselves on TV without having to do anything degrading like going on the Jerry Springer show," said South in 2003.[71]

What many young women were unlikely to have with their boyfriends was something called "dirty sex." A number of models liked it, not necessarily meaning dirty talk or anal, but a forceful kind of aggressiveness and unleashed energy that is close to the BDSM basin but not quite (BDSM can be very controlled and unenergetic). Veteran model Julia Tavella (Julia Ann) said in 2008 that she didn't like on-screen sex, "getting fucked at about 10,000 miles per hour...I find it kind of boring." She had done "anal and DP [double penetration] and interracial for Wicked" and liked them all. "I think dirty is the way you attack it, not necessarily how quickly or how hard you attack it. I've done dirty scenes, but they were dirty just because the energy was dirty. To me, that's gritty sex. That's the kind of sex that I want to have, that's raw."[72] Tavella, who had in fact entered the industry as a mud wrestler, was much in demand because she managed to communicate this on camera.

Escorting and Dancing

*"Isn't being a porn star nowadays only a marketing instrument
to increase the prices for escorting?"*[73]

STEFAN G, AMAZINGCONTENT, 2010

There is actually a difference between porn and prostitution. In the latter, the escorts seek to offer their partner (the client) a sexually satisfying experience. In porn, the models—male and female—seek to offer the viewer a satisfying experience, while their partners may or may not get off on it. On set it is not uncommon, after the word "cut," to hear someone say, "Get the fuck off me."

Since the birth of the industry in the 1970s, there had been some nexus between porn and escorting but, in the old days, many porn stars were indignant when asked to do "privates." In 1991, Taylor Wane, who gushed in interviews about how "I live and die for sex," vehemently denied engaging in prostitution; she later said, "You're trying so hard to be a professional, to be an actress. Sure, you have sex on camera but you don't consider yourself a prostitute.... I would get really angry when people asked me if I was an escort. How dare you!" Wane then continued with a really interesting observation, "Listen, I make movies. You don't think [famous actress named] is a whore but guess what—she's fucked every director that she's ever worked for to help her get all those starring roles. The only difference is I never got to see her pussy hole with a cock going in and out of it!"[74]

Then the economic crisis around 2008 spilled many more models over into prostitution, where the money was better and working conditions easier. Now-retired adult performer Mariah Milano, who started out in the industry around 1998, told journalist EJ Dickson that at that time, an adult performer openly escorting was quite rare. Milano said, "Escorts were considered dirty, bottom of the barrel. Nobody was open to admitting they did it."

Then Milano took a time out and returned to industry a few years later. Said Milano after coming back, "Girls would text me all the time like, 'Hey Mariah, what's your rate?' I'd get hit up on Twitter, through email, asking how much. People were just assuming that I escorted." Even her agent asked her if she did.

As English journalist and TV host Louis Theroux said, in 2012, after revisiting Porn Valley, "For many female performers nowadays, the movies are merely a sideline, a kind of advertising for their real business of prostitution."[75]

Lacey Blake, who in December 2013 had recently started working for the adult industry as an accountant, was describing a number of shocks she had as she learned about some of the seamier aspects. "Shortly after, I learned of the rather large number of performers who escorted and were prostitutes on the side. I'm still not sure why this surprised me so much, but it did. I felt so naïve."[76]

Naïve, for sure. The industry's involvement with escorting was anything but a secret! In January 2001, Dennis Hof's Moonlite BunnyRanch in Carson City, Nevada, advertised in *AVN* for other porn stars to come and join Sunset Thomas, "the Queen of the Bunny Ranch," who in 1999 had opened up the practice of famous porn stars escorting at the Ranch—for $2000 a night. In another ad, the Ranch pointed out that a popular porn star could earn over $100,000 a month: "Sunset Thomas, in the FLESH, right next to you, right now." The Ranch called Thomas the "first adult film star, in her prime, to work at a brothel so her fans can be with her."[77] No beating about the bush here. Thomas went on to star in 6 of the 20 episodes of the HBO series *Cathouse*, which the network broadcast from 2005 to 2008.

But Thomas (born Diane Fowler) was not the only porn star at the Ranch. In July 2001, the Ranch further summoned performers to "join our team! Not just sex—an adventure!" The Ranch listed by porn name 163 of the "adult features" who had worked at the Ranch, "and 46 that don't want their moms or hypocritical asshole directors to know." The list included some well-known performers, such as Kendra Jade, Porsche Lynn, and Teri Weigel. Bianca Trump had also headlined at the Ranch.[78]

So much interest did the ads generate that *AVN* itself felt compelled to run a feature on "Porn Star Prostitutes" in April 2002. "Formerly in the closet, they're now peeking out thanks to Moonlite Bunnyranch's Hof." The story called escorting "one of the most controversial subjects that adult video...has ever had to deal with," and listed a number of other models who escorted. The journal sent a reporter to the Ranch to interview Sunset and Hof. "When you have a party with me," said Sunset, "I'm going to give you one hell of a party, guys.... I'll have fans that are so excited seeing me, they'll pop in 20 minutes."

"Two minutes, more like," said Hof.

Sunset continued, "And I'm like, 'You're not done yet. You've got an hour with me.' So I keep partying with them and sometimes they cum twice. I give them a really good party."[79]

Why this increase in models who escort? There was the economic crisis caused by the free tubesites, for sure. A porner with the handle "Deemented" said in May, 2011, "I know one porn star who has been getting next to no work. She shot maybe 5 scenes this entire year so far. Years back she would have been shooting 10 scenes PER WEEK. Now she's just escorting in Vegas instead."[80]

But it was more than just the business crisis. Webcamming as well opened the door part way for escorting, as models gained the expectation of routinely interacting with clients. Interacting with them in person seemed an easy transition from masturbating for them online. Said Stormi Mountain, spokesperson for adult entertainer directory Eros.com, "Before, you just had to look good on film. Today's bigger stars are more comfortable with...interaction, and that sometimes means they're more willing to go on paid dates."[81]

As well, modeling agencies began specifically advertising for escorts as well as porn stars, legitimating the lateral career move. In 2004, Pretty Girl International, a modeling agency, teamed up with Escort Support, an adult escort community site, to sponsor "an adult model search contest." Applications would be submitted through the EscortSupport.com website, then presumably judged by Pretty Girl International. "Contestants do not need to be an escort or sex worker to enter the contest," said the promo copy, which ran as a news story in *Adult Video News*.[82] But, once you sign up with Escort Support, guess what....

Word got out that escorting was actually an easier, and safer, way to make a living than performing. One high-end "courtesan" told Mike South she'd never go back to porn. "Escorting is much easier. Half the time the customer doesn't even want sex, when he does he has to use a condom, he doesn't have to shoot up his dick to get hard, he doesn't choke me, spit on me, slap me, abuse me, degrade or berate me, and my environment is clean and safe. He has to play by my rules or he doesn't play. I can choose not to see him, essentially everything is under my control; this is much better than when I was doing porn." The last time she had an STD, she said, "was the last porn set I was on. I have yet to have an escorting client give me anything, even a cold."[83] (To discourage escorting, the official industry response was, you might bring onto the set infections you've received from your private clients who, unlike male talent, are not tested, but this seems rarely to have happened.)

Escorting could certainly be more lucrative! Robbie, who produced in Las Vegas the website Claudia-Marie.com starring Claudia-Marie of the giant breasts, said in 2010, "Claudia-Marie can make $10,000 a night with the right customers coming to town. Let a girl try to get that shooting a scene for a company. lol." He added, "The only reason girls do porn movies is to be able to charge a big fee to escort and/ or to make more money feature dancing at clubs. Guys love to have a real porn star on their arm and get to brag to their friends that they fucked her."[84]

In the "biz," being known as a prostitute was definitely not a key to advancement— not for moral reasons but because prostitutes quickly became very tired of sex, and porn needed young women who were sex enthusiasts. A feature called "Zero Tolerance Entertainment" in *AVN* listed, among the components of bad porn, "Hookers who hate fucking." [85]

Porner David Jennings, on one of his early shoots in LA in 1978 involving Rita, a prostitute, said Rita had "a hard, glazed look. She spoke in the languid manner of a veteran hooker."

What don't you like about working in sex films? she was asked.

"Fucking," said Rita.[86]

Hence it was true that, as Mike South put it, "Although most porn agencies have ties to escorting very few escorting agencies have ties to porn."[87]

To be fair, an unknown number of models did deny escorting. Ariana Jollee, who was not exactly prudish ("I love two dicks in my fucking ass," she said), was asked by an interviewer in 2004, "Do any escort work?"

She responded, "No. I'll bang a fan that really wants to have sex with me, but I'm not gonna get paid for it. They really have to convince me."[88]

Kayden Kross advised correspondent Darrah, a fellow female performer who expressed outrage at being propositioned, "You need a thicker skin honey if you want to be in porn. Why are you surprised that a man assumes that you also hook on the side when you make your living having sex on camera with strangers?... If you don't hook like most other male and female porn stars, then just delete the email and walk away." A final dig at Darrah: "I'm sooooo sure if George Clooney was offering you $25,0000 an hour or Brad Pitt offered you a starring role opposite him in exchange for sex, that you would gladly say yes."[89]

For models, the other time-honored way of making ends meet was feature dancing (meaning your name is on the club's marquee), which could be much more profitable than performing, provided that one first made a name for oneself as a performer. "Men, and not a few women, drive for miles to see their fantasies in the flesh," said an *XBIZ* writer in 2005. "They pay to have stars pose for Polaroids with them or sign copies of their latest DVDs." In addition to fee and travel expenses, many clubs also paid for "a personal assistant/bodyguard called a roadie."

Many models got into the industry as strippers, or "exotic dancers." (In California alone, exotic dancing employed 7,500 women full-time and another 5,000 part-time.[90]) But feature dancing is a bigger deal than regular dancing. It was said in 2005, that for top talent, a good weekend might harvest up to $27,000, and lesser-known talent, as one journalist reported, "can still garner $2000 for two 20-minute sets per night, plus high dollar lap dances and poster and box cover signing cash, and all of that without actual sex." Said Courtney Cummz, a contract girl for Zero Tolerance, in an interview, "Now a lot of girls ask me if I can hook them up with a dance agent." In fact, so many that "they're oversaturating our market."

The deal was that mega-stars like Nikki Benz would get the house aroused, then the local talent would offer lap dances and privates. After Benz had left the stage, the manager would "call all of the house dancers to the floor to solicit lap dances from the men that Benz had worked up."

"Twenty for topless, forty for nude," the manager called, as men followed the dancers into the private booths. Benz herself did lap dances for a higher fee, and the "porn vixens" loved the action. "I get to shake my ass in my fan's face," said Cummz. "It puts me up on stage, where I'm really happy, said Jessica Drake, a contract star for Wicked Pictures. "I love performing and I think it really gives me a chance to connect with the fans in a laid-back-party atmosphere...."[91]

In feature-dance appearances, the porn stars brought glamour to the hinterland. "In Los Angeles, it's no big deal to see one of the girls eating sushi," said Dave Michaels of a booking agency in St Petersburg, Florida. "In Omaha, if you see Brianna Banks walking down the street, that's a big deal."[92]

Chapter 6:
Pioneering Women

*"These women are smart. They have a contribution to make.
I'm in awe of the women in this industry. They are hardly a victim."[1]*

ANGIE ROWNTREE, PUBLISHER OF SSSH.COM, 2015

T he porn business before the 1980s was run by men, and the great majority
of porn stars were female twenty-somethings. But not all of them.

A First Generation

One has to distinguish between female pioneers of the earlier years, say 1970 to
1986, many of whom were strong women but had never heard of feminism, and
the later generation of articulate feminists. Jim Holliday, creator of the adult film
almanac, identified 16 women who "had worked in front of the camera for at
least ten years during the 1970–1986 adult era." These sixteen names, some of
whom remain well known today—include Marilyn Chambers (*Behind the Green
Door* 1972), Annette Haven (*Charli* 1981), Gloria Leonard (*The Opening of Misty
Beethoven* 1976), and Annie Sprinkle (*Honeypie* 1975).[2] (*Charli* is considered by
some "the first true woman's picture in the adult genre."[3])

Simultaneously arrived a group of explicitly feminist pioneers, including
Candida Royalle (Candice Vitala), "the Grace Kelly of Porn," who entered the
business in 1974 at 24—shortly thereafter starring in Alex de Renzy's *Femmes
de Sade* (1976), and in 1981 played in expressly feminist *Outlaw Ladies*, directed

by Ron Sullivan (Henri Pachard). In 1984, she began "producing erotica from a woman's perspective" with her Manhattan-based company Femme Distribution (for more on Royalle, see Chapter 3). Royalle's life traced the whole career arc of an early porn actress: from growing up in an Italian-Irish family in New York—where there were "certain mores and standards," as she later said—to therapy in San Francisco in order to deal with the guilt she felt from her first involvement in industry, to reaching the "conclusion that there really is nothing wrong with it. Sex is such an incredible life force. We're curious about it. We want to know. We want to see what it looks like. It doesn't turn us into mad rapists and killers. There's nothing inherently wrong with it."[4]

So this is how Royalle became a pioneering feminist figure in porn: "I felt there was really room here for a new kind of porn and we need something that gives women permission to explore our sexuality in a way that doesn't make us feel ashamed. We need to reclaim our sexuality, our right to pleasure, and not worry about being judged." Thus, in 1984, Royalle created Femme Productions.[5]

Some of these early figures, such as Constance Money (Susan Jensen), got out at the top of their game: After co-starring with Gloria Leonard in *Misty Beethoven* and *A Taste of Money* (1983), she bailed at 27 in favor of running an air freight business (or a restaurant, depending on the source) in Alaska. Stacey Bernstein, born in Glendale, California of a Mexican mother and a Jewish father, stayed in a bit longer: She began performing in 1996 at 19, became a contract girl as "Raylene" for Vivid (she married Vivid owner Steve Hirsch's brother Brad, and became Stacey Hirsch), shot for Vivid for three years then, restive, made a lateral move into feature dancing. Restive there, too, she left the industry for real estate. She was never wild about adult but made enough money to buy a house in her early 20s. Was she ashamed of her past? Not at all. "Always be proud," she said.[6]

Other women continued to perform into their fifties and sixties. Seka (Dorothea Hundley Patton), the "Marilyn Monroe of Porn," broke into filming in 1977, retired officially with *American Garter* in 1993, then returned at 53 for a hardcore reprise in 2007. (Old-timers still consider Seka the number one porn star of all.) Veronica Hart (Jane Esther Hamilton), born in 1956, played a hip woman in Roberta Findlay's sex-positive classic *The Playgirl* (1982), then went on to become a prominent director at VCA Pictures. As late as 2009, she was still winning industry awards for "best non-sex performance." (She retired from sexual performances in the mid-80s.)

It was around 2007 that the demand for older women really seemed to come alive with the concept of the MILFs ("mothers I'd like to fuck"). Shayla LaVeaux, who'd been big in the 1990s, thought her career was over until she came in demand again, shooting in 2014 at age 45 with Sean Michaels in the series *Legendary Players*. "Twenty years ago it would have been impossible for [a star her age] to come back," she said. "There was no MILF genre, now there's a demand for cougars."[7] (The concept of "cougar" is thought to have been born when actress Joan Collins, at age 50, posed for the cover of *Playboy* in December 1983.[8])

And cougar paid off. In 2014, "Robbie" told the *XBIZ* board that, from 1998 to 2002, he had shot for Pure Candy Images, a site that he also owned. "It was mostly teen stuff that I was shooting. And then, just for the hell of it, I shot a very mature looking milf. I sold more copies of that set than all of the teen ones put together. It taught me a lesson."[9] The company Naughty America's CEO Eddie Arenas said in 2013, "There's just something sexy about an older woman who knows what she's doing," and such Naughty America titles as *My Friend's Hot Mom* (2010) and *My First Sex Teacher* (2008, which went to 43 parts by 2014) were big money spinners.[10]

Older men often disliked the feeling that they were masturbating to a woman young enough to be their daughter, and it was frequently women over 25 who starred in this market. Among male viewers on the whole, there does seem to have been a preference for older women. For men visiting the abovementioned Freeones site between 1998 and 2013, 51 percent "preferred MILFs and Cougars over Teens."[11] Nina Hartley (Marie Louise Hartman), who made her first porn film in San Francisco in 1984, reflected in 2015 on the influx of older women into the business. "We can thank *American Pie* (1999) for making up the word MILF. Porn capitalized on that concept very well and came up with a category, Cougars and MILFs—it's been going on for about 10 years. A lot of decent, middle-age, middle-class married guys are parents, and it creeps them out to watch women who are their daughters' ages." Also, said Hartley, wives who might not be OK with videos featuring 20-year-olds could accept their husbands watching fifty-somethings.[12] "Boomers are aging, and a lot of boomers would rather look at someone who looks more like them!" (Confirming Hartley's observation, the proportion of people on Pornhub searching for "MILF," as opposed to "teen," rose with age.[13])

It was from this band of feminist veterans such as Hartley that the few performers' organizations in the industry were constituted. A performers' group called Club 90, after Annie Sprinkle's address on Lexington Avenue in Manhattan where they met, originated in 1983. It arose out of a baby shower, and then when all the straight guests left, the porn stars stayed on and, said Candida Royalle later, "We had the best time."[14] In 1984, the club put on an off-Broadway show called *Deep Inside Porn Stars*, a dramatization of the Club 90 meetings, which portrayed performers as people rather than as victims. (Until 2005, at least, the club continued to meet, if only online.) In the late 1980s, Nina Hartley co-founded with Porsche Lynn and others a short-lived support group for feature dancers called The Pink Ladies Social Club. The producers shunned it as a potential performers' union and tried to deny its members work.[15]

In 2015, at the 12th annual CineKink Film Festival in New York, the porn stars of Club 90 held a reunion, where their reminiscences were fond rather than bitter.[16] By this time, this concept of "feminist pioneers of porn" had finally taken root as a direction in which enlightened women might be heading.

A Second Generation

This first generation paved the way for a younger generation of feminist porn stars, the Jenna Jamesons and Vicky Vettes. Jameson (Jenna Marie Massoli), "the Queen of Porn," started performing in adult in 1993 at nineteen, and after winning a series of awards, started the adult entertainment company Club Jenna in 2000, with Jay Grdina (whom she later married and divorced). She was rocketed to fame in mainstream by Club Jenna; her 2004 autobiography, *How to Make Love Like a Porn Star*, said to have been ghost-written by *New York Times* music critic Neil Strauss,[17] zoomed to best-seller status. Appearances on Howard Stern's show and in his 1997 film, *Private Parts*, all made her the single most recognizable name in adult entertainment. In January 2014, Fleshlight released her signature "masturbatory sleeve" (artificial vagina).

In terms of feminism, Jenna Jameson didn't have much in common with Candida Royalle, who was a militant and articulate sex-positive feminist. Yet both had the same resentment of how the industry had treated women and the same resoluteness to go one better. Jameson said, "Over the years, I had noticed that women in the adult industry didn't seem to be valued. The stars were just disposable products with a shelf life of a few years." Jameson realized that she did not, in fact, have to work for someone else. "I could blaze a path I had seen no other woman take and start a successful company of my own. I could run my own website, produce my own content, call my own shots. I could be not just a porn star, but a porn CEO."[18] Unlike some porn stars who had crossed into mainline, such as Traci Lords and Stacy Valentine, Jameson had few social pretentions. "The porn industry made me what I am," she said in 2001. "And I am proud of what I do for it.... My prime concern is the adult industry. End of story. I'm a porn star. I'm not Sharon Stone."[19]

Vicky Vette entered the industry in 2003 at age 38, "repeatedly told by agents that she was too old to succeed in adult." But she made her name in movies, shot almost 150 scenes in three years, then exited the performing side to become an entrepreneur. She started a line of toys with Doc Johnson in 2009, headlining the "Vickie Quickie—Double Ender," "molded straight from Vette's pussy and ass and using Doc Johnson's patented UR3 [Ultra-Realistic] material." (For more on this, see Toys, Chapter 17.) She then set up her own network, VNAGirls.com, for 19 of the coming generation of porn stars to feature their own sites.[20]

These women were the original porn stars. But then the star system took a dive, and "porn star" became a generic term for any young woman paid to perform on set rather than an identifier for a real star. It was probably Jenna Jameson, developed by Joy King at Wicked, who wrecked it by leaving Wicked as a contract girl in 2002 for Vivid. "Wicked put like 5 million dollars into Jenna," said Brittany Andrews, her former roommate. "And the day that she left and went to Vivid, the star system absolutely collapsed, because everybody knew who Jenna was, but nobody knew what Wicked was, and after that...they became the 'Vivid girls' or the 'Wicked girls.'

"It opened up every major company's eyes, and they said, 'Oh shit. We can't make the bitch bigger than the brand.'"[21]

Chapter 7:
Abuse?

The shadow side of Porn Valley is that some performers really are abused and exploited. This abuse probably increased as a result of the transition from feature films to action-packed gonzo (see Chapter 10). In the feature era, the values on set tended to resemble more those of mainstream, and the actresses were on the whole treated with respect.

Abusive behavior rose with gonzo. Longtime actor Eric Edwards, who had entered porn in New York in 1969, recalled in 2006 the "onslaught of video." "It's a totally different animal. I'm not very fond of the new animal. It's demeaning to women, rougher. It's not like the lovemaking we did in the 1970s and 1980s."[1]

As gonzo peaked around 2000, the level of abuse in videos seemed to peak as well. Powerful voices in the industry said that the violence and the pissing should be dialed back. In March 2000, Frank Kay, owner of New Jersey's International Video Distributors, said that he didn't want to see the era of the obscenity prosecutions return. "I don't want to sit in front of a jury watching another peeing tape.... Stores are making money on the product, no doubt; but in the long run, if they're making a thousand bucks, what's a thousand when the court can cost you $100,000 in legal fees?"[2] Directors such as Khan Tusion, Rob Black, and Max Hardcore were making the entire industry nervous—in 2001, Rob Black and Tom Byron were banned from mention in *AVN*.[3] Even John T. Bone (the Englishman John Gilbert Bowen), who had led the charge into degradation (*The World's Biggest Gang Bang*, 1995), turned his back on it: "It's gone beyond consenting adults," he said in 2001.... I don't believe in violating women beyond sex play." He said that he regretted some of his own past work. So, some of the abusive scenes did subside.

Misogyny

Within the industry, virtually nobody behind the camera wanted their children to become performers. This is a sign that the porn stars were absolutely at the bottom rung of the prestige ladder. Asked in 2014 to comment on the question, "Would you let your kids enter the industry?" the majority view of the twenty-nine directors, producers and back-end executives who did answer was that working behind the camera was an acceptable choice for one's children, even one to be encouraged given how quickly one could make a lot of money. Not one of the twenty-nine, however, indicated even vague approval of one's children opting to become performers. The respondents used rationalizations of various kinds, but the undertone was that performing would be a degrading choice for children of wealthy parents who, in fact, could do much better in life.[4] Within industry, the performers were viewed as a kind of downstairs class of Edwardian domestics. (This does not change the reality that the performers often upgraded their own social status.)

A kind of residual misogyny lingered. This began with the contemptuous attitude many male directors had towards the female talent. A male humor of derogation permeated the industry. A sample:

"Top 10 list of topics covered in the typical porn girl's book [the premise is that all young women in porn are 'writing a book']:

1. How to sprill you're [sic] porn name.

2. It's OK for your tits to be 1/3 your total body weight.

10. Porn is better than Hooters because you don't have to work the fryer."[5]

This reflexive degradation of female talent often appeared in the language. One insider said in 2007, "We need to be very clear about the difference between what we sell and who we are." In the non-vanilla product, the female bottom may be called on screen "whore," "bitch," and so forth. People understand this is part of the fantasy. But, in reality, it is degrading, continued the insider, to "speak of the models as 'sluts' in business conversations.... I shudder every time I see on the boards, 'What do you think of this whore we just shot?'"[6]

Mixed martial artist and woodsman, Dick Delaware (Aaron Brink), later described his first scene. He said this much later after getting off meth and amphetamine—and it captures the feeling of degradation. Remember, this is now the "good" Delaware talking: "I was working with a...black chick. I'd never fucked a black chick before. Plus, I had to do an internal pop-shot [ejaculating inside the model for a cream-pie scene].... When I tore that whore a new one that day I knew I had a future in the business."[7] The man was physically massive. The account is terrifying.

In fairness, many directors bend over backwards to treat the models with respect; companies such as Wasteland.com and Sssh.com are exemplary and would *never* tolerate a Dick Delaware. Dee Severe's editorial in *XBIZ* in 2015 castigating such practices had a wide uptake.[8]

Some directors wouldn't even let the budding porn stars continue to use the same professional name because they wanted the models to appear fresh. So the models didn't have the chance to build their brand. Alexia Vosse said of previous shoots, "The crappy part is all the older scenes have different names. They didn't want me to use the names I used with other companies. I didn't know any better."[9]

And the nasty stuff! Janet Mason, who had her own "amateurs" website back East featuring herself and her husband among other couples, moved in 2009 to Los Angeles to try the pro side. She didn't like it. There was just too many nasty scenes she was asked to do. She wanted to do "only those types of scenes which accurately reflect the 'real me' and what I am genuinely into: very well-endowed black men, clean-cut and very fit younger white guys, other women, and my personal kinks such as handjobs, facials. foot fetish, etc. At no point will I *ever* consider doing another scene that is *not* something I'd do in my personal life again (such as bondage, sex with guys I find unattractive, etc.), and, if I am ever deliberately misled by a director again, I will simply walk off the set."[10]

Even though official industry spokespersons pretended otherwise, a kind of physical degradation was a reality. In 2011, Mike South doubted the insistence of Diane Duke, chief of the industry lobby, Free Speech Coalition, that porn had "a code of ethics." He mocked, "We would never do anything to endanger the lives of our most valuable asset, the performers...choking the performers until they lose consciousness, infect them with potentially fatal diseases with practices like ass to mouth, or mentally or physically assaulting them...ooops."[11] (To retain balance here, many performers readily accepted facials and anal as part of the job. In a 2013 analysis of the profiles of 7,000 female porn stars in the IAFD data base, which was started in 1981, 87 percent said they were ready to "take a facial," and 62 percent were set for anal.[12])

To their credit, many models pushed back against the misogyny, refusing to be treated as "two legs and a hole." In 2009, after a discouraging exchange about how disrespectfully the female performers were often treated, Sophia St. James, an Afro-American performer, blew up: "I DEMAND respect. Period! I am an ethnic, EDUCATED, woman who has lots of experience in many fields. I CHOOSE to be in the adult industry. I DON'T have to be. I am not a high school drop out. I am not a poor single mother just trying to keep a roof over my head. I have skills in the medical field, [am] a mother of a FABULOUS little one, and currently am going to school.... I may be a sex worker, but I deserve respect and manners shown to me. I will not have it any other way."[13]

The only conceivable response to this is, "Yes, ma'am."

Casting Couch

AVN question:
"Is there a casting couch in the legit as well as in the porn field?"
Porn star Marlene Willoughby answer:
"There's a casting couch in everything."[14]

You, as a model, were expected to have sex as though you were a kind of party favor. Tina Tyler, herself a director at Mercenary Pictures and former model, once performed a scene in the back of a Cesena airplane with her then-husband. After the scene was over, its director said, "Once you're finished cleaning up, you don't mind going up in the cockpit, right?"

"Why would I want to go in the cockpit?"

"Well. I promised the pilot he could get a blowjob if he gave me a deal on the plane."

Tyler replied, "Well, then you better get your knee pads out, because you're the one that made the promise."[15]

It was totally demeaning that many models were expected to have sex with the directors or the male staff on the set. Director Anthony Spinelli (Samuel Weinstein) told Dave Jennings of a scam he might pull with neophyte models. "After the guy delivers his pop shot, she looks at me and asks if she's done. I keep a straight face and say, 'Not yet. For new girls it's a long-standing tradition that the entire crew gets in on the action.' She ponders this for a moment, then asks, 'I get extra for that, don't I?'"[16]

Porn star Papillon said the couch was an industry standard, yet she refused to do it if the director was totally gross; she complained of one director as "an overweight, long haired hippie with a stuttering problem and also has a major alcohol addiction," who told her she'd get a contract only if she "slept with him on a regular basis." She hated that. But, "the sad thing about this is that I have given many a director a Bl*w Job just because I wanted too."[17]

But not all porn stars gave directors sex. Porn megastar Georgina Spelvin said that she never had to sleep with anyone to get a role in porn, unlike mainline where, "I ran the gamut of casting couches. I got tired of having to fuck the receptionist in order to get to screw the second assistant director [etc.]...in order to meet somebody to maybe get a walk-on."[18] Memphis Monroe, born in New Orleans and raised in Kentucky, entered the industry around 2005 at 21. She said in 2008, "The rumors of a casting couch were true in my experience, but I kept my dignity and politely refused. It was important for me to keep things strictly business. I might have lost some jobs because I didn't put out, but it didn't matter to me."[19] (Memphis Monroe did, however, take up escorting and was featured on "Premium New York City Escorts"[20]— yet sex for money was entirely voluntary on her part, unlike the more or less involuntary casting-couch scenario.)

Rough Sex vs. Degrading Sex

"There's a difference between rough sex and degrading sex. I love rough sex. Degrading is where men are taking advantage of the women [porn stars], and you can tell on the women's faces that they don't like this—that they're getting smacked and hit and getting things put up their butt, and they didn't expect to get pee'd on. That's degrading sex."[21]

BRIDGET POWERZ, PORN STAR, 2000

And here is some real violence, real exploitative sexual harassment that is not consensual. When Bridgette Kerkove was on a shoot, [male actor A] "was having problems getting wood during the scene.

"Bridgette was bent over doggy, she had [male actor B's] dick in her mouth and [male actor A] was trying to slam his limp cock into her ass.

"Apparently, during the frustration, [male actor A] slammed her to the ground once, forcefully, but not intentionally. They set up and tried again, assuming the same positions. With [the male actor B's] pecker back in Kerkove's mouth, [male actor A] began slamming her backside again, without the assistance of a hard on.

"He got really frustrated and slammed her again, this time knocking her down hard, and he stormed off the set saying, 'I'm outta here!'

"No one was seriously hurt in the incident, but the scene was a bust." The producer said, "I don't think I'll be using [male actor A] in any scenes for a while." Bridgette had bloody knees and male actor B's penis "was nearly severed...as it was in her mouth while she was slammed to the floor."[22]

That was an abusive male talent. It wasn't planned. But sometimes the violence is planned, and director Jerome Tanner was all too aware of this and furious about it. He said at a directors' roundtable in 2003, "If you've been on a set where the guy is mouth-fucking her and the woman is throwing up—not voluntarily; involuntarily—she's tearing, she's convulsing; now that's not—to me, *to me*, that's not sex. To me, that's violence."[23]

At this point in the directors' discussion, Veronica Hart made a point often used by the antiporners, and it may have some validity. Certainly, it's not to be dismissed out of hand. She said, "I know that people do view this stuff and get affected. It's not politically correct as pornographers to ever say that. We've been hiding behind that defense that what we do doesn't do anything, but we're sitting in here with a room of people who have been brought up on pornography, and I see it getting more and more and more and more extreme."[24]

So, rough scenes should be banned? Women who like them be slut-shamed? It was a rough scene that caused Amber Lynn to get off on camera for the first time, in a shoot with Billy Dee, "He had to fuck me while chasing me up a ladder. When he caught me, he trapped my head between the rungs, and held my hands behind my back so that I couldn't move...and he screwed me from behind like a mad bull. When he'd stroke really hard, my tits would press up against the rungs of the ladder—the pinching hurt them—I loved it. When I tried to climb up and away he grabbed my hair and pulled me to him and fucked me harder. That was the first time I really came on film."[25]

Amber Lynn may have enjoyed the rough stuff but Vivian Valentine, 21 when she entered the industry in 1998 (4 feet, 11 inches, 99 pounds), didn't, or at least not always. (She played in a number of "extreme" movies.) While filming for

RedBoard Video's *Torment 1* in 1999, her first extreme shoot, fellow actors Jamie Gillis and Jewel Valmont (Ava Vincent) began to bang her around. "We kept going," said director Duck Dumont (Alan Shustak). "It was never told to me that this was her first time.... At a certain point, twenty minutes into the scene, she pulls the tape off her mouth and says stop it. I can't take it." Dumont stopped shooting at once. "Off camera, she sobbed somewhat uncontrollably. I cleared the room. She was laying on the floor and I just held her for 15 or 20 minutes."[26]

So, this kind of thing gave many directors the willies who realized they were dealing with the futures of 18-year-olds! Samantha38G (Samantha Anderson) said on the *XBIZ* board in 2014 to a newbie producer who was asking advice, "[You should keep in mind that you are] booking such young females in something that affects their career choices for the rest of their life. Much less losing relationships with family members & friends when they do porn.... Personally, I don't think anyone under the age of 24 should do porn." She, herself, had offers from age 18 on, but didn't enter the industry until she was 30.[27]

Indeed, some of the "rough stuff" turned out to be even more involuntary than the industry imagined. In December 2015, male performer James Deen (Bryan M. Sevilla) was accused by several female performers of sexual abuse. The response of the industry was virtually instantaneous: almost every studio and institution with which he had been involved severed contact with him. The headline in the online press was, "The porn industry handles rape better than Hollywood."[28]

If one were to strip away all the other evidence in this book and include only the abuse stories in this chapter, one would come up with a stunning indictment of the adult industry. And this is precisely what many antiporners have done. Similarly, if one dwelt on the abuse stories coming from the pharmaceutical industry and neglected the many important agents brought to market and the intensive pursuit of science of the companies, one would construct a similar indictment.[29] Both porn and pharmaceuticals, in my view, have contributed much to society, the former by expanding the sexual imagination and thereby encouraging personal growth. At the end of the day, one tries to deliver a balanced account of both industries.

Chapter 8:
Internet

"The internet was made for three particular things: It was meant to check your email, to check your stocks and investments, and to check your adult content."[1]

GREG CLAYMAN, VIDEO SECRETS, 2004

D irector Holly Randall missed the *XBIZ* awards in 2007 because she was in rehab for her alcoholism. But she attended in 2008, and there were two very different nights. The first night was a select dinner including senior people in the field, offered in a lovely quiet ambiance. The second night was for webmasters and the *XBIZ* awards. It was a riotous mob around the bar that paid no attention to the awards ceremony proceeding on stage. What was the difference between the two nights?

"I realized," said Randall, "that the *XBIZ* Awards was a show that mainly honored webmasters, a crowd of people quite different from the old-school DVD producers from the previous night's dinner. These are two markedly different groups—the webmasters are mainly young computer whiz kids whose skills granted them a sudden income way beyond what they made in any previous line of work. This, coupled with their youth and easy access to beautiful women, gives them an exaggerated sense of self-importance that really manifests itself after a few drinks."

By contrast the DVD producers, said Randall, were people with memories "who are now watching the once-dominant DVD market crumble under the massive weight of the internet juggernaut."[2]

Going Online Begins

The year is 1996. Sean Shap is a second-year student at Concordia University in Montreal who's just been thrown off the hockey team and has his evenings now free. He starts playing around with his computer and discovers Persian Kitty's porn website; he learns from her online counter that she's getting "some insanely high number" of hits. He decides to organize his own site entitled "Wow Big Breast World" and post a link to it on PK's page. "PK listed my site around 5pm and the hits started pouring in." Shap's buddy, who was sitting there on the couch "couldn't believe THAT many people around the world were coming to view my collection of boob pics! The hits kept coming in all weekend long...."

Oh, oh. Fast forward to Monday morning. At 8 am, Shap got a call from "the geek at the head of the [university] computer department. The geek was 'all pissed.' He told me that over the weekend I had used 99% of the bandwidth that the school had used in the past 6 years. I had pushed over 250,000 hits in less than 3 days." Shap was banned from the university computer, banned from everything having to do with computers. He figured out he'd have to set up a site like Persian Kitty's and see if he could make money from it. By 2001, the site would be called Twistys. The rest, as they say, "is history."[3]

Let's back up a bit. In the late 1980s, entrepreneurs began using the Bulletin Board System (BBS) to sell images online. In 1989, Rich at FreshDVDFeeds, as his company was later called, began selling content online. "Credit card processing required a brick and mortar business of some type—banks actually inspected many businesses prior to accepting them, I had to set up a small lingerie store to get a merchant account to use for the bbs." Then around 1994, he said, "the web started to take off and for a while running an online adult business got easy, REALLY easy. Back then it seemed like doing anything with porn made money. Throw a few softcore pics on a page, they came in droves. Build a simple list of adult websites and you could clean up in advertising." Over the years, Rich built sites that sold adult toys, videotapes and, later, DVDs. Chat rooms, live feeds, video galleries: "Everything I did made money. By the late 90s there was a true 'gold rush' in online adult, everyone was doing it because it was so damn easy."[4]

Some of these early startups such as Gamelink became huge. In 1993, the CEO Ilan Bunimovitz began the firm after stumbling across a Bulletin Board System that let users dial in via a phone line permitting them to download software and exchange messages. Bunimovitz began by putting up video games, realized he could make little headway against ToysRUs, and switched over to adult videotapes. "Within six months, I started hiring employees," he later said. (In 1993 as well, San Franciscan Magnus Sullivan founded eLine, the technology firm that went on to manage Gamelink.com.) In 1999, Bunimovitz became the first to offer "video-on-demand for broadband."[5]

In 1997, Lensman (Joe Lackey) entered the industry from a design background. He saw the success the early webmasters were having and said, "Well, if they can do it, I can do it." Amateur Pages became his first adult site, featuring lots of little thumbnail images (thumbnail gallery posts, TGPs). Nobody else had been able to make money off this, but Lensman did. Then, in 2001, he acquired Adult.com, a huge affiliate program (for feeding traffic); next, he set up the chatboard GFY.com ("Go Fuck Yourself"), which made money from running ads: people chatted for free. In 2005, Playboy Enterprises bought out his entire operation, called ICS Inc., for $12 million.[6]

Thus, many of these early entrepreneurs became very wealthy. There was just so much money to be made as the nation discovered online porn. Looking back in 2011 on the golden years, Robbie, who together with his wife, Claudia- Marie, had built in 2007 a highly successful website based on the big-breasted woman theme, told aspirants, "If you can build a members area of 1,000 paying fans at $29.99 a month you are going to be a big success as a husband/wife team. Claudia-Marie and I own a 5,200 square foot home in Vegas with a beautiful swimming pool, a sport court, and some very nice vehicles in the garage." Between 2007 and 2011, Robbie and CM had made over $2 million [annually is evidently meant] on the basis of CM's giant breasts. "So yes, it can still be done," concluded Robbie."[7] And was done by those in at the beginning.

YNOT

In 1996, a new era began when the adult industry acquired a collective online presence in the form of the site YNOT.com, founded by Rick Muenyong (Rick Moby), whom Jay Kopita, today an administrator and part-owner of YNOT, describes as "a very intelligent, early internet visionary type whiz kid fresh out of high school."[8] YNOT was intended as "an organization for top adult site webmasters."[9] The elite group, which one could only join by membership vote, included Colin Rowntree, who had founded in 1994 the oldest adult site on the internet, the BDSM-oriented Wasteland.com; Richard Nash (Bangwang) of the site Pornholio; Jonathan Lieberman (Naughty.com); a member known by the handle "Pushrod," whose real name has been embarrassingly forgotten by old hands (his YNOT member site was Pushrod's Utter Filth though he was probably better known for his later site, Anarchy Links[10]); Alec Helmy, a multi-site webmaster who established the trade journal *4 Adults Only* in 1996, which turned into *XBIZ* in 1998; and David Van der Poel (Python.com).[11]

The founding members included a considerable number of women: Beth Mansfield, a 34-year-old accountant who established the highly successful site Persian Kitty in 1995[12] ; Carol Cox, creator of Wild Rose's Explicit Amateur Homepage in 1994 (see below); Danni Ashe, whose epochally successful site Danni's Hard Drive—the first megasite debuted by a model—launched in 1995; Angela Rowntree, who had begun building her site Sssh, the first porn-for-women site, in 1998 and launched in 1999; and Asia Carrera, whom Rick Muenyong remembers fondly as "the biggest nerd in porn; she could assemble a computer from scratch;"[13] born Jessica Steinhauser, she had begun her adult acting career in 1993.

"We relied heavily on each other for ideas, support, and assistance," said Rowntree later, "as we made our many mistakes and grew our businesses into the first online adult sites."[14] YNOT soon settled down as a chatboard but spawned a number of other YNOT-branded sites and awards programs, to become one of the classic names in online porn. (Muenyong went on to found TheBestPorn and MyPorn, and is now celebrated as "the Zuckerberg of Porn."[15])

The early days are still referred to in industry as "the YNOT days," even though YNOT continues to flourish. Robert Jenkins (Khan) says of that period, "The adult web in those days was quite different than it is today or even what it was just a few years later. YNOT members were a very exclusive group of mainly just regular folk. Entrepreneurial folks to be sure, but real people who were willing to help each other grow not only their individual sites, but also the YNOT Network and the new adult online industry."[16] (In 2005 the YNOT Network transformed the old resource, YNOT Masters, into YNOT.com.)

A New Era

For better or worse, a new era had begun. In 1997, only 18 percent of Americans used the internet at home. By 2011, it was over 71 percent.[17] With pay-per-minute, video-on-demand, and the electronic delivery methods of the internet, you could download or stream porn into your own living room without joining the raincoat crowd at the Pussycat Theater or having to buy videotapes or discs at the local adult shop. In the privacy of your own home, the vast world of adult pleasures lay open to you, the average surfer getting off in less than 10 minutes (9 minutes and 11 seconds for the younger crowd; over-35 males take fully one minute longer—according to 2015 data from Pornhub[18]). "No more skulking around the wrong part of town to buy a video, much less waiting for the mail carrier to bring a plain brown envelope with an 8mm film," said *XBIZ* writer Erik Jay. "Today, a $75 used PC and a $12.95-a-month DSL [digital subscriber line] connection sucks the universe of sex with its constellations of willing nymphs right into the consumer's home."[19]

The net was flooded with images; image sites behind a pay wall started to become infeasible. David, a professional photographer, said in 2016, "Trying to sell sand in the desert is generally a bad idea, but that is close to what this business model looks like. It's very hard to sell sets of photos alone as simply sets of great photos. No one cares. If I want to jack off to three girls giving one guy a blowjob, I'll just type "3 girls bj" into Google's image search and be done with it in around five minutes."[20]

The new era also meant the death of the quality porn flicks of the 1970s. "The internet TOTALLY killed the market that really supported high end porn," said Mike South in 2014. He mentioned pay-per-view (PPV), cable TV and so forth: all killed by the internet. "Hard to justify a big budget now when...you can get it on say Netflix. The money you get for it is a fraction of what it cost to make. It used to be that the cable and PPV deals alone paid for the high end features and the DVDs were just gravy—the times have a changed."[21] Authorities talked of internet porn creating "an electronic version of Gresham's Law [bad money drives out good]."[22] Cheap, poorly produced made-for-internet porn was driving out the 35mm features.

The cozy little world of Porn Valley, with its Thursday night poker games at agent Jim South's, began to give way in the 1990s to a mega-scene, involving numerous agents, dozens of directors and producers, and hundreds of models and would-be models. Said journalist Acme Anderson, "The '90s brought the internet, Viagra and inexpensive cameras, changing not only the way business was done, but who was doing it." LA Direct Models, the big new agency, had a roster of about 125 female performers and 30 males. "The bigger agencies all boast more than 100 performers on their sites," said Anderson. Another agent said he turned down "around 80 percent of the people who contact him."[23]

Things Pick Up

Things moved really quickly: internet porn began with still images, then, as the *AVN* technology writer put it, "slow, grainy video clips arrived on the scene," and from there to full-length videos, and then high-definition, full-screen full-length videos. And now, writing in 2005, "streaming videos viewable on cell phones."[24] Yet each step required successively faster frame rates, and that meant ever great bandwidth. Porn moved on line at the pace that the techies grew bandwidth.

Among the first studios to transition to the internet was Montreal-based Gamma Entertainment, founded by Karl Bernard in 1996. Bernard, an 18-year-old techie who had just dropped out of computer school, was pursuing his hobby of finding sexy images and putting them up on a web page. "Suddenly, people started visiting my site," he said. Bernard then acquired a number of other sites and thousands of "free hosted galleries." Thus, Gamma Entertainment was born, one of the big success stories in adult internet history. Bernard's own site featured women 18-21 under the labels "Web's Youngest Women" and "All Teens."[25] (These sites are at great pains to ensure that the models are in fact 18 and over.)

Accordingly, in the world of fantasy, 18-year-olds led the charge onto the net. (As we saw in Chapter 5, the actual models tended to be older.) In 1999, Hustler Video debuted its *Barely Legal* series featuring teens. In 2001, Steve Lightspeed (Steve Jones) pioneered the "teen solo-girl niche," scarcely legal models whose allure attracted an enormous following. Tawneee Stone was the first "Lightspeed Girl," and Lightspeed Media became a network of similar sites for "barely teen legal models." Reproached (unjustly) for using under-age models, Lightspeed responded, "I wish someone would show me a picture of what an 18-year-old girl is supposed to look like. If you put makeup on them, everyone says they look too old, if you don't put makeup on them, people say they look too young."[26]

By 2000, the internet was moving to broadband transmission, where download speeds at about 30 frames per second were comparable to those of television. Now it became possible to download quickly high-quality videos and to stream live feeds, and the shift from DVD to the net began in earnest. Moreover, in 2001, the Adult Entertainment Broadcast Network began PPV. AEBN was founded by Scott Coffman in Charlotte, North Carolina; in 1999; it piggybacked on streaming video in the form of porn pay-per-view, and Coffman figured out a way to let internet surfers "buy as many minutes of viewing as they want and to use those minutes to watch scenes from up to 12,000 movies." By November, 2002, almost 10,000 websites had joined AEBN's pay-per-view program. Surfers could also download entire movies on a rental basis, though it was another company, Bluebare Entertainment in Van Nuys, California, that introduced this.[27] These innovations made it possible for the raincoat crowd to stay home and download seven-minute segments, and for couples to curl up on the sofa and download adult movies.

DVDs continued to be sold, but their hegemony dissolved. On the one hand, we have what *XBIZ* editor Stephen Yagielowicz referred to as "the traditional video guys" in DVD, and on the other "legions of young, tech-savvy newcomers flooding onto the scene with their bright ideas [about the internet]." The newcomers saw the old video guys as "dinosaurs doomed to rapid extinction." And that turned out to be quite right. John Stagliano at Evil Angel was one of the dinosaurs. "I never knew how to put software onto computers," he said. "I didn't know this sort of stuff because I didn't have to. I was fat and happy.... I have to work 10 times harder for much less money right now," he said in 2009.[28]

The internet was the future of industry. JoJo Rufus, owner of a large paysite, went to the Internext [internet] meeting in Florida in 2002 and found Jesus. "The immediacy is what matters. Shoot with the Net in mind. Don't pigeonhole yourself into thinking about measly video distribution. So you sell 1000 units out the door if you're lucky. Half the distributors don't pay you on time. You have to beg, borrow and steal.... Meanwhile you ain't got enough money to pay rent...."

He continued, "The Internext tells us one thing. If you don't embrace the net, you are doomed. Like when people didn't embrace the VCR. Or the camcorder. Or DVDs. But guess what? The Internet requires a hell of more skills than those past technological advances...."[29] That was the thing: taping for VCR required little skill, moving to DVD scarcely a great deal more. But the internet called for programming skills, which few content providers had. They wanted badly to cling to DVD, but they couldn't.

In 2007 Vivid put up its first movies on the internet.[30] By 2006, Gamma's Karl Bernard was managing and designing the websites of male megastar Peter North (known for his gigantic ejaculates) and of Czech-born Silvia Saint. In 2008, the website of Tara Patrick—the new number one model after Jenna Jameson left the industry—moved into the Gamma fold, followed by the website of the famous Italian woodsman Rocco Siffredi. In 2011, Gamma debuted a large webcam model broadcast network. By 2015, Gamma was directly managing sixteen partner websites. The Gamma affiliates—partner websites with which

Gamma shared surfers' fees—were managed by the Gamma affiliate program FameDollars.[31] (Gamma entered the production side by creating Gamma Films Group, to launch such brands as Girlsway.)

Another early giant, PimpRoll, started out in Dave's dormitory bedroom in 1998 and became PimpRoll in 2001, an aggregator that offered over 450 sites. PimpRoll bought the domain name Porn.com for $9 million in May 2007, and so strong was the name that, by 2008, PimpRoll was getting 50,000 hits per day through type-in traffic alone.[32] This was a scale that just blew DVDs off the map.

So the young internet techies beat out the dinosaurs. But the great irony is that the internet gang found that "the pervasive 'culture of free'...left them with nothing of value to sell."[33] Technical change had conspired to diminish both the DVD dinosaurs and the technies. In the 1990s, the DVD era had been a gold mine, creating many millionaires. In the new millennium, internet people had to struggle to make a living in porn.

Amateur

"Amateur" videos first came out when Jim Enright (James Enright Shanahan), then national circulation director for *Hustler*, and Steven Vlottes, at Dreamland Entertainment, formed their own company, Homes Movies Limited; they started shooting in 1982, finding talent through swingers clubs. Essex Video distributed the four volumes of product. "They sell a lot in the blue collar communities," Enright said later. "They aren't all beauties out there. And these features are for them, for the people who maybe could never get a girl as pretty as a porn star in bed."[34] Enright later became a major director and producer.

There was often something performative, or stagey, about commercial video. But as the world moved online, amateur began to sweep the adult web. Amateur has the advantage over commercial of featuring real people who obviously are enjoying themselves, or otherwise they wouldn't be doing it. Said Dan Savage, author of the wildly popular syndicated column "Savage Love," in 2017, "The films are made by people for the fun and pleasure and joy of it."[35]

In the Canadian province of Alberta, Carol and Danny Cox began the earliest sustained amateur site in 1988 as an Adult BBS (Bulletin Board System) featuring pictures of Carol. That site soon became Wild Rose Amateurs with Carol. In 1992, the Coxes moved to Montreal for reasons of Danny's job in aerospace, and in the spring of 1994, they launched their first website, Wild Rose Fireplace Chat with free pictures of Carol. (This was the first of what would later be called the "solo-girl" sites.) They also started shooting amateur videos to pay for bandwidth, which was really expensive in those days. Carol's first video sold 30,000 tapes; within a few months, they were shipping between 600 to 800 videos a week. In January 1996, they started the CarolCox.com site, as it exists today. (The Coxes organized in 1997 a highly successful "cam ring," or group site for solo camgirls (see Chapter 18). "We did get lucky," Danny later said, "being in the right place at the right time.... Those really were 'the good old days.'"[36] By 2001, amateurs originated around 70 percent of all porn sites.[37]

Amateur was real, raw, and overwhelming. Now that feature films were out of style, surfers wanted to see real sex up close. "You have these college girls and these good-looking college guys," said veteran performer and website operator Nicole Sheridan, "and they think it'd be kind of nasty and cool to make a porn video in the dorm or wherever, and then put it on the net for free. Obviously, a lot of people are going to think, 'Why should I drop $30 on a feature with only a handful of sex scenes?' when they can get nonstop sex for nothing."[38] Once people could post their amateur creations on the internet, and surfers could download the suburban bedroom scenes on smartphones, homemade erotica went through the ceiling—so much so that many professionals downgraded their own shots in order to make them appear amateur. Cameras were getting cheaper, you could slap up your own website, and suddenly a brilliant new opportunity for making a living was on offer. Holly Randall: "Suddenly everyone could become a pornographer!"[39]

That is roughly what happened to *Bang Bus,* one of the most successful ever amateur series filmed in Miami in gonzo style—helping to make Miami a porn center second only to the Valley. In 2000, two school pals at the University of Florida, Kristopher Hinson and Penn David, conceived the idea of making amateur porn, and, after several false starts, ended up with the concept of a couple of "dudes" just driving around town looking for random "chicks" they could inveigle into hopping into the Volkswagen camper with tinted windows and having sex. Much of it was, of course, prearranged—often with professional models or local people responding to newspaper ads—but filmed to look amateur: "Oh, I've never given a blow-job before!" Most of the 40-minute films are taken up with persuading the young women to have sex for money; the last part of the video records the occupants of the moving van, except for cameraperson Greg Entner (Dirty Sanchez) and the driver, having sex in various combinations, and then dropping the surprised young woman off, unpaid, at a distant location while she curses at the disappearing van and the laughing dudes. *Bang Bus* harvested several *AVN* awards, making the owners of the production company, Ox Ideas, into millionaires.[40]

Amateur aggregators sprang up, so great was the demand for something that looked homemade. According to Webmaster Central, amateur was the top-selling adult category in 2014.[41] The performers were "Mom and pop [on a] Saturday night with a sixpack," said Farrell Timlake, owner of Homegrown Video, an amateur service founded in 1982. "The cat jumps on the bed. It's very raw and not produced to be anything but a fun testament of what they did that evening."[42] But amateur was a bit of a cultivated taste. Timlake said, "We always run into people who say, 'But what do you have that's professional? Like Playboy girls?' And we always say, 'Playboy is where people start to watch adult, but they always end up at amateur when it's all over.'"[43]

The Internet and Porn Valley

It was the best of times, it was the worst of times. The new internet technology made it possible to move into the living rooms of people worldwide and feast them with sexual images they would have previously considered unimaginable. For millions of men and women, this was wonderful.

At the same time, the new internet technology made possible the pirating of much content and depositing it on new "tubesites," so named after the ability of people to download YouTube content for free. Or webmasters might donate content to the tubes for the sake of publicity. The tubesites made their money on advertising from dating sites and webcam sites, not on fees from traffic. It started to become unprofitable to shoot in Chatsworth, and production began drifting away.

Pirating was, in a sense, the ultimate triumph of the new technology. Mike South said, "Here comes DSL [digital subscriber line] and cable, soon lots and lots of people had access to internet connections that were very fast, fast enough to download high quality video clips." Meanwhile, Porn Valley was pouring videos onto the market at about 20 per day. "It didn't take long before you could download and burn a perfect copy of a DVD in less time than it takes to drive to the porn store and buy it."

But surely people were just downloading amateur porn, so it didn't matter? No. "[Soon] you were seeing full quality DVDs appearing the same day they were released, mainstream movies and porn and piracy, got rampant, because now you didn't even have to buy the DVD to make a perfect copy of it." Tubesites, or free streaming video, could be set up with minimal technical skills. "Not porn made and submitted by so-called users," said South, "but porn made in Porn Valley. Suddenly it hit home."[44] In the olden days, when organized crime controlled distribution, piracy did not occur. Recalled producer Will Ryder, "With East Coast money there would not have been a problem. There'd be a Louisville Slugger [baseball bat] going through someone's office door."[45] But now, it was different.

Piracy was not exactly a new problem for the adult industry. Video cassettes had been massively pirated. But you would have to find a bootlegger who sold them. With the internet, you could download pirated product with a keystroke. Around 2008, this began to sink in. One producer, who didn't want to be named because he thought it might start a rumor that his company was in trouble, told *XBIZ*, "It doesn't matter whether you produce content for the web or DVD, piracy is rampant, and it's costing us millions of dollars a year. Add to that the volume of amateur content out there...and it just becomes backbreaking. I don't know whether to be depressed or mad, but I do know it's not easy to make a living anymore. The money and the fun are gone for a lot of people."[46]

But then, various developments solved the piracy problem without solving the cashflow problems of the content providers. One, the shift from downloading to streaming ended much piracy, as pay-per-view streaming is difficult to pirate. Master Ryan said in 2013, "I have years of real-world proof that PPV puts a huge stop to piracy. For example, go search for videos from Lad's Feet (www.Ladsfeet.com). They have thousands of videos for sale on their site, yet there are no site rips available on the net...pretty rare in porn! that a site is still making 2001-style piles of money, specifically because he chose a PPV setup."[47]

Secondly, industry began giving away porn free to "affiliates" (other websites with links to your own). The affiliates were supposed to put up free shots as teasers, but the teasers got longer and longer, and all of a sudden, you didn't have to visit the pay site in order to watch enough to get off. "That's how it started," said Joe D, a billing specialist. "But then a couple of big programs [studios] took the ball, each thinking they would convert [sell] the best if they gave just a little more and it snowballed from there...."[48]

The result of these developments was that young people, in particular, got out of the habit of paying for porn. But others did continue to pay, and this—in addition to camming—is what helped the industry keep going. There were two kinds of people who kept reaching for their Visas, as Dee Severe said in 2014:

One, those who "don't have any time to surf a lot of tubesites (for instance, they're married and they have the half hour after putting the kids to bed to retire to their home office for some 'work.')" They go right to familiar sources "that have material that will get them off."

Two, "[Those who] have a particular fetish that's not so readily available on tube sites." Dee Severe, as a fetish producer, was well informed about this. "[They] tend to be somewhat older and higher income than the group who would never pay for porn. This group would rather just go straight to their favorite Clips4Sale store or membership site that features their fetish, get some new porn and have fun."[49]

Tubesites

Around 2007, the first adult tubesites started to take off. And even though the economy recovered after 2009, the tubesites continued to dominate traffic.

Of the various tubesites, largest by far was MindGeek, which began life in 2007 when German-born Fabian Thylmann, who had been accumulating porn websites, registered the domain name Manwin.com. Simultaneously in Montreal, three entrepreneurs, who knew one another from college, created the Brazzers website, in addition to several others. They called the holding company Mansef. One of the partners, Matt Keezer, started Pornhub in 2007 within a company owned by Brazzers. Pornhub was to become a huge aggregator. In November 2013, it had over one billion visitors per month.

Now, in March 2010, Thylmann bought all these Montreal properties—Mansef, Brazzers, etc.—and changed the company name to his own Manwin. Manwin quickly partnered with Wicked Pictures to manage Wicked's paysites. Manwin took control of a number of Playboy channels (and started out by managing all of Playboy.com). They acquired Digital Playground, and they made globe-spanning distribution deals. In 2013, Thylmann sold his stake in Manwin, and the company's name was again changed to MindGeek. (MindGeek is headquartered in Montreal and Luxembourg.) At this point, MindGeek took control of a great deal of the online industry.

Thus, MindGeek became a vast holding company that managed communication (Playboy TV); content production (Brazzers, Digital Playground, Twistys, etc.); online access (Pornhub and many more aggregators); and DVD distribution (Pulse Distribution). Pornhub briefly had a billboard in Times Square.[50] MindGeek's sites have been criticized for their alleged extensively pirated content, and there is no doubt that the Manwin-MindGeek consolidation of production that took place after 2008 was partially responsible for the decline in work for models in Porn Valley, a decline that pushed many of them into escorting.[51]

So, You're Getting on the Bus...

So, you're getting on the bus in 2011. Where do you buy a ticket for? Chatsworth? Shooting today is a bad choice, said Mike South in 2011. "There is no longer any money in it. Shooting in Porn Valley has all but dried up.... I steer them [models] to the internet side of things. It's easy enough to set up a Clips4Sale store and she will have total control over her content. Or shoot for internet sites." Mike South thought that shooting would return—and it did, following *Fifty Shades of Grey* in the form of features. But "until then I would only encourage a girl I thought had a shot at a contract with Digital Playground or someone, a situation where she would be secure and reasonably safe."[52]

"Stay out of LA if you're a performer," porn star Brooke Tyler, a longstanding MILF veteran in her 40s who lived in Miami (and whose vast knowledge of the industry included escorting) advised aspirants in 2014. "If you...think that Porn Valley is the only one capable of producing adult entertainment...it's being made from one end of the U.S. to the other, and it doesn't stop there, it is being produced across the world." [53]

Chapter 9:
New Tastes

DVD and the internet had a huge impact on enlarging the palette of sexual tastes. The privacy of DVD and the net guaranteed the surfers' anonymity. Nothing could be done against internet porn that violated community standards. It was anything goes. And precisely this anything-goes atmosphere ended up exposing the public to all kinds of new tastes that previously had been the province of secretive elites. (New tastes in the area of dominance-submission and roleplaying are considered in Chapters 13 and 14; anal in Chapter 15.)

Starting Slow

Let's start slow. Lotza Ed and Lori Anderson, a self-described mom-and-pop shop, found a niche when a number of surfers started commenting on the profusion of blonde hair on Lori's arms. "More requests came in where members would want to see other girls or guys play, lick and touch her arm hair in video and digital photos. We aim to please, so we did that and these members became very satisfied."[1]

Moving up a peg, threesomes are pretty tame compared to blowbangs. Many couples can identify with having another partner in the bed in a way they can't identify with multiple penises squirting semen on the female player. In 2014, Richard Buss (Rochard) at Dating Factory—and therefore in a position to know something about it—said that threesomes were becoming quite popular, especially among women. "Women are much more open to new sexual adventures these days.... If you told a woman that you wanted to have a threesome, there was a good chance she would look at you like you were crazy. Now it's common."[2] (This is not polyamory, the new buzzword for "ethical non-monogamy." In non-monogamy, all the partners are not necessarily in bed at the same time.)

People sought information on threesomes. According to 2015 data from Pornhub, "threesome" figures in the middle of the pack of porn search terms, beaten out by "Japanese," "stepsister," "squirt," and "teen," among other winning terms.[3] Kelly Madison began as a threesomes website. In 1999 Kelly, the vice president of sales at a graphics firm, 33, and Ryan, eleven years her junior and a graphic artist on her staff, started seeing each other after hours, fell in love, and struck out on their own, deciding to set up a porn site (since Kelly had a cousin who was a porn star and knew the business). KellyMadison.com was Kelly's original site and Pornfidelity.com grew out of it. "It began as just a few random scenes that we did for my personal site," said Kelly later, "and we enjoyed it so much we decided to make an entire website dedicated to threesomes." It is interesting that both Kelly and Ryan fell upon the threesomes ideas with such glee, while maintaining a strong, monogamous marriage when not shooting. (This did later turn into an open relationship.[4]) Pornfidelity showed how Kelly and Ryan "met" girls (talent) and seduced them into bed. The response was huge. (This is not to be confused with the dating site AshleyMadison.)

Then there is swallowing the ejaculate in oral sex. In the real world, many are squeamish about swallowing, but in the porn space, the demand was great. Producer Peter North realized this after the success of *Deep Throat* in 1972, where Linda Lovelace of course swallows; he began producing the *B.J.* series. "Every fourth volume we'd do a swallowing edition because people were requesting that. I started to notice that there was such a high demand for the swallowing [scenes] that I started the Swallow [which] broke all of our sales projections."[5]

Female ejaculation, or squirting, is a natural phenomenon and has doubtless always been known. But it was not really celebrated before the 1980s; today, it is an obsession in online porn. Ivan Crozier, a historian of sexuality, calls it "the female equivalent to the 'money shot,'" meaning the male ejaculation outside the woman's body.[6] Returning to porn after a three-year furlough at the BunnyRanch in Nevada, veteran porn star Ray Veness had apparently just squirted a fountain over fellow performer Chris Cannon in a scene. "I don't normally," she told *AVN*. "It's not something you can do on command. It just has to be right. Don't expect it all the time. It just happens when it happens." That's why she picked the male talent she performed with. "I like to be in control—always have, always will." And that makes for a fountain: "I've got to pick my guys, guys I'm attracted to and I'm comfortable with, and I'm going to have a good, hot sex scene with."[7]

Golden Showers

Urination might be the next step up. "Golden showers" had always been known in the sex world and were considered a form of hideous perversity, not a normal variant. It was probably the great Spanish director Pedro Almodóvar who put the concept into the cinematic imagination in his 1980 movie *Pepi, Luci, Bom y Otras Chicas del Montón* (*Pepi, Luci, Bom and Other Girls of the Heap*). Unfortunately, this particular movie was never translated into English. Nonetheless, Almodóvar became hugely influential, and this flick, created in the exuberance of liberation from the dictator Franco, experimented with ideas that had been repressed for half a century. In the action, a policeman rapes Pepi; to avenge herself, she and her friends introduce their punk singer friend Bom "to the policeman's masochistic wife Luciana, and when Bom urinates on Luciana's face, she falls in love with Bom and leaves her husband."[8] The concept of golden showers was thus not totally unfamiliar to the middle class of Madrid in 1980.

But that was Spain. In the U.S., the feds and the LAPD had been alert to urination as a form of obscenity, said to be "an absolute no-no" in Porn Valley in the 1980s.[9] Yet in the 1990s, we start edging towards urination as a form of sex play. This begins with the thrill of male viewers watching women urinate on the ground, which surfaces with the *Barely Legal* series in 1999. Here, British director Clive McLean, at one time a manager of Cat Stevens and later living in Chatsworth, made urination a steady theme. One reviewer said of number 3: "The action is pretty hot but there's nothing here that really breaks new ground, unless you're counting the number of urination scenes." Adrianna, one of the performers, "pulls up to a secluded beach in an old pick-up truck. Wasting no time, she immediately removes her clothes and squats to take a piss."[10] This is new, erotic urination brought to you in the 1990s on DVD.

In the mass media, urination became a reality with the photo of model Andrea Kurtz in the May issue of *Penthouse* in 1997 as the first centerfold to urinate on camera. The issue sold the most magazines that year, and Kurtz enjoyed a brief moment of fame because of it.[11]

With the internet, performers began to urinate not just on the ground but on each other. A search in 2015 for golden showers on the website xvideos produced 1998 results.[12] Just weirdos on the web? In December 2014, *Cosmopolitan* ran a big feature on "Sex Talk Realness: Golden Showers," so people out there are listening.[13] Yet as niches go, golden showers was not huge. Peter Acworth, owner of Kink.com, said in 2012, "We tried a site called Pissing.com but realized that the number of people actually into this fetish is too small."[14]

Blowbangs and Gangbangs

"Blowbangs" are a coming theme, of interest as an exercise in "total body carnality," reveling in sexual experiences that embrace the entire body. These seem to represent the content themes of the future, no longer mere b/g or g/g but multiple orgiastic carnivals. In a blowbang, as in a gangbang, "typically a single woman performs blow jobs on a gang of men, eventually," as the site blowbanggirls explained, "becoming a sticky, cum-drenched mess."[15] That site, launched in 2015 in Chandler, Arizona, began "attracting a sizable European fan base." This sounds as far away from righteous morality as it is possible to get. Yet many models love working blowbangs—showering afterwards!—because it gives them control of the action. They are in charge of how quickly the male talent become erect and pop. It's not that couples in the privacy of their condos will aspire to blowbangs on a Saturday night. Rather, this material is expanding people's erotic imaginations. From fantasies excited by images of blowbangs may come actual bedroom scenes untypical of the 1960s.

A gangbang is slightly different; the male actors don't ostentatiously ejaculate on the model's face but penetrate her orifices while she manipulates them. Gangbangs reach way back in the history of adult cinema. A new theme, however, was the model in charge of the scene, not just the passive recipient of multiple loads of semen. John T. Bone directed an early example of this in 1993, with Savannah and eight male actors. Bone told an interviewer, "In my opinion, the normal run-of-the-mill gang bang tapes are offensive. It's just a lot of guys fucking a girl. I didn't want Savannah to be an object, but totally in control of eight men." (*Starbangers I* came out of this effort.)[16]

In 2015, Keisha Grey, who had joined the industry two years previously at 19, became "the new gangbang girl." In a scene helmed by Mason, a female director for HardX, Keisha said, "I was super excited!" about beginning it, a group sex fest with five men. She did several scenes with all three orifices filled, and simultaneously masturbating by hand the other two male performers.

Q: "Was this the most intense sexual experience of your life?"

A: "Definitely the most intense by far."

Q: "What was your favorite moment of the gangbang?"

A: "Getting DP'd [double penetration] in the standing position. Or when all the guys stood in a line and took turns fucking me."

Q: "How many times did you cum in this gangbang?"

A: "More than I ever have during any scene."

Q: "Will anal now be a regular part of your scenes?"

A: "I feel it already is a regular part of my scenes."[17]

Added model Eva Lovia in 2017, who was just building her site, "I'm entertaining the idea of doing a gangbang. I think there's something really taboo about it. For the same reason a guy wants 10 girls, a woman can want 10 guys for all that attention and lust on just you. It's got to be really empowering feeling." There were two ways to do it, she said. "A girl can be made to look like an object, or the girl is taking it and it's about her pleasure. If I were to do it...I [would] be absolutely in control. Make sure that I had a great time."[18]

The summit of this kind of multiple scene would be gangbang plus multiple penetration. In 2015, Australian porn star Angela White directed a scene in which she simultaneously performed with five men. "Not only did I get a gangbang done," she said later, "I did a double penetration, double anal, double vag and a triple penetration with two in my pussy and one in my butt and one in my mouth as well. It was actually quadruple penetration. It was very airtight."

And how did this feel, Angela?

"It was one of the best days of my life, not just one of the best shooting days. Doing this was a dream come true."[19]

Thus, this shift in the focus of gangbang films from the pleasure of the man to the pleasure of the woman shows how women on the internet were capturing a traditional male-dominated form, the gangbang, and turning it into a new erotic experience for themselves. The entire trend is much in line with the theme of women becoming sexually dominant in the last thirty years.

Fisting

We are now a number of pegs up the ladder as we come to fisting, inserting one's whole fist—and forearm—into a partner's anus or vagina. This had long been known in the gay community, and some of the early stags did feature fisting. But then it vanished from porn for years. In recent heterosexual adult content, fisting goes back at least to Linda Lovelace's loops in the early 1970s. Jim Holliday was able to list 22 titles involving fisting by 1986, so the practice was scarcely obscure.[20]

A kind of fisting revival stemmed from Chloe (Chloe Hoffman), who highlighted vaginal fisting in 2000 at age 29 with *The Fist*, directed by Patrick Collins and co-starring Keisha. She moved on soon thereafter to anal. Chloe began as a director as well as a performer, helming a gonzo for VCA in 1999 entitled *What Makes You Cum?* Fisting became a main theme in 2000 and continued thereafter. Chloe said later in an interview, "Now I've turned the whole industry on to it. I've got girls running up to me going, 'Chloe, guess what? My boyfriend fisted me for the first time!' They're just dying to tell me about it. They see how much fun I'm having and they want to try it, too. I've started a fisting movement."[21] Chloe became a major director and performer, with over four hundred credits, many of them anally focused and some given over to fisting, although VCA wasn't thrilled about this latter part.

Fisting remained controversial during the subsequent years. Adam Glasser (Seymore Butts) triggered an obscenity charge in 2001 with a vaginal and anal fisting scene in *Tampa Tushy Fest I*;[22] the LA City Attorney settled the case after Glasser argued that fisting was widespread in the gay and straight communities. Fisting became definitively anchored in the porn repertoire in 2011 when lesbian feminists Courtney Trouble and Jizz Lee designated October 21 as "International Fisting Day."[23]

It is of interest that none of the themes discussed in this chapter except threesomes is even mentioned in Steven Ziplow's *Film Maker's Guide to Pornography*, published in 1977. Ziplow's subject matter seems positively quaint compared to what has become routine today. He covers masturbation ("It's always a lot of fun to watch a pretty lady getting off on her own body."), "straight sex," oral, anal, and "orgies."[24] But one searches Ziplow in vain for anything more daring.

Chapter 10:
Gonzo

Gonzo began in 1989 when John Stagliano at Evil Angel filmed *The Adventures of Buttman*. Stagliano told Randy Spears to "look right into the camera to say something," and Randy says, "Look into the lens? Are you serious?"[2]

Amateur Revisited

Now, gonzo, the in-your-face loops with no plot shot with a hand-held camera, had a predecessor in Homegrown Video, which featured genuine amateur loops, shot often by the participants themselves with a camera on a tripod. The essence was hot, dirty action, and even though gonzo began with a slightly different premise, its core, too, was raunchy direct sex.

Homegrown Video began in 1982 in the backroom of a small mom-and-pop video store in San Diego run by Greg Swaim. VHS was just coming into its own, and Swaim began to tape the popular sex parties that he threw. He turned this into a business and advertised for amateur exhibitionists to send in their tapes, to be reimbursed at the rate of $15 per minute. In 1993, Swaim sold Homegrown Video to Farrell Timlake, who with his wife had previously submitted their own videos, and Homegrown Video went on to become immensely popular. As

Farrell's brother Moffitt Timlake, the Homegrown CEO, told *Adult Video News* in 2008, "With [the initial Homegrown Video releases] the pros saw firsthand that such conventions as 'plot,' however shaky and ill-conceived, weren't indispensable. They discovered you could ditch the story and go straight to the sex, and suddenly genres like gonzo started popping up."[3]

"Angel" was living hand-to-mouth in Boston in 2000, when he shot a couple having sex. "The male talent was horrible, it got to the point where I had to jump in and shoot it POV [point of view, meaning he had sex with the female talent while he held the camera]. I thought the video was a disaster."

Then Angel sent it off to Moffitt Timlake. Six months later, Moffitt called him saying, "Can you shoot some more?"

"I then went out and spent every spare second casting everywhere I could. I would take my own money and shoot a scene, send that to Homegrown and wait for the check to come back, then I would go out and shoot another one." Finally, Angel started his own website.

"And let's just say at that time in 2002 it was insane with signups [purchases]. 1 in 100 and 1 in 200 ratio signups. Made so much money off that site I started another one...."[4]

Rise of Gonzo

So a page was turned. The feature-film era gave way in the late 1980s to gonzo. Gonzo is a video story, and it began when Bruce Seven (Bruce Behan) started working with Stagliano. Seven, just starting out as a BDSM cameraman and director, walked into the office of Roy Karch, who had just arrived from New York, and said, "Tell me about this video thing."[5] This got Seven started in video, and he hooked up with Stagliano in the early 1980s.

Stagliano, called "the Italian Stallion" and also "Buttman" because of his own taste for buttock-worshipping (not initially anal sex), said of the first time he worked with Seven, "Bruce helped me a lot, having shot about four or five videos. We talked for hours about how to make videos. It was a great experience because that afternoon that I met Bruce Seven and saw what he was shooting, I went crazy. He was shooting really hot sex. It was the best stuff I had ever seen in my life at that point."[6]

In 1983, Stagliano founded the studio Evil Angel, taking the name of a newspaper he had brought out the previous year. Evil Angel was a video company, just as video was displacing 35mm film. In 1989 came the manufacturing business, and the first movie, *The Adventures of Buttman*, which is credited with sparking the gonzo vogue. A long series of Buttman films then followed. (The famous male performer and director Rocco Siffredi—Rocco Antonio Tano—was often Buttman's sidekick.) These were highly influential. Journalist Acme Anderson later wrote, "Finding a director in adult today who wasn't directly influenced by Stagliano may be impossible."[7] What Stagliano originally meant by gonzo, borrowed from the self-referential style of journalist Hunter S. Thompson, was the performers' recognition of the camera.[8] The term later shifted to signify brief, raw sex. (There would, inevitably, be "Buttwoman," and Alexis Texas acquired that sobriquet in 2015 as a contract girl for Elegant Angel.[9])

Yet gonzo quickly came to mean you-are-there, as well as demolition of the wall between audience and performers. It was apparently *AVN* editor Gene Ross who suggested applying the term to films of this nature.[10] Gonzo pioneer Ed Powers saw gonzo coming as amateur started to take off. "We just knew it was what people wanted, a more direct feel," he said later. "They want to feel like it's them in the action."[11]

Among Stagliano's protégés was Adam Glasser, who adopted the porn name Seymore Butts ("see-more-butts"), and acquired as well Stagliano's fixation on the derriere. Born in the Bronx but raised in Santa Monica, Glasser had a role in an early Buttman video of Stagliano's (*Buttman's Ultimate Workout*, 1991), then struck out on his own as a producer and director. Outside of the industry, he is best remembered for Showtime's popular reality series from 2003, *Family Business*, about the Seymore Butts' porn enterprise.

Several other notable gonzo directors debuted in 1989. Jamie Gillis (Jamey Ira Gurman), introduced to the gonzo concept by Stagliano, became known for his pioneering reality series, *On the Prowl* (1989), "in which he takes a porn star around in a limousine looking for regular Joes off the street to fuck her."[12] Indeed, some authorities consider *On the Prowl*, shot in San Francisco, the first gonzo film.

In 1989, Ed Powers (Mark Arnold Krinsky) launched his series *Dirty Debutantes*, with himself and Gillis in front of the camera. An old hand in the sex industry, Powers had come up performing in live sex shows at Show World in Manhattan. "I'm not big—but I always could get it to work," he said.[13] Powers is often given credit for introducing point-of-view (POV) shooting to porn, as an actor, rather than the cameraperson, holds the camera filming the scene. The *Dirty Debutantes* concept was so successful that it gave rise to the series *Deep Inside Dirty Debutantes* in 1993, which ended with its 47ᵗʰ part in 2002; the series *Dirty Dirty Debutantes* began in 1996, and so forth. Many were point-of-view products.

Nineteen eighty-nine was a big year in gonzo for another reason as well. Sony began selling its lightweight CCD-V900 Hi-8 camera, known for its picture and audio quality; a price of $1,850 made it "affordable to an army of potential shooters."[14] Homegrown Video began uploading these creations, a clear departure from either the feature films or the loops that had previously predominated. Gonzo appeared in *AVN* as a review category only in November 1992, mainly because they didn't know where to class Ed Powers' *Dirty Debutantes* and *Bus Stop Tales*.[15]

The gonzo directors, as noted, often themselves performed in front of the camera. Jules Jordan got his start directing at Pleasure Productions in 1998 with *Live Bait 1*, then moved to Evil Angel, finally in 2002 founding his own company, Jules Jordan Video (he performed in *Flesh Hunter* in 2002 and directed *Once You Go Black* in 2003). He was widely celebrated among gonzo fans for anal scenes. Senior figures like Ira Levine lauded the studio for its simplicity and directness: "The sex is always high-energy, hot and nasty without being ugly or mean-spirited and cast with great care. Jordan...delivers on the promise of maximum strokability in every title."[16]

Rodney Moore, who entered the industry in 1992 as a virtual student of Buttman-Stagliano, was among the first gonzo directors to shoot "facials" in his famous *Rodney Blasts* (1997). In an interview in 1999 he said, "No one who loves facial cumshots will ever be disappointed by a Rodney movie.... I do think that I'm very much responsible for the trend towards almost 100% facials in porn today."[17]

At the beginning of the vogue, only a few companies—Evil Angel, Anabolic, Diabolic, and Red Light District—were producing gonzo. But then the wave of amateur porn hit. As John Desjardins, director of online operations for Evil Angel Cash, said in 2007: "People are shooting gonzo out of their houses. When I think gonzo I think of someone just grabbing a camera and shooting people having sex. And when the internet came, amateur websites are what followed. People surfing just wanted to get to the good scenes. So the internet provided a way to get gonzo out there on a massive worldwide level."[18]

All this triggered much regret among veterans. Old-school director Jim Powers (James Lane), famous for shooting "one movie every ten days," said in 2008 that gonzo represented the passing of a era. "When we used to watch movies—real movies, like *Talk Dirty to Me, Part III*...the whole thing, the sex and the setting, all worked together.... When I first came [to the industry] it was different. The old guys with the New York accents, you know, the guys around in 1990, they're all dead now."

Powers continued, "Lots of porn is just garbage nowadays, not necessarily the competency of what is shot, but the boring stuff that's there. Porn has lost its flair... the way porn sites break up scenes and deal in little clips, like little law library citations."[19]

Gonzo was totally different from the feature films such as *Debbie Does Dallas* that Porn Valley had been turning out. It was the difference between sexuality and sensuality. Gonzo was plenty sexual, plenty of penetration. But Charlie Latour, a professional fluffer in the feature-film era of the 70s, missed the sensual. (Long delays in shooting 35mm meant that this semi-mythical figure, the "fluffer," was in fact sometimes needed to get the wood erect again.) She mentioned Jamie Gillis, Ron Jeremy and John Holmes. "They were men who knew how to sexually *be* with a woman. They knew how to touch. Did you ever see Jamie Gillis stroke his cock?" By contrast, in gonzo there was no sensuality. Said Charlie, "I've witnessed this on set where the girl says to the guy, 'We're getting ready to do penetration. You go off into that corner and stroke your cock. When you're hard and ready, you come back over and we'll do the fuck scene.'"[20]

Gonzo Sells

"Get in, get off and get out."[21]

RICHARD COHEN, PRESIDENT OF NATIONAL A-I INTERNET, 2009

But gonzo sells, and the seventies features sold less. Paul Fishbein, publisher of *Adult Video News*, was a college student at Temple University in Philadelphia in 1982 when he started working for a video store. The following year, he founded his own newsletter, *AVN*, to review for retailers the flood of new offerings. In 1989, he offered a somewhat bitter retro look at how the industry had changed: "We rode the wave. We watched the adult portion of the industry go from a huge multi-conglomerate hit-oriented feature film industry...to a price-driven, price-conscious, mostly inferior, legally retarded, shot-on-video network, with product carried by a precious few wholesalers at ridiculous [low] prices."[22] From *Green Door* to gonzo, in other words.

Gonzo showed considerable staying power in the years before *Fifty Shades of Grey*. Managers at a number of Los Angeles video stores surveyed late in 2007 said, "Their Top 10 rentals were all all-sex titles, with couples' movies like Digital Playground's *Pirates* down on the list."[23] The DVDs in the stores were for the deep-pocket "raincoat boys." Features, such as Stormy Daniels' big-budget epics at Wicked, did better on the net. But the *Fifty Shades of Grey* market had not yet sprung to life, and for years, it looked as though the artsy full-length treatment was dead.

The market for gonzo was quite specifically the 18-35-year-old male set plus tired businessmen in hotel rooms. How could you tell? Marc Bruder of Cable Entertainment Distribution said in 2006, "Younger [demographic] means sex and rock n' roll and quick satisfaction, like MTV—constantly in your face.... Taking a lesson from the internet, people are buying clips. Are they buying clips of people engaged in dialogue? No. They're buying clips of people fucking. Sometimes just the climax scene or the blowjob for the climax. Is the adult aficionado any different on the internet than he is on pay-per-view or VOD or a hotel room? Usually not." Bruder said that the "end user has become...very sex hungry."[24]

So, gotta give 'em gonzo. Otherwise talented directors shrugged their shoulders and shot gonzo. Said Jim Powers, a prolific filmmaker, "Porn is what it is. Guys watch porn for five to seven minutes at a pop, then hide the DVD, then watch it the next day. I guess your dialogue needs to fit in there somewhere."[25] Or not.

The advantages of gonzo were that it conveyed a sense of immediacy and was cheap to produce. Ira Levine said that many directors solved the problem of crew shortages by doing everything themselves. "They bring in a mini-cam and a couple of Lowel packs [lights], one PA [personal assistant], maybe someone for make-up and DIY [Do It Yourself] the whole show.... For the ultra-hard, all-sex format where the director's perspective through the lens is the key to creating a spontaneous, rough-cut, raw-edged atmosphere, the lone-gunman approach may actually be superior." One could get this up on the internet, but the poor production values made it less suitable for DVD, Levine said.[26]

For models, the disadvantage was that they were stuck in a gonzo ghetto. It was hard to move from gonzo to feature films because in gonzo there was little dialogue and nobody really knew if you could act. Trina Michaels, who by 2008 had performed in several hundred gonzo scenes in more than three years in the industry, was finding it difficult to get a role in features. But in 2007, she had a small part in SexZ Pictures' *Upload*. "Hopefully people will see that and think that I can do more than hot sex scenes," she said.[27]

But many less-ambitious models were just as glad there was no dialogue. "You can put on airs and talk about Nabokov all you want in your porn movie," said agent Wayne Hental. "But if you can't get your lead actress to pronounce 'Lolita' properly, the jig's up." The models weren't being paid for dialogue, anyway. They were being paid for what was on the worksheet: "BJ, DP or interracial," meaning blow-job, double penetration (anus-vagina) and—this is an astonishing comment on the racism in adult until recently—having to have sex with blacks.[28] Many thought, the less like a feature film and the more gonzo-like, the better, because you could get onto the next shoot later that day (Features took up the whole day.).[29]

In retrospect, gonzo dragged porn downmarket. It brought in a vast new demographic that didn't want to sit through a feature film, as the raincoats were willing to do, or dabble in niches such as fetish-BDSM because they didn't really have those essentially upper-middle-class tastes. Bitter were the lamentations from those who deplored the loss of the old-style feature films. Proper videographers, said Roy Karch, one of the founders of feature filming in the Valley, "have been replaced by point and click wannabes who will work for half a dollar and a piece of good pussy at the end of the day. Nuance replaced by overkill.... Love scenes have become handjobs, single girl masturbation scenes, a mainstay in all of porndom, are now referred to as solos. Where did all the passion go?"[30]

The Decline of Gonzo

Well, this was pretty dismal. But then, all of a sudden gonzo wasn't so popular anymore. The market became flooded with cheap, low-quality videos that were, in any event, easily pirated. According to Joe Gallant, owner of New York-based Black Mirror Productions, writing on New Year's Day 2007, gonzo now consisted of "endless titles of airless pool/couch/stairwell routines all done by Vicodin zombies who bat their eyes and do constant variations of 'sex face' mugging for the camera.... Then, here comes the Viagra dick with no shot of the guy's face and we go into the movie's theme—[anal] gape, ATM [ass-to-mouth], creampie [exuding an internal ejaculation]. No sweating, no hugging, no laughter, just endless dick riding. That's what's so over."[31]

The money began to drain away. Firms in the "gonzo pool" began folding. What was next? In an early reaction to gonzo, in 1993, Steve Orenstein founded Wicked Pictures in Canoga Park in the Valley because of the "lack of story-driven films," as a Wicked publicist later said. Orenstein started to open up the couples market and began producing films with traditional feature big budgets. *Dreamquest* in 2000 had a quarter-million dollar price tag.[32] (And it rocketed Jenna Jameson who starred in the film to prominence.)

In 2006, Mike South cited the "wild success of feature-driven porn like Adam & Eve and Digital Playground's *Pirates* [as] the last nail in the coffin for all but a few of the gonzo companies."[33] Director Ira Levine (Ernest Greene) let fly in 2008 at the gonzo producers; he scorned the man-cave audience whose noisy demands on adult chatboards for "evermore double-anals and cumfarts," were turning off the larger and more prosperous audience on which the long-term prosperity of the industry depended. "How much appetite remains for 'Choke and Puke 54' and all its clones is hard to assess, but it's noteworthy that some of the biggest moneymakers over the past few years have been big features."[34]

The growing feminist impulse within adult had absolutely no patience with traditional gonzo. This marks the first time that women in the industry started pushing back against male-oriented content. The feminist position was that porn should be for women, too, and gonzo as previously filmed wasn't. Feminist filmmaker Erika Lust, in business by 2015 for eleven years, supported this point in *Fortune* with her critique of "virtual reality" (VR) porn, the inheritor of gonzo. VR, she said, "creates the same repetitive, boring adult content we've seen for years. It's still just mechanical sex made by men, for men: gynecological shots, fake orgasms, tacky costumes and settings and zero narrative." In bed, she said, this would be a sexual anesthetic rather than a stimulant, "turning us into porn-consuming zombie junkies, sitting next to our lovers in the same bed, but not ever speaking to or touching one another."[35]

Thus, gonzo began to change. In 2003, Stagliano himself helped re-ignite the feature era with *The Fashionistas,* a four-hour heavily plot-driven fetish-fest. Ending an era, in 2005 Stagliano said goodbye to Buttman, a figure who had started gonzo, with 60-plus Buttman episodes since 1989 (*Buttman Goes To Rio,* etc.). Stagliano said, I'm over shooting Buttman. It's just not interesting to me anymore.... All I want to do is story-oriented stuff."[36]

But here's the thing. The gonzo concept was not intrinsically misogynist, violent, or lacking in interest for women. At its core was a celebration of the body, even the imperfect one, not abuse or exploitation. At a directors' roundtable in 2003, Mason, a female director, said she loved it. "I think that there's so much beauty to be found in gonzo, I believe it's very forgiving. It allows women that are less than perfect and don't fit the stereotype of what a woman should be...and I think women really learn a lot from watching it."[37] When in 2004 photographer-director Suze Randall returned to filming porn, after a seventeen-year hiatus, it was to gonzo. She was relieved she didn't have to create a plot. "We're not having to pretend we're something we're not," she said.... "We want to do really erotic, hot, sexual scenes. Nobody really wants acting: you want the beauty, the passion."[38]

In retrospect, the larger significance of gonzo is not its decimation of taste in the industry but its capture of the very carnality of desire. For the first time, with gonzo the sexual body is flung onto the screen—the buttocks, the penis in its exciting urgency, the powerful driving of intercourse—and all in high-definition reality. If one single stream within the industry could be said to have enlarged the sexual palette, it would be gonzo.

Chapter 11:
Shooting

L ate in June 2002, Tim Case arrived in LA for a week of shooting with his girlfriend, Felicia Fox. Ohio-born Felicia, then 28, had entered the industry four years previously and had already a number of films under her belt. Tim managed a stripper bar in Dayton, where Felicia also worked as a feature dancer. (It was in Dayton that Larry Flynt had founded the first Hustler Club in 1965.)

From Tim's Journal:

Thursday. Tim awakens Felicia early "with some coffee from the Quickee Mart," then packs her bag while she is in the shower: "Marilyn Monroe robe, furry slippers, hair crimper, condom & lube bag...cosmetic case, jewelry bag, lingerie for the stills, high heels, copy of current HIV test, copy of two forms of ID, hairspray, pic, camera, deodorant, baby wipes (for post-scene removal of jism), towel, magazines, cosmetic sponges."

They arrive on the set, at Sin City Studios. Male talent is Steve H., "the man who will soon be violating my girlfriend.... Steve's a nice guy—we've hung out with him on several sets when he's been working with other actresses. This will be Felicia's first scene with him." Tim sits down alongside the agent's rep on a couch watching the monitors. "The set is invisible from where we are, around the corner behind a barrier. The monitors show a wrestling ring from two different angles.... I find out later that the way the scene went was this—Felicia and Rhiannon [the other female performer] were catfighting, wrestling in this ring in their skimpy outfits. Steve H. and Kyle S. are the commentators, sitting at a table just outside the ring.

(The catfighting, I find out later, almost got out of hand, with both girls getting cut and bruised, body slams etc. Felicia, as is already well known, is a badass). One of the girls gets tossed out of the ring and onto the table into the commentators... whereupon the sex scenes follow. Felicia, getting into it, grabs a handful of Steve's hair and seems to be trying to pull it out by the roots."

The agent's rep "seems pleased with the scene. She remarks to me how much she loves Felicia's natural breasts bouncing all over the place. The scene ends with the requisite pop shots, with Steve H. launching a salvo of semen from between Felicia's legs that winds up all over her forehead and hair, narrowly missing her eyes. 'Oh my god, I'm sorry,' he tells her.

"'Thank god for false eyelashes,' she laughs."[1]

Next Monday. Tim got Felicia to the set on time, where she went immediately into makeup, getting ready for a boy/boy/girl schedule for that afternoon. "It turned out that she would be working with Eric Everhard and a new guy named Trent Desoro. Erik "proved why he's named...'The Jackhammer' by pounding Felicia from below while she was in the reverse cowgirl position with Trent's erect penis in her mouth. Several times Eric's hammering caused her jaws to clamp together, and I was afraid the other boy's porn career might be ended prematurely by I.O.P.D. (inadvertent oral penile detachment). Felicia, to her credit, kept trying to rein the enthusiastic Eric in by kicking him, slapping him, and telling him to 'Stop, goddammit!'"

On the way back to the hotel in the rented car, Tim asked, "You okay?"

"Yeah. Tired. Jesus, that was a tough one."

"Really? You did well. I'm proud of how you handled yourself."

"Thanks." She smiled at Tim. "God, I am so sore. I swear I think my pussy is going to fall off."[2]

A Porn Set

What strikes many is the complete normality of a porn set. "It's just like a scene in a regular movie," said Julie Meadows, with a background in mainstream film, who moved to Porn Valley to shoot in adult. "These creative types get to stand around some food and laugh with the same people they see every time they work, and when the time comes to perform, it's not weird! Someone walks up dispassionately and says, 'Are you ready?' and then they say, 'Yes,' or 'No, I have to go do my girlie things,' and then eventually things start."[3]

Ummm, well, not exactly normal in other ways. After-hours, for example. Steven St. Croix was filming in Europe. As Holly Randall tells the story, "Every evening after work, the crew and talent would hang out in the bar at the hotel they were staying at. After a few drinks and general friskiness all around, Steven and one of the girls began to have public sex in the bar. When the host came over to protest the girl grabbed him, unzipped his pants, and began to blow him. Needless to say, he stopped protesting." Holly's point: "These were the kinds of girls that put the word 'star' in 'porn star'—women who just liked to have sex and lots of it. Holly contrasted them with the eighteen-year-olds who had just hopped off the bus today (in 2008), and filmed with an eye on the clock. Twenty more minutes! Oh, no.[4]

How do you break in as a director? Greg Lansky, who had just graduated from high school in Paris, teamed up in Spain with his buddy Mike Adriano to shoot a quick movie. "We had no clue what we were doing," said Lansky later. They flew some girls down from France, filmed in a couple of homes to which Adriano had access (but not permission to shoot porn) and, in October 2005, marketed the product at the Venus Show in Berlin where they made a thousand bucks.

In Berlin, they met the remarkably open-minded Scott Taylor from New Sensations. Continued Lansky, "We came up to his booth to see if we could maybe direct movies for him. Scott wasn't too sure about it but he did ask us to come back later. Since he didn't give us a firm 'no,' we came back five times that day and the last one he just smiled and said, 'If you ever make it to Los Angeles, I'll give you one movie to try.'" The duo were in LA a month later, where Lansky and Adriano shot *Slut Diaries* (2006) with Adriano as the male talent. Taylor was pleased with the result and took them on staff.[5]

And youthful! In an *XBIZ* poll of readers in 2003 (almost all of whom were site owners or employees), only 10 percent were over 45, and 22 percent under 21.[6] What does this mean? High-school kids on the chatboard at *XBIZ* (where very explicit subjects were often discussed)? No, it means that late adolescents and young men often began careers in industry early.

Oh, so you're a porn director? "Say the words 'porn director,'" said porn star Nica Noelle (Monica Jensen), herself turned director, "and most people chuckle at the high-falutin' title. Don't they just pick up a camcorder, point it at a naked couple and tell them to do it 'doggy-style'?"[7] No, said Noelle, there's more to it than that.

Getting Going

It's no longer 1994, when large amounts of money could be made just by you getting in front of the camera with a girl and having sex. It's 2014. You've got a small amount of capital, some knowledge about lighting, and a desire to succeed with your own site. Is that enough?

In 2014 "Nightblaze," a male, 27, told the YNOT chatboard he was all set to go. He had about $10,000 and thought maybe he could get by with a camcorder and a couple of lights. "Fortunately for me, I have a bunch of credit card points and unused sick days from work saved up."

The old hands laughed. "You will fail," said Hardball.

Roberto said, "Oh geez. The fact that you're even considering $300 Best Buy camcorders as an option is just one of the many red flags that you're got no idea about this stuff." Roberto advised Nightblaze "to splurge on some working girls to work these fantasies out."

But Paul Markham, one of the oldest and most experienced directors in the business, had a different take. He advised Nightblaze to ignore all the static about cameras and the like. "Unless you have a model who can bring something worth paying for to the project [you're wasting your money]. Go and find one.... The key is HER. [You need a model who] appeals to her audience in such a way that they're addicted to HER. If you find a model like that, a cheap camera, lighting, little porn skill become secondary. They can all be picked up."

Are such models easy to find?

Markham said, "In the 35 years of producing porn, the number of girls I've found who can do this I can count on the fingers of both hands and have fingers left over. And yet without that girl...you're going to fail and lose all your money. The problem will also be, does this level of girl need you? I would say no."[8]

Shooting Sex

"Sex changes everything."[9]

PAUL THOMAS, A DIRECTOR AT VIVID VIDEO

Old-hand director Paul Thomas at Vivid—whom Harris Gaffin describes as "tall and slender...moving with catlike grace and aloofness"[10]—thought mainstream and hardcore incompatible because hardcore hijacked the product. "Once Meryl Streep is sucking Jack Nicholson's cock the whole mind thing and the whole vibe changes, and that becomes the point of the film. I mean, you can't have a karate fight in the middle of *As Good as It Gets* and ever hope to get back to the original story. And hardcore sex changes the vibe of a piece more than anything.... Sex changes everything."[11]

So, how do you shoot sex?

An important issue is getting the talent to relax. Often, female directors tried to cultivate an atmosphere of spontaneity. Belladonna (Michelle Anne Sinclair), the young actress who at 22 started directing for Evil Angel in 2003, was the wave of the future for female directors. "I really want the girls to be able to do what *they* want to do. I want the camera to be like a guy watching the girls as they do things to get him fucking crazy. We're involving the camera the whole time.... I was doing a g/g with Avy Scott but at the end of the scene I told the cameraman to cum on me and she [Avy] just sucked it up like a vacuum. It was really great because it wasn't planned. It was just real...I don't have a label for what I want. I just want everybody to have fun."[12]

Herbert Streicher, who as Harry Reems had played opposite Linda Lovelace in *Deep Throat*, entered the biz at 25, terminally horny but at last able to control his orgasms. "People, especially when they've never made one [porno] before, don't know how to handle the situation," he told Luke Ford. "I had an ability to relax people, especially new girls coming into the business. We'd sit and talk; it made people feel comfortable. I brought hundreds of people into the business."[13]

How about drugs to relax? Directors, when speaking for publication, swore up and down that their sets are drug-free, but guess what? Cocaine was widely used. Director David Jennings said, "Many ladies 'prepare' for screen sex by snorting coke, sometimes causing impotence in men whose penis glans have been numbed by the drug in their partners' saliva."[14]

Many directors emphasized having a "fun" set. But old-timers scarcely recognized all this talk about "fun." For them, sex on camera was business, which is to say, work. Ron Jeremy, who said he had slept with over 4,000 women, said on the subject of shooting, "Do you see those positions? Notice how the woman's legs are being thrust into the air at odd angles, how the guy's torso is twisted around like a pretzel.... Does it look like we're having fun?... The answer is no. We're doing it because it's *required* of us. We need to give you, the audience, the best possible view of what's happening. If you can't see the penetration then a porno flick isn't doing its job."

Jeremy continued on the subject of the "porn blow-job." For verisimilitude, you can see the model's cheeks bulge. "It doesn't hurt to have visual evidence that a cock is in her mouth, and for guys, this means ramming your cock straight into her cheekbones. You're not really fucking her mouth, you're going through two rows of her *teeth*."[15]

So much did Vivid director Paul Thomas recognize sex as a business that, after a scene had started, as a visiting reporter put it, "[he] takes a seat at a desk several feet away, puts on his glasses and opens a copy of the *Los Angeles Times*."[16]

A regular porn shoot (not a niche shoot) would involve four or five standard scenes. On a Rob Spallone set (Star World Productions), that would entail "10 minutes of pussy-eating, 10 minutes of blowjob, 12 to 14 minutes of sex in three different positions."[17] The positions might be: doggie-style, cowboy or reverse cowboy (this latter with the model on top, facing the male talent's knees), and missionary position with the bodies well separated. Not that I, an academic historian, am attempting to tell Mr. Spallone his job. But all this changing would require a lot of directing, much starting and stopping of the action, and risking the male talent losing wood (see below).

How do you choose your content? Chris Streams, a BDSM director, said, "I shoot what I would personally jack off to."[18] Director Bruce Seven (Bruce Behan), who began shooting amateur BDSM in 1970—and started work as a professional videographer a decade later—once remarked, "Behind every successful video is one guy's hard-on."[19] This is what made Seven such a classically good director and cameraman. John Stagliano, who counts as the originator of gonzo but was really a student and then business partner of Seven's, said, "[Bruce's] skill was not in how he shot. He shot nastier but what he would do was get inside the heads of the models. He'd get them to perform for him. Bruce was the first person I ever saw do that. Rocco [Siffredi] does that now. Because Bruce was into bondage and nasty sex, he'd hire Porsche Lynn and all these girls who were into nasty sex. He'd get them to do harder and nastier stuff than they ever did before.... He was the first person to shoot hard, nasty sex consistently."[20] ("Nasty" in gonzo means rough, possibly anal, sex.)

So, the director should not forget that he's not doing art, he's doing sex. Jim Holliday, the film historian who also directed, said in 1986, "A sex film should never lose sight of the fact that it is a sex film. The primary purpose is arousal, not entertainment."[21]

What Not to Do

The director can talk too much. Directors such as Anthony Spinelli strive for perfection, getting exactly the right angle, the right lighting. But interrupting the action is a bad idea. Director and former porn star Veronica Hart learned this the hard way in the course of shooting 43 films. At a reunion of older porn stars, she advised aspirant directors in the audience, "Keep your mouth shut. The one thing I used to do was kill any kind of chemistry my actors might have had for one another. In my mind I had to get this shot. We had to get the hard version; we had to get the soft version. So the one thing that I have learned in the over 30 something years of doing it, keep your mouth shut when you're directing. Set it up. Tell them about the kind of sex that you want to see, what your ideas are, but once they start going, 'shut up.' If you don't get the exact angle, the exact everything, the passion and the intensity of the couple are going to carry you through. That's just something that took me a long time to learn and boy, do I know it now."[22]

This is how you do it. Here, Gloria Leonard is directing *Vow of Passion* (1991) for Vivid: "As a hush of concentration falls over the set, the only sounds that can be heard are tiny rustles from Savannah and Tom [Byron]. Gradually, their exchange of emotions and caresses builds a sexual tension that hits the viewer like a tidal wave, as the pair approach mutual orgasm. Savannah matches Tom thrust for thrust, while Gloria watches wordlessly from the sidelines. Tom begins to peak, and the couple now seem welded together in an embrace that suspends the moment in time.... The set remains quiet as the couple separate; no one wants to break the spell. Savannah and Tom curl together and smile softly at each other."[23] This is totally hot, and the only surprise is that the crew did not break into applause afterwards. (But in real life, Savannah (Shannon Wilsey) had a troubled history and suicided in 1994.)

Alexander DeVoe, who directed heavily black-themed titles, had potential models fill out a questionnaire detailing their previous sexual activity. DeVoe said, "I chose female performers for my movies who are sexual freaks at heart.

If they're not sexual beings then I am not interested in shooting them." But they're actors. Couldn't they act like sexual beings? No, said DeVoe, because he gave them no stage directions at all. "I just tell my talent to enjoy each other.... In my world, once the sex starts the camera doesn't exist. I'm a fly on the wall, privileged enough to get a sneak peek at some volcanically hot action."[24] So this is the direct opposite of the constant-intervention policy with which Veronica Hart began.

Even though many models came to the industry via stripping, setting out deliberately to recruit strippers was probably not a good idea. Paul Markham had this to say to newbie directors: "Strippers usually make very bad models, especially for someone just starting out. They think all men who want to look at them naked are jerks. They are rarely desperate for the money, used to being in control, and prone to not show up. Added to the fact that she could have been dancing until 4:00 am and this all goes to make a recipe for disaster."[25]

And don't come across as an incompetent loser! Markham emphasized that you have to appear to know what you're doing and be professional. Don't make it seem as though your first desire is to get into her pants. "You don't want pictures of girls thinking, 'Get lost you loser; this is one pussy you can't even dream about!' What you want are pictures of girls thinking, 'Can I buy YOU a drink?'" (Markham had a huge reputation of sleeping with his models.)[26]

Interestingly, in the abovementioned 2003 *XBIZ* poll, a full 17 percent of site operators said "sex with models" was their main motivation for being a webmaster.[27] As Dawn Yagielowicz, who had a background in modeling, put it, "If your true desire was to have sex with her, then you should have hired a prostitute."[28]

Most importantly, if you're an incompetent loser, you might end up injuring the model. In a bondage shoot, for example, you totally have to know what you're doing. One physician who often treated on-set injuries was called to a bondage set in late 1999 because the director had "covered [the model] in clothespins and hung her on a nail. The nail gave way. One of the clothespins went through her labia and gave her a very nasty labial tear." Said Gene Ross, editor of *AVN*, "If you're going to do a domination movie...you need to know that there are professional riggers out there.... The hooks and the ropes are specific equipment. You just can't hang people on regular nails...."[29] Duh.

Projecting Desire

"The women always have to look insatiable."[30]

RUSS MEYER, *VIXEN* (1968)

You're going to a porn shoot? Hey hey, be prepared for a wild time! Or not. There is a general consensus that shooting porn is often boring precisely because porn sex is not real sex (even though the models may nonetheless enjoy it—see Chapter 5). The interesting point here is not whether the models really get off in front of the camera. Some do, some don't. What is at issue is the sensual voluptuousness that their supposed hedonism projects for the viewers. Said "Matt," one of Mike South's guest bloggers, "[The pornographer should] make me want to fuck the model on the screen instead of making fun of her or remembering some crack whore on the corner who reminds me of her."[31] Want to know why the surfers are so irresistibly drawn to the world of the models? It's because the models themselves very often draw the surfer into their sensuality.

Porn-megastar Nina Hartley understood this perfectly, and projected enthusiasm because it was so natural for her. Here she is, at age 25, talking to psychiatrist Robert Stoller around 1985. At a minimum, she says, you can just lie there. "[But] you're not going to get very far in the business if you do just that, unless you're very beautiful. People in the audience and people in the production end of it *want* to see a woman having a good time. If she can *really* have a good time [i.e., orgasm], great! You are in the right business. [The male talent] love the fact that I can take control of a situation without appearing to, just by turning up my enthusiasm, going, 'Wait, how about this? I'll try this.' 'Okay.' And I'll just start doing it and everyone starts filming it, and it moves things. That's easy. My work is very easy to me, it's natural to me."[32]

Thus, what gives porn its power is conveying to the viewer that this is real, the models are genuinely turned on. One surfer writes in, "How about actually looking like you want to fuck and enjoy getting fucked? Is that too much to ask? If I want to jerk it to someone who isn't enthused about being fucked, I'll go jerk it to my ex-wife."[33]

This isn't really a debate because people don't set up affirmative and negative sides, but in fact there is little agreement on whether porn sex is real sex. Addie Juniper, a porn star from Atlanta, said in 2015 about on-screen sex, "I have always enjoyed performing. Sex (at least good sex) feels artistic to me and I strive to let that come across on film. What it doesn't feel like is REAL sex, whether it's with my boyfriend or not. And that's because it's NOT! PORN is usually male-centric, brightly lit sex at 9 in the morning where you have to wear HUGE fake eyelashes and hold your butt cheeks up and out of the way. There is very little, if any, kissing and oral on the girl is often not even a part of it. And then they pour creamy face wash on your face and take pictures. Ta da! It's a JOB."[34]

There are, in fact, lots of shoots where nobody is really turned on at all. The key to this is all the obviously fake moaning and shrieking that goes on. Industry insider Angels Royal commented in 2014, "I have never understood why the hell (in most porn anyway) the female talent starts shrieking and screaming in blatant fake ecstasy the minute they get touched, and they don't stop until the end. Who actually believes this shit? I keep the volume very low when I do watch HC [hardcore], because I cannot stand it."[35] Director Holly Randall, daughter of famous feminist photographer Suzie Randall, found all this contrived passion particularly unnerving. "Growing up with parents who are in the porn industry and now being in it myself, I've secured a pretty healthy distinction between the fantasy of porn sex and the reality of real sex. Because I see the way most performers act in between rolling: the girl is bored and examining her nails, while the guy... is feverishly masturbating, trying to get hard so we can finish the scene and go home. When the cameras aren't on, she usually isn't paying the guy any attention whatsoever. But once I yell 'action' again, suddenly she can't get enough of his throbbing cock. That is not real sex...."[36] Indeed, the real problem with porn is that many viewers think that it is real sex, and find themselves sadly deficient when measured against it.

So this is a whole school of thought: seeing porn sex as different from real sex. Said model Casey Calvert in 2016, "Sex on camera is inherently a performance. You have to position your body in a way that the camera and lights can see, to get the hardcore [shots] that they need to get. I don't know anyone who has sex like that at home—and if they do, I would love to know why. It's not comfy."[37]

But the cinematic aspects work best when, in fact, porn sex is real sex. (See Chapter 5.) What directors strive for is models who are comfortable enough that on-screen sex feels like real sex. It is a need for verisimilitude. Does this sound like verisimilitude? Director and performer Rodney Moore was being interviewed about memorable sex encounters. "I did a scene early this year with Robin Wood, who I hit it off with. I had my camera girl Scarlett filming us, but she had to leave after taping about 30 minutes of sex on camera. So we went to the bedroom and had about two hours of sex off camera in the dark, then went back out and filmed the pop shot. That was very nice."[38]

The important point here is not the reality of being turned on but projecting that appearance. Clearly, Robin Wood was, in fact, turned on. This is what Nica Noelle, a director for Mile High Media who tries to cultivate on the set the feeling that women are "appreciated, respected and loved," was aiming for. She said, "I'm trying to get them to be passionate and intimate and vulnerable." When she watches director Manuel Ferrara's gonzo movies, "I can see that the girls want to be there, they want to have sex and they're truly turned on. You can see it in their body language, their facial expressions." For director Jim Enright, it was in the eyes: the eyes had to meet and lock. "I drop a lot of footage on the floor when I see eyes that don't register," he said.[39] This sense of being genuinely turned on is the key to sensuousness, as opposed to the ceaseless pounding of the eight-minute loop.

So for many of the top models, the ability to project enthusiasm was real—and this is how they got to be top models. Veruca James, from Chicago (and with a BA in finance), was 22 when she did her first adult scenes in 2011. Does she like blowbangs? "Yes, definitely yes. It's just really hard to compare blowbangs to other sex scenes because it's so different. If I had to choose between blowbangs and regular sex for the rest of my life, I'm obviously going to choose regular sex but I love blowbangs.... The idea that you're getting all these dicks off. I'm a giver so I love that. I get really excited turning somebody else on. That gets me off. I get off on other people getting off on me."

How about "being DP'd?" a journalist asked her (double penetration, anus, and vagina).

She answered, "It is this overwhelming feeling of being filled and fucked at the same time. And it triggers the orgasm anally and vaginally back and forth. It's a feeling of also being like out of control and being helpless in a way. You're just being forced and forced to orgasm. [Laughs.] It's hard to explain to a guy...."[40]

Hard to explain it might be, but visually it comes across as this intensely erotic scene. Surfers are watching this, and simultaneously masturbating.

Chapter 12:
Woodsmen

"Not just anybody can do this. It's a rare breed that can pop on cue."

EVAN DANIELS, FILM EDITOR AT VIVID[1]

It isn't even noon yet," wrote master-woodsman Ron Jeremy, "and I've already had sex with fourteen women.... I'm not so jaded that I don't feel incredibly fortunate. How often does a guy get to be the center of attention, the 'meat' in an all-girl sex sandwich?" The director asked him if he needed Viagra? They had a case in back. No way![2]

Getting Started

Why would a guy go into porn? For many of the young women, the reasons are complex: rebellion, better than working at the Piggly Wiggly, a touch of exhibitionism. For guys, the reasons often boil down, in Harris Gaffin's view, to one thing: a chance to meet chicks, not so much for the sex on set, which generally is more work than fun, but at the parties afterwards. "They do it to date the girls," said Gaffin. "They tolerate work for the party afterwards. Hot action with sexy chicks."[3] HepMan (evidently producer Harold Epstein) on the *XBIZ* board agreed: "Most guys get in it to get laid—as the quality of the finished product demonstrates."[4] Given that many of the models are gorgeous, these motives do not seem altogether illogical, though somewhat limited.

For male models, as for female, the path began at the door of Jim South's World Modeling Agency in Chatsworth. Tom Byron, who became a porn superstar, arrived there in May 1982. He had dropped out of college and had been working in auto parts, waiting to turn 21. Director Bobby Hollander was there, just hanging out. "[Hollander] didn't take my first Polaroid but he brought in a girl to dance for me to, you know...." Byron's voice trailed off. "So I got a little chub and [Hollander] goes, 'Christ, look at the hammer on that kid.'" So that was the beginning of Byron's thirty-year career in porn." (Hollander wanted Byron to do a d.p. the next day. "Oh, it was a horrible scene. The d.p. never happened—I popped too soon.")[5]

Soft Wood

> *"I stopped shooting couples because there's nothing more boring than sitting with a video camera in your hand waiting for some guy to get his dick hard."*[6]
>
> DIRECTOR RODNEY MOORE, 1999

Being male talent sounds pretty good, doesn't it, guys? People pay you to have sex with beautiful women. But are you up to the test? Here is what porn star Tianna Taylor (*Totally Teri, Heavenly Hooters*) told a male friend of hers who wanted to get into the biz: "Get a video camera and a dozen of your best male friends. Stand them in a circle around you, take off your clothes and videotape yourself in the center of the circle with an erection that you can keep standing for 15 minutes. If you can do that, then you can think about applying for the job."[7]

Producer David Jennings said in 2000, "Most new men, no matter how horny, can't 'get wood' when faced with probing cameras, harried directors, hot lights and cold ladies. With thousands of dollars at stake, producers—myself included—prefer to hire only the 'reliables.'" So it was always "the same five guys" (John Holmes would have been number five but he died in 1988): Jamie Gillis, John Leslie, Ron Jeremy and Eric Edwards.[8] Or rush in an extra. When the male talent failed on Rob Spallone, owner of Star World Productions, Spallone had to "hire a guy off the local lunch wagon to finish a facial pop shot."[9] Talent agent Jim South is said to have kept a factotum on staff "in case," as Jennings put it, "a stud out on location suffered penis limpus."[10]

It is 1992, and Mike South has just decided to start shooting porn in his hometown Atlanta; he has rented lights and brought a stripper and her boyfriend on set. "For two hours the stripper serviced her boyfriend orally, but he couldn't get it up," reports a journalist. "This is how South ended up starring in the first porn film he ever shot."

South continued, "So finally, the guy looks at me and says, 'You fuck the bitch and I'll film it.'

"And I'm like, 'Um, that wasn't really what I had planned; but the show must go on.' The whole concept of stage fright had never even occurred to me," said South.[11]

The frequent inability of woodsmen to have an erection can ruin an entire shoot and cost the director lots of money because he has to pay everyone else on the set whether he gets a usable scene or not. Ten years later in 2002, Mike South, now a veteran pornographer, was introducing "two hot girls" from Florida to porn, who had come up to Atlanta to try shooting for him. "I decided to give a new guy a try, Doug. Doug had done a few gangbangs and was convinced he had what it takes to be a porn star. Doug gets there and we get through the oral on her just fine, we get through the oral on him fine. We take a break to freshen the makeup, and when we come back, Doug has wood problems all of a sudden."

Mike's assistant gives Doug 50 mg of Viagra and "30 minutes later he has wood. He starts in a missionary position, I am filming the close up from behind, after maybe two minutes he says, 'I'm gonna come.'"

So Mike missed the pop shot (he was inside her), and of course, the scene was over. "All we can do to salvage it is turn it into a girl girl. Neither of the girls (who are best friends) had ever done girl girl before so it's awkward but we get through it, 12 hours after we started."

So Mike "took a BEATING on this shoot," because he had to pay Doug and both women.

And Doug's reaction? He claimed that he lost wood because "the girl wasn't helping him, that he is USED to being with girls who want to fuck him."

Mike South was furious. "Listen up, guys, this is NOT a fucking girlfriend experience. She does not want to fuck you because you are such a stud.... When you are on my payroll...you fuck a dead, limp fucking body if that's what I tell you to do.

"Don't quit your fucking day job, Doug."[12]

Thus, the industry depended on a handful of reliable woodsmen. According to Millward's analysis of 3000 male porn stars in the IAFD database, "of the 100 most prolific porn stars of all time...96 are men." Of these men, the ten most prolific performers have slept on screen with an average of 1,013 women—for an average career length of 22.4 years. That works out to sex with 45 women a year. (By contrast, the 10 most prolific women have slept with an average of 148 different men—for an average career length of 17.7 years. That works out to sex with 8 men a year.) Millward contrasted two champions: Tom Byron, whose career began in 1982 and had 2,549 film credits, who slept on film with 1,127 different women; and Nina Hartley, whose porn debut was in 1984, who performed in 938 films and slept on camera with 199 different men.[13] It is not that men were in greater demand with the public! Most male viewers could have cared less about the identity of the male talent. It was that directors cast the same men again and again because they could be relied upon.

Indeed, in a pinch, one of these old reliable woodsmen could be called in, such as Dave Cummings, a retired lieutenant-colonel in the U.S. Army, who at 54 first appeared on camera in 1994 in *Nina Hartley's Guide to Better Cunnilingus,* then in 1995 in his first feature appearance, *The Devil in Miss Jones 5: The Inferno.* His reputation for sexual stamina won him a place in 2007 in the *AVN* Hall of Fame. "Under the right circumstances," he said in 2014 at 74, "I could get back in front of the cameras again."[14]

Erik Everhard (Mitchell Hartwell), a native of Calgary, Alberta, saw an ad for porn models one day in the paper. "This guy says come on down, maybe they'll use me. I knock on the door, they open it and say, 'Can you fuck a chick right now?' They had a girl ready to go and needed somebody to do this scene with her. 'Can you pop in about five minutes?' they ask me. So I did, and that was that. I thought, 'No big deal, that was easy!' And I got $50, too."[15] This skill, actually, was very unusual, and Everhard became a standard woodsman (see below).

How many failures are you allowed? Three, one insider told Robert Stoller around 1985. "Anyone can have a one-day washout. Of course, that will immediately get around. And they might be allowed a second at bat. But if they strike out three times, they're out. They're gone. So that's tremendous pressure to be under."[16]

Size

"There are only so many professions in which being called 'a big dick' is a compliment, and porn is one of them."[17]

XBIZ JOURNALIST ACME ANDERSON, 2005

When people asked Ron Jeremy how large his organ was, he would respond, "Two inches [pause] from the floor."[18] (In fact, his member erect measured 9¾".) Men as well as women seemed hypnotized by the sight of these great cocks. Joey Silvera coined the term "woodsman" in 1995.[19] The top woodsmen have big penises, and an ability to make them erect at will. Director and film-historian Jim Holliday put together a list of twelve talent "at least packing 10 [inches] at peak arousal," including the famous John C. Holmes heading the list. (Back in the early days of black and white loops, said co-performer Ric Lutze, "A lot of girls were actually scared of his size." Gene Ross, who interviewed Lutze, added, "A story goes round that one blonde model named Rita said that doing it with Holmes was like 'fucking a baseball bat.'"[20] (Holmes was said to be almost 13" long—but Jim Holliday opined that it was only 11."[21]) There followed Tony "The Hook" Perez, Dick Rambone (reputedly 15 ½"[22]), Ron Jeremy, Bill Margold, and other stars.[23]

A later arrival to this list was Italian star Rocco Siffredi with his 13" "sword." Models did not necessarily crave these titans with their huge organs, as constant banging against the vaginal end of the cervix quickly made them sore. ("I will not work with Ron Jeremy," screamed Carol Z. at a shoot as Jeremy was about to help out in a wood-failure emergency.[24]) Yet these well-endowed men constitute a kind of honor roll, "the hung jury," entirely untypical of the normal male talent who, like the normal male population, have penises averaging about 5½" in length erect.[25]

Writer-director-actor Bill Margold boasted to psychiatrist Robert Stoller around 1985 of his own 10 ½" organ, "They say it's big. At one point it was the second biggest in the industry and now it's maybe the third.... I don't really give a shit, you know, it does what it has to do. One of the nicknames for it is 'The Hose.'" Margold said that it worked reliably and that he needed no help in getting hard.[26]

No help in getting hard? Standards must vary quite a bit from set to set, but the expectation does seem to be common that the females on some sets will "fluff" the male talent, getting them erect by giving them a hand-job or a b-j. Fluffing was common in the features era because delays associated with changing film and so forth caused male talent to lose wood. Many sets, however, continued to use fluffers even in the video era. In his first scene ever, Ron Jeremy was supposed to "bone" the famous porn star Samantha. But there was one thing to do before.

The director led him into a room. "Samantha is in the middle of a scene right now, but we'll probably be ready for you in another fifteen minutes or so. In the meantime, feel free to enjoy Christine here."

Christine was sitting naked on a couch. Jeremy began worrying about his lines. (It worried him that he didn't have any.)

"You okay, sweetie?" she asked.

She took his hand. "Don't you worry, I'm going to make sure you have a nice, big erection."

Samantha herself realized she was dealing with a newbie. "Don't worry kid," she said, "I promise I'll be gentle."[27]

In this scene, Jeremy, who had been holding himself back for a week, ejaculated in torrents. The crew burst into applause, then asked him how he did it.

"Chicken soup," joked the Jewish Jeremy. "A bowl of chicken soup two hours before sex. Works every time."

Little did he then know, but Jeremy had started a huge myth in the New York porn scene. "Years later, chicken soup would become a common sight on porn sets. I'd show up for a shoot and find cans littering the dressing room."

Actors explained to Jeremy, "Oh yeah, it makes you cum like a volcano."[28]

Did Viagra greatly enlarge the talent pool? Not really. Performance anxiety could overpower even Viagra, and in 2015 director Brad Armstrong at Wicked said there was too little male talent for too much work. "Some of the [male talent] are doing two to three scenes a day because, even with the male enhancement drugs, there are still only a number of guys who are in demand who can do scene after scene no matter who the girl is and pull it all off to the specifications that the directors need."[29]

Fame?

In retailing video tapes and DVDs, there were only a couple of male names that counted, but they really drew in the crowds.[30] In the 1980s, John Leslie (John Leslie Nuzzo) was often requested—he would have been 40 by 1985. He started in porn in 1975 playing Clint Eastwood. The premise of the flick *Venture Into the Bizarre* was that "Clint Eastwood" walks into a plaster-casting shop in New York's Greenwich Village and asks for a cast to be made of his organ. Over his life, Leslie accumulated 310 film credits and numerous more as a director (after 1988) and a producer with his own company in the 1990s. Like many of the top male talent, Leslie got wood by fantasizing during a shoot rather than responding to the model. Pornographer David Jennings recalled a Leslie shoot, "as [Leslie] pumped himself into coming on Kellee's face. His eyes had been closed; she'd been no stimulus to him at all."[31] But as a testimonial to his endurance, he was still performing (*Brianna Love*, 2007) until shortly before his death in 2010 of a heart attack at age 65.

The most legendary male talent was John Holmes. Yet word had it that Holmes never really got hard. Annette Haven said, "It was like doing it with a big soft loofah sponge. You had to kind of stuff it in."[32] Holmes was born as John Curtis Estes in Ashville, Ohio, in 1944 and was recruited to porn shoots in 1967 when a photographer for a porn magazine, standing beside him at a urinal, noticed his unusually "large member." Notable peep-show loops began to feature Holmes in *Pretty Girl*, around 1971 and possibly before, an 8mm silent stag filmed in the Valley; and *Playmate 11*, also around 1971. Holmes began to move out of the loop category with *Turn-on-Orgy* in 1971, which ran 29 minutes, then *The Winning Stroke* in 1973, a 58-minute flick directed by Simon L. Egree (these are, of course, "porn names"), and distributed by Noel Bloom's Caballero Classics, a studio for which Holmes did much work. Best-known of the early Holmes oeuvre is probably *Tell Them Johnny Wadd is Here* (1976), directed by Bob Chinn and co-starring the famous Annette Haven. (In this series that started in 1971, Johnny Wadd was one of Holmes's stage names.) The International Adult Film Database lists 526 entries for him, one of which was a compilation, *John Holmes Goes Gay*, released in 2002. (In the 70s, Holmes did a number of gay loops[33] and was thought to have died of AIDS[34]).

According to Al Goldstein, Holmes had a magnetic effect upon female performers. "To see Holmes loops and films was to see hundreds of beautiful women driven to sloe-eyed ecstasy with his cock buried in them. His fourteen inches [sic] of dangling death was an instrument of shuddering awe to porn starlets, who succumbed weakly under its powers."[35] Holmes ended up starring in over 2,000 loops, stags, and adult features, in addition to traveling around the world where his famous member was available for private engagements. Holmes's career dimmed when he was arrested for the famous Laurel Canyon murders in Los Angeles, acquitted in 1982, and died six years later. The movie *Boogie Nights* (1997), directed by Paul Thomas Anderson and starring Mark Wahlberg and Burt Reynolds, was shot in the Valley and is based on Holmes's life.

A third famous woodsman was the rotund, unchiseled, hirsute Ron Jeremy, also known as "the Hedgehog," who took the baton from the faltering fingers of

Holmes. Jeremy's member put him in the star ballpark. (And yes, Pipedream has molded him.) Ron Jeremy Hyatt was born on Long Island, and after a girlfriend sent a picture of him off to *Playgirl* in 1978, he was "deluged with female fan mail, and letters of interest from adult filmmakers!"[36] From 1979 on, he appeared in over 800 adult feature films, performed well into his fifties—and prides himself on not needing Viagra.

The interesting thing about Jeremy is that, even after he developed a big gut and became physically unhandsome, he remained famous and in demand. You thought only stallions became woodsmen? Not at all. Jeremy said that surfers could identify with him. "I am living proof that anybody can get laid.... When people see me in a porno, they think, If *this* guy is getting lucky in the sack, maybe there's hope for me!"[37] Here's what young, fresh Ginger Lynn thought of Jeremy when she walked into the little apartment in Santa Monica where they were shooting for Vivid. She was nervous about this her first shoot. "Ron was sweating and smelly and hairy and fat...I looked at him and I almost left. Then I thought, 'You know what? If I can do it with this guy, I can do it with *anybody*.'"[38]

The good times came to an end for the woodsmen around the same age as for the porn models—maybe a bit older. With 40, you were washed up (with the notable exception of a few megastars like Ron Jeremy). Tom Byron, himself a legend, told *AVN* in 2003, "I'm really self-conscious about my body now. I'm 42 years old. Even though I work out and stuff, you can't stop the midriff. You just can't stop it. Plus I have arthritis.... I can't do a sex scene—but maybe a P.O.V. [point of view] scene. Just so I can get laid."[39]

Yet the abovementioned big four were exceptions. As hard as many female talent found it to get their name in lights, male talent had it, in general, even harder. Said journalist Acme Anderson in 2008, "Guys are typically treated as props by everyone from the talent to the producers to the fans." Men who download porn do not do it in order to see other men, and the identity of the male talent is of relative uninterest. Similarly, male performers receive less for a shoot than female. Male prima donnas are virtually unheard of. "I'm just there to do my job," said woodsman Alec Knight. "To keep my dick hard, open up for the camera, give the director what they want and that's what keeps me busy. I don't really have an ego about it. It's just a job for me."[40] This is in contrast to the dreams of many female performers about becoming literal porn stars.

That said, in the new century there was a trend to see male talent as something more than "stunt cocks," to give them co-billing as stars. Ironically, this began with Candida Royalle's founding of Femme Productions in the 1980s, with box covers that depicted the male stars alongside the female in order to make the point that this was more about couples than pounding. Later, Royalle said, "It's taken over twenty years since I started Femme Productions, and a whole new young generation of women who are openly interested in porn, but it doesn't surprise me one bit that men in hetero porn will begin to have their own billboards."[41]

Chapter 13:
Dominance

"There has been a big change in my membership. Women are now saying, 'I want.'"[1]

ANGIE ROWNTREE, ADMINISTRATOR OF FEMINIST ADULT WEBSITE Sssh.com:

Interest in women-on-top has exploded at the same time as rage against sexual harassment. Both are sides of the same coin: Women's new fury about abuse and subordination has become one of the main drivers of twenty-first century culture. This public fury converts into a private refusal to accept being the passive partner.

Dominance and submission are actually psychological concepts requiring no gear or toys: a woman can be dominant in her flannel nightie and pink bunny slippers. In the BDSM area, one partner is almost always dominant, the other submissive, yet they may switch. It is not about giving or receiving pain. The exchange of power is the key idea.[2]

How big is this, really? Big. On the hook-up site for married people VictoriaMilan. com, of the first 50 consecutive profiles of married or partnered Canadian women seeking temporary liaisons, twenty indicated an interest in dominant-submissive roleplaying of some kind: Of these, six said they found "blindfolding" a turn-on, eight opted for domination-domineering or switching, and six signaled an interest in "being dominated." This is a special population of women in sexually-unfulfilling marriages who long for sensuality, but 40 percent long for roleplaying of some kind.

Another special population are the subscribers to the online website of the Swedish toymaker LELO. When polled, this group, consisting heavily of young females, said that 20 percent of them preferred the dominant role, a third wanted submissive, but 45 percent opted for "taking turns." So the dominant, plus part-time dominant, constituted two-thirds of the group.[3]

Consensual sadism and masochism have both been subject to a certain misunderstanding in the media and among academics unfamiliar with the roleplaying scene[4]—and this is why participants prefer the term "roleplaying" to the fearsome-sounding "S & M." Masochism in sex does not mean taking pleasure in pain as such, but rather in accepting pain as evidence of the top's dominance. The point of the exercise is to enhance her psychological authority, not to leave the bottom with welts and bruises. Similarly, sexual sadism is not pleasure in inflicting pain as such (unlike real sadism), but ensuring that the submissive bends absolutely to your will, and we'll test that with a few strokes of the riding crop. If the experience is genuinely unpleasant for the bottom, he or she will not return.

One shouldn't create the impression that the dominant woman is a new idea. In pornography, we've had female dominance since the Marquis de Sade's "Juliette" around 1800 or Leopold von Sacher-Masoch's "Wanda" in 1870. Yet, historically, the dominant gender was once male. British physician and sexologist Havelock Ellis wrote in 1913, "The masculine tendency to delight in domination, the feminine tendency to delight in submission, still maintain the ancient traditions when the male animal pursued the female."[5] Yet this was Victorian culture, and not biology, speaking, for after the First World War, the notion of female dominance emerged. The early twentieth century threw up a tight little subculture organized about the image of the professional, leather-clad domme (see below). But these were fantasy images, designed to inflame the male imagination.

It was in the 1960s and after that the notion of the dominant woman began to take off in the real world.[6] And, for the average woman, this is indeed a new role.

How does this work? People require guidance. What exactly does one do as a top? This is a kind of where-do-the-legs-go-in-sex question for newbies. But the world of dominance and submission has its own codes that exist to enhance the dominance of the woman and the submissiveness of her partner, and there are scripts in this kind of roleplaying that wannabe femdoms should learn. (Of course, the man may be the top, but historically new here is women topping men.[7]) A feminist editorial team led by author Barbara Ehrenreich said, "For heterosexual women who desired more control over the sexual act—a common enough request—S/M offered a method of binding each partner to play by a set of mutually agreed rules."[8]

But within the context of those rules you, as a dominant, have a free hand— in this particular bedroom on this particular afternoon —and that may or may not involve handcuffing him to the bed, spitting in his mouth and calling him your "bitch," and flogging him until his backside is red. You decide...because you are dominant. (In dealing with a professional, however, there might be a preliminary conversation about "limits.") The point is that the top is in total and complete control of the scene. Power has been transferred. This is why it is so thrilling for the bottom. Said Dee Severe, producer and co-owner of BDSM-oriented Severe Society Films, "My joke is that one of my most frequent lines as a director is, 'Pretend you don't like this.'" [9]

The dominance of either gender goes profoundly against the idea of the 50-50 marriage, where both partners share all duties and pleasures. But many find the 50-50 marriage a recipe for bed death. "I know what a 50-50 marriage should be like," one man said to *The New York Times*. "But what is 50-50 sex supposed to be like?"[10] I am not arguing against the concept of marital equality, but simply saying that dominance may be more intrinsic to sexual satisfaction than is often realized. That might account for its soaring popularity today on the internet.

Female Dominance

The irresistible woman is a common archetype. But to be irresistible is not necessarily to be in command. Here is what being in command feels like: One young woman in Toronto first started to feel dominant at 14, when she got her first motorcycle jacket. "The jacket made me feel strong." Then she started stripping ("dancing"). "When I was dancing, I did a lot of domination. Guys would come in so I could... slap them, bite them, step on genitals with my heels, squeeze their nipples as hard as I could. They got off, and I felt like I was in complete control, which was fantastic."

Some were married. "Wives wouldn't do this at home?"

"Absolutely not, hands down."[11]

Dominant women have dressed up for the role ever since Count Leopold von Sacher-Masoch's fictional Wanda in *Venus in Furs* in 1870. What is different about the dominant woman today is that she doesn't have to dress in leather or latex to be the commanding figure in the relationship. The classic dominatrix that emerges in the 1920s, clad in leather from head to toe, derived her dominance from her gear. (She was also a professional.) The historic dominatrix was costumed for the role, in other words. Today's dominant female derives her commanding authority from her personality, from her income, from the general view of the Zeitgeist today of women as being somehow "on top." She may well opt to dress for the role, but even if not, she will still be dominant over her submissive partner.

Even outside of porn, magazines have flourished for the dominant woman. In 1991, mistress Dianna Vesta began bringing out *Attitude,* the first femdom journal by and for women. Keri Pentauk's *WHAP! Women Who Administer Punishment* followed from 1994 to 1998. (She distilled the wisdom of WHAP! in her 1998 book *Spanked Husbands Satisfied Wives.*[12]) The appeal here was to dominant women in the real world, not to pro-dommes or subordinate males, though some of the latter might have perused the pages as well.

Dominance erupted into TV in 2016 in the series *Submission,* produced by Paul Fishbein, the former publisher of *AVN,* and written and directed by Jacky St. James, who had originated in 2013 the hardcore domination-submission classic, *The Submission of Emma Marx.*[13]

Today, in the real world, the dominant woman is a common figure. In a survey of 1,516 adults by three investigators in departments of psychology in the Canadian province of Quebec, 47 percent of the female respondents had "fantasized about dominating someone sexually" (60 percent of the males—but the difference between the genders was not statistically significant). To be sure, 65 percent of the women had fantasized about being dominated (53 percent of the men).[14] But the interesting figure here is that almost half of the women in this sample had fancied themselves, in their secret thoughts, as sexually dominant. It is not unusual for fantasies to "switch," as the submissives become dominant and vice-versa. Roleplaying was clearly on the fantasy table in Quebec.

The larger social context here is that in the early twenty-first century in the United States, the increasingly popular "female led relationship" (FLR), also called "femdom," is emerging as a distinctive domestic lifestyle. (The male-dominant version is often called the "discipline relationship."[15]). An FLR is not the same thing as BDSM, because bondage and domination are roleplay; an FLR is not a role but a lifestyle. Female leadership may range from receiving mild deference to imposing a chastity cage (a "cock cage") upon the male (see Chapter 17).

FLRs appear to be commoner than discipline relationships, to go by search choices on the massive website Pornhub: In 2015, search terms reflecting female dominance or control were sought out vastly more often by women than men. "Guy eating pussy" and the like were searched by women around nine time more often than by men. Women went for "lesbian threesome" 353 percent more often than men and "lesbian strap on" 192 percent more often. As a search category, "lesbian" outpaced even "big dick." These are porn choices in which the guy is simply switched out.[16]

As stated, this projection of dominance is a psychological quality quite separate from roleplay (BDSM) or gear (fetish). Here there have been several intriguing studies. Donald McCreary and Nancy D. Rhodes, two academic researchers, found in 2001 that "student participants were more likely to believe that submissiveness was more desirable in men than in women," although not by a lot.[17]

These young people were the wave of the future. In 2014, Chad Braverman, COO at toymaker Doc Johnson, said their BDSM line was really taking off, and that the fans were "extremely vocal" which, said Braverman, was a new development. "What's even more impressive is that the majority of [the fans of a BDSM toy line] are women from the ages of 18-25, a demographic that nearly every business wants a piece of. It's interesting how quickly barriers are being broken down as far as what's taboo and what's vanilla."[18]

Dominance in Porn

Here is smoking as dominance: In one variety of "smoking porn," the woman, is portrayed with a cigarette, exhaling casually as the man penetrates her or performs oral sex. The image conveys the message, "Actually, my smoking is more important to me than you are, you worm." It is a very dominant message.

The dominant female as a sexually-arousing figure has a recent history in the adult industry and in the culture. Exchange of power entered adult film in the "kinkies" of the 1960s, the first being *White Slaves of Chinatown* in 1964, followed by such creations as *The Sadistic Hypnotist* (1969) and *Ilsa: She Wolf of the SS* in 1974. They were a mixture of femdom and femsub, and attracted large followings.[19]

Russ Meyer's films feature a series of dominant women, starting with the three sadistic go-go dancers in *Faster Pussycat Kill Kill* (1965), in which a black-leather-gloved-and-jumpsuited Tura Satana roughs up the male lead; then Meyer shot *Vixen!* in 1968, which he called "the first sex picture in which a woman called all the shots."[20] Erica Gavin played Vixen Palmer, and she would star in one more Meyer film, *Beyond the Valley of the Dolls* (1970), before leaving the industry several years later.

In Anthony Riverton's *The Other Side of Julie* (1978), Julie comes to show her dominant side. Said Jim Holliday in 1986 of the film, "Some men may become threatened to see a woman in control. I personally think this is where adult films must head if they want to appeal to women and couples." But even though the woman was in control and not just, as Holliday said, a "sex object," the film was sexually appealing and did not lose sight of Holliday's "cardinal rule of sex films": They must be arousing.[21] Radley Metzger offered more specific instruction on BDSM in *Maraschino Cherry* (1978).

Female dominance started to become a common adult theme, reversing the classic historic figure of the female performer as the trinket of the male porn star. In 1987, the concept powered onto the newsstands when veteran "girlie mag" editor Dian Hanson helmed a book called *Leg Show*. Previous editors had been gay and the magazine had a campy sensibility, but with Hanson, it became known for its portrayals of leggy, dominant women. Hanson ran photos of herself, though never showing her face, in domme gear. (The last issue was published in 2012.)

In 1992, Vivid Video launched the two-part series *Dominant Dames*, in line with its general policy of female-friendly flicks. "Don't be misled by the title," said the reviewer. "There's no B&D...just a lot of ladies who know what they want sexually and don't mind telling their partners what to do and how to do it."[22]

But let's not get carried away. Until *Fifty Shades of Grey*, the great majority of men and women in the U.S. were not really interested in kink. As late as 1993, video marketers in the Valley continually received messages about the undesirability of specialty tapes from merchants in the small towns and suburbs of the South and Midwest: "It wouldn't be right for our community," or "I just don't think there's any market for it here. Nobody wants to buy that stuff." Or, even more emphatically, "Hey—I can't even sell hardcore tapes here; you think they'll let me sell tapes where women get tied up?"[23]

Now, an interesting thing that did happen in the 1990s was that women who felt themselves dominant began pouring into the industry. Irene Boss, a lifestyle Pittsburgh domme, got the first pro-domme site up in 1994.[24]

Later, among the most prominent BDSM sites of the pro-dommes was that of Dee Severe (Dee Manning) at Severe Society Films; Severe encountered BDSM in adolescence and spent her time tying up boyfriends. "I always had a dark sensibility," she said in an interview. "When other little girls had their favorite Disney princess, my favorite character was Maleficent. She wore black! She lived in a castle and had minions and power.... Starting in my teens, my sexual fantasies always had a power exchange quality to them. I dabbled around in BDSM in my early 20s, but then I had a vanilla marriage that didn't last.... I think I'm hard wired to be kinky, it's just what I am, and it's the core of my sexuality." Dee Severe got a part-time job as a pro-domme in 2005, and she and her husband Michael Manning founded their own company two years later.[25]

Isabella Sinclaire, owner of GwenMedia, felt drawn to BDSM as a teen in Birmingham. "The first realization that I was different from all of my friends was when I was in high school and a couple of us were watching the movie *Nine 1/2 Weeks*. All of my girlfriends seemed to associate more with Kim Basinger's character [the bottom], and I wanted to be just like Mickey Rourke. Needless to say, the first time I dressed in fetish clothing and picked up a whip, I felt like a latex-clad fish in water."

Then she moved to New York and bumped into a woman who turned out to be a bottom. "When I told her my interests were as a dominant, she took me to a few fetish stores and clubs. I was hooked." Later, Sinclaire set up GwenMedia, with the view that "when the fans buy our movies or sign up to our site, they know what they are getting is the real thing, because we are fetishists too." She advised aspiring dominants: Practice on your boyfriends![26]

Scraping the outer edge of female domination were femdoms such as Saharah Eve who could be very rough with their male bottoms. "The hits are real," she told the *XBIZ* chatboard. "The smothering is real. Sometimes I get pretty violent.... Want to see a naked and shivering guy kicked square in the balls hard by a dominant female?"[27] If there was any trend on the net towards rough sex, it was these femdoms who demonstrated their control by beating up consenting male clients who longed for this kind of experience.

In 2015, the industry recognized the importance of femdom when Clips4Sale. com established the first annual Femdom Awards; the winning femdom site was MeanBitches.com, and award categories included Cuckold Scene of the Year and Strapon Scene of the Year[28] (see below).

Fifty Shades of Grey

Fifty Shades of Grey had a large impact on the sex realm.[29] We are in Montreal, summer 2015, on the set of a pornshoot. Angie Rowntree, the webmaster of a feminist site called Sssh.com and producer of the shoot, is chatting with Starla, a

Montreal domme and female talent in the shoot. Both have decades of experience in the industry:

Angie said there was huge interest on the site in BDSM, women dominating men and the reverse. Yet, "the number one question [of the site's members] is, 'Am I normal?' If she sees it on Sssh, she says, 'That is exactly what I want. I want to try that.'"

Starla: "After the session, my clients too ask me, 'Am I normal?' After *Fifty Shades*, all of a sudden it was OK. They stopped asking if they were normal."

Angie: "*Fifty Shades* really gave them permission."[30]

Thus, part of the new interest in female dominance comes from a literary production, a novel.[31] In 2011, an obscure publishing house in Australia brought out the first volume of English novelist E.L. James's trilogy, *Fifty Shades of Grey*. Dealing with dominance and submission—an incandescent affair between the shop clerk, Ana, and the masterful billionaire, Christian—the novel was an unlikely candidate for world success. Yet *Fifty Shades of Grey* soon became the subject of excited internet chatter, and by June 2015, the Vintage Books edition that came out in 2012 had sold more than 125 million copies worldwide, making it one of the best-selling novels in modern times. Movies followed the trilogy and, by the summer of 2015, the first of what would be at least three films themed on the novel had become a blockbuster. Just imagine: Christian's dungeon, "the Red Room," floggers, handcuffs, and the whole apparatus of light bondage—a blockbuster.

Of course, *Fifty Shades of Grey* does not initiate the concepts of dominance and submission. What the novel does, however, is to place the concept of "transfer of power" on the breakfast table for discussion. It gives women the option of choosing to be bottoms, like Ana, or choosing to be tops. And this is new: the advent of the dominant woman, not as a pro-domme working for wages in the escort sector, but as a partner in a normal relationship.

The novel's spin-off was enormous. The entire toy sector was energized, Toymaker Lovehoney, founded in 2002 in Bath, England, captured the *Fifty Shades* license from E. L. James in 2012. Lovehoney then sublicensed out some of the product line and, in 2015, Williams Trading began upselling, or adding to the shopping cart, such products as "exclusive Fifty Shades After Spanking Cream" and "Christian Grey Aftershave."[32]

After the release of the *Fifty Shades of Grey* movie, at the website Pornhub, the number of women searching for terms such as "submission" and "dominant" increased about 50 percent. The terms "whip," "master," and "leather"—all used in the novel—spiked after the debut as well.[33] At Sheri's Ranch, a brothel just outside Las Vegas, the courtesans began offering "introductory training in sadomasochistic erotic acts involving dominance and submission." The ranch's "dungeon room" became increasingly booked by "women and couples between the ages of 35 and 50." Dena, the brothel's madam, said that of her 144 courtesans, "I need to make sure that I have at least four to eight women in each week's lineup who specialize in BDSM activities and education."[34]

The novel essentially romanticized the bondage market, and the mainstream media ate it up. Public interest in domination and submission became intense. The chain Good Vibrations had a couple of fetish titles, including Tristan Taormino's book *50 Shades of Kink*. Vice president Jackie Strano said of the *Fifty Shades of Grey* phenomenon, "I think it taps into some psyche zeitgeist of folks exploring submission more as surrender and bondage and fetish play as a way to push for deeper sensation.... It's become more acceptable for mainstream and is not relegated to a back room." Michael Stabile , marketing director at Kink.com, confirmed that *Fifty Shades of Grey* had expanded the fetish audience: "We're seeing lots of interest in exploring BDSM from all areas—from mainstream stars, from younger gay men, from women, as well as our more traditional audience. We're seeing a demystification of BDSM and fetish in popular culture, and that's helping lower the stigma about it." [35]

Fifty Shades of Grey had an interesting impact on Kink.com itself, convincing owner Peter Acworth to move away from such extreme material as the public humiliation and gangbang sites and to develop more educational sites. Acworth said in the fall of 2014, "We're shifting our energies to things like Kink University, enhancing the social aspects of our websites, events in our community center, and adding the ability to buy kink-branded BDSM gear on our sites." The motive? "With the mainstreaming of kink as evidenced by the huge popularity of *50 Shades of Grey*, we feel there is an opportunity to serve a wider customer base in the future."[36] Of these new fans, he said, on another occasion, "We have a small, but growing and dedicated female fan base."[37] In 2017, Kink.com sold its San Francisco headquarters, the Armory, and moved to Las Vegas; Acworth told the press, "It's the end of an era."[38]

Porn and toys in the dominance space began to expand to mainstream. Said Lovehoney, co-founder Neal Slateford, in 2015, *Fifty Shades of Grey* "has made BDSM much more accessible to a mainstream audience. We always sold a lot of BDSM products but *FSOG* made us world leaders in that format.... Three summers ago, there wasn't a beach or a train where you could not see perfectly ordinary women enjoying pretty hardcore erotic literature without a trace of embarrassment. Clearly, a lot of these women and their partners wanted to do more than just enjoy the books—they wanted to experiment sexually in the same way that Anastasia Steele does in particular in the books." Marketing director Ray Hayes said that Lovehoney's Official Pleasures Collection was sold "in every developed country in the world," including Target in the U.S., where the Collection was stocked "alongside products like toothbrushes." We have now sold, said Slateford in June 2015, more than two million units, including handcuffs, blindfolds, and above all, nipple clamps, which Slateford thought "would be fairly niche but not at all."[39]

Meanwhile, across the Pond, in 2012 the popular daytime show *The View* was featuring fetish on a segment called "Favorite Things." Co-host Sherri Shepherd held up a bondage kit and said, "This is my new favorite." Pipedream's PR manager Kevin Johnson looked on in bemusement as the show presented Pipedream's inflatable bondage chair. "Even five years ago, you simply wouldn't have seen these types of goods on daytime TV," he said.[40]

Fifty Shades of Grey permitted toymaker Sportsheets to take it up a notch from "soft bondage products" to harder-edged stuff in a line they called "Edge" featuring more advanced restraints and floggers. Said one of their executives, "For years BDSM has been considered a taboo area of the adult novelty industry, but as it has gotten more and more mainstream...the demand for our products has skyrocketed."[41]

Within adult, *Fifty Shades of Grey* was considered by some actually to have saved the industry. For John Stagliano at Evil Angel, *Fifty Shades of Grey* came as though heaven-sent. Stagliano was one of the most respected producers in the business, had done federal time on an obscenity conviction, and was determined to keep fetish-BDSM in the forefront of the erotic imagination. "The success of *Fifty Shades*," he said in an interview with *XBIZ* in 2015, "exposes the inherent lust of the American people—and particularly of women who long for kinky play." It was the internet driving this forward, he said, "allowing people to explore more and more fetishes. New media stuff, Facebook, Instagram, Twitter gives people more and more places to discuss these previously hidden desires." Femdom was all over the amateur market, said his colleague at Evil Angel Aiden Riley. Director Dana Vespoli at Angel, who had just released *Fluid 3*, said, "The market is definitely growing. You look at Clips4Sale.com [an online site for short loops], which is almost entirely fetish-based, and how successful it is...I certainly think that *Fifty Shades* had a big influence." [42]

In fetish-themed lingerie, *Fifty Shades of Grey* played perfectly into the new dominance theme. "It's no surprise," said one biz journalist, "that women are taking control in the bedroom with dominatrix-influenced lingerie cast in rich jewel tones and basic black." What kind of lingerie would that be? Straps were the big new theme in the spring of 2015. Said Emily Bendell, whose Bluebella Black Label had the official *Fifty Shades* lingerie license, "That means more strap-detailing and lingerie with ties." Added Wilson Kello of International Intimates, "Straps are here to stay." In some stores, "harnesses and handcuffs were strategically placed alongside *Fifty Shades'*-inspired lingerie sets."[43] The marketing theme here was not the subservience of Ana in the novel, but female dominance.

In the continuing long tail of the *Fifty Shades* fervor, many couples entered the scene who had previously been unfamiliar with kink, basically, who did not know what to do. Several companies filled this gap with "instructionals," movies hosted by players such as Tristan Taormino or Jessica Drake, covering not just bondage but anal, lesbian sex, fellatio, the use of toys, threesomes, and roleplaying. (See, for example, Wicked's *Guide to Anal* or Adam & Eve's *Guide to Bondage for Couples.*[44])

For the adult industry, *Fifty Shades of Grey* had been like putting your head inside a bell and having a crazed giant with a hammer pound it repeatedly. It is not too strong to say that the industry has been stunned by the novel and the overwhelming outpouring of interest among women in domination and submission.

The Dominance Niches

"If you have a narrow niche, the guys who find your site were looking for exactly what you have and want more of it. So they pay." [45]

SunFunBill, 2014

Did the niches always exist in people's minds in latent form and the industry merely activated them? Or did the industry create the niches in order to earn a buck? One must be careful about attributing novelty to anything in the area of sexuality, because the ingenuity of humankind over thousands of years of experience has been enormous. After all, as early as 1886, in his great compendium of sexuality, Vienna psychiatrist and sexologist Richard von Krafft-Ebing described "shoe and foot fetishism."[46] So, yes, many desires have always existed, slumbering latently in breasts burdened by religious fanaticism or social convention.

But there is evidence that much in the world of adult desire today has recently arisen, has been created de novo. The word "niche" entered the industry's vocabulary around 2000 when the flood of free vanilla material, often shot by amateurs whose cameras now permitted high-quality (but low artistic) filming. Serving the granularity of niche and sub-niche markets turned out to be a fine new way of making money, given that the tubes would dominate more generic searches. A.J. Hall, founder and CEO of the software company Elevated X, said in 2015, "If a husband and wife run their own swinger site, and they go *from* swapping and group sex videos *to* videos where the wife is one-on-one with other men, the husband is made to watch, the wife is blindfolded and surprised with a new partner—that content just went from covering one or two highly competitive niches to several less competitive ones...[so] the only way someone can see a lot more of it and in good quality is to visit the site and pay."[47]

Industry insiders speculate that dominance niches may be more industry-led than surfer-led, meaning the content is more created by the studios rather than demanded by the clients. *XBIZ* journalist Stewart Tongue, writing in 2013, said there had been recently a "critical change." "Now...studios are not only quickly filling any voids in the marketplace, they have also become the primary driving force in the creation of new niches and popularity of existing ones." Tongue mentioned "selling BDSM fantasies" as a way of selling your site to your fans. [48]

Among the early niche producers were the Timlake brothers at Homegrown Video (see Chapter 10), who began marketing the scads of amateur videos they received in "something like 32 different niches," as Farrell Timlake said in a 2005 interview. Their *Cream Pie* series was "the first continuing internal pop line," and other Timlake niches included *Horny Over 40* and *Housewives Unleashed*.[49] None of these were dominance niches, but Homegrown put the idea out there that niche-ing was a way to make money.

Important among the niches were the fetishes, as many different ones as the sparks fly upward. At New Sensations, Scott Taylor said we're going to have to figure out exactly what the market will support. "We plan to explore themes such as light bondage, sensory deprivation, fem-dom as well as hotwifing and swinging. There is also a plan to mix fetishes."[50] Said another industry exec, "If you have content of girls getting beans poured on them, my guess is, if you understand that fetish and can deliver it to the fans, you will be able to still make a good ROI [return on investment]."[51] It was like the beginning of the Gold Rush. Which creeks had the golden seams?

The list of fetishes that are internet search categories goes on for pages, and the fetishes themselves split into micro-variants. Take foot fetish. Just naked feet? Noooo. Said fetish-director Larry Ross, "There's people who want bare feet, people who want stockings on, people who have black stockings, brown stockings, people in sweat socks, feet that smell, feet that don't smell...."[52] "Barefootsies" is the handle of the porner who has a foot fetish, which he quite unabashedly mentions on the *XBIZ* chatboard as he jokes with women porners about taking off their shoes. When Holly Randall went to do a photo shoot with a hetero male model, she wondered how she was going to get him hard, given the absence of a fluffer on the set that day. So she brought a bunch of porn magazines. He scarcely glanced at them.

"'Could you take off your shoes for me?' he asked me inquisitively.

"What? Did I hear him right?"

And yes, he had a foot fetish. He kept glancing at her toes during the shoot, hard as steel.[53]

What niches do sell? Jeremy, CEO of the BDSM internet studio DarkCircus. com, said in 2008, "Chastity and cuckolding is really what launched us." Those niches quadrupled his company's sales in one month. Chastity means restrictive devices that a dominant woman can lock on a submissive male's penis to ensure that only she has access to it (see below). Cuckolding is the fantasy that some other man, usually a well-endowed African-American, will penetrate your wife while you are "forced" to sit and watch.[54] This fantasy is so popular that content-provider "dcgohard," an African-American at Chocolate Empire Media, had a special site "for people in the cuckold lifestyle and I have found over time a lot of white couples and females on my site are looking for black men that are well endowed aka referred to as bulls."[55]

Were these cuckolding and chastity tastes just latent, waiting to be activated by DarkCircus's images? Or did the image of a dominant woman, locking on a chastity device and saying she might remove it next month, create a taste in male partners for this kind of submissiveness they had not previously even fantasized about? If always latent, surely there would be some residue in pre-internet porn.

But neither I, nor other investigators, have been able to find pre-1970 images for any of these niches.

In October 2000, Jay Kopita, the administrator of the YNOT chatboard, asked, "Are there any popular fetishes you just don't 'get'?"

Richard Buss (Rochard), an executive at Dating Factory, replied, "What I really don't get is men being dominated by women. That just goes against everything to me. Women kicking men in the balls, who is into that?"

SunFunBill said, "Ha, cuckold, sissification and humiliation are the main niches I push. They convert [sell] like crazy. I 'get' them but they are not what I prefer. The video I once made with a lesbian friend was sissification."

Housekeeper, who lived in New York, added, "I 'get' all of those niches and understand why they are popular and desirous." But, he noted, "I wouldn't invest in them as interests."[56]

Topping Your Partner in the Real World: Niches

These niches play out in the real world as well, not just among professionals. Clearly, an ever-growing minority of women wanted to top their partners. How does one go about dominating one's mate?

Telling him he can't ejaculate without your permission would be an entry-level command. Spanking is also a kind of entry-level activity; a bit of pain, a red bottom, are age-old.

Eve Howard ran a Valley production company called Shadow Lane that specialized in spanking videos and brought out a glossy magazine, *Stand Corrected*. She envisioned spanking as female-focused, a patriarchal residue from the days when stern male figures such as Gary Cooper looked as though they might spank the female lead if she wasn't good.[57] But when women spank?

"Forced" Events

In reality, porn is 100 percent consensual. But there is the psychodrama that porn creates, and in that fantasy land, relations for some viewers become more appealing when they seem to be "forced." It is within this forced category that we encounter several fetish niches that absolutely did not exist some decades ago (or if they did exist, I have not seen them despite exhaustive searching). For heterosexuals in relationships, the forced events are: "forced sissification," forced bi, forced chastity, kicking, and heterosexual pegging, the "forced" penetration of the male's anus with a strapon.

Strapons

Lesbians have used strapons since time out of mind. A Google-image search for "vintage lesbian strapon" produced a photo of what seems to be real lesbians using a strapon from "c. 1890."[58] (Corresponding Google-image searches for "vintage heterosexual strapon" and "vintage girl-boy strapon" produced nothing that appeared to antedate 1970.)

Pegging, or women strapping on a harness in order to penetrate their male partners anally, is not at all new; nor is pegging confined to lesbian sex, where the historical record is rich.[59] In a personal communication to the author, BDSM historian Judson Rosebush says, "Textual and visual documentation of women penetrating men anally with strapons in the context of heterosexual relations dates from antiquity, although documentation is more scarce than lesbian strapon depictions or traditional coitus. The appeal of the practice, then and now, involves a kind of sexual inversion, in which a female dominates and penetrates the male. The pleasures are both psychological and physical, because the male prostate is stimulated by the action. Femdom malesub strapon sex should not be confused with anal sex with a man, which has a different sexual basis entirely."[60]

Clearly, therefore, strapons go back a long ways and were used in lesbian culture since time out of mind. But for heterosexuals, there does seem to be a historical change here. The female heroes in the Marquis de Sade's novel *Juliette* (1796) are strong female characters—without being necessarily psychologically dominant. Juliette and her friend, Clairwil, penetrate a number of men and women anally with dildos yet, in general, without the use of harnesses. It is precisely a harness that gives the top all her force in anal penetration. Moreover, the sex scenes, strapon ones included, in Sade are highly mechanical (probably because he was interested in writing allegory, not pornography).[61] There is no sense of psychological domination. We have to wait another century for this.

Some academic authorities see pegging as interesting, because it shifts the point of masculine erotic interest from the penis to the anus.[62] Yet more to the point, pegging shifts dominance in male-female relations from the male to the female.

In 1998, pegging received a great promotional boost in the instructional video *Bend Over Boyfriend*, starring sexologist Carol Queen, directed by Shar Rednour, and produced by Nan Kinney and Fatale Media (see Chapter 16); it explained how pegging stimulates the prostate gland; this helped popularize the "bend-over-boyfriend" concept as another term for penetrating men anally. "*BOB*" also prompted a great increase in the sales of strapons.[63]

On the basis of my own research, over the past thirty years as compared to the period before the Second World War, pegging does seem greatly to have increased in frequency. (The term is used as early as 1985, and it is incorrect that columnist Dan Savage was first to propose it in 2001.[64]) One of the earliest references in the pulp novels occurs in *Anal Eroticism: Greek Style* (1968) where, on their wedding night, Cynthia performs anal sex on Harry using a strapon dildo and refers to him as a "slave."[65]

As far as I know, the first vague, suggestive cinematic representation of pegging is found in director Michael Sarne's *Myra Breckinridge* (1970), starring a glitter cast including Mae West and Raquel Welch. A strapon is featured in Peter Locke's 1973 release *It Happened in Hollywood* (notable also because publisher Al Goldstein gets on-screen oral sex from Tanya Tickler). *The Opening of Misty Beethoven* (1975) is said to be "the first explicit pegging seen in a film." (There is a close-up.) Even in the erotic films of the 1980s, strapons were used so infrequently as to prompt film critic Mark Kernes to say of a Jimmy Holliday 80s compilation, in which Sharon Kane deployed a strapon on Lee Caroll, "These actions were so rare in the old days that they come complete with elaboration explanations of what's happening."[66]

Even in the early 90s, male talent was largely unfamiliar with strapons. Director Henri Pachard was in agent Jim South's office one day in 1991, as porn star Taylor Wane tells the story, "and [Pachard] asked if there were any guys in the business who would let a girl fuck them up the ass with a strapon."

South said no and asked "who the girl in the scene was." (When South said Taylor Wane, two male actors in the room stood up.)

Wane ended up penetrating Candice Heart's boyfriend in the scene. She said, "I really enjoyed that, actually. And I really wanted to do it. I get into this whole trip where I go into this fantasy world where I have a dick."[67] For Wane, the strapon was an instrument of power.

Strapons were the object of big color ads in *AVN* first in 1993, as Nasstoys launched The Boss, and illustrated the ad with a leather-clad domme and the text,

"The ultimate—that puts you in command."[68] The meaning could not have been clearer: strapons meant dominance.

"All girl! All strap-on," screamed a Pleasure Productions ad in December 1993 for *Strap-on Sally* and its "nine-girl cast"[69] And then, of course, there was Fatale Media's *Bend Over Boyfriend* (1998), mentioned above, an instructional video on pegging.

Thus, within porn, by 2002, strapons had become a familiar concept. When journalist Paul McFarland interviewed internet domme Brittany Andrews ("The Niche Bitch"), 27, from Milwaukee and creator of a live-feed content on one of her sites called *The Brittany Andrews Show*, she told him, "We had Warren Cuccurullo from Duran Duran [an English band] come on the show, who's recently had a molding made of his cock. Mind you, I do a strapon series called *Brittany's Bitchboys* where me and my girlfriends wear strapons and rape men's asses. So I said to him, 'Too bad the motherfucking [molding] isn't a strap on.' He goes 'it [is].' 'Oh my God, you've gotta let me rape your ass with your own fucking cock."[70]

One of the pegging classics was Francesca Lé's (Erika Sherwood) *His Ass is Mine*, which debuted Lé's femdom strapon series in 2005. Lé produced, directed, and starred in the title, and told *AVN* of the contents, "This is definitely a movie for guys who love dominant women taking control and showing who's boss because we all really know that women are the superior sex."[71] Lé's first domination-themed title had been *Dressing Room Domination* (1998), and she deviated from her usual ass-lesbian themes, to produce several further femdom flicks as well.

Porn star Devinn Lane came to production company Shane's World in 2005 with the idea of shooting a *Guide to Strap-on Sex*, and in January 2006, the DVD debuted. Said Shane's World owner Jennie Grant, "We are very excited about stepping into this niche"; the *Guide* featured a number of male talents such as Kurt Lockwood and "a real college student" "taking" a strapon for the first time.[72]

In the real world as well, pegging seemed in those years to be on the uptake. Julie Stewart president of Sportsheets, said in 2015, "The suburban housewife is our new best friend. And one of the biggest shifts we're seeing is with heterosexual couples pegging, where the woman will put on a strapon and fuck her husband in the ass with it. We've been making strapons for over 15 years, and way back when, they were sold primarily to lesbians. But the demographic has shifted, and the majority of strapon sales now are to heterosexual couples."[73] A former pro-domme in the U.K. wrote the author in 2014, "I enjoyed wearing my strapon with my last boyfriend because I knew how much he loved it. It was naughty and I could always make him come quick.... I enjoyed being the man sometimes and it was rather big, he screamed. I liked that. I guess I'm slightly sadistic."[74]

These are anecdotes from the front lines rather than hard statistical data (which do not exist), yet they have some value. Said porn star Aria (Marie Silva) in 2003, when asked what she had in her nightstand, "I do have JoJo the Dildo in my drawer. JoJo is my strapon. He's in my drawer just in case there's company, because you never know who's going to come by."[75] So true.

Other "Forced" Events

Forced bi, also called "bi-sex," is premised on the male partner being submissive. She then orders him to give oral sex to another man. The fans, in other words, are not gay but rather are males who long to be "humiliated" by women, "forced" into actions that they as presumable heterosexuals would never undertake on their own. Tina Tyler starred in her first "bi-sex" film in 1994, after Chi Chi LaRue (born Larry David Paciotti) in Cannes introduced her to the concept (she had never heard of it before). Tyler thought the market for "bisexual" was considerable, and likened it "to the wily and elusive women's market in that no one thought it existed until people began making movies that women wanted to see. Now you can't turn around without seeing a website devoted to porn for women."[76] (Interestingly, a stigma hovers over the term "bisexual" in industry, and today, "forced bi" is preferred.) Yet again, a shade on the palette of desire seldom glimpsed before 1970 becomes huge today.

Still more dominant: women are able to buy special "male chastity" devices—intricate locks around the penis and testicles—to insure that your guy's only sexual release will be at your command and with you alone (for details see Chapter 17 on Toys). The woman is referred to as the "keyholder," the guy as "the slave."

"Forced" sissification belongs, of course, in quotes because the men being turned into housemaids and the like by dominatrixes ardently desire this all along; it represents an intensification of the experience of being dominated, being "forced" to wear a frilly dress, high heels, and makeup. Historically, gay men often sought out feminine roles, and for that reason were called "queens" and "sissies," and indeed, many called one another cattily "Mary"—but now we are talking about heterosexuals who aspire to sissification. It is unclear how many couples do sissification play, but in the world of professional domination, it looms large. The earliest example of which I am aware goes back to Leonard Burtman's magazine *Bizarre Desires* that he began publishing in 1958.[77] But there were few other such early examples. In 1967, in the dime novel *The Punishment Complex*, Bertha, 29, is a domme who advertises in the papers that she can help men who want to dress as women.[78] But non-dommes forcing (or appearing to force) their partners to cross-dress? I have not seen this in the early writing.

Kicking and CBT ("Cock and Ball Torture")

Viewing these scenes is really not for the faint of heart, because the booted dommes who kick the males—men who evidently are genuine customers rather than male models—seem to hold little back. And there are scenes in which the female models seem to take fiendish glee in wedging a high heel down onto the man's erect penis or flailing it with a whip. Hitting his ball sack while wearing boxing gloves...the list of tortures visited upon the poor male organ of generation is really quite extensive. But the demand for this among male surfers seems virtually inexhaustible. A Google search for "cock and ball torture" in the late winter of 2016 produced over 800,000 hits. "AngelsRoyale" shared with the *XBIZ* chatboard in 2012 about the Detroit stripper he had been dating, "She seemed to really attract the guys who wanted their balls stepped on and crushed with high-heeled shoes, to be told they were worthless, etc....I found it vastly amusing that she loved doing it so much, to the guys who wanted it."[79]

We have surely shaded over into the gear and techniques of BDSM here, which is the subject of the next chapter. But the psychology of dominance involved here is of equal interest: In many videos, the male bottom is not restrained, as in BDSM, and either stands upright alone, awaiting his fate, or is held in place by fetish-y looking female accomplices. So the underlying logic is, "I own you, bitch, and I can do anything I want with you," rather than, "You are under my control because I have restrained you." (The male bottoms are referred to as "bitch.")

Breath Control

Breath control games represent another pseudo-forced event, the dominant woman obstructing the breathing of the supposedly resistant male. Asphyxiation games have a long and unhappy history in erotica, and numerous are the tragedies of people accidently hanging themselves when attempting breath control on their own. Suffocation, or pseudo-suffocation, to the point of darkening consciousness, is the objective. Yet historically, representations of breath control have been very few.

Today, breath control with a partner is big, though quite frowned upon by the authorities. Porn-megastar Kayden Kross, for example, loved breath control games but her employer Adam & Eve, motivated doubtless by a sense of responsibility, wouldn't run them. She said in November 2008, "I have no complaints [about Adam & Eve]. Actually, I have one—sometimes I want to get choked out during sex but their standards prohibit that so I've learned to do it on my own time. Or do it anyway and let them edit it out."[80] Breath control, of course, is all over the internet. A Google search for "autoerotic asphyxiation" produced 340,000 results. Yet the commonest form seems to be not self-erotic (autoerotic) but a dominant partner inducing the asphyxia as part of a roleplaying scene. Such is the veil of social disapproval of the practice that the partnered version has not really been studied, and we know little about it aside from countless images on Flickr. On the internet, it is much more the women who are in control of the breathing of the males than vice-versa.

Cuckolding

"I have a crazy theory that men are slowly beginning to evolve into women and women are beginning to take over the dominant role in relationships. I think the cuckolding thing plays into that."[81]

JASON KIDD, ON *XBIZ* BOARD, 2011

Almost at the top of the domination-submission ladder we have cuckolding, also called hotwifing. Men have always gotten off on adultery, of course, but how about getting off on *their wife's* adultery, and how about them staging it? Men who voyeuristically arrange their wives' adulterous relationships while they themselves are "forced," or thrilled, to watch is new. The men are "cuckolds," a traditional term; their wives are "hotwifes," or "hotwives," a new expression for women who accept—or create—voyeuristic scenes either to satisfy their mates or themselves.

Cuckolding has become very popular. "Adult Blog Writer" said on the *XBIZ* chatboard in 2013, "It's one of the most popular types of phone sex call requests I get, so LOTS of guys are into it."[82] On the huge website Pornhub, "cuckold" is the 23rd most common search term—and the 13th most popular in West Virginia! Alabama and Kentucky follow close behind, although some in New England are curious about cuckoldry as well.[83] In the adult industry's enactment of these fantasies, the outside males are often black studs with large penises; the husband might be shackled as the scene plays out (which reinforces it as a BDSM niche), or forced to listen downstairs through the open bedroom door. Or he might be trembling with anticipation of himself participating in the scene. Any of these variants embodies the theme of female dominance, male subordination. As one pro-domme noted: "He gets pleasure from Her pleasure, he becomes addicted to Her power.... [This is] why such a relationship has a powerful place in the Femdom lifestyle." So cuckolding was definitely for dominant female players.[84]

A poll in 2014 of the members of the Spanish website FemDom captures perfectly the world of these pseudo-forced events. The poll was organized by "one of Ama Nadya's submissives," Ama Nadya being one of the dominant females on the site. The pollster was "a man who frequented bars and nightclubs to meet women for sex. Until I met Mistress (Ama) Nadya, that day I stop being a man to become her toy, her cuckold chaste and humble slave 24/7." (The pollster and many respondents had English as a second language.)

Q: "Male slaves...in enforced chastity are more docile and obedient?" 58 percent of 681 respondents gave the majority response, "Yes, always in permanent and long-term chastity."

Q: "What future should be in store for a submissive husband/boyfriend with a small dick unable to pleasure the Dominant Wife/Girlfriend?" The responses were split between "Turn him into a sissy maid in chastity," and "Turn him into a little slut [who is] allowed to participate in sexual activities of the Mistress and her bulls."

Q: "The Mistress/Keyholder should always have the key to her chastity slave [placed where]?" Answers: "On a gold chain on her neck between her beautiful tits": 42 percent; "On a gold chain placed on her ankle": 19 percent; "Give the keys to your lover, so he [can] decide when the sissy cuckold be released from the chastity cage": 13 percent.[85]

Naturally, the cuckold is secretly squirming with delight as he contemplates these various possibilities: his girlfriend's bull-like lover making the decision about when the cuckold might possibly have an orgasm (the Spanish don't apparently share the racism of comparable U.S. sites in which the bull-like lover is invariably black); being turned into a sissy maid with a lock around his organ; cleaning up the mistress and her bull after they have sex in front of him. For submissive males and dominant women, one can see what vast horizons of pleasure open up, horizons that historically are unprecedented for people in the heartland.

In 2015, the niches and forced events all came together as The King Adult Broadcast Network inaugurated a First Annual Femdom Awards Show. "It's about time we had an award show for the femdom genre," said Glenn King, head of the network. "The femdom industry has been a huge part of adult entertainment for many years with very little publicity." The award categories included strapon, facesitting, ass worship and cuckold.[86]

Thirty years ago, none of this existed.

Chapter 14:
Fetish and BDSM

P aul Markham, in the 1960s a young sex-photographer in London, remembers well how fetish went from zero to sixty. He said, quite correctly, that niches such as fetish-BDSM "have always been around so why didn't we shoot them back in the day?" The demand was too small, he said. "The problem...is a return on the investment. Today it's tough, back in the day it was nearly impossible or not as lucrative as mainstream porn." And they were shooting on 35mm film with no monitor "to see what's being shot." "Not a good time to find out the camera man, lighting or sound man had screwed up.... When running the risk of producing and selling porn, why go for a market that sold 1% of what a mainstream niche would?"

The VCR and the internet changed all this, said Markham. You could become your own pornographer, and many became their own fetish videographers. To get on the net, all you needed was a digital camera and people were "able to make money in a niche they loved.... Some stayed Ma & Pa operations, a few grew to the size of Kink.com and many failed. With sites like Clips4Sale all they need is a camera."[1]

So the market for fetish exploded. A Lovehoney poll of 2,000 people in 2014 in the U.K. found that 66 percent of university graduates had tried out bondage, only 37 percent of non-graduates.[2] Is that because all the surfers harbored secret fetish desires in their hearts, or because they came across Kink.com, Wasteland.com, or *Fifty Shades of Grey* and found that they loved it?

In 2015, the Swedish toymaker LELO conducted a survey of its international clientele; 1,100 subscribers to its online newsletter responded, two-thirds of them female, one half ages 18-25. "Do you feel s&m is part of a normal healthy sex life?" Ninety percent said yes! (Meanwhile, the American Psychiatric Association still considers s&m a "paraphilia," or perversion.)

Have you read *Fifty Shades?* One half had.

Did *Fifty Shades* make you "more adventurous"? Eighty percent said yes.

But *Fifty Shades of Grey* wasn't the crucial factor for this heavily young female group.

Have you tried BDSM yourself? Around 75 percent said yes.

What encouraged you to try BDSM? Seventy-five percent said they had "always wanted to try it." Only 15 percent credited the novel with getting them into roleplaying.

So, for these young women, the desire had long been latent; the novel may have activated their curiosity, but it didn't create it.

They were drawn by the concept of dominance and submission, and by the practices and the gear. (Almost all who had tried BDSM had begun with spanking and restraint, half with whipping, a third with gagging.)[3]

What's up with that?

Dominance is about psychology. Fetish and BDSM are about practice: behavior and gear. Fetish is everywhere. Fashion ads show dominant women in leather. The clubs are crawling with latex. High-shaft black boots have replaced galoshes as the standard winter footwear. As an *XBIZ* journalist put it, "From the catwalks of Paris to comic book superheroes clad in skintight cat suits, the subliminal suggestion of fetish is ingrained into the psyche of contemporary society."[4]

An important point: fetish and BDSM are consensual sex. There is a distinction between "rough sex," which may or may not be completely consensual, and kinky sex, which is *always* consensual. Colin Rowntree, CEO of Wasteland.com, explained in 2016, "So much of what has been produced over the past seven years for the Internet under the guise of BDSM is simply very rough porn star sex, with bondage sets and gear thrown in for shock value. I call this the 'Flog and Fuck School of Filmmaking,' which has very little to do with the realities of consensual D/S relationships and activities."[5] In the real world, the distinction between rough and kink may be blurred as well, and practitioners of the former may end up being charged by the police.

Fetish Is Different from BDSM

Almost anything can become a fetish, a sexual accelerant. The book *Psychopathia Sexualis* of Austrian psychiatrist Richard von Krafft-Ebing is full of tales about how men became aroused at the sight of women's hair and the like.[6] Here I am going to use the term "fetish" in a much narrower sense to mean gear, and here latex is very definitely on the upswing at the cost of leather. Moreover, color blossoms today at the cost of severe-looking black.[7] The top two fetish categories on the site Clips4Sale.com, with its almost five million total clips (as of April 2015), are "bondage" and "female domination," both essentially fetish sites because the players are almost always either garbed in leather and latex, or feature leather gear prominently.[8]

Sheila Rae, owner of a fetish boutique, said of fetish gear in 2007, "The average American knows that it's sexy. They know it's kinky. They might not understand the whole submissive/dominant theme, but when they see it, they get it. They just don't know why they get it."[9]

So, we are bathed in fetish. But we are not necessarily bathed in BDSM, which is a more specialized space, with rules and codes of its own, such as everything must be absolutely consensual and, yes, there is an exchange of power.

Though BDSM and fetish are often lumped together, they represent two separate domains of activity, however much they overlap. Montreal domme Mistress Hellkitty, a femdom of vast experience, was explicit that BDSM and fetish are separate domains. "The difference is real," she emphasized in an interview. "BDSM addresses the body and mind. Fetish is objectification, it's about things. Fetishists tell me they aren't into pain or submission. They really like nylon or boots. They're just really happy if you have the boots on. In a session, they might just masturbate."[10]

BDSM, on the other hand, involves the whole psychology of the transfer of power plus the material world of restraint. In an early feminist appreciation of BDSM, Barbara Ehrenreich and co-authors write, "S/M...is innately fetishistic; it *requires* paraphernalia."[11] As well, BDSM is edgier than the mere psychology of domination and submission. "I think that in BDSM we get real," said Ming Destiny, one of the designers at toymaker Williams Trading. "We are demanding more from our sex than just feel-good feelings and tender kisses. We want it to hurt, we want it to push us.... The people drawn to BDSM are edge-walkers, they want raw and they want primal, and in a society that is seeking to always corporatize and homogenize our body image and our interactions with each other, BDSM is about real bodies, playing hard, messy sex and primal lust."[12]

The Narrative

BDSM, once called "sadomasochism," is as old as time and is first documented, to the best of my knowledge, in the 15th century.[13] Fetish by contrast arrives on the sexual scene only with the publication of Count Leopold von Sacher-Masoch's *Venus in Furs* in 1870. With the exception of makeup and tight-lacing in court circles, previously few inanimate objects, such as fur and leather, were used as sexual accelerants. The Marquis de Sade's two novels, *Justine* (the submissive one) and *Juliette* (the dominant one), were written around 1800— and in them there is no hint of fetish, however much the protagonists bang one another around.

French psychologist Alfred Binet, co-inventor of an IQ test named after him, put sexual "fetishism" on the radar in 1888, distinguishing between "major" and "minor" fetishism, the former being extravagant acts, the latter "the secret of strange loves."[14] The distinction was subsequently lost, but the term remained.[15]

The popularity of leather as a fetish seems to begin around 1900, supplanting fur which, of course, gave Count von Sacher-Masoch his thrills in *Venus in Furs*. And the figure of the dominatrix, clad head to toe in leather, dates from the years between the two world wars.

It is likely that that BDSM represents some hardcoded aspect of human sexuality, present in all times and places, while leather and fur fetish are whims of the time, although adepts of these fetishes feel their need very deeply, as though somehow biologically embedded in nervous tissue. But the practical absence of fetish before 1870 means that it cannot have this deep kind of biological baking.

Over the last thirty years, there have been two fetish/BDSM narratives:

The first is how the practice of BDSM itself actually changes, and here the big story is the advent of penetration.

The second is how "fetish-y," or fetishistic, porn itself becomes. By 2000, there is leather and bondage-like imagery everywhere; even when the content is straight-up vanilla, the model on the box cover may be portrayed as carrying a whip. Fetish-y imagery engulfs the entire field, without the vanilla sections of the field necessarily changing their content at all. (This development is parallel to how fetish-y fashion has become since the 1960s, without women, who are booted fall, winter, and spring, being mindful of the message that boots once conveyed.)

The U.S. history of fetish practices and their images goes back to the beginning of the twentieth century and is intimately associated with the concept of female domination. In the U.K., such publications as *London Life* opened up the world of fetish in the 1920s and 30s.[16] In the United States, the Australian John Coutts (John Willie) began publishing *Bizarre* in 1946 as a dedicated BDSM magazine. Evidently, it was Coutts who introduced Irving Klaw to the concept of fetish publication.[17] Klaw's story began in the 1940s in a studio above his used "bookstore," soon renamed Movie Star News, on East 14th Street in Manhattan, where he and his sister Paula sold photos of starlets. Receiving frequent requests for "Damsel-in-Distress" photos, around 1949, he began shooting fetish and enlisted a pin-up model named Bettie Page. He was at pains not to show nudity or sexual contact, and the photos usually featured a leather-clad Bettie beating up on some other model. He also filmed several fetish features, as well as 8mm and 16mm loops, including *Varietease* (1954) and *Teaserama* (1955), which starred several noted strippers, plus Bettie. All this could be sent through the mails until the Kefauver Hearings of the Senate Subcommittee on Juvenile Delinquency in 1955. Klaw's work was, thus, BDSM with a heavy fetish overlay.

A protégé of Klaw's was BDSM illustrator Eric Stanton (Ernest Stanten), who specialized in leather-clad Amazonian women, just Klaw's cup of tea. Starting around 1949, Klaw began publishing some of Stanton's drawings in *Movie Star News* and pulp novels. Many of Stanton's drawings illustrated Klaw's later booklet imprint called Nutrix.[18] Stanton, Klaw, and Page have all since become cult figures, evidence of the power of fetish and BDSM within U.S. culture.

The relationship between Klaw and Stanton didn't last, and Stanton began selling his drawings to Lenny Burtman, who had started publishing another key fetish magazine, *Exotique*, in 1955. In 1958, according to Johnny J., who has penned a careful history of fetish publications, "Burtman and his business associates produced the first entirely FemDom magazine, called *Bizarre Desires*." *Bizarre Life* followed in 1964. This opened the floodgates to femdom-fetish publication in the 1970s and later.[19]

In 1970, Burtman and Reuben Sturman, the "porn king," formed the company Eros-Goldstripe, which launched a variety of fetish-femdom magazines. After Burtman retired in the 1980s, Sturman continued to run Eros-Goldstripe. Johnny J. speaks of the "clamor for more FemDom" that became loud in the 1970s, echoing in a number of what had previously been "girlie" magazines.[20] All of this publication was focused on professional dommes and their male clients, not on couples. As pointed out in the previous chapter, Dianna Vesta's *Attitude* magazine founded in 1991 was the first publication by, and for, dominant women.

Leather fetish made it into the living room in the form of the British ITV series *The Avengers*, debuting in 1961 with Patrick Macnee as the suave John Steed, and actress Diana Rigg as the leather-catsuited Mrs. Peel. This was the mainline. The international following of the series was enormous, and even after Diana Rigg left the series in 1967 (which ended in 1969), it was reprised as *The New Avengers* in 1976-77. One episode in 1966, *A Touch of Brimstone*, which featured Mrs. Peel in an actual dominatrix outfit with opera-length gloves, knee-high boots, a body-suit, a spiked collar and a flogger, was deemed too risqué to air in the U.S. Leather went on to have an above-ground career as a fashion item, and a subterranean existence as cult gear.[21]

The Avengers brushed the margins of soft-core bondage. But right at the center of the soft-core bondage market sat Robert Harmon's studio Harmony Concepts, which opened in 1976 and published *Bondage Life*. About a year later, the company started shooting super 8 and 16mm films, then moved with the rest of industry into videotapes and DVDs. "We characterize what we do as love bondage," Harmon said. "Very soft. We're really just pin up cheesecake."[22] This corresponded to the concept of "vanilla bondage" that toymaker Sportsheets was pushing in the toy space (see Chapter 17). But the market soon moved beyond soft bondage, and Harmony Concepts stopped shooting in 2003.

Quality gear stores began when Kathy Williams opened Stormy Leather in San Francisco in 1983, specializing in leather corsets and dildo harnesses for women.[23] Spartacus Leathers in Portland, Oregon, by "Big Al" Bedrosian and Northbound Leather in Toronto by Anna and George Giaouris, both followed in 1987. Both stores now have huge international mail order businesses. Latex did even better than leather, especially in fashion and the club scene. By 2014, Joel Tucker, owner of longstanding fetish-supplier The Stockroom, said that "over 75 percent of the fashion items we sell are latex." Latex, he noted, had moved from "heavy gauge black rubber" into "a rainbow of colors and textures that are equal parts fashion and fetish."[24]

Meanwhile, a regular bondage culture was developing. Bettie Page roared back into fashion, at first underground in the 1970s, then as a full-blown cult figure in the 1990s. Indeed, Bettie's look of long black hair and bangs became a kind of template for fetish models, and many Bettie Pages sprang to life in the dungeon. Industry veteran Bill Margold said in 2006, "I would say that Bettie Page was the grandmother of adult entertainment or the grandmother of modern-day erotica."[25] None of these films featured penetration.

In the world of serious bondage, the 1970s saw a quickening of interest in what BDSM historian Judson Rosebush called "the old-style bondage," with clothesline-style rope work that, if tied too tightly, could cut off the circulation. The old-style bondage was on offer in the publications of the House of Milan and Centurion Press, in addition to tabloids such as the *SM Express* in New York. *The Story of O*, by Dominique Aury (Pauline Réage), which debuted as a fetish novel in 1954, came out in France in 1975 as a full-length feature. (Both Dominique Aury and Pauline Réage are pseudonyms of Anne Declos.)

Penetration

Until the 1990s, BDSM films typically did not mix penetration and bondage. Radley Metzger's *The Punishment of Anne* (1975)—the only film Metzger directed under his own name—was electric with eroticism yet contained only three oral scenes, and no penetration. (The two urination scenes in the original were said to have been cut owing to fear of the censors.[26]) In 1993, *AVN* told the retail merchants that bondage tapes "...contain no hardcore sex acts—and therefore are unlikely to be prosecuted under the Supreme Court's three-prong test for obscenity."[27] So, lots of pain and screaming, but little sex. As Boston domme Isobel Wren later explained, "In real fetish stuff, the climax scene would be centered around that fetish rather than the sex. In regular porn, the climax is the sex. In mainstream porn, you might have someone getting handcuffed or spanked—I'm seeing a lot of spanking in mainstream porn—but it's still centered around the sex. [But] in real fetish stuff, you might not even have sex, you might not even see genitals at all because the fetish is the most important part."[28]

Then BDSM cinema drifted ever closer to showing penetration. Director Ira Levine, who specialized in BDSM, recalled, "My first porn gig was tying up a young and luscious Marilyn Chambers for a deluxe shot-on-film series called *Private Fantasies* back in 1984.... Crawling all over Marilyn on a giant bed, lashing her down as if for a typhoon, a world of limitless possibilities seemed to open before me."[29]

These possibilities were brutally terminated by the Meese Report in 1986. Attorney General Edwin Meese (a Reagan appointee who, in 1988, resigned under a cloud) pontificated, "The pain is very real," and thus illegitimate. Levine said of the Meese Report, "From this off-hand boorishness an urban legend was born to the effect that showing sex and bondage simultaneously was 'against the law.'" In fact, no such provision had ever been written into federal statutes.

The effect of the Meese Report, however, was to stimulate a new genre of BDSM films offering fetish only, "a sort of masquerade approach to bondage play," Levine continued, "that implied what went on by the performer's dress and manner before the usual vanilla sex broke out. These boring 'bondage videos,' in which the performers squirmed and struggled rather pointlessly, were a throwback to the old 8 and 16mm loops of New York bondage photographer Irwin Klaw showing "bound babes thrashing about fully dressed without risking too much interference from the postal inspectors."[30]

Further militating against penetration in the 1980s was the AIDS epidemic, and BDSM shifted in the direction of "safer sex." The entire bondage culture militated against penetration. Rosebush: "In the professional environment old school [dommes] still prevailed, where the House recruit is first trained as a submissive because only by learning the inner experience can one become a meaningful domme." In the old school, the subservient definitely did not penetrate the domme! He was often not permitted even to touch her.

Then the Meese doctrine was overturned, and BDSM began featuring penetration. Levine: "It became more common to see big-name porn stars taking a turn in bondage videos, and bondage videos sexing themselves up more and more." It was Hustler's *Taboo* magazine in 1998 that "officially destroyed," in Levine's view, "the bondage-with-penetration restrictions for adult publication." In the "dungeon melodramas...open sex play was increasingly bold."[31]

Many couples started BDSM play without being aware that what they were doing was considered "sadomasochism," a fearful term. Said Susan Wright, founder of the New-York-based National Coalition for Sexual Freedom, "Those are the people who are buying so much vanilla porn, and they are loving all these BDSM behaviors in their porn."[32]

Other players quickly rushed through the penetration breach. With his soon-to-be wife Nina Hartley, in 2002, Levine created the series *Nina Hartley's Private Sessions* for Bizarre Video. "Now I had a well-known lead player just coming into her own as the new kind of domina: smooth and seductive, with her own approach to securing the obedience of her subservient darlings." Levine directed the 2005 award-winning *Jenna Loves Pain*, shattering earnings records; "the wall came tumbling down between BDSM and hardcore, never to rise again."[33] (Levine, or Ernest Greene, was also instrumental, beginning in 2005, in producing Hartley's popular *Guide To* series, which reached sales of 500,000 units with the title, *Nina Hartley's Guide to Erotic Bondage* (2005)[34]; the series began in 1996.

A new note was struck by bondage enthusiast Peter Acworth, mentioned above as the developer of Kink.com. His first website, which he founded while a graduate student in business at Columbia in 1997, was Hogtied.com. In 1998, he moved to San Francisco and, together with Tony Pirelli, went into bondage production full-time. Initially, they shot in a two-bedroom apartment using daylight. Acworth shunned DVD because of the risk of obscenity prosecutions if he showed penetration, but online, it was unproblematic.[35] He began to create a series of specialty sites, such as FuckingMachines.com in 2001. Inspired by Levine, Acworth was said to have purchased every fucking-machine he could find, and on Craigslist, he encouraged builders to invent more. (At this point, Acworth was using the pseudonym Peter Rogers.)[36] *Sex and Submission, Men in Pain*, and *Whipped Ass* soon followed. The company was known as CyberNet Entertainment until Acworth acquired the Kink.com domain in 2006. By 2007, he had 51 employees editing footage alone, when the company was averaging 60 shoots a month to keep the content fresh on these various sites.[37] Kink.com at its State Armory and Arsenal building on Mission Street in San Francisco, acquired in 2007, was in many ways the high citadel of BDSM porn and was committed to safe, consensual scenes that on screen look anything but.[38] (In 2017, as mentioned, Kink moved all production from the Armory to Las Vegas.)

Evidently, by 2005, Acworth felt he could risk mixing BDSM and penetration, and founded the site "SexandSubmission.com."[39] Kink.com's Michael Stabile said of the penetration barrier, "Historically fetish and BDSM content was really limited in terms of physical distribution, because of the increased risk of obscenity prosecution. In fact, one of the factors that really caused Kink to thrive in the early days was that, as an online outlet, we were one of the few places where you could see BDSM and sex mixed."[40]

Other BDSM producers followed suit. Jimmy Broadway (Michael Manning), co-owner of Severe Society Films, a premier fetish destination, said in 2014, "We started out in more traditional BDSM, but now we're combining it more with sex."[41] He put this in a larger perspective: "Fetish film used to be the realm of leather-clad masters and dominatrixes in shiny latex, leading their slaves around a dark dungeon on a chain. But that's not how a lot of people play in real life. As fetish moves more into the cultural mainstream, we want to present an authentic experience that more people can relate to."[42]

Rosebush confirmed the point about penetration: "Kink gingerly crossed this line, got away with it, and thus now we are all able to range in a relatively free space across a wide variety of sexual practices that are limited by our imagination."[43] Precisely. The BDSM story heads in the same direction as the other sexual stories. New areas of sexuality opened up, and the intensity of bondage and domination deepened even further with full intercourse.

Kink on the Internet

Desire doesn't change by itself. There have to be images for people to learn from, or be inspired by. Here, industry seized the internet as a platform. DVDs had to be sold in stores and to owners leery of obscenity prosecutions. (Said Julie Simone, a well-known BDSM webmaster, "Distributors are scared to carry real BDSM. It aggravates me no end that double anal is fine but god forbid you hit someone."[44])

The internet meant freedom. Colin and Angie Rowntree put the site Wasteland on the internet in 1994 after attending a New York Fashion Boutique Show and noting a leather lingerie wholesaler called Ecstasy Leather. The Rowntrees were already running a jewelry mail-order business, and they thought they might supplement it with a leather line of underwear. "So we took some pictures of girls in the outfits that looked very lovely." The Rowntrees then discovered that nobody was buying the outfits but they were looking at the catalogue like crazy. So, they put the catalogue and some more photos of models in leather behind a pay wall, and they charged $50 a year, thinking, as Colin said later, "the world would laugh at this obscenely greedy folly. A little search engine called Yahoo listed us, and people came. Then a new little link list called Persian Kitty listed us [see Chapter 8]. And then they came in droves, phoning and faxing in, and, yes, even emailing their credit cards numbers. Wasteland was born."[45]

Colin Rowntree said that what differentiated Wasteland from other sites is moving into the psychological side of things. "We are into consensual bondage: the kinds of things that lots and lots of people are doing in their own bedrooms. They're playing slap and tickle, things along those lines...clean, healthy, family-value bondage and discipline. It's the 'darker side of desire,' ...erotic power exchange. It's the psychological interplay between the dominant personality and the submissive personality in a sexually charged atmosphere."[46]

The demand for dominant males and dominant females alike began to soar. Industry executive James Medina commented in 2008 on the "huge number of couples who are interested in exploring their sexuality a little more. They don't always identify themselves as being kinky, but they may be just as willing to purchase a strap-on harness or some good leather cuffs...or a fucking machine for between $450 and $1,200" instead of "a $20 vibrator." [47] Remember, this is four years before the launch of *Fifty Shades of Grey*. Moe Styles, the New York-based administrator of an amateur bondage website that he started in 1999, said in 2009 that "AmateurBound.com experienced an average of 15–20 percent growth every year." Such sites tend to be high-end and the fans, Styles said, "can be extremely passionate and extremely loyal."[48]

At a time when the tubes were demolishing non-kink pay sites, fetish and BDSM remained profitable. Master Ryan commented in 2014, "Solo and fetish sells millions of dollars of subs [subscriptions] every day. If you think porn doesn't sell anymore, it means you aren't doing any business in those two areas."[49]

Several Events Were Fueling the Kink Vogue

First, there was a take-off in fetish sparkplugged by Madonna's book *Sex*, published in 1992, which sold over 150,000 copies on the first day of its release and jetted onto *The New York Times* bestseller list. The publisher was said to have had grave reservations about the explicit photographs, but Madonna pushed ahead anyway. The critics, of course, hated it—just as they hated *Screw* publisher Al Goldstein— yet the book "still remains the best and fastest-selling coffee table book of all time."[50] Since neither Ana nor Christian in *Fifty Shades of Grey* swans about in leather; the Madonna volume clearly cues the fetish vogue.

Secondly, youth was driving kink. The internet opened up possibilities for a younger generation of amateur BDSM home-videographers who didn't care a fig for Meese and his absurd views. "Blissfully unaware of the local taboos against showing tied-up people getting fucked," said Levine, "they did it gleefully—and the sky failed to fall."[51] Dee Severe agreed that the younger generation was hugely different from the older: "The big difference between 35-54 and 18-34 is, the older group, being kinky has always been VERY VERY secret, like, life could be destroyed if people found out. So those guys are mostly married to vanilla women, don't have an outlet for their kink except for porn (and pro dommes if that's their thing)." For the younger group, by contrast, Severe said, "Being kinky is no longer super secret, every big city has fetish clubs...."[52]

Also, you could make money shooting fetish for the web whereas, by 2000, this was no longer the case for simple boy/girl and girl/girl, so much had the free tubesites hosed up all the oxygen in the room. Even if they had no personal inclination towards fetish, industry legalist Michael Fattorosi urged newbies to shoot fetish. He said in 2000, "I have numerous clients over the past five years that have failed at BG [boy/girl] and have succeeded at fetish." He urged them to get their material up on Clips4Sale and collect email addresses. "If anything BG/BGG [boy/girl/girl] porn is dominated by a few companies and/or tubes. Fetish is the last area that the average person can get into production without a huge amount of capital."[53]

The taste palette thus expanded beyond simple penetration. In the 1990s, said Rosebush, the sites began offering, among other techniques, "forced climax." "The forced climax does not appear in the old-school product and the concept of pleasing the sub comes to the forefront: restrained and brought to climax."[54] This is essentially the sensualizing of BDSM, transforming it from an exercise in flogging to a rush of orgasmic pleasure. This trend brought BDSM into line with the other new trends of the last thirty years, breaking through the old sex codes and making sexuality a delicious experience. Today, said industry consultant Alex Parker in 2015, we are selling "merchandise to a public who are curious about BDSM play in a way that they never have been before.... The public is smart, savvy and sexually switched on in a way that in the 1970s was unheard of."[55]

Chapter 15:
Anal

"Culturally, ass is the new pussy." [1]

PORN STAR ASA AKIRA (2015)

Ron Jeremy is on set with a number of female performers. It's time for anal. The director says, "Who signed up for anal?"

Several young women raise their hands.

"A pretty black girl drops to her knees. She's ready to go, her asshole lubed and stretched out about as far as it'll go. I put the head of my cock in at first." Jeremy doesn't want to hurt her.

"Is that okay, honey?" he asks her. "Tell me if that's too much, okay, sweetie?"

"Oh, Jesus Christ, Ron," she says, pushing her pelvis at him. "Just ram it in, will you?"[2]

Anal sex is on the rise; August is now "Anal Sex Month."[3] In Britain, according to the National Surveys of Sexual Attitudes and Lifestyles, the number of men aged 16-44 having had anal sex in the past year rose from 7.0 percent in 1990–91 to 17.0 percent in 2010-12, women up from 6.5 percent to 15.1 percent in that time span.[4] In the U.S., according to a survey in 2011-2013 by the National Center for Health Statistics, on a lifetime basis, for people aged 18-44, 42 percent of men (up from 26 percent in 1992) and 36 percent of women (up from 20 percent) have had anal sex with the opposite sex.[5] These dramatic increases are reflected, too, in industry perceptions: Jahaziel Perez, owner of DickzToyz.com, said in 2014, "I have seen an increase in the number of bisexual and straight women asking questions about anal sex."[6]

"Anything with 'anal' in the title sells well here," said Jerry in 1993, a clerk at Rocky's Entertainment Emporium in Cleveland.[7] "I told her that I want anal sex," screamed a female-written story at the feminist porn site Sssh.com.[8] So, increasingly the response seems to be, OK, hey, no problem. According to 2015 data from Pornhub, millennials are 69 percent more likely to view "big ass" videos than the older generation, and "anal" is number nine on the list of most popular videos for the 18–34 year-old set. Data are not given for older surfers into "anal.") Moreover, straights search for "anal" more than twice as often as gays.[9]

Thus, word got around. In the new millennium, the Upper East Side location of the Manhattan toystore Pleasure Chest began offering an "Anal August State Fairground," featuring take-offs on "such beloved state fair food...[as] butt-shaped cupcakes" and games such as "Bobbing for Butt Plugs."[10] By 2014, *Cosmo* had placidly accepted anal on behalf of its readers. A piece quoted Julie Stewart, president of bondage-toymaker Sportsheets: "The perfect thing to start with anal is your hand because you can feel it. If you're pushing on your partner's muscles and you are hitting the right spot, you can feel that. If you're grabbing a toy or an object, you might just keep pushing."[11] This is in contrast to the 1980s, when the standard advice in women's magazines was that your husband should see a psychiatrist if he wanted to touch you "back there."

Bill Margold, an actor and director based in West Hollywood, recalled interviewing male talent in the 1980s about whether they would do anal sex. The feeling seemed to be yes.

"You'd take a dig up the ass?

"No, *no*!

"Would you fuck someone in the ass?

"Oh, no *no*!

"So I'd ask, what's anal sex?

"Going to the bathroom."

Margold was astonished that male talent then did not even know what anal sex was![12]

But the mid-1980s seem to have been a kind of turning point. Anal was not much featured in the first issues of *AVN*, which started publication in 1983. Yet, by January 1986, anal got a prominent advertising display on the back cover (ditto for double penetration, which seems to erupt in a Rambone ad in August 1986). Luke Ford also dates the take-off of anal as the 1980s and emphasizes Max Hardcore's *Anal Adventures* that streeted in 1992.[13]

"Will you do anal?" interviewers asked Barbara Dare, who was on her way to becoming a porn-megastar, in 1986. "No anal," she said. (And no blacks.) "The booty's being saved for the man I marry. (Laughs) I gotta save something."[14]

In the industry today, anal is not to every model's taste, yet many do it. Earlier, a number of performers were ambivalent and would consent to it for the payday, but not because they cherished the sensation. Yet more now accept it. The length of time before a female porn star would consent to anal has decreased, according to Millward's analysis of the IAFD data base, from "about two years" in the 1980s to six months today.[15]

Unlike in many scenes, in anal, small male organs were preferred. Michael Morrison, whom *Screw* publisher Al Goldstein identifies otherwise as a "fat slob," nonetheless "did fuck Seka and Marilyn Chambers and got paid for it. He had a small cock, but became a leading lady's top choice for anal intercourse because of it."[16]

Jewel De'Nyle, 23, did her first anal scene, with woodsman Peter North, in 1999. Gene Ross of *AVN* said to her: "Knowing that Peter packs the luggage that he does. This is not a little carry-on."

Jewel: "I know! And I'm a tiny girl."

Ross: "Did anyone try to give you horror stories beforehand?"

Jewel: "Yeah. Everybody tried to freak me out about it. Oh you can't do your first anal with Peter. You got to warm up."

But then Jewel said, "The first penetration shot was like painful and scary. But he took it slow and was easy on me. After we got it going I didn't want to stop. I was a bad girl. I was like, yeah, I want to do more anal positions."[17]

There was a subset of U.S. professionals that specialized in anal and said that they liked it. This subset included such performers as Jada Stevens, 27, "the booty queen" and a contract girl for Arch Angel who was also known as "Buttwoman." (In Pornhub searches for anal, Madison Ivy, Lisa Ann, and Alexis Texas led the list.[18])

Among male talent, the enormously prolific Tom Byron (Thomas Bryan Taliaferro, Jr.) became known as "Lord of Asses," because in an acting career that began in 1981 at age 20, he had starred in, and later produced, so much anal content. (Byron acted in over 3000 adult films.[19]) His first explicitly anal title was Hal Freeman's *Caught From Behind 2* (1983), with Ron Jeremy, showing double penetration. (Hal Freeman's first *Caught From Behind* in 1982 also featured anal, but lacked Byron and Jeremy. Freeman directed much of the 25-part *Caught From Behind* series, which ended in 1997, and it was with *Caught 1* and *2* that Jeremy thought the whole anal fascination began.[20] Freeman's name goes down in the annals of industry history, however, not for this series but for his brave stand on behalf of the First Amendment against the California "pandering" prosecutions— see Chapter 4).

As the years went on, anal became an increasingly popular theme for Byron; after he and colleagues formed Extreme Associates in 1998, the *Lord of Asses* series, which debuted that same year with Byron as director and star, reached 15 titles by 2010. *House of Ass* began in 2005 (and reached 14 videos by 2011), and *Ass Eaters Unanimous*, which began in 2003, reached 23 installments by 2011. Byron directed and starred in all of these, which featured anal intercourse, often with anilingual moments as well. It was probably Freeman who sparked the anal vogue—and director Bobby Hollander with *Anything Goes* in 1984 the anilingual vogue. These two directors plus Byron placed anal on center stage in Porn Valley and hallmarked the growing eroticization of the body taking place in these years.

Such is the consumer demand for anal images that, within porn, anal is now standard. Here again, we find a dramatic break with thirty years ago. In the memory of old hands, anal was once much less common. In 2003, "RD" weighed in, "Let's go back about 10 years when anal was rarely filmed and considered taboo."[21] "Hardball," writing in 2015 said there is even more anal now: "Ten years ago, it was kind of a high priced specialty item. Now for about 50 per cent of girls it is just another arrow in their quiver that they can make a few bucks more out of."[22]

Another blogger pointed out it was largely a function of gonzo: "I'll concede that there's probably more anal today than in the past if you watch gonzo flicks. But gonzo is a pretty new phenomenon." The nameless guest blogger said that ten years ago, "Ginger Lynn almost always did an anal scene. Ashlyn Gere did many anal scenes."[23] He cited several other examples. Starting in 1993, the X-Rated Critics Organization (XRCO) began giving an annual award for "the best anal or DP scene," and winning the sweepstakes in the first year was Wicked Pictures' *Arabian Nights*.[24] So certainly, by then, anal was a familiar category.

Contributing, finally, to the growing popularity of anal play was its intimate association with the rapidly increasing concept of dominance. The power to play with someone's anus is, essentially, the power to dominate them. Curve Novelties wised to this theme in 2016 when introducing its new Rooster butt plug in its Alpha Advanced line: "Assert your dominance!" it instructed users.[25]

By 2015, anal had become virtually standard for aspiring young models. Producer Jules Jordan said, "A lot of these new young girls are doing anal. If you're shooting those types of movies it's definitely beneficial. It's kind of refreshing to have some of these young girls out there doing everything."[26]

Meanwhile, in the real world, there was an ignorance gap. Many curious people were unaware that an enema beforehand was a good idea, and that lube was definitely preferred. As sex-counselor Charlie Glickman put it in 2015, "Nobody should be learning to have anal sex from watching porn."[27] The anal guide for women in the real world was Tristan Taormino, who at 27 wrote the pioneering *The Ultimate Guide to Anal Sex for Women* (1998)[28]. Then, for ten years, she penned a sex-porn column for the *Village Voice* in New York. In Porn Valley, she directed or wrote 23 titles for Evil Angel and, after 2006, for Vivid, including the *Expert Guide* series to such subjects as "the g-spot" (2007), "anal pleasure for men," (2009), and "pegging" (2012). It was Taormino who, more than any other figure except perhaps Stagliano, put anal on the heterosexual radar. Stagliano and Ernest Greene (Ira Levine) directed in 1999 for Evil Angel Tristan Taormino's *Ultimate Guide to Anal Sex for Women,* starring Nina Hartley. (On fisting, see Chapter 9.)

Rosebud and Risk

Max Hardcore (Paul F. Little), in his anal series beginning in 1992 with *The Anal Adventures of Max Hardcore,* is said to have initiated the popularity of "rosebud," in which the inner walls of the rectum become externally visible, or "gape." As journalist Michelle Lhooq explains, "The bright red internal tissue blooms out of your anus like a desert rose." Out there among the surfers, there is a keen new taste for rosebud, which big porn companies like Evil Angel have started to gratify with high-budget films. Jay Sin (Jason Wade Dejournett), a director at Evil Angel since 2007, perfected these anal gape scenes, and by 2014 his *Anal Buffet,* one of Evil Angel's numerous rosebud hits, was in its *ninth* sequel.

The appeal of rosebud for the surfers is obscure, but for the industry it is clear. Says Lhooq, "Why would you reach into your wallet to purchase a film when thousands of videos of couples banging in their bedrooms are just a few clicks away? In response, the industry has turned towards niche markets that can't be found easily online for free. After all, the average girl next door might be able to take dick like Sasha Grey, but she most likely won't be able to rosebud on command."[29] Indeed, the models who do rosebud prepare themselves in extensive training, and the night before, might well sleep with a butt plug to expand the anus.

Is rosebud healthy? Of course not, no more than professional football is healthy, the players risking concussions week after week—and the porn stars make much less money than the football players. Cautions rosebud veteran Amy Brooke, "OK, girls, keep it up and you're going to be a spokesperson for adult diapers."[30]

Even short of rosebud, many forms of anal sex are not without risk. Models who submit to prolonged anal sex may end up fecally incontinent. Colin Rowntree, who together with his wife, Angie, often served as the voice of prudence for the industry, noted in 2015 that anal has become so popular with viewers, most studios and webmasters are integrating this content into offerings to consumers.... The primary risk [of this] 'anal pounding' is 'anal prolapse' which currently has many porn starts in adult diapers and colostomy bags. Forever." He said that among porn directors and performers in his own circle, "there is much horror about this as it is permanently physically damaging performers in our industry."[31]

Nor is "ATM" (ass-to-mouth) necessarily safe, although many performers take elaborate precautions. "Whenever we have shot one," said Robbie, his partner Claudia-Marie "has anal douched to the point that you could eat out of her ass."[32] Yet others were not always as meticulous and ATM and ATP (ass-to-pussy) counted in the industry as unhygienic but something the surfers, who would never be able to do it at home, much wanted.

Chapter 16:
Gays and Lesbians

*"Desire is constructed through fantasy—and it is through fantasy
that we learn how to desire."* [1]

JEFFREY ESCOFFIER, HISTORIAN OF GAY PORN CINEMA (2009)

Much has changed in gay life since the days of the "queen" and the "nance," when many gays self-identified as cross-dressers and referred to one another as "Mary." Mary is dead, and the twinks—or slightly-built young men—and muscle jocks and leatherman-clones have rushed into her place. And when the jocks and twinks come together, look out!

Helix, a mainly twink producer, brought some of its models together with the jocks from the Dominic Ford studio, who flew down to San Diego for the movie shoot. At Helix, said Deniz Bilgin, director of Helix operations, "So many of them had expressed fantasies about getting fucked by big muscular jock types. We knew if we encouraged them to play out these fantasies in front of the camera, the results would be electric." Dominic Ford added, "We wanted to put the Helix boys in an environment that brought out their more masculine sides and really showed them enjoying getting fucked by hot muscle jocks."

So the shoot began. Ford continued, "The Helix exclusives [contract performers] were loving it. They tend to interact only with other similar-looking boys in their day-to-day life. But that doesn't mean they don't hunger for hot jocks to pound them."

As for the jocks, "They'd never been on a twink set and were really amused at how much time is spent on hair and makeup."[2]

This shoot ended up on the internet. But the history of gay sex on the internet is not necessarily the history of actual gay sex. In fact, oral sex in the gay community is much commoner than anal penetration ("fucking").[3] Yet one would never gather that from internet porn.

As with straight porn, gay porn began with mass-produced pulp novels, such as *Torment,* in the late 1940s, a retitled reprint of Richard Meeker's *The Better Angel (*1933). Thomas Hal Phillips' *The Bitterweed Path* (Avon, 1950) is "about three men and their love for one another," as the jacket announced; it typifies the budding genre.[4]

Yet the biggest gay icon of the twentieth century owed nothing to the internet. It was the Tom of Finland, "Leatherman." Touko Laaksonen (Tom of Finland) was born in the small town of Kaarina, Finland, in 1920. Because homosexuality at that time was deeply illegal, he drew a secret stash of art that, after the Second World War began to find international diffusion. The look characterized the gay BDSM scene for half a century. As Rebecca Weinberg, an executive for XR Brands, which brought out Tom of Finland-themed lubricants and toys beginning in 2014, put it, "This hyper-masculine man—clad in leather gear, including chaps, jackets and accessories—inspired a look, lifestyle and attitude that not only influenced the gay community, but also made its way to the straight leather biker clubs around Europe and eventually, the U.S." The Tom of Finland clone, a gay male wearing leather jeans and a harness on top of a naked torso—together with a leather motorcycle cap—displaced the "sissy" or "fairy" as the gay icon of the 1960s and remains so today. In 1984, Laaksonen, now sixty, and Durk Dehner established in Los Angeles the Tom of Finland Foundation, which premiered the first exhibit of its permanent collection in August 1999.[5]

Gay Films

As in straight porn, in gay adult films the emphasis over time changes from the straightforward to the sensual, from sex in the missionary position (for straights) or from uncomplicated buggery (for gays), to a veritable Arabian Nights of variety.

Gay films, in the beginning highly tabooed, were about buggery. The first gay porn film produced in the United States is thought to be *Surprise of a Knight*, aired in 1929 (or 1930 according to some authorities). Because hardcore porn was illegal, no credits are given for the direction or the acting, which in any event, in the film's ten-minute span, is not a great deal. A gay man in drag lets himself be anally penetrated twice by a gentleman caller in a business suit, which rather encapsulates the beginning of the transformation of sexual activity that gays have undergone: the bottom is a "drag queen," and the only physical contact was down-and-dirty anal sex—unlike today when gays, as straights, navigate the entire panoply of sensuousness. Few gay films followed that were not equally underground.

Then, in the 1960s, just as the hetero adult films started hitting the mainline theaters, gay films began surfacing in "specialty" cinemas, cantonized because of the total unacceptability of depicting sex between men. Kenneth Anger's *Scorpio Rising*, with its macho motorcycle gang imagery, streeted in 1963. Andy Warhol's softcore *The Chelsea Girls* (1966) and *Lonesome Cowboys* (1969) played to packed (art) houses. Steven Toushin, owner of Bijou Video in Chicago, was a major producer and distributor of hardcore gay in the 1970s and after. Relentlessly hounded in anti-obscenity prosecutions, he was arrested 35 times, leading to five federal trials and state and local trials so numerous that he was unable to recall many for an interviewer.[6] (The Bijou Theater later became to go-to address for classic gay porn that the company had restored.[7])

Giants of Gay Cinema

Yet, above ground, things were mellowing. On the East Coast, Wakefield Poole's *Boys in the Sand* (1971) is seen as the beginning of the gay breakout; the film is filled with passionate and erotic sex scenes—and lensed on Fire Island off the coast of Long Island. Sadly, the lead, John Calvin Culver (whose stage name was Casey Donovan), most famous of the early iconic gay actors, died in 1987 of AIDS.

But, on the West Coast, the main bastion of porn remained San Francisco, which had been the cradle of straight porn as well. First off the mark was the Colt Studio Group, founded by Jim French under the pseudonym Rip Colt in 1967 as a photographic studio. (French: "I don't think anyone has ever photographed the male butt better than I."[8]) French managed the Colt Studio brand until 2003. As Colt Studios flourished, it was said to be "the face of a specific moment in gay history—one that was wedged between Stonewall [1969] and the AIDS crisis."[9]

In 1971, Chuck Holmes purchased a handful of gay loops and established Falcon Studios as a mail-order company; this essentially, as director Chris Ward said, "gave birth to the modern gay porn era." Holmes, known as "the gay Hugh

Hefner," realized "that for gay men to truly imagine equality, they needed to see positive representations of themselves."[10]

Falcon's first release was *Muscle Sweat and Brawn* in 1978. In 1978 as well, Falcon debuted *The Other Side of Aspen*, directed by Colin Meyer, and starring Casey Donovan from *Boys in the Sand* and Al Parker—an iconic "Marlboro Man"; the flick became Falcon's first blockbuster. Chris Ward calls it "a watermark in the history of porn," with the close camera work focusing on penetration that became a standard for gay cinema.[11] Five more installments in the *Other Side* series followed, the last, *The Other Side of Aspen 6* (2011), directed by Ward.

In 1988, Holmes's friend and lover Steven Scarborough, who owned a health-food store in San Francisco, came on board as a director at Falcon; Scarborough tightened up operations, introduced a contract system, and moved filming along at a good clip, beginning with *Perfect Summer* and *Touch Me*, both in 1988. In 1993, Scarborough commenced the famous *Redemption* series for Falcon.

Meanwhile, a struggle for control between Holmes and Scarborough had begun. Scarborough had remade Falcon as a first-rank studio, but fighting with Holmes was too much for him, and in 1993, he left Falcon to establish his own company, Hot House Entertainment. *On the Mark* (1993) was its first hit.

While at Falcon, Scarborough had hired or influenced a number of junior directors who went on to become seminal figures in gay porn: Chi Chi LaRue (Larry Paciotti), a famous drag queen who became the founder of Channel 1 Releasing, had begun directing in 1987 and occasionally shot for Scarborough (he usually did not direct in drag); John Rutherford, who would become head of production for Falcon after Scarborough; Bruce Cam, who later founded Titan; and Chris Ward, who started at Hot House in 1998, directing and starring in *Powerfist* (1998). This was one of the three *Power* titles that initiated the Hot House Club Inferno fisting series in 1998. Ward horrified the industry by showcasing the "unshaved, tattooed, and pierced men" that he himself found appealing, up to then "unthinkable in the world of mainstream gay porn," as Ward later said.[12]

Ward then co-founded with J.D. Slater Raging Stallion Studios in 1999. Ward and Scarborough had a huge falling out over the creation of Raging Stallion. So Ward joined Falcon in 2004, initially in charge of finance. "During the golden years of porn—by golden I mean when money was coming in faster than we could count it," said Ward later, "we were all very competitive."[13] But Scarborough and Ward reconciled, and when Scarborough retired in 2014, Ward called him "one of the great directors…[He] has had a large part in defining gay erotica, and thereby gay culture."[14]

After Rutherford left Falcon in 2003 for Colt, Chi Chi LaRue became the de facto director of production. He left Falcon a year later, in 2004, to concentrate on his own company, Rascal Video. LaRue directed some of the Falcon classics of these years, including *Heaven to Hell* (2005), which starred all-Falcon exclusive talent and streeted just after LaRue's departure.

But the story had further legs. Chuck Holmes died of AIDS in 2000 and Falcon passed into the hands of a charitable trust named after him. In 2003, Steve Johnson, Terry Mahaffey, and Todd Montgomery took leadership roles at Falcon and the following year formed a company, called 3M, that bought Falcon from the foundation. Meanwhile, times were becoming more difficult, and studios began merging. AEBN acquired Falcon in 2010, merging it with Raging Stallion. This formed, as Chris Ward said, "the single largest all-male erotic production company in the world."[15] Yet the identities of the two labels were kept separate. Ward said in 2013, "Falcon guys are mainly smooth, younger men—the boy-next-door type—whereas Raging Stallion guys are muscular, hairy and often sport amazing tattoos."[16]

With Scarborough's retirement, in 2014 Falcon/Raging Stallion bought Hot House.[17] And just to show that the gay market was heading in the same direction as the straight, in 2015 the company relaunched Hot House as "the Ass Authority," with a commitment to offering "the best all-male ass action" in the world[18] (see Chapter 15 on Anal).

Now that Hot House and Falcon were under the same roof, Ward assembled within the Falcon Studios Group, 13 exclusive contract performers into the A-Team, and the members of the A-Team highlighted for Ward the exquisite side of gay porn: "Boomer Banks has the biggest dick in porn. Dario Beck has the most perfectly hairy ass of all time. Brian Bonds has a hole that can take just about anything. Ryan Rose is the archetypical all-American Falcon man. Johnny V has a jaw-dropping physique."[19] (It is interesting that, to aggregate these qualities, Ward had to assemble a team of five actors. Chi Chi LaRue described his own search as director for the perfect gay actor: "It has to be someone who has all-American good looks, someone who has a huge dick and a great body—and that's really hard to find."[20])

Then, in 2014, Ward moved the A-Team, Hot House, Falcon, and Raging, all from San Francisco, to Vegas! From the gay capital of the universe to a place that was, as Hot House producer Christian Owen put it, "a little bit more on the quiet side.... You think it's going to be very gay, but it's not—at least not yet."[21]

The relentless process of concentration among the major gay studios continued in 2016, when Ward retired as president of the Falcon Studios Group and was replaced by Tim Valenti, who simultaneously was co-owner of another studio called Naked Sword. Valenti retained that post after joining Falcon, while Ward, a History Ph.D., indicated a desire to return to France for further studies. The background: Naked Sword was founded in 1996 and shortly started the first gay online streaming service, producing the hugely popular gay soap opera *Wet Palms*. As well, for years, Sword had streamed the videos of the Falcon group. The gay porn scene thus throbbed with vitality, with these huge San Francisco-Vegas powerhouses flanked by effervescing smaller studios popping up everywhere.

Gay Websites

The first gay internet sites seem to have launched in 1995; according to gay webmaster Keith Griffith in New Orleans, they included AbsolutelyMale. com, MountEquinox.com, and Badpuppy.com (which had started in 1992 as a bulletin board). His own Bedfellow.com began appearing in 1996, and he quit his daytime job to "cruisemaster" it fulltime the following year. These early gay sites were oriented towards community services, especially keeping track of the ever-changing cruising locales. Griffith said much later, "I made a pact with the men who visited the site: You give me the information about where you have sex, and I'll place it online for other men to see."[22]

Gay webcamming followed close behind. In 1997, Douglas Richter started working with Portfolio Studios in Minneapolis, an adult modeling agency that supplied photos to gay magazines. "It turned out to be more than a 'modeling agency' because they were also one of the early live cam studios and operated a small stable of models broadcasting feeds from their digs in the warehouse district." Richter said that he found the webcams "beyond interesting; you could literally connect live to beautiful people from your home or office. It brought real interactivity to web chatting; people could no longer hide behind false profile pictures." So Richter started typing messages to the users while the models did their live sex shows."[23] This was, as far as I know, the beginning of interactivity on gay webcams.

Gay and Straight

Looks, as we know, matter in straight porn. But they matter for the female performers. They matter in gay porn, too, but this time, of course, for the males. But unlike straight, in gay, looks are not necessarily the main thing that matters. Here is director Jasun Mark at Titan Media, talking about porn-megastar Landon Conrad, whom Mark had shot many times. "We've all seen those beautiful guys who look great until you see them on video and it's like watching a mannequin. Landon's best asset isn't just a handsome face, a big dick and a great body—although those sure do help. It's his facial expressions. His personality and the character all come out there. That's what makes him so hot to watch. And those eyes? Just beautiful. There's a shot in *Hardly Working* [2015] where I got an extreme close-up on his face, and his eyes look like blue lasers. They're amazing."[24] I cannot recall seeing a description of this in straight, where nobody really cares what the male talent looks like—witness the success of Ron Jeremy—and where breast size certainly trumps eyes.

Director Chi Chi LaRue called attention in 2007 to the presence of faces in gay, their frequent absence in gonzo. "In gonzo there's no faces shown, just bodies and genitals. For me, people's faces turn me on by their reactions, so when I am doing rimming or sucking or whatever I really need to see the face of the person it's happening to. And that's a big difference between gay and straight turn-ons."[25]

Meanwhile, in the real world, anal sex turns out to be commoner among straight males than gay. In a survey for 2011–13 of the National Center for Health Statistics, 42.7 percent of heterosexual men reported having had anal sex, 33.9 percent of gay men. This is a complete shocker, in view of stereotypes about gay males and "buggery" (the buggers turn out to be heteros!). For heterosexual women, 35.4 percent reported "any anal sex"; for homosexual or bisexual women, 44.2 percent. This, also, is surprising in terms of traditional stereotypes of female fastidiousness surrounding the anus.[26]

There is one other real-world difference between gay and straight: Fisting reached the gay male world far earlier than the straight. "There's tons of fisting out there," said Christian Owen in 2014, Hot House's main fisting director in charge of the Club Inferno line, which had begun in 1998 (Owen came on board in 2010). Owen saw himself as upholding Steve Scarborough's tradition of good viewing angles and lighting, to create premium product. "I'll hold the camera in a way that it can make the guy at home feel like that's actually him in the scene. A lot of times, I'll put the camera right over the top's hand, so the guy that's at home can visually think that's his hand." And the fisting models? "They're all into it," said Owen. "They're fisting performers at home, so when they come to shoot a movie, they love it. It's their passion."[27]

Shooting is not all that different between gays and straights. Just as Veronica Hart learned on the hetero side to keep her mouth shut (see Chapter 11), Hot House director Nick Foxx, who shoots anal gay, learned it on the gay side: Don't interrupt the action. Foxx refrains from asking the models to change position. "The viewer," Foxx said in an interview, "doesn't need to see models moving around—especially if it's not sexy. And what the viewer doesn't know is, models hate moving from position to position—and sometimes it takes an excessive amount of time to make it look seamless and set up the lights for a three-second shot. I like to keep things fast and sexy."[28]

Another similarity is performance anxiety, the inability of the talent to get and hold an erection. This came home to "sexalicious" gay performer David Dakota at his first shoot. "I was extremely nervous. I couldn't get hard or stay hard, which is unusual for me! I'm erect all the time! It took me over four hours to shoot the scene."

How did you finally get it done?

"By the time it was over I had a blister on the head of my dick from jacking off for so long. Painful!"[29]

Just as female talent, gay male actors might fill in the idle hours with escorting, a practice that, said one well-informed insider in 2014, "has increased dramatically in the past 5-10 years."[30] Gay executives cotton to the idea of a gay porn star as an evening companion, and, says journalist Harris Gaffin, they tend to be quite intimidated by their date's celebrity. In 1989, the escort rate was $150 an hour. One service that gay-talent agent David Forest offered was "private meeting" connections.[31] Like the female performers as well, gay talent went on the road to dance at gay clubs, headliners known from their porn films commanding huge sums.[32]

A New Porousness in Gender Identity?

There is a fantasy that many gay men apparently harbor: "I can be the one that can make them cross over. Or at least have fun trying!"[33] In 2015, Nica Noelle directed for Icon Male *Straight Boy Seductions,* enacting the seduction of a straight guy. Said Noelle, "My personal favorite is the scene where [straight] Ty Roderick reluctantly agrees to let [gay] Asa Shaw 'practice' his blowjob skills on him, which results in Ty becoming the sexual aggressor."[34] Straight content was a hot new item in gay porn, and shows one of the new trends: increasing fluidity across what was once a firewall between gay and straight. This porousness appears on the screen, and in the real world, as well.

In 2011, "Vegas Barbie" asked on the *XBIZ* board, "Is it worthwhile to market across the 'gay-straight' border?" "Pinkhelmut," an older gay guy, responded, "I'm only learning NOW that there are indeed HORDES, and I mean HORDES, of married men who live two lives, totally in the closet, have NO physical connection to stereotypical gay life, bars, etc, and a very large portion of them, to my surprise, appear to be GENUINELY bisexual and actively participate BOTH AC and DC.... This is a type of male that gay men used to scoff at for years, whispering, 'Just give him time—He'll figure it out.'" Many members agreed that it was a huge, unexploited market, one highly wary of having their wives "out" them by seeing them watch other men.[35]

As for women, many are becoming increasingly excited by images that once were destined for men. We visited this above for lesbian women. The gay film production company Corbin Fisher enlarged its market with "gay porn for straight women." Company COO Brian Dunlap said in 2011, "The feedback from women indicates that they simply like to look at good-looking men and their passion involved in the [gay] sex." With the Fisher company, there was a progression of sites that led from homosexual to mixed heterosexual experiences to straight heterosexual, beginning with *Amateur College Men* (gay) to *Guys Gone Bi,* to the straight site *Corbin's Coeds.* These sites proved so popular that, by 2011, the company expanded from two or three to a staff of 25 in a newly acquired building in Las Vegas.

Dunlap said, "It's not only gay men who are purchasing company content but also bi-curious men, straight men and a considerable amount of women."[36] This new perspective about crossing sex-orientation boundaries—today at a crescendo—fits with the larger motive of breaking down barriers between genders and between sexual orientations. This kind of porousness is entirely in keeping with a Zeitgeist today that scorns "binary" sexuality. There are many stations in the pathway from straight to gay.

Porousness is the theme that Shine Louise Houston seized and made her own. She was the founder in 2005 of Pink and White Productions, a studio noted for "explicit queer feature films." For Houston, gender was anything but a fixed concept. "Part of the joy in the work we do," she said in an interview, "is the chaos we hope we're throwing in the face of any idea that sexuality and gender are a fixed or predetermined inner essence, as if the functions of our holes were inscribed on our DNA, as if queer women are all perpetually stuck in a sexual universe of softly-lit feminine lesbians caressing each other...in a mutual embrace of gentle tribadism."[37] Houston was a major influence on Nica Noelle at Mile High Media, noted for "forbidden" gay themes.

In 2006, Colt Studio started introducing product into such mass-market chains as Virgin Megastores. This was a breakthrough. Yet the smaller mom-and-pop shops were reluctant to accept gay material. Was this logical, asked Colt President John Rutherford. No. "We find that most men who purchase our products in rural America don't necessarily identify as 'gay'—they can be gay-curious and just happen to stumble upon gay product that intrigues them." So carrying gay products will boost your sales among apparent straights, was the argument.[38] This is remarkable. I have never seen before the view that large numbers of straight men are buying gay product, and if Rutherford's analysis is correct, it marks a sea change.

A 2015 YouGov poll in the U.K. found that a stunning 46 percent of youth ages 18-24 considered themselves "not exclusively heterosexual."[39] Although, for many, this pliability will be largely theoretical, the statistic shows that the traditional barriers between masculinity and femininity are breaking down. The older age groups were much less accepting of their inner gayness, but this youth cohort will carry these attitudes within them as they grow older—and those who come behind may be even more liberal. Thus, a big recent change in the U.K. in sexuality is this new porousness between the genders.

Meanwhile, American data show the same trends, though more pronounced for women. Are you attracted at all to members of the same sex? asked a survey of the National Center for Health Statistics in 2002, and again in 2011-2013. (The question actually was "Sexual attraction: Mostly opposite sex?") In 2002, 10.2 percent of women 18-44 felt some attraction to the same sex; in 2011-2013, 12.9 percent. (As for men in that age group, in 2002, only 3.9 reported some same-sex attraction; in 2011-2013, 4.1 percent.) Thus, stirrings of same-sex attraction were almost three times commoner in women than men, and in both sexes, these stirrings increased slightly over a six-year period.[40]

Gay Niches Arise

"Not all gay men are attracted to the muscle-bound, all-American, athletic jock....
You have bears, daddies, twinks, jocks, leather and ethnic." [41]

JAHAZIEL PEREZ, OWNER OF DICKZTOYZ.COM, 2014

In line with larger changes over the last thirty years, in the gay market there have been important trends. In the past, gay porn meant mainly buggery, anal penetration. The 1970s, for example, were known as the "gay glory hole era."[42] The models themselves were pretty much of a piece, "the pretty-boy California surfer-types," as director William Higgins put it. "If dark hair wasn't bleached blonde, the market wasn't interested."[43]

Gay porn then enlarged the sexual palette, opening up the erotic imagination. One gay content producer, whose sales increased 280 percent during the brutal recession of 2008 and after, "attributed this success to his catalog of controversial harder to find gay genres such as barebacking and swallowing. The jack shacks sell through his titles almost immediately upon hitting the shelves." [Gay-themed video stores sell out.] Nor does he need to hustle for business: "The clients contact him."[44] (Barebacking means doing without a condom, and, for safety reasons, is generally filmed with established couples whose HIV status is ascertained. The term gained popularity in the 1990s.)

There is no single "gay" market. Over the last thirty years, taste has exploded into a variety of niches: hairy gay men ("bears"), young men and late adolescents ("twinks"), more mature gay men ("daddies"), and musclemen, to say nothing of covering them all with leather. In 2001, Mike Zillion and Ken Slater in San Francisco organized a genuine bear site, CyberBears.com. Slater: "We show real bears who are big and heavyset and also masculine, sexual and hairy."[45] Members of the bear community tended to avoid Gay Pride parades but flocked to Convergence, an annual bear convention in Palm Springs, and had their own purchasing tastes. Jahaziel Perez at DicksToyz.com said, "You can't show up to a chubby convention with a paddle and ball gag." Nor were the bears interested in "sexy underwear." "I [don't] want anyone to face public shame. Everyone wants to feel sexy regardless of their size."[46]

Thus, the niches were extensive: ethnic, military, and combos, such as "Latin twinks," and "Leather-bound dungeon." Servicing these niches gave the webmasters their edge over the free gay sites featuring homogeneous "gay sex." In the industry as a whole, maybe one surfer in five hundred would "convert," or type in his credit card number. In gay niches, the conversion rate for a micro-niche could easily be 1:20 and "retain for 6-8 months at a minimum."[47]

Another Niche: Gay BDSM

On the basis of an analysis of 1.9 million ads on Craigslist in 2010 of gay men seeking partners, Ogas and Gaddam concluded that around one-third of gay men who advertised in this milieu were tops, two-thirds bottoms.[48] (This is roughly true among heteros as well, where the great majority seek to bottom.) Growing up in a "very conservative and intensely religious" part of North Carolina, Paul Wilde, later an influential director, knew he was gay. Sean Connery was one of his "childhood crushes." But he didn't know about kink until his first boyfriend took him to the AA Meat Market in Chicago, where he found the tape *Fallen Angel* (1981). A light went on. "I pretty much played that VHS tape until it gave out," Wilde later said. "It introduced me to a fantasy world that has become a very real part of my personal life." He relished San Francisco's "vibrant kink community."[49] But while in North Carolina, he couldn't even have suspected it existed.

BDSM became an integral part of the gay experience. "There are clear criteria for being a star," said Chris Steele, who had worked as a booking agent for gay bars in Dallas. "You need to possess three elements: a handsome face, a nice body and a big dick." But on stage, Steele continued, you need to go beyond that. "The tops are the stars. If you want to be a big name in gay porn, fuck like one. Learn to talk dirty. Take control and be a pushy, nasty top. If you do that, you'll be on your way—big time."

But what if you're a bottom?

Steele had an answer for that, too. "You can still be a big name but you'll have to work harder at it. Keep your dick hard while you're getting fucked and then turn around and give as hard as you took. Don't wait for the director to tell you what to do, take charge and fuck your co-star's brains out."[50] Aggressiveness was the keynote here, for both top and bottom. Gay BDSM strikes a different note than straight, where control rather than aggression rings the chime. The basic non-fetish (vanilla) gay activities, said Brian Mills, a director at Titan Media, are "kiss, lick, rim, suck, and fuck." What separates gay fetish from gay vanilla Mills continued, is "over-aggressiveness."[51]

Suddenly, BDSM was everywhere: The muscle-bound, leather-clad "clone," who surfaced after Stonewall in 1969, now ruled the gay bars; the "nance" and the "queen" were hidden away in dresser drawers forever. Said one observer, "The amount of BDSM fetish niches on the gay adult internet is endless. From flogging, caning and spanking to tickle torture to CBT [cock and ball torture], just about every BDSM activity imaginable can be found in gay erotica. Gay BDSM sites can be incredibly specific: one might focus on steel bondage exclusively, while another might cater to rubber fetishists."[52]

Over time, the concept of a "leather culture" elaborated itself within the gay and lesbian communities much more so than within the heterosexuals. Chi Chi LaRue said in 2009 that, in contrast to regular gay porn that "sells okay...you make these big leather fetish movies and they pay for themselves (snaps fingers) right away."[53] When heteros think about leather, it is usually in the specific BDSM context. For gay men, the leather culture helps to define the orientation itself, "identifying itself by dressing in leather gear, including harnesses, caps, chaps, etc. The leather community," continued the lexicographer, "is made up of mostly gay men, but also includes some women and transgender participants. Internationally known leather events include San Francisco's Folsom Street Fair...."[54] As far as I know— with the exception of such rare events as Denver's Thunder in the Mountains— there is no heterosexual equivalent.

Lesbian and Girl/Girl

Many lesbians definitely did not wish to see lesbian porn abolished by the sex-negative feminists![55] The first lesbian film was apparently *The Third Sex* (1934), also known as *Children of Loneliness*, with Richard C. Kahn as director; it was based on the 1928 Radclyffe Hall novel, *The Well of Loneliness*. The film was little seen in the day because, as one might imagine, the upholders of righteous morality banned it as quickly as possible, and today, it is considered "lost," with no surviving copies.

It's unclear whether the film was genuinely lesbian, or else equivalent to what Porn Valley would later call girl/girl. Lesbian porn is made by and for lesbians, and girl/girl porn uses heterosexual female models at shoots directed by men aimed at the male market. "The problem," said journalist Anne Winter, was that girl/girl is "just not real. The pretty girls performing in these videos are what many in the business call 'gay-for-pay' actresses, and they're certainly not having authentic lesbian sex—they're heterosexuals having sex the way directors instruct them."[56]

Like the straight market, in the 1950s and 60s, the lesbian market as well was served by pulp-fiction novels. In fact, the first pulp bestseller of any kind was Polish-French writer Tereska Torrès's *Women's Barracks*, published in the U.S. in 1950, which reached two million copies (reissued in 2011 by She Winked Press). Others soon followed, such as Marijane Meaker's (pen name Vin Packer) *Spring Fire* (1952). To avoid prosecution for obscenity, the novels were often obliged to end tragically.[57] The pulps of the 1950s and 60s saw many "lesbian" novels—most, but not all, aimed at the male market.

Modern lesbian porn began in 1984 when Susie Bright, Nan Kinney, and Debbie Sundahl founded a lesbian-centered erotica magazine, *On Our Backs*, a take-off on the politically-correct antiporn publication of the 1970s and after, *Off Our Backs*. A year later, in 1985, Kinney and Sundahl founded the studio Fatale Video to make lesbian porn films. They launched *How To Female Ejaculate* in 1985 showing, as *XBIZ* put it, "a gushing G-spot orgasm."[58] In 1985, Fatale debuted *Private Pleasures* and *Shadows*; shown at a film festival, the antiporn feminists and pro-sex feminists in the audience almost came to blows.[59] Fatale's next big hit was *Bend Over Boyfriend* in 1998, a smash hit among the strapon curious directed by Shar Rednour and produced by Kinney. *Suburban Dykes* in 1991, directed by Sundahl, starred Sharon Mitchell as a "chains n'leather biker bitch"[60] and Nina Hartley (who campaigned in the coming years for lesbian flicks).

Simultaneously, Pleasure Productions, then headquartered in New Jersey and known for gay and transsexual lines, began producing lesbian porn. *Lesbian Passion* debuted in 1985. And it was genuine lesbian, as exemplified in such series as *San Francisco Lesbians*, which began in 1993, not just girl/girl. A 1997 ad for the series, "Part I," announced "True Dykes, right off the street. They're incredible—and they're real." [61] The studio's *Strap-On Sally* series, with an all-female cast, began in 1994.

Until the new century, girl/girl content had been in bad odor among the big studios and the cable companies, turned off by the previous gonzo approach to girl/girl, which was, as Levine put it, "how-big-a-toy-can-these-girls-get-up their-butts."[62] But the demand for genuine lesbian product was such that, when Dan O'Connell, together with a partner porn-named Moose, founded Girlfriends Films in 2002 in Valencia, California, it was no longer necessary to put quotation marks around lesbian. With the help of several lesbian staffers, O'Connell intended to offer titles "that stressed sensuality, intimacy, chemistry, performed by gay or bisexual women who really got off having sex with other [women]." His *Women Seeking Women* series became a classic[63].

Around 2001, Sherry Halloway, a mortgage banker, decided to open a distribution company, Girlfriends Distributing, with Girlfriends Films as her first client. Halloway had a problem with male-produced girl/girl. "Their take is, why pay the extra money to film quality lesbian content when you can do girl-on-girl action for less...? Our company supports films that portray the real lesbian life: how they feel, how they hook up, the challenges they face." Halloway distributed the DVDs of a number of young lesbian producers moving into this market segment. (She knew their fears and anxieties because she had second-mortgaged her own house to open the company.)[64] By 2011, when Girlfriends partnered with AbbyWinters.com to create a membership site, it had "the largest library of lesbian-themed video content in the world."[65] A major figure came on board in 2012, when B. Skow ended a twenty-year tenure at Vivid to shoot lesbian for Girlfriends.

Some lines and studios were helmed by genuine lesbians. Dana Dane, founder of Erocktavision in 2002, said, "I am a lesbian but without every single politic up my ass. I don't get trapped in a forum that thinks every film needs a butch and a femme." Julie DeRoot, part of the creative team at HotMoviesForHer.com, said in 2006 that Valley lesbian producers had shed the 70s feminist antiporn optic. "For a long time, there was an anti-pornography component in the lesbian community being driven by feminists. Now we're getting away from that, especially with the younger audience...."[66] In 2007, DeRoot at HotMovies teamed up with Kinney to begin shifting some of Kinney's material online.[67] Yet in general, the lesbian space was far slower than the gay space to embrace the internet.

Lesbian films reached the acme of high production-value features in 2011 when writer-director Kay Brandt brought out for Samantha Lewis's Digital Playground, under the line Jewel Box Films, two episodes of *Cherry*. (Brandt herself had been earlier so timid about shooting porn that she watched the scenes from a monitor rather than entering the bedroom.[68]) The concept of the series: Cherry (mainstream performer Judith Thompson in a non-sex role) runs a strip-club in which the dancers cater to the exotic wishes of the lesbian clientele. The plot was rich and complex; the fans loved it.

Meanwhile, the demand for girl/girl among heterosexual males started to dry up in favor of more exotic carnal combinations, such as girl/girl/boy and the like. As Mike South told the *Independent Florida Alligator* newspaper in 2011, "Every girl is like 'I wanna do girl-girl' and I'm like 'Honey, I can't even give that away.'"[69] It was the advance of technology that had extinguished some of this "girl" market. The demand for watching a solo female masturbate herself had ebbed, as Jesse

FameDollars at Gamma Entertainment explained, "because of how prevalent and advanced camming has gotten. If I wanted to watch a solo girl, I would just go to a cam site because I have the added bonus of possibly interacting with the girl."[70]

Dee Severe, who specialized in producing BDSM for all sexual orientations, added, "I agree, solos are a yawn." Yet, "it depends on the lesbian. If you do sweet girlie content and cast porn girls who are not really bisexual in real life, they're just being lesbians for pay for your shoot, you're not going to get very interesting or realistic content." (Severe included herself in this generalization and said, on another occasion, that she shot lesbian content poorly "because I'm a mostly heterosexual kinky person and I don't have those hot buttons. Which is why we don't shoot g/g unless it's g/g BDSM, which is a different thing."[71])

Yet, Dee Severe added, hot lesbian BDSM still moved: "If you cast fabulously dirty girls who genuinely love to fuck other women and like to go hard, and give them some strap-ons and other fun toys, you're going to get a scene that's every bit as hot as any boy/girl."

And, ah yes, there was one more advantage to shooting girl/girl. Severe said, "Nobody ever has a problem with their wiener."[72]

What turned a corner in shooting lesbian content was the advent of a number of female directors who had a feeling for navigating the shoals of young female talent. In 2015, former performer Tori Black (Michelle Chapman), now turned director for ArchAngel, shot her first full-length lesbian feature, *True Lust,* starring Kendra Lust and distributed by Girlfriends Films. She said the secret was talking with the models beforehand, getting a sense of their own fantasies, and then letting them act the fantasies out in front of the camera. This is something that the whole generation of male directors from New York definitely did not do. So, said Black, in shooting lesbian, we're going to press them but we have to be careful. "Girl/girl scenes are very complicated and difficult because women in general are very complicated and difficult.... Tapping into what makes girls tick was a good challenge. Guys are so much easier to please. We want to push boundaries, but we can't push too hard or you'll have a horrible scene with the girls looking at each other like, 'Ew, I don't want to be with her.'"[73]

With "lesbian porn noir," the lesbian space moved further into the enlargement of erotic tastes that the straights and gay males had been experiencing. In 2015, an "all-girl adult studio," Girlsway in Montreal in the Gamma Films Group (the production arm of Gamma Entertainment), introduced "lesbian porn noir as part of the *Business of Women* series. The first movie, produced by Bree Mills, featured a number of hardcore sex scenes, including a BDSM threeway,[74] that gave girl/girl BDSM the power to appeal to a core lesbian community and to the larger market for girl/girl at the same time. Within thirty years, the cinema of lesbianism had thus migrated from demure Vaseline-on-the-lens productions to total-body hardcore.

Chapter 17:
Toys

"I just watched a video with an older woman (+65) talking about sex toys and the Shades *phenomenon. She says her peers are really interested in it, are talking about it, and think sex toys are new, fun and exciting. She lives in a retirement community in Florida and her son owns a sex toy store, so she has become 'Sex Toy Mom' in her community."* [1]

DOMINA DOLL, 2012

Women in the booming "sex tech" industry, primarily situated in New York City, reject any identification with "pornography." [2] And properly so. Pornography is images while sex toys are pleasure extenders. Given that only about a third of all women have orgasms during penetrative sex, the demand for toys that extend the orgasm experience is enormous. Yet sex toys have always been a major part of the adult entertainment industry, and the toymakers are amply represented at industry meetings and in ads.

There is, for example, a plaster mold of Stormy Daniels' private parts available for sale as well as a "Realdoll" in Stormy's image. Promo copy: "You've probably wondered what it would be like to have sex with this luscious starlet. As you contemplated the notion of making it with this beautiful sex vixen, you most likely felt the need to pleasure yourself, stroking to your wildest fantasy." And now you can make your fantasy a reality! "Stormy Daniel's Precious Private Parts—an actual mold of the star's hottest erogenous zones—looks and feels real. Slide and thrust your penis inside of this replica sleeve...." [3] Thus, "Stormy's World" included moldings of her perineum.

When Susan Colvin opened California Exotic Novelties in 1994 in Los Angeles, the toys available at that time were mainly dongs, "artificial pussies," anatomically correct anuses and vaginas, and vibrators. "Very few items were geared for couples," Colvin later said. Yet she believed "that toys were fun, and I thought they were just going to open up to couples and to women." Couples-friendly videos were just catching on. "People were becoming more open-minded to the control of their sexual experiences," Colvin said.[4] Colvin had been general manager for a distribution company that had a small novelty unit called Swedish Erotica. The products were crummy, such as noisy vibrators with "basic" packaging. Colvin saw "potential in the market and knew things could be done differently."

When the distribution company folded in 1994, Colvin bought Swedish Erotica and changed the named to California Exotic Novelties with an all-female team of product developers.[5] "I had to tap into the female psyche," she said in a 2008 interview, "and develop products that (a) women could understand, and (b) are easy-to-use, maintenance-free and reliable." Moving from Los Angeles to Chino, she hired models to shoot the catalogue, an industry first. She introduced colors into the packaging and the products. "The industry was a bit of an 'old boys club' back then," she later said. "For example, it was common to hear people say, 'We have three plastic vibes in two styles, why do we need more colors or styles?'" The old boys didn't understand why toys needed to be waterproof! (So you can clean them and use them in the shower.) CalEx introduced waterproofing.[6] She was seen as a bit of an oddity at first, she said, but "now the industry is loaded with other women with similar philosophies."[7]

Sex toys are not new, and have been around ever since the Upper Paleolithic Era.[8] Yet only in the last thirty years have toys emerged to suck, vibrate, and penetrate every erogenous zone of the body. The narrative here is enlarging the erotic imagination with toys. This is new, and the sexual moralists have received sex toys as poorly as they received porn. Within recent memory, sex toys have been banned for various periods in Alabama, Georgia, Indiana, Louisiana, Mississippi, Texas, and Virginia.[9] So there is no doubt that sex toys threatened the whole system of righteous morality. "If the purchase of dildos is a crime, then only criminals will have dildos," quipped one commentator.[10]

Early Toys

In the late 1960s, Gene Wallace founded Love Toys in Las Vegas. New York's Duane Colglazier, a former Wall Street trader, opened the gay-axised toystore Pleasure Chest in 1971. Lovecraft in Toronto opened in 1972. This was retail.

Adam & Eve was founded in 1970 by Phil Harvey and Tim Black in Hillsborough, North Carolina, as a condom mail-order house that soon moved into toys. It became the "first wave of the new model" of adult store, as Bob Christian of Adam & Eve later put it, with a polished look that was considered women-friendly.[11]

There followed in the 1970s a whole series of toymakers and toy stores whose rise coincided with the erotic quickening of those years. Marty Tucker launched Topco Sales in North Hollywood in 1973 (later moved to the Valley, then in 2003 to Chatsworth). In 1974, Dell Williams in New York established Eve's Garden, the first sex shop owned by a woman and specifically aimed at the female market. It arose from an embarrassing encounter at Macy's department store, where she went to buy a Hitachi Magic Wand and was humiliated by a young male sales clerk who, in a penetrating voice, asked her, "What do you want it for?" She vowed that women in New York would not have to go through this again.[12]

Teddy Rothstein, who had been with Mafia-influenced Star Distributors, debuted Nasstoys in Brooklyn together with his cousins Elliot and Irwin Schwartz in 1975. They started selling Spanish Fly and Sta-Hard cream, and, its most popular product even decades later, the All American Whopper dildo.[13] Reuben Sturman founded Doc Johnson—making old school pal Ron Braverman president—in North Hollywood in 1976. (Sturman incorporated toymaker Marche Manufacturing as the product supplier.)[14] Doc Johnson's most important initial innovation was decorative packaging, "the silent salesman," as Braverman later put it. People could understand how to use the device without the hassle of asking the salesperson for all the details.[15]

Companies such as Topco, Doc Johnson and Nasstoys were giants of the industry; they arose in the "golden age of porn" hallmarked by *Deep Throat* and *Behind the Green Door*.

But this chronology makes the toy market sound livelier than it was. Doc Johnson, recalled Braverman, was really just an adult book business in the early years. "For a very long time, all adult stores were primarily focused on magazines and 8mm films; novelties [toys] were such a small segment of the market." This started to change with videotapes in the 1980s, then DVDs in the 90s, as people's eyes were opened to the erotic possibilities inherent in toys. Braverman said, "It wasn't until the end of the 90s that sex toys really started to be considered as a viable focus for stores. In the last ten years," he said in 2011, "the market for these products has just exploded."[16]

As with much else that was erotic in the age of righteous morality, male masturbation, too, carried its own particular shame. Icon Brands felt obliged to bring out its line of butt plugs and kegel balls in fake books that one could put "high on a bookshelf and never be discovered," as sales manager Joanie Lee said in a 2014 interview. The volume labeled *Perfecting Your Stroke* contained male-masturbation toys, the volume *The Other Door*, anal appliances, and so forth.[17] But, by 2014, male masturbation toys began receiving media coverage, and sex toys started to lose their aspect of "perversion."[18] Screaming O spokesperson Conde Aumann told *XBIZ* in 2014, "Sex toys are no longer seen as the solutions to an intimate problem; and instead more shoppers treat sex toys as exciting sexual enhancements. They build intimacy and keep things fun and fresh."[19] The toy box became a standard appurtenance in the bedroom, toy play a delicious component of the sexual encounter.

Toys Move on Line

The earliest toymaker to move online seems to have been JT's Stockroom, called simply "JT Toys" after its founder Joel Tucker, who in 1988, as a student at Occidental College in Los Angeles, posted a small catalogue of products on his school email account, later on the online bulletin board Usenet. He thought that after putting up a text version of the catalogue on the Alt.sex bondage newsgroup, sales would take off—but they didn't because, at this point, customers were too wary to hand over their credit card numbers. Once word spread that he was trustworthy, "It's been a steady evolution since," said Tucker. JT's Stockroom became "the number one supplier for fetish giant Kink.com."[20] The firm's motto: "It only seems kinky the first time."[21]

As the DVD and video markets tanked because of free porn online, a number of studios moved into the toy market, where new customers awaited who never previously would have bought porn. Jocelyn Saurini took the San Francisco sex-toy store MyPleasure online in 2001 to find an entirely new audience; the typical customer was "a woman, early 30s, located in a suburban area," said Sandor Gardos, the company's president. "A lot of people aren't within a hundred miles of a sex toy store, and if they are, they sure as hell don't want to tell the clerk, 'No, no, not that one—the bigger one!'"[22] By 2005, there were an estimated 25,000 websites selling toys on the net.[23]

One early initiative rocked much more couple-oriented than guy-oriented, Tom Stewart's Sportsheets, which he began in 1988 and incorporated in 1993 with the slogan "keeping couples connected." The founding appliance was a simple restraint device that could be spread on a bed, so that couples could stick each other to a velcro sheet with velcro cuffs that attached to anchor pads (which then attached to the sheet). This was really the beginning of the concept of "non-threatening, affordable, couples oriented restraint play," as company executive Joanne Queenin put it. Women were reassured in being able to pull free from the velcro restraints if they so desired.[24] Indeed, the company's later publicity showed women in the dominant position. Sportsheets then moved to a less conspicuous under-the-bed restraint system—and its whole business received a terrific bump up, of course, with *Fifty Shades of Grey*[25] (see below).

Sportsheets prided itself on selling the theme of "vanilla bondage." (Their ads showed a carton of ice cream with "vanilla bondage" on the label.[26]) "We're not so extreme," said president Julie Stewart. "Being restrained is a big fantasy. Whatever it is about being tied up reaches a lot of people, but not everyone wants to experience the extremes of that fetish."[27] The company's Sex and Mischief line, said Stewart, was an entry-level brand aimed at newbies with *Fifty-Shades*-driven curiosity.[28]

Molds

The male masturbation market had once been moribund, limited to a few "clunky penis pumps" and "outmoded sex dolls."[29] In 1965, the chair of a House subcommittee said of an artificial vagina, "Anyone who would judge this not to be obscene ought to be investigated, and by a psychiatrist, too."[30] But the availability of silicone—which Metis Black at Tantus popularized for toys in 1997—and other materials meant that molding for the masses lay just around the corner. Making molds of male performers' organs goes back at least to 1975, when it was the premise of the movie *Venture into the Bizarre*, as an actor playing Clint Eastwood goes into a plaster-modeling shop and asks that a cast of his member be made. In 1977, aspiring pornographer David Jennings toured the mob-run S&L Distributors in LA that featured "pocket pussies" and "pocket assholes."[31] So, these things had been around.

There were, for example, the "real dolls," life-size replicas of someone like model Teri Diver that Doc Johnson Enterprises produced in 1992[32]—clearly not the first. These found a large following. In 1993, California Exotic marketed what must have been one of the earliest examples of a personalized "pussy mold," a vagina "molded precisely to the luscious perfection of Racquel Darrian." Racquel herself was featured in a suggestive pose on the box, as an added treat.[33] Later that same year, 1993, Doc Johnson advertised "the realistic vagina," based on porn star Jacqueline's "pussy." It was said to be the "next best thing" to Jacqueline herself.[34]

Then came Fleshlight. In 1998, Steve Shubin patented an artificial anus-vagina masturbation device called Fleshlight and marketed it in the form of a flashlight with his company Interactive Life Forms in Austin, Texas. The inner sleeve was made with a substance called Cyberskin and mimicked the feeling of anal or vaginal intercourse. ("Some men say it's even better than the real thing," screamed the marketing copy.) Sales limped until Shubin ditched the distributors and in 2002 put it directly on the internet, making $1.9 million in the first year.[35] The marketing twist was modeling the perineums of famous porn stars and selling the mold as an authentic representation of Tori Black's anus or Riley Steele's vagina. Models knew they had arrived when they were selected to be fleshlighted (Fleshjack was the gay version). In 2009, Kayden Kross described her own experience. "Sooooo I got molded today....It was probably the easiest recurring paycheck I will ever make. I read a book for four hours while uninterested men mixed and poured yellow and blue goo on me and I held still as it heated and cooled and heated again and left hard. Yet there was one (semi) saddening moment: "The thing I can't stand in this equation is the passage of time, because eventually Kayden Kross's pussy and ass will not be a new toy and I feel like small parts of me will die with them when they are retired."[36] Lovehoney's sales of Fleshlights were 73 percent "pussy" and 9 percent butt—with one in three being molded after a given porn star.[37]

The mold market took off quickly. In 1999, Serenity, a contract girl for Wicked, founded her own toy company, Las Vegas Novelties, in Las Vegas. She marketed molds of her own "derriere," and of porn star Jewel De'Nyle's butt and vagina.[38] Taylor Wane gave her "very good friend" Gene Simmons of the group Kiss some marketing tips. You have to brand yourself. She marketed in her name "pussy soap that's actually molded from my pussy, paper weights that were molded from my pussy, a business card holder that was molded from my pussy and my asshole." There was so much more, including "vibrating anal grapes, strapon dildos...and an anatomically correct doll. It's not a blow-up doll, it's made of silicone. The pussy vibrates, the anus vibrates, she talks, she has a heartbeat! It just goes on and on!"[39] Some readers may be alarmed by the mind-blowing vulgarity of the account. Yet that is not the point. In terms of expanding the palette of desire, this tale of all the toys shaped in the manner of her pussy shows a significant leap forward over the past decades.

In 2006, Doc Johnson founded a Club Jenna Line, named after the porn star, and featuring "ass and pussy molds" fashioned from UR3 rubber based on Jenna's contract models, as well as a whole doll based on Jenna herself. (Jenna's "realistic pussy" followed in 2011.) After the ass-and-pussy mold of porn star Vicky Vette in March 2011, Doc Johnson launched the Vickie Quickie, a hand-held vagina.[40] The ass-and-pussy molds were hand-painted "to look exactly like the real thing." When porn star Casey Parker received her mold, she said "it felt like holding her own vagina."[41] Dani Daniels, who produced a mold with Doc Johnson, said, "It's awesome, because not only will my fans be able to fuck my 'holes' molds (ummmm, excuse me how rad is it that my fans can be among the first to fuck my ass?!), my fans will also be able to purchase toys for men and women that will be of my own design."[42] Later, the Doc Johnson line of masturbation sleeves became Pussy Pocket Pal.

For the aspiring young models, getting molded (becoming a "toy") is a big deal. Porn star Eva Lovia, 26, enthused after Fleshlight molded her in 2016, "It's a milestone! Girls wait their whole career to get a toy and Fleshlight is one of the biggest brands out there. I have a toy alongside legends like Tera Patrick and Asa Akira—to say I'm honored is an understatement."[43]

Nipple Toys, Anal Toys

The last thirty years did not exactly discover the erotic pleasures of nipple play—which is documentable at the end of the nineteenth century—but it was once uncommon. In 1899, German psychiatrist Paul Näcke, himself gay, reported that sexual arousal from stimulating the nipples was "unusual." Näcke may have been reporting experiences in the gay community, though he did include women in the observation. He recounted with wonderment, "On a trip I once met an English Jew, who told me that as soon as he rubbed his nipples, he felt feelings of desire."[44] By the 1970s, nipple play had become much commoner.[45] And recently the nipples have become a major focus, overcoming the shame once attached to getting pleasure from this area of the body. (One merchant at Pleasure Chest reports "customers who feel embarrassed about their sexual preferences and ask me questions like, 'Is it weird that I like wearing nipple clamps?'" The answer, of course, is "not at all!"[46])

Indeed, in the last thirty years, the toymakers have discovered the profits of nipple play. In 2013, nipple clamps were said at Spartacus Leathers to be "the company's fastest growing product category."[47] Riding the *Fifty Shades of Grey* vibe, in 2014 Lovehoney debuted a line of Pleasure and Pain Nipple Rings, "include[ing] a triple weighted bead chain for a little added pain, as they tug on the wearer's nipples."[48] The following year, in 2015, CalEx launched a complete line of nipple play items, including nipple jells, suckers, clamps of various kinds including vibrating, and nipple jewelry.[49]" In 2015, the best seller of the toy store Tyes by Tara in Greenwood Village, Colorado, was the Teddy Niplace, which, said owner Tara Christine, is "a necklace with nipple rings attached.... I love wearing it and even have customers who wear it under a loose shirt because it makes them feel a little naughty in public."[50] Specialists did nipple piercing, inserting silver bars or rings in the nipples (from which weights could be dangled in nipple play). Women have always known from breast-feeding that their nipples were erotic zones; men discovered it during the past few decades, but only recently have merchandisers been able to put nipple merchandising displays on offer.

And the anus! Butt plugs were a popular item in Toyland, but caution: enthusiastically inserted butt plugs might disappear into the anus, necessitating an emergency-room visit, of which 6,899 between 1995 and 2006 in the U.S. were sex-toy related.[51] Butt plugs in the late-nineteenth-century did in fact have flanges to prevent misadventure, but with the years, this precaution was somehow lost track of. Around 2012, it was Lucy Vonne at Evolved Novelties who was said to have re-invented the idea of a butt plug with a protective flange "that prevents your toy from going too far during anal play." [52]

Contrary to popular belief, butt plugs were not at all a gay monopoly. According to Jon Millward's analysis of data on Lovehoney's sales, of one million items during five months of 2013, butt plugs were purchased by 34 percent of Lovehoney's single gay or bisexual male clients, and fully 20 percent of straight men (but only 12 percent of single straight female clients).[53] These were mail-order sales. But this kind of toy demonstrates the helpfulness of brick-and-mortar adult stores in expanding people's erotic horizons, as opposed to buying more cheaply on line. Mark Espinosa, an executive at a toy wholesaler, gave this example of "a seemingly casual customer interaction [that] turns into a life-altering conversation." "I never thought about putting something up my ass before and thanks to the patience and education of that sales associate, [now] I can't imagine something not being up there."[54]

Vibrators

"When I started in 1981, people...had never seen a vibrator, never mind held one." [55]

JO THORNE, 71, SEX-TOY SALES IN TAUNTON, ENGLAND

Vibrators for masturbation reach way back to the end of the nineteenth century. Their revival in the 1980s, in the face of much state legislation declaring them obscene,[56] was linked to women's new sexual activation. An early bump up for vibrators was Howard Stern's recommendation of a Japanese product called the Pocket Rocket on his radio show beginning January 13, 1999, and then continuing for years. The publicity the Pocket Rocket, a small but powerful plastic device, received from the Stern show was enormous, and led to a number of U.S. toy companies bringing it out under various labels. (On the show, Stern recommended the Pocket Rocket for "amateur" masturbators, and hyped the Hitachi Magic Wand—see below—for more serious endeavors.[57])

Vibrators, though apparently innocuous, can be so deeply subversive of the sexual order that, as we have seen, in 1989 the Alabama legislature banned their sale ("any device designed...for the stimulation of human genital organs"). The legislation was overturned the following year in federal court.[58] Thus, a page was turned when in 1977 Joani Blank, a publisher who had worked with feminist sex therapist Lonnie Barbach at the University of California Medical Center to support "preorgasmic women," opened Good Vibrations in San Francisco; she wanted to sell them vibrators.[59] (Sexologist Lynn Comella at the University of Nevada has described these developments in *Vibrator Nation*.[60]) Good Vibrations established an online store, Goodvibes.com, in 1996 and estimated that 60 percent of its buyers were women. The site offered 150 different models of battery-powered vibrators.[61]

It was vibrators that gave the toy market a decided female spin, if only because the women's movement directed many women towards control over their own orgasms. In Millward's analysis of the Lovehoney data, vibrators were the second-commonest item (after lubes and creams).[62] Just watching women buy vibrators in one of his stores was a source of satisfaction for *Hustler*'s Larry Flynt. "The sexual revolution gave women permission to enjoy sex and it's fun to watch a woman come into the store and buy a deluxe vibrator and walk up to the cash register and slam it down, no shame, no guilt. But a guy who wants to buy a sex toy will stick it inside his coat and walk up to the cash register and kind of slip it to the [clerk]."[63]

Vibrators offered a kind of core orgasmic experience and were the keystone of the bedroom toy box. An episode of HBO's *Sex and the City* featured the character Charlotte obsessing about her Rabbit Pearl vibrator, a Vibratex product. Bunny vibrators offered, as Dawn Yagielowicz said, a two-in-one product: "a rotating shaft for vaginal stimulation and a vibrating bunny simultaneously stimulating the clitoris. Why not go for two erogenous zones instead of one?"[64]

Of all toys, the Hitachi Magic Wand had the greatest impact, a vibrator with a big round head that plugs into the wall socket for use at two speeds: slow is 5,000 vibrations per minute, fast is 6,000. Launched in 1968 and popularized by sex educator Betty Dodson, the Hitachi Magic Wand was voted in 2005 by readers of *Mobile Magazine* "the no. 1 greatest gadget of all time."[65] (In 2013, the device was renamed the Original Magic Wand after Hitachi spun it off to Eldorado as unflattering to the corporate image. Vibratex distributed it.) The Magic Wand has become the favorite vibrator of industry professionals—on screen and off. Members of the website Sssh.com were said by site administrator Angie Rowntree to have a special fondness for it. And Montreal domme Starla added, "It's not just a vibrator. It's a life changer." The first time she used it, she was shocked. "I didn't know that was possible."[66]

LELO, the Swedish toymaker, had such crossover success with their vibrator that it became featured in huge displays at Brookstone stores in airports. Colin Rowntree asked the clerk at the branch at the Los Angeles airport how many they sold a week. "A week," he replied, "I'm not sure, but at least 12 per day. After AA batteries, those are by far our best selling products at Brookstone."[67]

Vibrators and porn together could change lives, not just of Montreal dommes but of 70-year-old women such as Lynn Brown Rosenberg, a widow who had not had sex in the decade since her husband had died nor an orgasm "in a very long time." (Her mother had once told her, "Only prostitutes enjoy sex.") Finally, she grew tired of not having any sexual release and approached her therapist. "Get some porn and a vibrator," the therapist said. Rosenberg was shocked but was willing to try extreme measures "to feel like a sexual woman again." So she went, with great trepidation, to The Pleasure Chest, where a young woman helped her to select a vibrator and steered her to the porn section. Rosenberg, who had at first wanted to escape as quickly as possible, "wound up lingering, totally engrossed in all the DVDs." About an hour later, she took her purchases home and "started having pleasure twice a day!"

"This was a whole new world for me. I was watching porn and enjoying it. She never looked back. "It was the first part of my journey toward sexual freedom."[68]

Toys and Fifty Shades of Grey

"My husband and I had more sex for that month than we'd had in the last five years."[69]

JULIE STEWART, SPORTSHEETS, AFTER READING *FIFTY SHADES OF GREY*

Fifty Shades of Grey, or "FSOG" as it was called, blew everyone's socks off in the toy space. Consumers were clamoring for everything mentioned in the novel; the Lovehoney firm in Bath, England, won the invaluable license. But Lovehoney was not the first to market a toy collection aimed at the middle classes. As early as 2001, California Exotic Novelties launched the Pleasure Bound collection, for apprentice bondagers who wanted a tidy set of restraints. Theirs, in well-designed boxes, featured cuffs, an eye mask, and a collar with cuffs. But it was all themed together and looked appealing on merchants' shelves.[70]

Yet Lovehoney was the most astute of the toy packagers because they knew how to market the product to middle-class women. When Neal Slateford and Richard Longhurst founded Lovehoney in 2002, they were appalled at the labels of some of the available products such as The Cunt Screw and Fuck Your Pussy Clean. So they re-photographed everything they put up for sale on their own website, emphasizing female-friendly themes, such as "Sex toys are good for you."[71] Lovehoney became "the sexual happiness people." Slateford later said of *Fifty Shades of Grey*, "The most important thing for E.L. James was that her vision of the toys and bondage items... was brought to life. It was really important to her that the millions of readers of her books were able to buy authentic products [mentioned in the novels]." By March 2013, Lovehoney's Official Pleasure Collection was primed to hit the market, and included the Inner Goddess Pleasure Balls as the most popular item, plus such "softer bondage items" as the Soft Limits Wrist Ties and the No Peeking Blindfolds.[72] This was a cute kind of bondage-lite, but pitched perfectly at newbie sex experimenters. In 2014, Lovehoney sold "more than a million *Fifty Shades of Grey* items." And from 2014 to 2015, sales were up 53 percent.[73]

Fifty Shades of Grey vastly empowered women in the world of toys. Everything could be obtained online, of course. But even at the brick-and-mortar level, the clever marketers of *Fifty Shades of Grey*-themed merchandise made the packaging attractive to women. Blindfolds and handcuffs now seemed almost natural. And moving up a peg in the bondage space, the stores were now attaching *Fifty Shades of Grey* to products for more serious players, such as the Trust Me adjustable leg spreader, or the Keep Still St. Andrew's cross (wrists and ankles spread and pinioned) in The Playroom collection. Soft Velcro arm restraints were promised, and "100-percent vegan" leather items. "The line's cuffs are lined with faux fur for a sensual accent."[74] XR Brands offered a GreyGasms line of masks, ticklers, "and other assorted gentle and effective BDSM products for the exploratory couple."[75] These products were not for brutes. By March 2015, The Love Store in Las Vegas was reporting, as owner Edward Wheeler said, "a decrease in single men but a huge increase in women and couples."[76]

There is no single development in the adult story that reached into the world of the soccer moms as decisively as *Fifty Shades of Grey*-themed toys. Layla Ross at The Stockroom said, "What *Sex and the City* did for vibrators, *Fifty Shades of Grey* has done for BDSM. We have been getting a lot of 'soccer moms' who are surprised they had the guts to shop at a BDSM/fetish store. We are impressed with their bravery and how quickly the conversation changes from asking about a blindfold and within minutes we are talking about more esoteric topics such as male chastity and electrical play."[77] The soccer moms putting their husbands in chastity: This is femdom in capitals.

The sound barrier that rocketed *Fifty-Shades*-driven bondage into mainstream merchandising was crossed in 2014 when two fetish toymakers—Sportsheets in the U.S. and Box of Grey (BXG) in the U.K. (established in 2012) teamed up to offer bondage equipment packaged in gleaming metal cases, to be marketed at the Selfridges department store in London's Oxford Street, the second largest in Britain after Harrods. The spin was total perv: one Box of Grey ad featured a model's long legs, clad in six-inch heels, sticking out of the door of a high-end sports car. Another showed a BXG do not disturb hotel-door card with the added line, "...unless you want to join in." The glistening Box of Grey cases—which contained cuffs, several masks and a "spread the love" bar (to spread the legs), among other accessories, cost almost seven hundred pounds a pop, about $1,000 U.S.; the ad copy invited clients to "reinvent the dirty weekend." The ultra-chic models were intended to look like playmates, not like spouses of the executives who could afford these toys.[78] None of this would have been out of place in a U.S. toy store, but Selfridges!

Toys and Dominance

Let's return to chastity for a second (mentioned in Chapter 13). In a female led relationship (FLR), the ultimate expression of dominance is "forcing" your partner to wear a chastity device that locks under the testicles and covers the head of the penis, with a hole permitting urination. A key-locked device, it does not permit a full erection or penetration. The idea is that the dominant woman, or "keyholder," has complete control of her partner's sexuality, so that an orgasm for him depends entirely on her will. Submissive men find this attractive and sometimes ask their partners to put them in chastity; and, of course, dominant women may simply compel their (submissive) partner to accept the device. Yet usually, the submissive male yearns for expressions of his degraded status and of his female partner's unchallengeable will. She might express this as well by cuckolding him as he wears his device. Although not everyone's cup of tea, some couples do find this a way of refreshing their sexual relations. Women, in particular, for whom the standard sex act has started to seem jaded, may find in their flaunting of the key, dangling perhaps from a gold band around their ankle, an unfamiliar thrill. One "locked" male said, "A week or so ago, my wife said she wanted to speak to me. She completely freaked me out when she told me what she wanted, an FLR and chastity play.... The fear of having to trust her and obey without question became arousing and appealing."[79]

Introduced in the 1990s, a number of commercial devices were on the market by the decade's end, including The Cell, available in 1997 from Fantigo.[80] Chastity cages now abound. Lovehoney offers 41 different male chastity devices, ranging from a simple steel-ribbed urethral dilator to the complex CB-6000 Designer Chronic Male Chastity Cage Kit. Nikki Yates, a spokesperson for A.L. Enterprises, explained that the CB-X series is also aimed at "the more vanilla market...couples looking to spice things up for a few hours or a weekend of tease play."[81] Yet even in this area, it is the woman who applies the cock cage to the man. It is she who is dominant.

But look out, slaves revolt! Mr. Feet, whose keyholder has imposed on him the Stockroom's Houdini Cock Cuff, shares, "I have found that when totally relaxed... while soaking in a warm bath, that I can slip my penis back out of the tube and that I could stroke it if I wanted to. The penis could then be reinserted back into the tube without discovery."[82] But the keyholder monitors his baths to prevent just this kind of trickery.

There are new ways male tops can control female bottoms. Here's one: Jimmy Jane's wearable vibrator, introduced in 2015, that your partner can control remotely. So that, say, when you're out having dinner, the top might switch it on at a given moment and vibrate the bottom remotely to orgasm as she consumes her salad.[83] (Remote-controlled "cybertoys for cybersex" go back to 2000,[84] but this wearable vibrator came later.)

Primed by women and their new toys, men, in turn, began bringing new gadgets into the bedroom. Said Sunny Rogers, marketing director at Doc Johnson, "Men are definitely using more sexual aids than ever before. Much of this is due to women bringing sexual aids into the bedroom via inspiration from *Fifty Shades of Grey* and other media influences." What toys? Male enhancement pills and vacuum-geared penis pumps. "It's all about boosting a man's confidence," said Jeff Bolanos, president of Beamonstar Products.[85] Isn't this interesting? Men need toys to build self-confidence, women use them to emphasize control.

Toys Go to House Parties

Starting in the 1980s, an important marketing channel for toys was adult home sales, which meant arranging for local sales reps, or "consultants" who were independent contractors, to stage house parties mostly for women (about 20 percent of the parties in one sales program included men). "Women who might have sold kitchenware 20 years ago," said journalist Joanne Cachapero, "are watching their friends fill out order blanks for vibrators, lubricants and even bondage gear. Home parties represent the fastest-growing area of the adult toy industry."[86] One of the heavy hitters, Pure Romance, began in Patty Brisben's Cincinnati basement in 1993 as Slumber Parties (name changed in 2004) and, by 2014, its 25,000 consultants were doing $130 million in sales. The house parties, said an industry spokesperson, "offered a safe environment for women to ask questions and learn more about improving relationships, which is gauzy talk for introducing an eager but unknowing audience to sex toys, lubes, and erotic lingerie. The consultants themselves were trained by industry staff, where the saying was current, 'Like it, place an order; love it, host a party; want it all, become a consultant.'"[87]

In 2005 Tamara, owner of the Home Party Network, organized the Home Pleasure Party Plan to bring consultants together with distributors and manufacturers. She proposed a prototype party: starting with a warm-up of passing around a dildo using only one's legs in a "variation on musical chairs," then a presentation of products, explaining what each does. Need an occasion? Link your party to a performance of *The Vagina Monologues*.[88] Sophisticates may smile at these antics, yet with the tens of thousands of house parties that took place every month, adult entertainment was penetrating deep into the American heartland.

Toys Move Mainline

It was in a climate of far greater openness than decades previously that toys moved mainline. In the new millennium, women might actually mention their dildos in the company of friends and relatives, or men respond with laughter in bars when the subject of Fleshlight came up. Glenn LeBoeuf shifted in 2002 from corporate America to run operations at toy distributor Nalpac. He later reflected, "People, on the whole, seem much more open about exploring their sexuality than ever before. It's much more acceptable to discuss and become educated on the goods we sell. I can remember when the average person didn't want to even admit to masturbating; now it's okay to talk about what to use to enhance the experience!"[89]

By 2015, sex toys had become a $15 billion a year business. According to the *Huffington Post*, by this time, 44 percent of women ages 18–60 had tried them.[90] "It's definitely due to exposure of the internet," said Pipedream's marketing director Brian Sofer. "People are talking about sex. Taboos are becoming less and less taboo because it's becoming more and more available to the public."[91] Instead of "novelties," the new buzz words were "pleasure products," "sexual wellness," and "intimate self-care."[92] Toys were becoming socially acceptable in situations that earlier produced mortification. Online toy wholesaler David Levine said, "Back when I started, all my mother cared about was that she couldn't brag about me to her friends. Now when she tells people what I do, everyone gets excited."[93]

The core of the toy story is not the advances in technology that make possible Fleshlight; it is, as Gram Ponante at *XBIZ* puts it, "the breakdown of shame."[76] Thanks to Facebook and other social media, people are no longer embarrassed to say "I use a vibrator." The toy company OhMiBod makes a special thong that will "transmit ambient club music directly to (the wearer's) clitoris. Hands can't do that," says co-founder Suki Dunham. This is the story of the last thirty years. The entire body becomes sexualized; people acquire thrilling new psychic roles as tops and bottoms; and toys pass from novelties to essentials for the expression of desire.

Chapter 18:
Camming

"When a man talks dirty to a woman, it's sexual harassment.
When a woman talks dirty to a man, it's $2.99 a minute." [1]

BLUSH BOSS, 2014

S tormy Daniels on webcam is something else. Naked, she lasciviously licks a glass dildo then masturbates herself with it. Meanwhile, a surfer, off camera, is having a conversation with her. "I thought I was the tease!" she joshes him. [2]

In the last thirty years, the male surfers have started to evolve from consumers to participants. Becoming a player with someone like Stormy—and not just the holder of a Visa card—would be the dream of many men. They feel so involved at every level in porn, that actually knowing the model and interacting with her, if only in cyberspace, would surely be the next step. Said Quentin Boyer, director of public relations for the company Pink Visual, "More than any other development, the expansion of the live feed and live chat markets gave the web something that the offline adult industry couldn't offer: the ability to interface directly and in real-time with the model the customer was viewing." [3]

Webcamming was the culmination of a development long in the making. The industry began in the 1960s and 70s with girlie magazines and toys. Both forms were low in interactivity and in what scholars call "media richness," or psychological involvement. Over the years, the various offerings become steadily higher in interactivity: phone sex and chat rooms, then DVDs, cable TV, and webstreaming video. The *nec plus ultra* of interactivity was live, interactive web-based camming filled with back-and-forth in the form of private chats, and psychologically hugely engaging for the client. [4]

Webcamming was, thus, a step the industry badly needed because the website behind a paywall was becoming unprofitable: too much free competition. Camming was a big piece of the industry's financial future. Gary Jackson, at CCBill, the biz equivalent of Visa, said in 2013, "Cams, dating, hook-up, social networking—all have been storming the industry. The paysites and content producers which are leveraging these connections...are the ones making more money."[5] In 2014, industry media specialist Kate Darling at MIT added, "The largest and most lucrative business model in the industry today is live camera shows." The live experience could not be pirated, and the clients especially liked the highly lucrative one-on-one sessions with the models, not wishing to share with other men, because of an "'oh, this is my girlfriend' type feeling."[6] In 2012, the revenues from webcamming in the U.S. were estimated to be about $2 billion a year, compared to an estimated $2.8 billion for online porn, a figure from a couple of years earlier.[7]

The Rise of Webcamming

Webcamming began, in a sense, with phone sex: reaching a recording or a live model by dialing a number. It is an interesting measure of how starved the male population was for sex of any kind that when, in 1983, the porn magazine *High Society* opened up the first "free phone sex" lines, the lines were jammed with hundreds of thousands of calls a day. Surfers got a breathless 57-second recording: "Hi, my name's Lori and I'm touching myself...." Gloria Leonard was the titular head of the magazine, but Carl Ruderman was the publisher, and the huge boost in circulation and profits from "free phone sex" on AT&T's 976 multi-call lines motivated imitators far and wide. Thus, electronically mediated live or recorded sex really began with *High Society*.[8] Phone sex experienced its own swift rise and fall, and by the late-1990s, was overtaken by webcamming.

Live feeds and chats date back to the mid-1990s. The first adult cam site was probably JenniCam, launched in 1996 as a look into Jenni's (Jennifer Ringley) daily life in a dorm room, including her sex life.[9] In 1996 as well, a then-small company, Video Secrets, began direct communication with models in what was called "live video chat." Said co-founder Chuck Tsiamis, "There are a lot of people who live really isolated lives out there. You'd be amazed. Half of the chat sessions that go on Flirt4Free aren't even about sex. They are about life. People filling a void for another person who is lonely." It was this void that live video chat, later called "webcamming," set out to fill. In 2001, Video Secrets got a huge boost when they lined up Jenna Jameson to do live chat. By 2004, they had over 1,000 models—on the guy side, 400-500—at twenty studios worldwide.[10]

In 1997, porn entrepreneurs Danny and Carol Cox organized in Montreal a highly successful cam ring, or aggregation of individual cam sites. They started updating Carol's site with new pics of Carol, launched under the name of Carolcox.com (RoseCam Network). It pioneered the idea of aggregating amateur sites, becoming the largest, most profitable such ring on the internet. Danny quit work to run it full time because they were making "ridiculous money," so much, in fact, that the Coxes began wintering in the Caribbean, summering back home in Montreal.[11] (They gave it up in 2003 after many other me-too sites jumped in.[12])

Large webcam networks arose, made possible by the advent of broadband, which could deliver much faster chat connection speeds, and larger video sizes and frame rates than the old dial-up. By 2007, Video Secrets was hosting sites, among others, for Playboylive.com and Falconlive.com. The sites were completely customized to look as though you were at a Playboy (straight) or Falcon (gay) site, but the "white-label" host was Video Secrets, which also hosted many of the camgirls and camboys. The talent was supplied by the 400 studios of independent contractors, or "broadcasters," with managers located worldwide from the Czech Republic and Russia to Canada and the U.S. Like Playboy and Falcon, the studios could market on their own network (hosted by Video Secrets), or on a Video Secrets network called Flirt4Free. VS did not provide "social networking," an introduction service for members. "We are more like a strip club," said Gregory Clayman, CEO of VS Media. "You see a performer, you have some fun and then you go home."[13]

By the new millennium, two polar types of webcam models had evolved. In one type, the models were pursuing a "total business package," as B.K. Boleyn, who ran an agency for webcam models, called it. The total package women were porn stars and had business models with a number of income streams, of which chat was only one.

At the opposite end of the spectrum were the non-porn star models who were working the high end and not seeking the limelight. "Full time, they work a small pool of high-paying clients in one-on-one shows, similar to a high-class online escort but without the legal issues." Jesse Quinn was an example. She said in 2013, "My most generous and loyal regs [regulars] visit me for personalized, unique experiences that could never occur in a chat room filled with lurkers and other participants. There are a ton of men out there willing to pay for that, despite Chaturbate [a big cam ring].... I essentially sell my undivided attention."[14] Five dollars a minute was the going rate in 2010. This type, said Boleyn, was five-to-ten times more numerous than the total package models.

Between these two opposite types were the webcammers on the rest of the spectrum, "either chipping away at it part time or working in a sweatshop studio."[15] Two dollars a minute was their typical rate. And in this vast middle mass would be the college students and other amateurs who dabbled in camming.

What the Clients Got Out of It

Q: "What can a pretty girl earn on Chaturbate?"

A: "Don't take it personal but just a pretty girl is worthless. All about personality." [16]

The advice sheet that Chaturbate, an aggregator of camsites, sent its models counseled, "Be yourself. Your personality is as important (maybe even more important) than your looks."[17] The successful webcam girls offered a personality that men could feel comfortable with and confide in. Looks were decidedly secondary. "The webcam business is one where you really need to create an emotional connection with the user," said "tripleXdigital" in 2012 to the *XBIZ* chatboard. "Guys come back when they perceive that they have formed a relationship with the model on the other side of their screen. The best way to make this connection is via social media sites like Facebook and Twitter. Keep communication open and consistent. Share intimate messages about your everyday life."[18]

You had to know how to deliver a kind of psychotherapy. Ben Clark of Webstream. co.uk told *XBIZ*, "We have models using our software that have clients coming back every single day. Why? Because they fulfill the client's needs by offering something he cannot get at home....We have models that don't even offer a sexual service, they simply offer a sympathetic ear, a kind of therapy the client can't get elsewhere."[19] "2Muchmark," who ran cam sites, told the *XBIZ* chatboard in 2014, "Speaking from experience, we see our own chat customers spending a lot more time and money with chat models who are 'just chatting', instead of jamming objects into their bodies."[20] Czech model Kyla Cole said about camming for her international following, "I do the chats every week and because I have fans that do not want me to get naked on the cam, we just chat. They have the opportunity to talk to me in real time and they make use of it."[21]

Blush Boss, a woman operating a cam network, added to the abovementioned post by Jessica Quinn, "We had a girl that worked for us almost three years, she was intelligent, quick witted, stunningly beautiful and kinky as hell in her real life, but the majority of her private shows were all talk. She was fantastic at continuing the conversation, so much so she would even lose track of time. Her work shift was seven hours and she was in private 87% of those hours every day, six days a week.... She hasn't cammed in two years now and several of her former clients are still trying to find her, desperate for a reconnection. They can get porn or sex anywhere, they can't get that connection anywhere."[22]

When Jesse Quinn read Blush Boss's post she replied—and it is a reply that points to porn's future, "There's as much if not more money in words than there is in pussy/tits/ass."

What Industry Got Out of It

Webcamming was probably the most successful business model in adult. Chuck Tsiamis said in 2004 that a surfer might easily spend $100,000 a year in chat. "Per capita no one spends as much money as a live chat customer on the Internet."[23] Clinton Cox, the organizer of Camming Con, a dedicated trade show, said in 2014, "The numbers are insane." He had seen a single model's free chat room with more than 7,000 viewers at one time. He estimated that a 15-minute snapshot of the cam space would show "about 15,000 models online with 250K fans."[24]

By 2015, live webcam revenues accounted for as much as a third of adult online total income, running into the billions of dollars. *Playboy* had a huge aggregation business and *Penthouse*'s own webcamming was tied to the giant AdultFriendFinder dating service (separating from it in 2016).

How does the math work out? Jack Avalanche at Cherry Pimps produces on the aggregator Streamate live shows for 40 to 60 porn stars a month, "and if you imagine each girl averaging 100,000-200,000 Twitter followers, then you can see us reaching a pretty diverse group of porn fans."[25] This is a powerful reach. (Bear in mind that Streamate, a huge operation, had over 1,500 active sites and featured camgirls from such big industry names as MindGeek and FreeOnes.) There are cam sites, such as LiveJasmin.com founded in 2001 (with its 40 million visitors a day), that globally can stream thousands of feeds simultaneously; its owner, Gyorgi

Gattyán, is said to be "Hungary's richest man."[26] CEO Karoly Papp said that, by 2015, the site had over 50,000 active models, and two million registered.[27]

For the operators of cam networks, the big downside was the hairpulling unreliability of many of the camgirls themselves. The owner of Media Originals, who went on the boards under the handle "Desperate Amateurs," said this was the reason she had kept her company out of webcamming: "I have the worst time getting them to show up for shoots. I can't imagine trying to get them to show up for cam shows.... Some work from home while others work from a location set up for this. Either way, the reliability factor here would be dismal."[28]

What the Models Got Out of It

After years of misogyny, many models were just smoking about the patronizing and contemptuous treatment they frequently were the butt of. In 2009, Samantha38G fumed on an industry chatboard, "After 13 years in the adult biz, we are just disposable sluts. Dealing with owners & power players of the porn industry the conversation I hear over & over again is what stupid whores we all are. There is no respect for the talent at all. Most just want to use us sexually & financially." But now, continued Samantha, the worm was turning. Social media meant the models could get their own brand out, and camming meant their political independence. "Porn stars due to their social media are becoming major power players of traffic that is needed for sales. Because ya'll have ignored me, told me I was too old, too fat, I went out & did things on my own.... Fact is, girls who went out & do their own sites, their own brand don't need ya'll anymore."[29]

Webcammers answered to no one. Here is Aria DeLaunay in 2011: "I don't do 'PORN'! But I'm a webcam model. And I love the freedom. Being my own boss. Working from home. I like the money. I've always been very open sexually. I enjoy the fun and attention. It's good times. Jobs outside the adult industry end up boring the hell out of me (and I've done everything from car sales to medical industry). It's really that simple."[30]

But camming attracted not just models and strippers. By the 2000s, the money was seeping out of pro-domination. A surplus of amateur dommes, greater willingness of partners to dominate, and the easy availability of domme images on the internet all conspired to make the traditional business model of domination unviable. A lateral move to camming was an obvious strategy for many dommes. Said Boston domme Vendetta in 2005, "Every pro-domme I know—which is probably at least 100—is also doing phone or cam work...because it's incredibly difficult now to support yourself being only a pro-domme."[31]

The intrinsic power of camming was such that, once sex workers in other areas discovered it, they did not return to their previous jobs. This appeal is why the idea of installing cams in strip clubs never really caught on. Once the dancers discovered camming, they were gone. Said cam model Daisy Destin in 2015, who came to industry three years earlier on the cam aggregator Streamate, "I know a few fellow camgirls who used to be dancers in clubs, until they discovered camming. Now they are full time camgirls and tell me that they make way more money camming and don't have to leave their house.... I do know that if I was a club owner, I wouldn't want my best dancers to quit so they can stay home camming. Introducing them to camming would be like introducing them to your competition." (In fairness, as another observer pointed out, "There are a lot of strippers who don't want to be on the internet. They like the anonymity of working in a club.... Put her on the internet...someone screen-captures the cam feed, then it's sent to her mom on Facebook.")[32]

Unemployed models discovered they could set up their own sites online taking, as Stephen Yagielowicz at *XBIZ* said, "their careers into their own hands, leveraging social media to promote the cam shows and other revenue streams, such as feature dancing, escorting, whatever. Live camming became the Millennial lifestyle."[33] From the viewpoint of camgirls, the great advantage of online camming was that you didn't have to live in Porn Valley, or Barcelona, or any of the other growing international porn hubs. You could webcam from, literally, any place on the globe—although good teeth and (almost) unaccented English would be auguries of success in the Atlantic community.

As the models gained confidence, they broke free of the big aggregators and set up their own Facetime and PayPal funded Skype videochats to keep more of the fees themselves. All this could be done on a smartphone via a high-speed internet connection. This was no longer the porn world of Reuben Sturman.

As well, the money in camming could be terrific. Leo Radvinsky, who debuted in 2004 one of the largest sites, MyFreeCams, said, "There are literally hundreds, if not thousands of models that have made $100,000 a year or even more on our site. Some of our top models will make over $200,000 a year."[34] Right. But the average cam model made somewhat less. One informed guesstimate was $60,000 a year, and "working their asses off for it...way more hours than most people...want to put in with camming."[35] Those dollars flowed through the site. But a number of camgirls got extra payments via Western Union for private sessions or nudity, so the money was not to be sneezed at.

How do you get started as a webcam girl? In 1999, Lori Anderson and her husband were sitting on the couch one evening watching a *20/20* special on webcamming.

"Hey, would you do that?" asked her husband.

"In the privacy of my own bedroom? For sure!"

Lori Anderson started out just being in front of the webcam. "Almost overnight, I was a cover girl for some of the more popular webcam companies on the Internet." Soon she had more than 8,000 paying customers. They started asking her to build a website of her own. She based hers on the micro-niches her customers were requesting. Then, "We started our affiliate program LotzaDollars.com with these sites and built up from there."[36]

The models could do "voyeur camming" from home. Naughty Allie began a 24/7 site in 2003. She offered five live sex sessions a week plus 24/7 coverage with four different cameras of whatever she happened to be doing at home at the time. Members could also email her.

Q: "Would you say you're an exhibitionist?"

A: "Without a doubt. I never miss an opportunity to get naked. I don't think anyone could have a site like mine with all the live cams and everything if they weren't truly an exhibitionist at heart.... It really gets me off having sex on a live cam knowing that there are literally hundred of people watching me."

These voyeur cams are such a departure from the past. We follow Allie from the shower into the bedroom: "I take an hour off of work and fuck myself senseless."[37]

Camming thus shifted power from the market makers to the models. As *The New York Times* noted in May 2018, "The rise of webcam work has opened up a style of performance that can be totally controlled by the model in her bedroom."[38] The demoralizing condescension of the men in industry ceded to the earnest supplications of men astonished to be in direct personal contact with these often gorgeous women: "Please take off your bra."

Chapter 19:
Black Porn

B lack performers have always had to fight the same prejudices that existed elsewhere in American society. When (white) porn star Ashley Moore was interviewed in 2003, she was asked, "Are your parents aware of your profession?" Yeah, her mom knew, and she had just told her dad. But there was a potential problem: "I don't know how my dad would take my sucking black cock."[1]

After decades of "goona goona" films, in which blacks were portrayed as lower orders of life, the pseudo-anthropological *Africanus Sexualis (Black is Beautiful)* in 1970 offered the first moderately decent representation, although the film did dwell on the "strange and erotic practices" of black men. Although Matt Cimber is often given credit for the title, it was produced by Cimber's partner Marvin Miller. The title initiated black hardcore. (This is the Miller of *Miller v California* in 1973—see Chapter 4.)

Melvin Van Peebles, who was African-American, wrote, directed, and starred in *Sweet Sweetback's Baadasssss Song* in 1971. This film really begins black porn cinema.

An early prominent black actor in porn was Desiree West, who at age 20 performed in 1974 in *The Pleasure Masters: Kikko & Lil*, directed by Alex de Renzy. She is thought the first black "movie star," departing from the pattern of black actors as "nameless bodies."[2] Yet *The Pleasure Masters* was overshadowed in fame by the more widely circulated *Lialeh*, a Barron Bercovichy film, also in 1974, set in New York and starring Jennifer Leigh in the title role and Lawrence Pertillar as Arlo. "Pink on the inside, black on the outside," read the ad copy.

Some see *Lialeh* as kicking off the "Blaxploitation" genre, yet that would ignore these earlier titles.[3]

The "big black dong" years followed, nameless black actors with supposedly massive equipment. (Even today, this remains a theme in cuckold porn: "Honey, do you mind if this huge black guy fucks me?") It is not that there were no blacks in the industry. The share of black performers in porn, in Millward's analysis of 10,000 profiles in the IADB, over the years 1981–2013 averages out to 14 percent, congruent with the proportion of blacks in the U.S. population.[4] Yet, for a long time, there were almost no blacks in *white* porn except for those who could be identified as having exceptionally large organs in order to create the thrill of transgression. In general, interracial was taboo (first violated when Johnny Keyes bedded Marilyn Chambers in *Behind the Green Door* in 1972). Interracial commanded a special premium. You, as a model, would have to be well rewarded to have sex with a black man; it was otherwise considered so degrading. (Many models were from small towns in the South and brought that particular set of prejudices with them.)

What was available for blacks often stank. The quality was poor, the audience treated with the back of the hand. "The problem with a lot of black product," said Tony Santoro of the production company Black Ice, "is that people weren't putting in a lot of effort. The technical quality was piss-poor, and the action was lazy. Real porn lovers are not going to be satisfied with cheap shit."[5] Thus, a market lay fallow.

Interracial continued its uptick with the Dark Brothers' *Let Me Tell Ya 'Bout White Chicks* in 1984 and *Let Me Tell Ya 'Bout Black Chicks* in 1985. The Dark Brothers were white, and they were not brothers. Greg Dark (Gregory Hippolyte Brown) teamed with Walter Gernert in telling the story "from a pimp and hustler point of view...about the joys of jumping white pussy," as one journalist said.[6] Gernert and Russ Hampshire ran Video Corporation of America—VCA. This was one approach to interracial film; as journalist Susie Bright put it in 1987, "We're the people momma told you about."[7] (Quite unrelated to interracial, the Dark Brothers' *New Wave Hookers* [1985], starring Traci Lords, became one of the best selling videos of all time and a huge embarrassment when it was discovered she was underage.)

The era of serious black porn was kicked off in 1988 when Sean Michaels, born Andre Allen in Brooklyn, appeared at age 30 in *Hate to See You Go*; Michaels would act in over a thousand further titles. His directorial career debuted in 1991 with *Girlz n Da Hood*, and his stint as a producer, soon to have his own company, began with *You Go Girl* in 1995. Michaels performed in much interracial filming and showed a marked affinity for anal.

Gonzo became the main theme that carried black porn forward in the 90s. In 1993, the prolific director Ed Powers (Mark Arnold Krinsky), 39—who is white and from Brooklyn—riffed on the interracial theme with a hugely popular series of gonzo titles called *Black Dirty Debutantes,* starring (with the exception of himself) an otherwise black cast. Powers was known for hundreds of *Debutante* films of various ilks, and the 1993 interracial title remained a one-off until he returned to the genre in 1995 with *More Black Dirty Debutantes,* filming thirty-two of them, the last in 2001. These films were an enormous venue for black talent. Said Jake Steed of the *Black Debutante* series at a 1999 meeting on black porn, "Almost every black man in America watched those movies." There was once scene in particular: "I did a scene with Janet Jacme, one scene, and more people have probably watched that scene than if I had done 300 movies. People watch that." And there was money to be made. Steed: "Then the same people who denied any kind of work or respect as far as black talent jumped on the bandwagon. What you see is a bunch of white guys trying to commercialize the new untapped market of blacks...."[8]

The breakthrough for blacks that Sean Michaels had begun widened with such figures as Mr. Marcus (Jesse Spencer), who entered the industry in 1994. Referring to the white-inspired black penis years, "I hate that shit," said Mr. Marcus in an interview. He particularly scorned the Cambria List of topics that porners were to avoid (see Chapter 4). Mr. Marcus later said in an interview, "The part that really struck a nerve with me was down on the list, it said 'No black men with white women.' Here I am, a good five to six years in the business, and I was upset because that was a lot of my work!" Indeed, Mr. Marcus said that he got into the industry because of the women. He had been driving a truck, "hungry," as Gaffin Harris said, "for porno-chick nookie." Mr. Marcus himself said, "I would go into these bookstores, pick up a magazine and I'm saying 'The bitch look good. She's fine.' I'm looking at the pictures and thinking, 'How do I get into this'? I mean, find some phone number, find some people. I want to see them. I want to be part of this."[9]

Among other male models, Mr. Marcus was himself something of a paragon, known for his "mental toughness" in blocking out such distractions as "lights, cameras and female body odor" (as another woodsman put it) in order to stay on set for 12 hours at a stretch. (Mr. Marcus also said that meeting the girl in advance for a nice conversation was essential to the chemistry and avoided what was known in the industry as a "hate fuck.")[10]

Just as white models were on the receiving end of male abuse scripted and unscripted, black woodsmen suffered from white models. Mr. Marcus: "The way they wanted it done is the girl would call the black guy she was having sex with 'nigger.' And I was like, 'Nah...she ain't gonna call me that.'"[11]

Mr. Marcus joined Sean Michaels as one of the first big black directors; Marcus's fan base were blacks. "When I'm on the street, I'm recognized by blacks. It's not a bunch of white guys. It's always minorities. Mexicans and blacks."[12]

But even at the abovementioned meeting in 1999, an earlier history of discrimination had left a bad taste in the mouth of black actors and directors.

Mr. Marcus: "You know the first movie I saw with a black guy in it? It was Jack Baker in an all-white movie, and he jacked off into a salad."

[laughter]

Mr. Marcus: "I was just like, why is a black man in there jacking off into a salad?"

Jake Steed: "'Cause no white girl's going to work with him."[13]

Mr. Marcus broke through this presumed stereotype in Jim Malibu's *The World's Luckiest Black Man* (1998), in which his character supposedly beds a hundred white girls. But a year later insiders were scandalized at the mere thought that Jenna Jameson might have had sex with Mr. Marcus. When queried by *AVN* editor Gene Ross about Jenna "doing renegade sex scenes," Joy King at Wicked found the rumor "highly unlikely." [14] As far as I know, Jenna never did have sex with Mr. Marcus.

Black female performers in particular hated this kind of dissing from the industry. When asked why she became a porn actress, India (Shamika Brown), answered that she was tired of "the negative stuff": "Dirty Black Bitch, or Yo Bitch Get On the Bus. For me, as a black woman, it's hard enough to get respect, and I wanted that respect...to show that every girl is not a ho, and every girl is not stupid. We have minds, we have thoughts, and we can come here and dominate and take over and be just as good as the blond girl...."[15] The reality for black women was that they continued for years to be victims of systematic discrimination. Diana DeVoe said in 2007, "It is accepted knowledge that a black woman in this industry will earn between 20 and 50 percent less than her white counterpart for the same scene because she is black."[16]

Mr. Marcus was determined to help make porn by black people and for black people, and in 2007, founded his own production and apparel company called

Daddy Inc. "I knew I could do this," he said, "and take the next step in my career. All my years in the business have prepared me for this moment."[17] (Mr. Marcus did blot his copybook in 2012 when he falsified a VD test result and was responsible for a small syphilis epidemic among performers. For this, he served a month in jail.[18])

Lexington Steele (Clifton Britt) began shooting adult in 1996 in New York, making a part-time move from Wall Street, where he worked as a stock broker. Two years later he relocated to Los Angeles to work full-time in the industry, initially with James Alexander at West Coast Productions (known as "the godfather of black porn"[19]), and Chris Alexander, whom Steele credits with helping him become a director. Steele revived in 2002 the *Women of Color* line that Sean Michaels had originally directed in 1994. After founding his own studio, Mercenary Pictures, in 2003, Steele had a string of black and interracial successes, including *Black Moon Risin 1* (2006), which spawned a whole series.

Jake Steed, hitherto a "fuckbeast," initiated his career as a director in 1998 with the first volume of the video series *Freaks Whoes and Flows*. It ultimately reached volume 35 in 2004 and was said to be "a must-stock for any store with black clientele, especially those who'd rather support a brother instead of throwing their money to the Man." Steed himself rapped in the ad copy for volume one, "So shake all those wack videos that was made by a buster and check out this fly shit masterminded by a hustler." The title was considered "the first widely available series to be directed and produced by a black man and targeted to a customer base within the black community."[20]

Heather Hunter was probably the first black woman to become a bona fide star. A New Yorker, she entered the biz in 1988 at 19 with her first video *Heather Hunter on Fire*. After moving to LA, she became the first black Vivid contract girl. *AVN* considered her "the best known black porn star in history.[21]

Stereotypes fell. By 1999, the stereotype was gone that said you couldn't show movies of black men having sex with white women. Director Christian Mann, who had done a lot to encourage black talent, said that the cable companies had not wanted to lose sales in the South and kept the prejudice in place. But then, "Video Team came along and broke that barrier with the help of the Adam & Eve Channel.... What they found was that the complaints that they were expecting, David Duke KKK guys calling to cancel their cable, just didn't happen."[22]

Around 2007, Hush Hush Entertainment created a distinctive internet presence with three black male contract performers: Shane Diesel as Blackzilla, Boz as

Daddy's Worst Nightmare, and Richard Mann as the Abominable Black Man. All three had DVD lines distributed by Digital Sin.[23] Shane Diesel had an "unbelievably large unit" and, for that reason, was called "Blackzilla." He fed off the stereotyping rather than challenging it: "I wanted to use all the stereotypes, pro and con of the interracial and well-endowed black guy," he said in a 2006 interview. "We're going to run with all the stereotypes and just have fun with it."[24]

Yet some stereotypes remained in place, described by scholar Jennifer Nash as the degradation of "racial fetishism."[25] First of all, lots of white *men* were riveted at the idea of black studs "gangbanging" white women. Robbie, one of the earliest webmasters, recalled his adventures with one prominent black site: "Then in 1997 I started promoting [the site] Blacks on Blondes—and of course since I had tons of traffic they gave me a user/pass and told me to use whatever I needed to make galleries.

"So I started using the most hardcore pics EVER—hot blonde bitches being gang fucked by 20 black guys in every hole. It was intense!

"And I made more sales than GOD! Up until then I had only used softcore images and had made a lot of money—but NOTHING like those Blacks on Blondes galleries I made back then."

"Dude," Robbie told another correspondent, "I was making $10,000 a month off of just running that ONE gallery per week!" [26]

Who knew the white male appetite for black gangbangs was so ravenous.

Then, the supposed potency of black males showed up in porn directed at white *women*. In the world of female sexual fantasy, "black" ranked high, number four in the list of "terms most often searched by women," compiled in 2015, with "ebony" and "big black cock" following closely behind. "Black thugs fucking raw" was up 269 percent on a year-to-year basis.[27] And, of course, there was gold in them thar' hills, on the principle, as Sean Michaels put it, "The more taboo they are, the bigger the sales."[28] James Melendy, owner of Black Market, said in 2009, "The bigger the dick, the smaller the white girl, the better. It's always been taboo, and it's always going to be a big seller."[29] Director Casey Calvert called this southern affinity for "big black cock" and white women a kind of fetish. "They want to see it. It gets their dick hard."[30]

There was a white *male* fantasy that that black women possessed an extraordinary potency. David Christopher (Bernard Cohen) portrayed black actresses as dominant over submissive white guys in a long series of films, beginning in the early 1980s, with *Hot Fudge* (1983) and *Black Angels* (1985), with himself featured in many videos as Pussyman. The black actresses then became even more dominant over Pussyman later on, with such titles as *Worship My Giant Black Ass* in 2012. The synopsis says, "White boy humiliation, extreme toilet facesitting!...They totally degrade and humiliate him to the ultimate."[31] Christopher said in an interview, "The Pussyman brand has not really gone away. It's just evolved into females using the power of their sexuality to gain pleasure from the male." Film critic Linda Williams remarked of this brew of stereotypes, "All depictions of interracial lust develop out of the relations of inequality that have prevailed between the races. They grow out of a history that has covertly permitted the white man's sexual access to black women and violently forbidden the black man's access to white women. The racist and sexist assumptions that underlie such unequal access to sex have generated forms of pornographic sexual fantasy with an important purchase on the American sexual imagination."[32]

"Racism flows through porn," said Luke Ford in 1999. He opined that "No black ranks among the industry's one hundred all-time leading performers."[33] Ford's harsh judgment would have to be modified today. Industry meetings are now filled with distinguished black performers and directors. Yet, even so, there are underlying racial currents that still flow strong. Asa Akira, who is Asian, said in 2014, "When I do a scene with a white guy, that's not considered interracial. But when I do a scene with a black guy, that's considered interracial. Which is the weirdest thing ever. But that's just the way it is." (She said, if you wait a while before doing your first interracial, you get a lot more money, maybe even a box cover. "Akira finally gives in!")[34]

Just as a footnote, did black male talent in fact have larger organs than white? Common as the fantasies of white females about blacks are, in fact, black and white Americans have exactly the same average erect penis size: 5.6 inches (reported self measurement).[35] There has never, to my knowledge, been a study comparing directly erect black penis size vs. white (the university ethics committee would go crazy over such a proposal).[36] But there is some testimony. In 1991, Johnny Steele of *AVN* asked Dominique Simone, a young Afro-American porn star from Atlanta, "C'mon, you mean to tell me that black men as a rule don't have bigger cocks than white men?"

Simone reflected for a moment and then said, "No, I don't think so. And I don't think they're better lovers."[37]

Millions of dollars of white money viewing black talent are riding on Simone being wrong.

Chapter 20:
Porn Today

For most couples, the devalorization of sex that characterized the 1960s is pretty well a thing of the past. If they flatline sexually, increasingly they break up, and that is that.[1] There is no doubt that porn has played a role in this kind of sexual activation, and those who oppose porn understand exactly what is happening. It *is* destabilizing. No doubt. But in a free society, individuals have the ability to choose desire, and to act on it. To insist that they don't, and that they must go to church on Sunday morning, or whatever, would be an act of scandalous condescension.

In a sense, porn has come full circle. It started out in the 1970s as feature-length movies that women could enjoy. Gonzo then took the industry in an entirely different direction that appealed to frenetic male masturbation. With the arrest of gonzo, the industry once again is returning to sex-positive, female-friendly full-length features. This promises to be the wave of the future. Women now have the possibility to choose desire, just as men have done for decades.

The New Porn

How porn has changed since the 1960s and early 70s! Then it was mainly straightforward boy/girl vaginal penetration. Gay and lesbian porn existed but deeply underground. It was unimaginative straight intercourse, the guy wearing black socks, the young woman usually a love-summer hippie or a prostitute. Today, the main categories are niche, gonzo, and feature, none of which existed in the era of the 7-minute loops.

Consider the porn video that directors Kayden Kross and Manuel Ferrara streeted in 2015 with Carter Cruise in the starring role: *Carter Cruise Wide Open*. It featured Cruise in four sexual encounters: "a boy/girl anal with Ferrara; a girl/girl anal with Kross; a blowbang with Eric John, Chad Alva, Chad Diamond and Filthy Rich; and a D.P. [double penetration, anus and vagina] with Mick Blue and Ramon Nomar."

Kross joked afterward, "I feel like I'm growing up. Now I do anal like the real girls. We used a really cool glass dildo. It was a solid, solid scene."

Cruise herself liked this blowbang better than a previous one, "where it was more just me getting destroyed." This one was different: "For this blowbang I was very much in control."[2]

Virtually none of this existed in the 1970s. The difference between these movies and the earlier 16mm loops is unimaginable. The actors revel in one another's bodies. The set is crowded with penises; one female talent penetrates the other female talent with a strapon harness. And the sales uptake is massive. One cannot contrast sex scenes then and now without thinking that something fundamental has changed in sexuality in the course of thirty years.

Does porn change tastes, or is it swept along by them? The evidence in this book points towards porn as an active part of the story, a driver of the changes in sexuality of the last thirty years. People may not know what they are until they see it on the screen. Christian Mann, a well-known fetish director for Evil Angel who had inspired many young colleagues including Colin Rowntree, attempted in 2012 a nuanced formulation, in this case of his studio's famous butt fetishism. He said it was a "chicken vs egg conundrum." "In some cases you have fetishists searching out movies that fill their need, and in some cases you have consumers who aren't fetishists discovering fetishes in the movies of their favorite directors and finding out that they're into something. So in some cases what Evil Angel provides is a catharsis, in other cases it's a catalyst."[3]

Gonzo is declining, and what the industry is struggling to do nowadays is to stay abreast of changing sexual tastes. Who knew that tastes could change so easily, after a thousand years of stability in the missionary position. Yet change is a constant preoccupation in the bar conversations after a shoot. What is the next wave, and how can we catch the crest of it?

Couples films are on the order of the day, which is to say features that women might find appealing. These had begun with Candida Royalle in the 1980s (see

Chapter 6). But the concept gained ground in the 1990s, struggling to avoid suffocation by gonzo. In 1993, Steve Orenstein founded Wicked Pictures, targeting the couples market, as a Wicked publicist explained, "with better scripts, elaborate locales, costumes, sophisticated packaging and quality post-production"; these are manifest in Wicked's lesbian-themed *Dream Quest* (2000), starring Jenna Jameson. In the late 1990s, Michael Ninn, whose background was not in porn but in emotional connections—creating music videos for advertising agencies[4]—began turning out couples films such as *Dream Catcher* (1998) for VCA that further amplified the feature concept.[5]

Two films that debuted in 2005 were a kind of double-barreled marker for the New Porn. *Pirates*, directed by Joone for Digital Playground, cost over a million dollars to produce, and starred Jesse Jane and Carmen Luvana; it offered highjinks in the eighteenth-century West Indies. The flick had a large following among middle-class women, and, according to marketer Howard Levine, "sold 65,000 copies out the door." In some ways, *Pirates* foreshadowed the success almost ten years later of the *Fifty Shades* films. As well, in 2005, the *New Devil in Miss Jones* bowed, directed by Paul Thomas for Vivid; it, too, was a kind of marker. Jenna Jameson is the Devil, and Miss Jones plunges once again into a cauldron of erotic adventure; the film secured for Thomas the *AVN* Best Director award in 2006, becoming one of X-Rated's "Greatest Adult Movies of All Time."

These feature films were hardcore. Meanwhile, hardcore pushed softcore onto the mainline "lads mags," as frontal male nudity and dildos became increasingly acceptable. As Steve Lick, one of the guest contributors to the Mike South blog, said in 2008, "Who the fuck is actually getting off to [softcore] when there are so many other opportunities to score real porn in today's technology culture. Why watch a guy fake hump a chick wearing a skin colored patch on her vag when you can easily walk over to your computer and within 15 seconds pull up a Russian farm girl blowing the Budweiser Clydesdales?"[6]

The Industry Contracts, the Surfers Explode

Looking back, the early 2000s were a kind of golden age for porn, as writer Michael Stabile put it (who evidently didn't realize that the 1970s had also been a golden age). For him and his partner, jetting around the world on industry's dime, the five years after 2002 "were a string of Christmas mornings."[7] Then came a great contraction that began around 2007 with oversupply and accelerated with the

Great Recession of 2008. This had a devastating effect on the small producers.[8] (Webcamming, toys, and dating remained highly profitable.)

The tubesites put an end to much of Porn Valley. To attract custom, the webmasters started giving away content to the tubes, and the tubes pirated a lot as well—and, all of a sudden, porn was free! Said Bill Asher, co-chair of Vivid, in 2009, "We always said that once the Internet took off, we'd be OK. It never crossed our minds that we'd be competing with people who just give it away for free."[9] Challenged to make money under these circumstances, many studios closed; Alec Helmy, editor of *XBIZ*, estimates that the number of content providers dropped from a previous 200 to 20 in 2015. By some estimates, industry revenues contracted a full three-quarters by 2015.[10]

Thinking about a career as a performer in porn? Better not, said Porno Dan (Dan Leal), CEO of Immoral Productions, in 2016. "Opportunities for a new model are approximately 25 percent of what they were from five, six years ago. In 2007, there were approximately 200 scenes a day shot in Los Angeles. Now, there are less than 50 scenes a day."[11]

The typical porno shrank from five scenes to four. (These would be, in industry parlance, one "blow-job" and one "pussy-eating," plus two penetration scenes, one of which would probably be "reverse cowgirl.") "Most companies simply can't afford to shoot more than four scenes at full prices," said Ivan (Slava Siderman), first at Evolution Erotica, then at Porn Star Empire. "DVD sales are dying and a majority of companies have gone out of business."[12]

Paradoxically, with the worldwide popularity of porn, traffic exploded. There may be 800 million individual porn pages on the web, three-fifths in America, according to *The Economist* in 2015. MindGeek alone got 100 million visitors a day.[13] This enormous expansion of traffic means that, on the whole, the industry is more profitable today than ever. Knowledgeable insiders, who have access to data from the billing services, say there is no comparison with the pre-internet days. "To think the internet has killed porn," said Damian in 2013, "is very amusing to me."[14] The margins, however, are concentrated among a handful of major players; the mom-and-pop operations have largely fallen off the edge.

There is no such thing as a typical porn viewer. In 2000, the audience, though still heavily male (see below), was scattered across all the demographics. According to Andrew Edmond, CEO of the online data base SexTracker, "There really isn't a cross section cut through our community where we can say these people look at porn and these people don't."[15] Data from SexTracker for 2000 show that the all-important demographic of 18 to 24-year-olds amounted to 20 percent of all viewers, and the 41 to 47-year-olds were at 18 percent (those over 56 only 7 percent).

Lonely raincoaters living in cold-water flats? Forty-six percent of the SexTracker group were married. Income? Edmond said the $30-40 thousand was the most frequent group, "right in the middle of the middle class."[16] Given that porn in general tends to lean upscale, it is rather difficult to accept the argument that adult films somehow epitomize the world of "white trash."[17] It is true that many in the industry are not highly educated, but to characterize them as white trash is inaccurate and judgmental. Similarly, when newspapers are included in the shot, it is most often the *Financial Times*. The whole world of fetish and BDSM tilts very much upper-middle-class because that is where those with such tastes seem to have landed socially. (Also, the gear may be quite expensive.) On balance, the epicenter of porn is not the rusting pickup in the backyard but the bedroom of the suburban ranch house.

Other social landmarks? According to Pornhub data, the "average visit duration" worldwide was 8:56 minutes. In 2013, Americans were the slowest to respond, at 10:39 minutes, Japanese the quickest at 7:14.[18] Within each country, there was doubtless huge variation, yet the general impression is that porn viewing remained a solitary masturbatory experience and not a couples' eros fest.

Mainstreaming and Stigma

"Non-industry girls I met 20 years ago were put off and sometimes repulsed by what I do. Now, they're more likely to say 'Cool!'"[19]

RODNEY MOORE, DIRECTOR, 2013

Will porn ever join mainstream cinema, so that the present dividing line between them is erased? Said *AVN* columnist Tripp Daniels in 2003, "Porn, as a business and lifestyle, has been called up from the minors to the big leagues of entertainment." Jenna Jameson, he noted, was everywhere. Pieces on the industry routinely ran in *The New York Times* and *Variety*, and the men's magazine *Maxim* was full of it.[20]

Thus, the interpenetration of porn and mainstream became ever more complete. Producer Magnus Sullivan said in 2015, "The only thing that separates adult now from mainstream is the ability to shoot hard cock, pink and penetration.

Mainstream goes right up to the edge, and I don't think it will be long until we see hard cock."[21] Sullivan thought that, if the porn industry were to remain alive, it had to stay competitive with Hollywood in terms of full-length features such as his *Marriage 2.0* (2015), a critically acclaimed film starring Ryan Driller, India Summer, and Nina Hartley about a couple's venture into open marriage; he wrote the script and produced it with the LionReach studio.

Sullivan, a thoughtful intellectual in an industry that has plenty of smart people but few intellectuals, said that prerecorded masturbation porn was dead. Starting around 2006, the net had moved massive amounts of free content on line and one scarcely needed pay for a five-to-seven-minute stroke loop. He concluded, "The age of masturbation porn as a lucrative business is behind us, but the opportunity to redefine the role and scope of adult cinema in mainstream society is staring us right in the face." We must move to mainstream techniques—and the ensuing budgets—before mainstream moves to penetration, in other words.[22]

Yet it is unclear if "hard cock" is in the nature of the mainline beast. The moment a mainstream film includes a hardcore scene, the scene becomes the story. As Mike South said of the movie *9 ½ Weeks*, "I'm sure tons of people would have flocked to see Kim Basinger give Mickey Rourke a hardcore blowjob...but in doing so the movie would have become secondary, it would simply be known as the movie where Kim Basinger sucked a dick." Hardcore sex overpowers the story. As Orson Welles reportedly said on The Dick Cavett Show in the 1970s, "Real sex is too powerful, it's like real death."[23]

The big companies such as Vivid in Los Angeles and Private in Barcelona were becoming the backbone of a mature industry. Private became listed on the Nasdaq in 1999, not to make fundraising easier but to "create the credibility," said Berth Milton Jr. in 2006. "We saw early on that all the big companies...were looking into adult, but dealing with small companies in the basement was really not what they wanted to do."[24] Having a public stock exchange listing made one seem like a serious company. (But let's not exaggerate. In 2005, one of Private's directors at a party in Cannes was "Ionie Luvcoxxx."[25])

What were once real worries about stigma seem today vastly overblown. Melody, who joined an online payment company, said in 2013 that when the company first approached her, "I had a lot of misgivings about taking that leap. I was worried about...the clients being 'scumbags,' merchants fraudulently sending through transactions, my stellar mainstream resume being destroyed limiting future opportunities, and my own reputation at risk with friends and family." A year later, she sat down with her boss and said, "Do you remember all of those fears I had when I joined. Now looking back they all seem so silly."[26]

Another approach to mainstream is to grab their advertising. Previously, major advertisers scrupulously avoided "smut." This may be changing, given the ability of the industry to deliver huge numbers of twenty- and thirty-somethings. Veronica Vain, a former Wall-Street intern who had retained her business sense, told the online news service BuzzFeed in 2015, "The younger generation has less qualms with porn, and most companies that aren't Folgers Coffee want porn watchers to buy their shit. They want them as the recurring revenue stream. Mommy and Daddy are dying soon."[27]

Even fetish is tiptoeing towards the mainstream, but not quite there yet. The novel *Fifty Shades of Grey* plunged a toe into the water. At a symposium at the University of Southern California in 2015 on "Fifty Shades of Erotica," porn star Casey Calvert said, in the words of a reporter, "When she started doing porn, fetish work was considered the hardest, most extreme niche in the industry, but nowadays 'fetish is a romance category.'"

"Everyone is shooting fetish," she said.

At the same conference, Wicked's Jessica Drake said that she had timed her *Instructional BDSM for Beginners* to coincide with the release of the *Fifty Shades* movie.[28]

The mainstream media now discuss porn, but it is usually the business side, leaving blowbangs out. (A Google search for "blowbang" in September 2015 produced 3,800,000 hits; in the first ten screens, none were mainstream media.) Jenna Jameson and Ron Jeremy serve as the poster-persons for the mainstream media, and then the journalists segue to the porn business model. While media coverage in the 1980s and 90s was unremittingly negative, Frank Rich's cover story in *The New York Times Magazine* in 2001 has been seen as a turning point, legitimizing business coverage of porn. Joy King at Wicked said in 2006, "That article was such a defining moment for the industry because we were acknowledged as a legitimate business."[29] (Yet even *The New York Times* has not left behind its former distaste for "smut," and a piece in 2016 on industry resistance to legislation mandating condoms made snide references to female performers at the hearings wearing form-fitting dresses and stiletto heels. The piece evoked a furious open letter from performer Lorelei Lee: "When we are fighting for our bodily safety, this dismissal of our humanity by a journalist amplifies our daily risk of harm.... We are not a parade. We are a battalion, and we are fighting for our lives."[30]) Thus, journalistic condescension infected even a business story.

But more than business is now in play. "Things are definitely moving," said Wicked's Steve Orenstein in 2000. "The mainstream and the adult side of the business are meeting somewhere in the middle." Wicked's rival Vivid had started to target couples and women with movies that are, as one report said, "nasty but romantic at the same time."

What was driving the train away from gonzo and towards the couples market? "Women," said Steve Hirsch at Vivid. "The business has grown because women now play a major role in front of the camera and behind the scenes."[31]

Women, eh?

Where Does the Future Lie? The Women's Market

"I love porn.... I've become increasingly seduced by its gushing celebration of the human body in all its variety; its capacity for pleasure beyond the bounds of moral, missionary stricture; and the fantasy outlet it provides."[32]

NICHI HODGSON, JOURNALIST, 2014

How paradoxical that women should turn out to be one of the heroes of the porn story, given that viewing pornography was, for decades and decades, just about the last thing any woman would do. Before understanding the cycle of ovulation around 1900, women had little interest in increasing the sexual ardor of men—because they could get pregnant at any time. Advances in birth control during the first half of the twentieth century lessened this risk somewhat, and the discovery of the Pill in 1962 virtually abolished it. The impact of the Pill was to open women up to the same kinds of sexual experiences that men had been having since the dawn of time. Quite coincidentally, the nature of those experiences began to change in the 1970s. That is the subject of the present book. But it means that women were able to participate in all this new sexual innovation on an equal footing with men, and today, younger women view porn almost as frequently as younger men.

Women as Producers of Porn

Since the 1980s, women have made steady progress in directing adult features. The concept of a female director is no longer an anomaly. Angie Rowntree, who in 1999 created Sssh.com, a major pro-porn feminist website, said in an interview in 2015, "Why should we expect a feminist born in 1990 to have the same perspective as one born in 1940?" She said of a feminist porn film, "It would emphasize mutual pleasure between performers, depict real intimacy and connection. So much of the time in porn, there's no smiling, no having fun. To me, I like to know the performers are enjoying themselves, which is about more than orgasms and climaxing."[33]

Feminist porn demanded to be recognized, and in 2006 Carlyle Jansen, owner of the Toronto adult toy store Good for Her, and Lorraine Hewitt, a burlesque performer with the stage name CoCo La Crème, founded the Feminist Porn Awards, with the slogan, "Mild to wild, straight to queer, smart sexy films for everybody." In 2013, Tristan Taormina, editor of *The Feminist Porn Book* that had just appeared,[34] began coordinating a Feminist Porn Conference linked to the awards. The program highlighted for the media indie productions that validated sex-positive adult entertainment, and offered the winners statuettes in the shape of a butt plug. (This may have been Taormina's idea.)

By 2016, women had become prominent producers of porn. Evil Angel hired a whole raft of female directors for whom dominance was a big note: Aiden Starr, Francesca Lé and Dana Vespoli. The common denominator here, in the words of an *XBIZ* journalist, was that "women have taken the opportunity to control their place in the adult industry without the persistent stigma of victimization.... Vespoli's primary interests are themes of gender and power transgression." [35]

In 2016, industry veteran Kelly Holland, previously the president of the Penthouse Broadcasting division, purchased Penthouse Entertainment, the parent of the Penthouse empire (which, alas, went bankrupt in 2018). She thus became the first woman solely to own a mainline adult magazine and media network. (Gloria Leonard had been the publisher of the magazine *High Society* but not the owner.)[36]

Women as Consumers of Porn

As consumers, there had been no women among the raincoaters in the Pussycat-style adult theaters. Porn in the early days was a male affair. Yet there was no intrinsic reason women would not be interested in porn. It is, after all, a gateway to expanded sexuality. And as soon as the locus shifted from the Pussycat to the living room, women begin viewing porn in significant numbers. Director Anthony Spinelli told *AVN* in 1987, "I was at a video store in Oak Park, Illinois, and it was packed. The women were picking out the shows, and the old man is standing there, ready with the credit card. It was incredible, yet there it is."[37]

That video store was ground zero for women watching porn. The number of women viewers began creeping up in the 1980s and after, when watching moved out of the sleazy art houses and into the privacy of the home. A survey in 1995 found that, of 500 general video stores, women alone counted for only 3 percent of the clients, women with men for another 19 percent.[38] But then, things started to change. Anecdotally, in 2000, Larry Flynt reported women shoppers crowding into his new upscale Hustler Hollywood sex emporium on Sunset Boulevard: "That's the thing to getting people in—you make them feel they're in a Neiman Marcus or Barnes & Noble. All of a sudden, it's not dirty anymore."[39]

Yet patronizing an adult store required a public appearance. In the privacy of one's living room, there were more female viewers. In 1998, Carla Paterson founded Purve, a pay website devoted to heterosexual women. "When I started this, I couldn't believe that no one had targeted adult material at women," she said in an interview. By 1999 there were, she said, about a hundred websites for women, up from three the year previously.[40] A 1999 survey of internet porn viewers found that 17 percent of them were women—two-thirds of them between ages 18 and 34.[41] Comscore Media Metrix, an internet research firm, found in January 2004, that 42 percent of all visitors were women, the highest rates being among women ages 18 to 24. Samantha Lewis, president of the DVD-company Digital Playground, said in February 2004 that "women account for 40 percent of retail sales of Digital's movies, double what it was just two years ago. At trade shows... half the fans are women, compared to maybe 10 percent five years ago."[42] An *Elle/*MSNBC poll in February 2004 found that, among those interested in computer dating, 75 percent of the men and 41 percent of the women had viewed "erotic images" online.[43] When the online website Tumblr, owned by Yahoo, checked its demographics in 2016, of the users ages 18 to 25, "men and women composed equal parts."[44] These figures suggest that the gender gap in porn is fast diminishing.

The first wave of female viewers arose in the 1980s (see Chapter 3). What fed a second wave of female viewers was the pushback against gonzo among women in industry and among viewers. It began when Andreas Hronopoulos established the studio SoCal Cash in San Diego in 2001, changing its name to

Naughty America in 2004. The guiding principle was "female-produced adult entertainment." Their third film, *My Friend's Hot Mom* (2004), initiated a long series under that title aimed at the MILF, or cougar, market. An early star was Vicky Vette. Ira Levine said of the company, "If a porn company could rightly be termed wholesome, Naughty America would be the one. You won't see anything shocking or disturbing in any of their releases, but you will see a kind of 'Desperate Housewives Do Dallas' style throughout the entire line. They know what mildly adventurous married suburbanites want to see, and that's what they give them." Levine noted that Naughty America hopped early on the MILF craze. "Their boomer audience grew up on *The Graduate* and was ripe for the idea of the hot mom next door."[45] It was a sort of "Ozzie and Harriet meet Jenna Jameson" market space, in other words, or, as company production manager Laura D put it in 2006, "hardcore vanilla...the kind of thing any midwestern housewife would be fantasizing about."[46]

Meanwhile, the lesbian market was widening, including straight women aroused by lesbian sex: Pornhub's 2014 survey of its viewership found that women were 132 percent more likely than men to search for "lesbian"[47]). Girlfriends Films big line, *Women Seeking Women*, was launched in 2002 and sat at number 122 by 2015 (see Chapter 16). In 2005, veteran producer and director Kelly Holland (see above; earlier Toni English), then at Chick Media, created the video series *My Sex Therapist*. It was one of the studio's four new lines that "will target the women's market," said Holland, "an area which has been overlooked by adult producers and distributors who have failed to provide products that are tailored to the tastes and sexual sensibilities of women." [48]

Maybe it was Naughty America, Girlfriends Films, or *Fifty Shades of Grey* that battered open the door, but somewhere around the beginning of the new century, it became acceptable for women actually to consume porn. As we have seen, in 1999, producer Angie Rowntree, co-owner of Wasteland, a BDSM production company, founded Sssh.com, a website featuring "porn for women by women." It is now the oldest current female porn site. Membership in the site, says Rowntree, has been increasing steadily.[49] It would be tedious to enumerate the many microsurveys that show young women downloading porn, but to illustrate: In 2008, a sample of 813 graduate and undergraduate students at six college sites across the U.S. (including Brigham Young University in Provo, Utah) were surveyed about porn viewing; 49 percent of the young women "agree[d] that viewing pornography is acceptable" (and two-thirds of the young men), and 31 percent of the women said that they used pornography (87 percent of the men).[50] No recent study of which I am aware has ever demonstrated that young women are overwhelmingly against porn and do not view it!

Then with *Fifty Shades of Grey*, women practically leapt into porn, especially the non-vanilla variety. John Stagliano's Evil Angel had long been the go-to address for kink, and Stagliano said in 2015, "The success of *Fifty Shades* exposes the inherent lust of the American people—and particularly of women who long for kinky play." He noted that the internet, Facebook, Instagram, and Twitter all gave "people more and more places to discuss these previously hidden desires."[51] Thus, post-*Fifty Shades of Grey*, women's use of porn has really shot up. Among Pornhub's users in 2015, 23 percent were women.[52] (Twenty-four percent of the millennials were women, 21 percent of the older crowd.[53]) And then this: xHamster reported that worldwide, by 2019, 30 percent of porn viewers would be women.[54]

According to unpublished data of the Print Measurement Bureau of Canada, there has been a very substantial sexual activation of young and mid-life women between 2004 and 2014.[55] In a random survey of the entire population, trained interviewers asked, for 2004, if the female respondents had visited adult sites at all, and for 2014, "within the last thirty days." In 2004, before *Fifty Shades of Grey*, very few Canadian women viewed porn: 2.2 percent of the population ages 18-24, 2.7 percent of those 25-34, and 2.0 percent of those 35-49; older women simply did not download or stream porn in 2004.

By 2014, these figures had changed remarkably. Among 18 to 24-year-old women, porn viewing increased more than sixfold, to 13.5 percent; among 25-34 year-olds, the increase was more than fourfold, to 12.0 percent; increases of a similar order of magnitude were registered for older women as well, going up to age 64 (after 65 the men and women in this survey lost interest in porn).

There were also big increases in the percent of Canadian men viewing porn, and the absolute percentages were higher than those of women at all ages. But the increase for men between 2004 and 2014 was of lesser magnitude: in the general age bracket 25-54, porn viewing rose just threefold, from 7.5 percent to 24.1 percent. This rise tells us that more than *Fifty Shades of Grey* was responsible for increased Canadian porn viewing because men as a whole displayed little interest in the novel. Yet it is inconceivable that the enormous female interest in *Fifty Shades of Grey* in Canada was not somehow implicated in women's increased porn viewing: a sixfold rise among younger women!

In October 2015, the mass-circulation women's magazine *Marie Claire* published a survey on porn viewing among its readers that makes most previous data on women and porn unreflective of the current situation. Three thousand readers responded. Gone was any talk of using porn to enhance the relationship or get an idea of what he might like. They wanted to get off. Said editor Amanda de Cadenet, "Here's what jumped out at us in our findings: Your relationship to porn is mostly about you—your sexuality, unencumbered by a partner. Most of you said you watch it regularly, and you watch it alone." Only 12 percent watched with a partner, and only 17 percent thought it helped them to "understand what your partner likes." Seventy-three percent agreed that "it's a quick road to an orgasm." Although most women were straight (83 percent), or bisexual (12 percent), 44 percent of the total liked lesbian content. "Has porn negatively influenced your sex life?" Seventy-six percent said, "It hasn't." The women were distributed across the young age groups (only 13 percent were over 42); 31 percent of the total watched "every week or so," another 30 percent "a few times a month."[56] That's two-thirds of *Marie Claire*'s readers who regularly watch porn. And they may have watched it on DVDs from the national adult retail chain Fascinations; seventy percent of whose retail DVD sales in 2009 were to women.[57]

There was a dawning that porn was not a threat to women, and that the earlier antiporn aversion stemmed from a prudish distaste for public images of sex. Sex-positive feminism produced a new kind of activist: women intent upon driving the sex culture in a productive direction rather than eliminating it. Stores in the Babeland chain offered educational workshops, which collectively were known as "Babeland University." Founders of Babeland, who opened the store in Seattle in 1993, Rachel Venning and Claire Cavanah, had been involved in feminist activism at college. A journalist noted that "women's studies departments and campus feminist centers are logical spawning grounds for [such] sex activists." Said Cavanah, "We're all interested in changing the culture around sexuality."[58]

By 2015, women and porn-positive feminism were all over the media, in place of the previous diet of "Intellectuals Oppose Porn." In July 2015, *Cosmopolitan* ran a feature by Jill Hamilton on "The 15 Best Porn Sites for Women." "As we all know (because we are women), women enjoy porn just as much as guys do. But it's shockingly hard to find good porn in which the woman is actually enjoying herself in a realistic way." "If you're into kink," the *Cosmo* piece said, Hamilton was "a good place to start. It's sort of like a big box store for BDSM, fetishes, and other kinks—they'll probably have what you want, and other things you didn't know you wanted may end up in your cart as well."[59]

Exactly. This is the most powerful theme of the last thirty years; porn awakens you to tastes that you didn't even know you wanted. And for women, who historically have wanted so little, this was throwing the door of desire wide open. Here is an example of awakening new tastes: On set, a young performer told director Mason, who is a female director, that she didn't want to do "any rough sex." OK, no problem. That was on a Friday. On Monday, that performer told Mason that she'd done a "Gag Factor" [rough deep-throating] over the weekend, and she said, "You know what? I loved it. I found it so liberating. I loved being a total filthy slut. I loved having my mouth fucked. I love it."

Mason said, "But you were so against it Friday."

The model said, "Well, you know I had to experience it and express myself." [60]

Taste Gendered?

"Pornography as a genre wants to be about sex.
On close inspection, however, it always proves to be more about gender." [61]

LINDA WILLIAMS, IN *HARD CORE.*

Does taste today remain gendered? Not clear. Male producers think that it does while some female producers, at least, size up women as ready for the hard stuff.

Women, says Jeff Dillon, an executive at GameLink, prefer "story lines, sexy characters, and romance that leads to hot sex. It's clear that women have a more romantic idea of the kind of porn they like to watch." Among the top ten adult movies watched by women, the studios Adam & Eve, Wicked Pictures, and New Sensations Romance are in the lead, and topping the list is the movie *Marriage 2.0.* There is one instructional film in the top ten, *Tristan Taormina's Expert Guide to Oral Sex #2.* This shows, says Dillon, "that women want to be entertained, but also want to learn new things to improve their relationships."[62] Television sex guru Susan Block, speaking in 1999, agreed with Dillon, "Women want sex to be related to other concepts: to beauty, to stories.... When they just see genitals, it's like 'Okay, so what?' while men go 'Wow! That's really cool!'"[63] But this may not be the cutting edge of younger female tastes.

Within the industry, among the new female directors and producers close to changing market demands, there is a different, pro-hardcore view. Kylie Ireland's company SlutWerkz produces "hardcore filth for men by women." Among her directors, such as Ginger Lynn, Katja Kassin, and Lorelei Lee, "fisting and hardcore bondage are being encouraged." Said alt-porn director Joanna Angel (Joanna Mostov), who founded Burning Angel, "There are girls who love rough, dirty stuff just as much as men do; they just want to see that the girl is enjoying it."[64] (Angel, the Mark Zuckerberg of the industry, turned her Burning Angel network of websites and movies into an industry leader.)

Alt-porn, or punk porn—in contrast to "Big Porn"— found a home at Vivid Alt, where Eon McKai and Dave Naz were the main auteurs; Joanna Angel figured in several of McKai's videos. (McKai began filming with *Art School Sluts* in 2004; *Girls Lie* was his first Vivid Alt production in 2006.)

Do you need a story to get off? Naah, says DWB, a female executive at Asian Money Machine. "All I need is a few good minutes, or even one that I can loop. That's all it takes. Everyone has their positions or angles that gets them off. You don't NEED a 25 or 30 minute scene to do the trick. A good tease buildup is indeed nice, but I don't need it to flip my trigger."[65]

For Erika Lust, a Swedish director based in Barcelona who is among the leaders of the new female porn directors, there is no question of smearing Vaseline on the lens. She wants to capture women's total orgasmic experience. "If someone is having an orgasm, we want to see how their entire body reacts.... The 'cuddly romances' of the porn world are in fact her least favorite to write and direct." (In her 2010 book *Good Porn: A Woman's Guide*, Lust declared, "Forget flowers, cozy fires, and romance—we want porn where we call the shots."[66]) Jessica Drake, who directs *Jessica Drake's Guide to Wicked Sex* for Wicked Pictures, says, "I know women that love erotic love stories that are very sensual." This would be more in Jeff Dillon's line of country. But then she adds, "I also know women that like to see—and write—rough sex."[67]

The big growth categories in porn definitely did not correspond to traditional notions of what women were supposed to want. Among women's searches on Pornhub from 2014 to 2015, such oral-sex terms as "hardcore pussy eating" more than doubled, and the Pornhub statisticians observed that terms involving hardcore or rough sex like "hard rough fuck" and "fucked hard screaming" saw growth of around 300%." Women searched for "gangbang" 104 percent more often than men, and "double penetration" 87 percent more often.[68] So much for women and gentleness. According to Ogi Ogas, co-author of *A Billion Wicked Thoughts*, there is a gap between what women are supposed to find enjoyable and what they actually watch: "Studies show that what turns women on is different to what they wish turned them on or how they politically should feel about it.... What is fascinating is that women commonly promote the idea of feminist porn and socially want to believe in it.... But when it comes down to it, that's just not what they are interested in looking at," he said.[69]

It goes against all of our stereotypes about women and their sexual tastes, but there was almost a consensus among women in the industry that Ogi Ogas was right and Jeff Dillon was wrong. Here is director Veronica Hart at a roundtable in 2003 defending her sex scenes: "I think my sex is just as hot as anybody else's sex. I have, if you want, five guys on a girl. I have that. The chick is digging it, though; there is that. She's asking for it. She's saying 'Come on and fuck me!'.... Women love hot sex too. Women love sex. They love to cum."[70]

So what do women want to watch? Kelly Holland and Mark Graff, then producers of a female-oriented series for Playgirl TV, discovered it was handbags. And shoes. "It turned out art direction was incredibly important," said Graff. "From the headboards to shoes to his haircut, her haircut, everything that was in the room was being closely examined [by the focus group], whether or not the bedspread was pretty. 'Why is she wearing those shoes?' was a big thing. Not why was she wearing shoes or not wearing shoes, but why is she wearing those shoes? Shoes were like—a big deal." If Playgirl TV did not turn out well, it was not because insufficient attention was given to the actors' nails and to special dresses for 1950s scenes set in diners.[71]

Social Media

In 2014 alone, sales of smartphones surpassed one billion units.[72]

Many have commented that the adult industry is often the first to adopt new technologies. Why is that? Just brighter? No, it's that technology adoption is often driven by desire. When a new technology becomes available, there's a tremendous consumer push to access porn with it. As industry tech guru Quentin Boyer pointed out in 2012, "After the first films were made it wasn't too long before dirty films followed. And the same went for the internet. As soon as they could, the adult industry was clamoring to get their content online." And just as soon as Pink

Visual could capitalize on mobile traffic they did so, "to provide," as he said, "a great mobile experience for their customers."[73] According to data on the 100 million users worldwide of the site Porn.com, in 2015, for the first time, more users viewed porn from mobile and tablet devices than from desktop and laptop computers.[74]

The rush into mobile had some interesting political consequences: It contributed to shifting the locus of control from the studios to the models. After around 2010 the models were able to leverage the fan bases that social media gave them into positions of greater power. Mike Quasar, a big gonzo director, said in 2015, "Social media has dramatically changed the landscape of the business and the girls themselves have become much more important than whoever is holding the camera.... A girl like Kendra Lust is far more important than whatever director she shoots for. I tweet out a box cover or a trailer to my 15K followers, and a girl like Kendra retweets it to 300K."[75]

The social media helped widen a kind of chasm between the age groups. With smartphones, you can easily download free porn from the tubes, and many young people do. According to data from Pornhub in 2015, 64 percent of the 18 to 24-year-old year-old group of Pornhub viewers watch adult entertainment on their smartphones, 17 percent of the 65-and-over group.[76] Entrepreneur Kelli Roberts said, "Stripper rules apply here—if you have a hot college guy or a fat, bald man in his like 50s who do you go sit with? Duh! The old guy of course. Young guys don't ever have money."[77]

Previously, the main audience for porn had been affluent westerners with desktops. The future audience would be all these young people walking around peering into their personal devices. And it's a mass global audience, not a middle-class western audience as with desktops. According to the abovementioned Porn.com data, in 2015, two Chinese cities—Jilin City and Baoding—topped the list of most searches for "Brazzers" on Porn.com. The only U.S. city to make the grade was New York, last at number thirteen. (The only other trans-Atlantic city to figure was London at number 8.)[78]

Smartphones democratized the adult world by making porn universally accessible: Apple's iPhone launched in June 2007, Google's Android system a year later. Traveling businesspeople could now view porn in their hotel rooms at night without worrying about giveaway entries on the bill. Men and women at work could download videos from Pornhub without leaving telltale traces on the office computer. In 2008, "sex" and "porno" were the eighth and ninth most popular of all search terms. Apple's 3G technology, unveiled in June 2008, greatly decreased download times. By 2008, 58 percent of U.S. smartphone owners downloaded the web on their phones, as opposed to 13 percent of other mobile users.[79] In 2008, the U.S. mobile porn market was still described as a "sleeping giant," because service providers were still unwilling to include adult in their direct (on portal) offerings.[80] Yet this was to change.

Today, shooting adult is moving from Porn Valley to a larger stage: the whole country, the whole world. With today's technology, porn can be shot anywhere; the webcam models who are supplanting the loop-carrier DVDs may set up their laptops anywhere; and the new websites with their amateur porn and local models may be based anywhere. Porn Valley, once needed to provide content, is now mainly needed for behind-the-camera services. Movies on celluloid were dead, digital tapes were dead, and DVD was heading toward the exits. By the new millennium, the world had moved from "hard goods" to online streaming, introduced to the web in 1994 by the Dutch porn company Red Light District.[81] This was a profound paradigm shift.

From Masturbation to Mainstream

"If you can't sell porn to a guy with his dick in one hand and a credit card in the other, go find another job."[82]

MASTER RYAN, *XBIZ* CHATBOARD, 2014

For decades, the adult industry has conceived of itself as offering a masturbatory experience. And why not? But there are two problems with masturbation as a business model. One is that it's impossible to make money with it because so much adult material is available free. The second is that the market appears to be heading in the direction of deepening relationships between people rather than offering ever more exciting ways of getting off. Ways of masturbating have, after all, a finite limit. Human interconnection has no limit.

At the abovementioned Eros conference at the University of Southern California, sex educator Elle Chase, said, "People are masturbating and cumming in 30 seconds, but what they miss is intimacy, the arousal process. The feeling of sensuality and what comes along with it. And that's where the money is."[83] This is also where older viewers are, especially older women, who are the market of the future. (Younger viewers, as we saw above, may be more about erotic release.)

We're talking here about the sensualizing of sexuality in terms of magnifying the erotic palette. Establishing micro-niches in the area of transgender, female domination, fetish/BDSM, blowbangs and other forms of eroticizing the whole body has driven the changes of the last thirty years. These all cater to very specific tastes that once either did not exist or were submerged in vast undifferentiated basins of lust. But they are micro-niches that converge on the concept of the sensualization of sexuality. What has the capacity to take porn mainstream is not penetration but sensuality, luxuriating in the sexual nature of the body as a whole. Adult entertainment has become a billion dollar industry by pushing America— and the entire world—towards an enlargement of these erotic horizons. New sexual tastes are being discovered, and sometimes acted upon, with the hedonic pleasure and the social wreckage that such enlargements often leave in their wake. Is this good or bad? Not for me to say, but it's happening right now.

Acknowledgments

I am grateful to *Adult Video News* in Chatsworth for several weeks of hospitality as I worked my way through back issues of that publication, which otherwise are terribly difficult to find. Mark Kernes proved an amusing and informative conversation partner.

Over the years, Susan Bélanger in the History of Medicine Program has captained a crew of researchers that included, for this volume, the very able Esther Atkinson, a doctoral candidate at the University of Toronto who shortly will be writing her own books.

For many years, the forward-looking foundation, Associated Medical Services (AMS), led by Gail Paech, has supported my work in various forms. AMS remains the structural backbone of the History of Medicine community in Canada, and we all who are active in this field owe them an immense debt of gratitude.

For helpful advice, I should like to thank Charles Campbell, Dee Manning, Judson Rosebush, Angie Rowntree, Colin Rowntree, and Valerie Webber. Steve Bennett and Tanya H. Lee helped on the technical side.

My dear friend and literary agent Beverly Slopen guided the book through much of its shaping, and I am indebted to Stacey J. Miller for shepherding it through production.

Glossary

Affiliate marketing: A cross-promotion system between competing companies. "Every referral [from one site to another] that converted into a paying customer resulted in a kickback for the referring site (which came to be known as an 'affiliate')."[1]

AVN: *Adult Video News*, a trade publication founded in 1983 by Paul Fishbein and two others.

Airtight: All three orifices filled.

B-G (B/G): Boy/Girl, a heterosexual scene; this would include BGG et cetera.

Blowbang: A female gives oral sex to a several men more or less at once.

Cream pie: Heterosexual terms for an internal ejaculation, possibly followed by lingual contact.

Cum dump: Homosexual term for an internal ejaculation.

DP: Double penetration, anus and vagina.

Facial: Ejaculation on the model's face.

Fish-hooking: The male pulling the corner of the female's mouth apart with two fingers when having sex from behind.

Gangbang: Multiple partners in play with one woman.

G—G (G/G): Girl/Girl, a "lesbian" scene.

Golden shower: Urinating on someone with erotic purpose.

Gonzo: Brief hardcore loops shot with a handheld camera; all action, no plot.

Hotwifing (Cuckoldry): "The practice of sharing one's wife sexually with other men and deriving pleasure only from her arousal." It may involve humiliation or dominance of the submissive male and is synonymous with the more traditional term cuckoldry.[2]

IAFD: International Adult Film Database, created by Peter van Aarle in The Hague, Netherlands, in 1981; it came online in 1999.

IMDb: International Movie Database, created by British computer programmer Col Needham in 1990, who moved it online as an independent website in 1993.

Loops: Very brief stag films: no plot, all action, as in gonzo.

MILF: A "Mommie I'd Like to Fuck," an acronym not exclusively reserved for mom-appearing types and cougars but for any female who appears to be over the age of 25.

Nasty sex: Alternatives to gentle vaginal sex. Tina Tyler on her motivation to direct porn: "It's to create porn that is intimate, yet hot and nasty at the same time."[3] Nasty may also mean "enjoys anal," as when Tom Byron said of the fresh young Ginger Lynn shooting for Vivid for the first time in the 1980s, "She was nasty, man. She'd fucking tongue your ass—and nobody that looked like that was nasty like that back then—you know what I mean?"[4]

NSFW: "Not Safe For Work," meaning an explicitly sexual topic or image that might cause offense around the water cooler.

Pegging: "What should we call it when a woman fucks a man in the ass with a strapon dildo?" Dan Savage, in a 2001 column, popularized the term "pegging."[5]

Point-of-view style (POV) in shooting porn: One of the performers, not a cameraperson, holds the camera and films the other performer in action; for example, a male performer receiving oral sex might point the camera downwards, framing the female performer's face.

Pop shot: Filming the male ejaculating onto the model's face or abdomen. It may also be called, though rarely is, the "money shot."

Reverse cowgirl position: The woman sits on the man's penis, facing his knees.

Rimming: Lingual-anal contact.

Suitcase pimp: (Definition supplied by Tim Case, who managed a stripper bar in Dayton, Ohio.) "The industry term for any boyfriend or husband of a porn chick.... [They] can usually be seen carrying the bags of the actresses when they arrive on a set (hence the term "suitcase"), and they are often to be found on the cell phone handling the business affairs of the girls (i.e. 'pimping' them out to whichever producer will pay the most money for a scene").[6]

TGP site: A Thumbnail Gallery Post is a kind of free website offering links to the paysites of the content producers.

Twink: Gay male aged 18-24. Said Andy Fair in 2006, "A twink is a young, slender gay boy with little or no body hair, the sexual equivalent of a sugary snack."[7]

White label: Someone lists his content on someone else's big site using the latter's format; the big site gets a percent of the revenue. Example: "I created a Chaturbate white label site two days ago and have traffic, first two days around 500 clicks per day. But I had not one single free registration and not one guy who spent money." [8]

XBIZ: A trade organization and newsletter founded by Alec Helmy in 1998 that sponsors a news website (Xbiz.com) and a chatboard (Xbiz.net).

References

Preface

1. https://www.huffingtonpost.com/entry/chelsea-handler-stormy-daniels-parkland_us_5abd2f50e4b003c304ca412c.

2. Alexander Poe, "Forward Progress: Directors Say Technology Shaping Future," *XBIZ* Feature, Sept 10, 2015, www.xbiz.com/articles/198598.

Ch. 1: Introduction

1. Roy Karch, "Before It Was Legal – Man, Did We Have Fun!" *XBIZ* Feature, Aug 23, 2010, www.xbiz.com/articles/124448.

2. Al Goldstein, *I, Goldstein: My Screwed Life* (New York: Thunder's Mouth Press, 2006), 16.

3. Robert J. Stoller, *Porn: Myths for the Twentieth Century* (New Haven: Yale University Press, 1991), viii.

4. Starla Sparklefox interview, Montreal Aug 19, 2015.

5. Alison Flood, www.theguardian.com/books/2014/feb/27/fifty-shades-of-grey-book-100m-sales.

6. Sam Williams, "Gloria Leonard," *XBIZ* Feature, Dec 6, 2006, www.xbiz.com/articles/18467.

7. Edward Shorter, *Written in the Flesh: A History of Desire* (Toronto: University of Toronto Press, 2005).

8. Dan Miller, "Day in the Life," *XBIZ Premiere*, Dec 2015, 78.

9. John F. Cuber and Peggy B. Harroff, *Sex and the Significant Americans: A Study of Sexual Behavior Among the Affluent* (New York: Penguin, 1965), 172.

10. Al Goldstein note in foreword, Larry Flynt, *An Unseemly Man* (Los Angeles: Dove, 1996), xviii.

11. Joanne Cachapero, "Joe Gallant's Dirty Movies," *XBIZ* Feature, Dec 10, 2005, www.xbiz.com/articles/11894.

12. Kurt Schneider, "Die Schichtung des emotionalen Lebens und der Aufbau der Depressionszustände," *Zeitschrift für die gesamte Neurologie und Psychiatrie*, 59 (1920), 281-286, 282. For a capsule summary, see Edward Shorter, *Historical Dictionary of Psychiatry* (New York: Oxford University Press, 2005), 83.

13. Edward Shorter, "Sexual Sunday School: The *DSM* and the Gatekeeping of Morality," *AMA Journal of Ethics* 16 (17) November 2014: 932–937, http://journalofethics.ama-assn. org/2014/11/pdf/mhst1-1411.pdf.

14. H. Montgomery Hyde, *A History of Pornography* (London: Heinemann, 1964); for a more scholarly history of pornography, see Edward Shorter, *Written in the Flesh: A History of Desire* (Toronto: University of Toronto Press, 2005), passim.

15. The phrase is Anne McClintock's, "Gonad the Barbarian and the Venus Flytrap: Portraying the Male and Female Orgasm," in L. Segal and M. McIntosh, eds., *Sex Exposed; Sexuality and the Pornography Debate* (London: Virago, 1992).

16. See, however, Georgina Voss, "'Treating It As a Normal Business': Researching the Pornography Industry," *Sexualities*, 15 (2012), 391-410; Chauntelle Tibbals has pioneered the close academic observation of the industry in *Exposure: A Sociologist Explores Sex, Society, and Adult Entertainment* (Austin: Greenleaf, 2015). For a scholarly but refreshingly open-minded appraisal of the industry, see the essays in Lynn Comella and Shira Tarrant, eds. *New Views on Pornography: Sexuality, Politics, and the Law* (Santa Barbara: Praeger, 2015). Important as well is Linda Williams, *Hard Core: Power, Pleasure, and "The Frenzy of the Visible,"* exp. ed. (Berkeley: University of California Press, 1999. On building bridges between academic research and pornography, see Juris Dilevko and Lisa Gottlieb, "Selection and Cataloging of Adult Pornography Web Sites for Academic Libraries," *Journal of Academic Librarianship*, 30 (2004), 36-50. For an annotated overview of the enormous secondary porn literature, see Damon Young, "Pornography" (2012), http://www.oxfordbibliographies.com/view/ document/obo-9780199791286/obo-9780199791286-0153.xml.

17. Dee Severe post of Feb 8, 2015, on thread "What if 50 Shades movie is really, really bad?" www.xbiz.net/index.php?c=discussion.view_thread&id=14341.

18. Srybchin post of Sept 7, 2012, on thread "Fifty Shades — a quick flame or a cultural awakening?" www.xbiz.net/index.php?c=discussionview_thread&id=7088.

19. "Film Critic Says 'Deep Throat' Could Expand Sexual Horizons," *NYT,* Dec 21, 1972, 40. The expert was Arthur Knight of the University of Southern California.

20. Paul L. Montgomery, "Pulp Sex Novels Thrive as Trade Comes Into Open," *NYT,* Sept 5, 1965, 1.

21. Mike South, "Holding Up a Mirror," July 30, 2008, http://mikesouth.com.

22. "BDSM and Affiliate Marketing," *XBIZ* Feature, Oct 2, 2008, www.xbiz.com/articles/99808.

23. Sharon Reed, Sept 1, 1999, "What Do Women Want on the Internet?" http://business.avn. com/articles/video/What-Do-Women-Want-On-The-Internet-41086.html. The blogger was KafkaFan.

24. Alison Marshall, "Mixing It Up," *XBIZ* Feature, Dec 23, 2008, www.xbiz.com/ articles/126976.

25. "WIA Profile: Holly Ruprecht," *XBIZ* Feature, July 17, 2011, www.xbiz.com/ articles/136344.

Ch. 2: East Coast, West Coast

1. Don Fernando post of Apr 11, 2011, on thread "Porn industry to flee California?" www.xbiz. net/index.php?c=discussion.view_thread&id=3638.

2. Deemented [sic], of Oliya Productions, post of May 11, 2014, on thread "Improving porn for modern times?" www.xbiz.net/index.php?c=discussion.view_thread&id=11762.

3. Ariana Rodriguez, WIA Profile: Kathryn Hartman," *XBIZ* Feature, June 11, 2012, www. xbiz.com/articles/149508.

4. "Denise LaFrance interview with Ron Sullivan" [Henri Pachard], Oct 8, 2008, www.pornsaints.org/blog/ron-sullivan-denise-lafrance.

5. Sept 16, 2004, http://business.avn.com/articles/video/I-AVNInsider-i-A-Pornographer-s-Journal-40388.html.

6. "Crime Cashing in on Pornography, *NYT*, Sept 28, 1969, 54.

7. Al Goldstein, *I, Goldstein: My Screwed Life* (New York: Thunder's Mouth Press, 2006), 26, 108.

8. Sam Roberts, "Richard Basciano Dies at 91," *NYT*, May 7, 2007, 28.

9. "7 Are Convicted on Pornography Charges," *NYT*, Nov 6, 1971, 35.

10. Howard1955 (Howard Levine) post of July 28, 2015, on thread, "How long have you been in the industry?" www.xbiz.net/index.php?c=discussion.view_thread&id=15635.

11. "10 Indicted by Grand Jury in Shipping Pornography," *NYT*, May 1, 1969, 53.

12. Ralph Blumenthal, "Porno Chic," *NYT*, Jan 21, 1973, E28.

13. Al Goldstein, *I, Goldstein: My Screwed Life* (New York: Thunder's Mouth Press, 2006), 112–113.

14. See, for example, Morris Kaplan, "Police Raid Huge Smut-Film Operation," *NYT*, Sept 8, 1973, 28; the murder of Paul Rothenberg, who ran a film reproduction lab, aroused a great deal of media attention. See, for example, Steven R. Weisman, "Reputed National Distributor of Smut Is Shot to Death Near Home in Nassau, *NYT*, July 30, 1973, 23.

15. See, for example, Legs McNeil and Jennifer Osborne, *The Other Hollywood* (New York: HarperCollins, 2005), 169-171.

16. For a brief biography of Sturman, see Eric Schlosser, *Reefer Madness: Sex, Drugs, and Cheap Labor in the American Black Market* (Boston: Houghton Mifflin, 2003), 116f.

17. Ariana Rodriguez, "In Full Bloom," *XBIZ* Feature, June 10, 2010, www.xbiz.com/articles/121621.

18. Edward Shorter interview with Max Allen, May 7, 2015.

19. For a re-hearing in 1992 of the original hearing in 1991, see http://law.justia.com/cases/federal/appellate-courts/F2/951/1466/257565/.

20. John Johnson, "No Heir Apparent for Toppled Porn King," http://articles.latimes.com/1989-12-04/local/me-27_1_van-nuys.

21. Luke Ford, *A History of X* (Amherst, NY: Prometheus, 1999), 75.

22. William Serrin, "Sex Is a Growing Multibillion Business," *NYT*, Feb 9, 1981.

23. Sept 1, 1999, http://business.avn.com/articles/video/LA-Times-Calls-Porn-LA-Economy-s-Dirty-Secret-35478.html.

24. Colin Rowntree, email to Edward Shorter, July 10, 2015.

25. "Fried Retires from Doc Johnson," *AVN*, 20 (1) (Jan 2004), 352. Doc Johnson, of course, had been co-founded by Mafia-affiliate Reuben Sturman.

26. Jeffrey Escoffier, *Bigger Than Life: The History of Gay Porn Cinema From Beefcake to Hardcore* (Philadelphia: Running Press, 2009), 124.

27. Richard Corliss, "That Old Feeling: When Porno Was Chic," *Time*, Mar 29, 2005.

28. William Murray, "The Porn Capital of America," *NYT*, Jan 3, 1971, SM 8.

29. Eddie Muller and Daniel Faris, *Grindhouse: The Forbidden World of "Adults Only" Cinema* (New York: St Martin's Press, 1996), 127.

30. Jim Holliday, *Only the Best* (Van Nuys, CA: Cal Vista Direct, 1986), 15.

31. Luke Ford, "Essays 1966–74, Scandinavian Porn," www.lukeisback.com/essays/essays/1966. htm.

32. Joe Kukura, "Remembering When San Francisco Was 'The Porn Capital of America,'" Apr 30, 2015. http://brokeassstuart.com/blog/2015/04/30/remembering-when-san-francisco-was-the-porn-capital-of-america/.

33. "Film Pornography Flourishes Despite Court Ruling," *NYT,* Nov 4, 1973, 22.

34. Tod Hunter, "*AVN* Hall of Fame, Class of 2001, Inductee: Bob Vosse," *AVN,* 17 (2) (Feb 2001), 80.

35. See on this Robert O. Self's, "Sex in the City: The Politics of Sexual Liberalism in Los Angeles, 1963-79," *Gender & History,* 20 (2008), 288–311.

36. David Jennings, *Skinflicks: The Inside Story of the X-Rated Video Industry* (Bloomington, IN: 1rst Books, 2000), 55.

37. David Houston, "The Birth of Porn Valley: 1," *XBIZ* Feature, June 15, 2005, www.xbiz. com/articles/9131.

38. See Paul Fishbein, "Freeman Wins One for the Industry," *AVN,* 3 (10) (Oct 1988), 18.

39. David Houston, "The Birth of Porn Valley: 2," *XBIZ* Feature, June 16, 2005, www.xbiz. com/articles/9149.

40. "Adult in the City of Angels," *XBIZ* Feature, Feb 28, 2007, www.xbiz.com/articles/19852.

41. Rodger Jacobs, "Unique Delivery," *XBIZ* Feature, Oct 9, 2006, www.xbiz.com/ articles/17520.

42. David Hebditch and Nick Anning, *Porn Gold: Inside the Pornography Business* (London: Faber and Faber, 1988), 227.

43. May 3, 2004, http://business.avn.com/articles/video/Noel-Bloom-Industry-Pioneer-Returns-to-Adult-with-Maximum-Xposure-38474.html. Another source gives the date of purchase of Caballero as 1985. Ariana Rodriguez, "In Full Bloom," *XBIZ* Feature, June 10, 2010, www.xzbiz.com/articles/121621. For an overview of these developments see Kevin Heffernan, "Seen as a Business: Adult Film's Historical Framework and Foundations," in Lynn Comella and Shira Tarrant, eds., *New Views on Pornography, Sexuality, Politics, and the Law* (Santa Barbara: Praeger, 2015), 36–56.

44. Matt O'Connor, "Original Roy Karch," *XBIZ* Feature, Apr 18, 2006, www.xbiz.com/ articles/80582.

45. Matt O'Connor, "Original Roy Karch," *XBIZ* Feature, Apr 18, 2006, www.xbiz.com/ articles/80582.

46. Robert Rosen, *Beaver Street: A History of Modern Pornography* (London: Headpress, 2012), 130.

47. Frank Rich, http://www.nytimes.com/2001/05/20/magazine/naked-capitalists. html?pagewanted=all.

48. Mark Kernes, "Adult Film: Golden Age Of," in Patricia Whelehan et al., eds., *The International Encyclopedia of Human Sexuality* (Chichester: Wiley, 2015), vol I, 29–35.

49. Jan 1, 2006, http://business.avn.com/articles/video/AVNONLINE-COLUMN-200601-EXECUTIVE-SUITE-Steven-Hirsch-CEO-Vivid-Entertainment-47087.html. Puzzlingly, Hirsch said that he had known Sturman well, yet denied any knowledge of the involvement of crime in the adult business.

50. Peter Alilunas, "Ginger's Private Party Flyer (circa 1985)," *Film History,* 26 (2014), 144–155, 148.

51. Joanne Cachapero,, "Women on Top: 1," *XBIZ* Feature, June 28, 2006, www.xbiz.com/ articles/15733.

52. Harris Gaffin, *Hollywood Blue: The Tinseltown Pornographers* (London: Batsford, 1997), 146.

53. Tim Connelly, "Vivid," *AVN*, 20 (1) (Jan 2004), 52.

54. Jan 1, 2005, http://business.avn.com/articles/video/AVN-COM-BUSINESS-PROFILE-Vivid-Marks-20th-Anniversary-by-Looking-Ahead-Not-Back-44428.html.

55. Jan 1, 2006, http://business.avn.com/articles/video/AVNONLINE-COLUMN-200601-EXECUTIVE-SUITE-Steven-Hirsch-CEO-Vivid-Entertainment-47087.html.

56. The sources for this section on Vivid also include: May 23, 2003, http://business.avn.com/articles/video/i-Business-2-0-i-Profiles-Vivid-Co-Founder-Steve-Hirsch-31855.html; Paul Keegan, "Prime-Time PORN," Business 2.0, June 2003, http://search.ebscohost.com/login.aspx?direct=true&db=buh&AN=9917005&site=ehost-live; Ralph Frammolino and P.J. Huffstutter, http://articles.latimes.com/2002/jan/06/magazine/tm-20634/2.

57. Joshua Chaffin, "The Rise of a Premiumporn Producer," Oct 4, 2005, http://www.ft.com/intl/cms/s/0/386ecc36-3473-11da-adae-00000e2511c8.html#axzz3vosltn1n; Peter Alilunas, "Ginger's Private Party Flyer (circa 1985)," *Film History*, 26 (2014), 144–155.

58. Darrick Danta, "Ambiguous Landscapes of the San Pornando Valley," [*sic*] *Yearbook of the Association of Pacific Coast Geographers*, 71 (2009), 15–30.

59. Sam Williams, "Gloria Leonard," *XBIZ* Feature, Dec 6, 2006, www.xbiz.com/articles/18467.

60. Tim Connelly, "Vivid," *AVN*, 20 (1) (Jan 2004), 54.

61. Trent Brown, "Sin City Films," *AVN*, 20 (2) (Feb 2004), 280–281.

62. John Paone, "Interview: Barbara Dare," *AVN*, 1 (45) (Nov 1986), 44. Inexplicably, she told Paone she had grown up in "Texas."

63. Harris Gaffin, *Hollywood Blue: The Tinseltown Pornographers* (London: Butler, 1997), 29.

64. Acme Anderson, "Old School Meets New," *XBIZ* Feature, Dec 19, 2008, www.xbiz.com/articles/126971.

65. On weighing these considerations, see Henri Pachard, "Where the Producers Are Shooting Adult Videos," *AVN*, 4 (5) (Apr 1989), 20.

66. Darrick Danta, "Ambiguous Landscapes of the San Pornando Valley," *Yearbook of the Association of Pacific Coast Geographers,* 71 (2009), 15–30.

67. Jeffrey Gettleman, "L.A. Economy's Dirty Secret: Porn Is Thriving," *Los Angeles Times*, Sept 1, 1999.

68. Gregory Piccionelli, "Golden State Jitters: 1," *XBIZ* Feature, Mar 8, 2007, www.xbiz.com/articles/20003.

69. Jeffrey Gettleman, "L.A. Economy's Dirty Secret: Porn Is Thriving," *Los Angeles Times*, Sept 1, 1999.

70. Rodger Jacobs, "Where Are They Now?" *XBIZ* Feature, Aug 1, 2005, www.xbixz.com/articles/80070. For a more nuanced perspective on this time, see his autobiography, Howie Gordon/Richard Pacheco, *Hindsight: True Love & Mischief in the Golden Age of Porn* (Albion, GA: BearManor Media, 2013), 248f.

71. Matt O'Connor, "Digital Playground's Joone," *XBIZ* Feature, June 3, 2005, www.xbiz.com/articles/8989.

72. Joanne Cachapero, "The Business of Being Brittany," *XBIZ* Feature, Feb 18, 2008, www.xbiz.com/articles/90305.

73. R. Verrier, "Porn Producers Are Latest to Leave LA," *Los Angeles Times*, Aug 6, 2014, www.neogaf.com/forum/showthread.php?t=869315.

74. Roy Karch, "Before It Was Legal — Man, Did We Have Fun!" *XBIZ* Feature, Aug 23, 2010, www.xbiz.com/articles/124448.

Ch. 3: From the Pussycat to the Living Room

1. Rodger Jacobs, "Eric Edwards," *XBIZ* Feature, Feb 10, 2006, www.xbiz.com/articles/13399.

2. See Al Di Lauro and Gerald Rabkin, *Dirty Movies: An Illustrated History of the Stag Film, 1915–1970* (New York: Chelsea House, 1976); Dave Thompson, *Black and White and Blue: Adult Cinema from the Victorian Age to the VCR* (Toronto: ECW Press, 2007).

3. Early stag films have given rise to a whole cottage industry of scholarship. For an overview see Nicola Simpson, "Coming Attractions: A Comparative History of the Hollywood Studio System and the Porn Business," *Historical Journal of Film, Radio and Television*, 24 (2004), 635-652, fn 32, 651.4 Eric Schaefer, "Gauging a Revolution: 16 mm Film and the Rise of the Pornographic Feature," in Linda Williams, ed., *Porn Studies* (Durham: Duke University Press, 2004), 370–400.

4. Robert Berkvist, "...And What About the Peeps?" *NYT*, Dec 9, 1973, 187.

5. Chrissie Bentley, "Foreword," in Dave Thompson, *Black and White and Blue: Adult Cinema from the Victorian Age to the VCR* (Toronto: ECW Press, 2007), viii-ix.

6. Steven V. Roberts, "Pornography in U.S.: A Big Business," *NYT*, Feb 22, 1970, 1, 66.

7. "SF Pornography: Listing by Publisher," www.philsp.com/homeville/KRJ/sfp-pub.htm.

8. Harrison E. Salisbury, "Senators Start Morals Hearings," *NYT*, May 25, 1955, 1.

9. Joanne Cachapero, "Women On Top: 3," *XBIZ* Feature, Aug 11, 2006, www.xbiz.com/articles/16476.

10. On Milton see David Hebditch and Nick Anning, *Porn Gold: Inside the Pornography Business* (London: Faber and Faber, 1988), 42–53.

11. Acme Anderson, "The Public World of Private," *XBIZ*, May 19, 2008, www.xbiz.com/articles/128505; John Stuart, "Executive Seat: Milton, Not So Private," *XBIZ* Feature, Aug 16, 2011, www.xbiz.com/articles/137538å; www.lukeisback.com/essays/essays/1966.htm.

12. Joanne Cachapero, "Women On Top: 3," *XBIZ* Feature, Aug 11, 2006, www.xbiz.com/articles/16476.

13. Larry Flynt, *An Unseemly Man* (Los Angeles: Dove, 1996), 88.

14. Dan Miller, "Beaver Fever," *XBIZ Premiere*, July 2015, 74.

15. Rhett Pardon, "Flynt: Playboy's Nude-Free Decision is 'Ludicrous,'" *XBIZ* News, Oct 13, 2015, www.xbiz.com/news/200075.

16. William Serrin, "Sex Is a Growing Multibillion Business," *NYT*, Feb 9, 1981, B1, 6.

17. William Serrin, "Sex Is a Growing Multibillion Business," *NYT*, Feb 9, 1981, B6.

18. "Peep Shows and Massage Parlors Are Targets...," *NYT*, July 13, 1972, 26.

19. Master Ryan post of Aug 13, 2013, www.xbiz.net/index.php?c=discussion.view_thread&id=9429.

20. See the analysis of J. D. Bauchery [sic], "Early Female Voices in Porn," June 24, 2010, www.blogher.com/early-female-voices-porn-scoundrels-here-hotmoviesforhercom.

21. Quoted in Eddie Muller and Daniel Faris, *Grindhouse: The Forbidden World of "Adults Only" Cinema* (New York: St Martin's Press, 1996), 60.

22. Eddie Muller and Daniel Faris, *Grindhouse: The Forbidden World of "Adults Only" Cinema* (New York: St Martin's Press, 1996), 82–83.

23. Eddie Muller and Daniel Faris, *Grindhouse: The Forbidden World of "Adults Only" Cinema* (New York: St Martin's Press, 1996), 85.

24. Legs McNeil and Jennifer Osborne, *The Other Hollywood* (New York: HarperCollins, 2005), 11.

25. Aug 27, 1999, http://business.avn.com/articles/video/LEGENDARY-ADULT-DIRECTOR-VOSSE-DIES-35502.html.

26. Legs McNeil and Jennifer Osborne, *The Other Hollywood* (New York: HarperCollins, 2005), 90.

27. https://en.wikipedia.org/wiki/I_Am_Curious_(Yellow); on the film as a hybrid between porn and art-cinema, see Kevin Heffernan, "Prurient (Dis)Interest: The American Release and Reception of *I Am Curious (Yellow),*" in Eric Schaefer, ed., *Sex Scene: Media and the Sexual Revolution* (Durham: Duke University Press, 2014), 105–125.

28. Mar 11, 2005, http://business.avn.com/articles/video/Battle-of-the-i-Deep-Throat-i-Numbers-42583.html.

29. Vincent Canby, "What Are We To Think of 'Deep Throat'?" *NYT,* Jan 21, 1973, A1.

30. Luke Ford, *A History of X* (Amherst, NY: Prometheus, 1999), 47–48.

31. http://www.theguardian.com/film/shortcuts/2013/aug/26/lovelace-movie-gloria-steinem-catherine-mackinnon.

32. Chauntelle Tibbals, *Exposure: A Sociologist Explores Sex, Society, and Adult Entertainment* (Austin, TX: Greenleaf, 2015), 125, 130. Lovelace later apparently recanted part of the "abuse" story. She told a friend of Ron Jeremy's "that some of the antipornographic feminists used her for their agenda. And actually she felt a little exploited by *them*." Ron Jeremy, *The Hardest (Working) Man in Showbiz* (New York: Harper Collins, 2008), 83n.

33. Feb 10, 2005, http://business.avn.com/articles/video/Ex-Porn-Star-Harry-Reems-Opens-Up-in-Exclusive-Interview-42164.html.

34. Conner Habib, http://www.slate.com/articles/arts/culturebox/2013/08/linda_lovelace_movie_is_bad_for_real_porn_stars.html.

35. Joanne Cachapero, "Women on Top: 1," *XBIZ* Feature, June 28, 2006, www.xbiz.com/articles/15733.

36. Jim Holliday, *Only the Best* (Van Nuys CA: Cal Vista Direct, 1986), 17.

37. Luke Ford, *A History of X* (Amherst, NY: Prometheus, 1999), 64.

38. Nicholas Gage, "Organized Crime Reaps Huge Profits From Dealing in Pornographic Films," *NYT,* Oct. 12, 1975, 1.

39. Eddie Muller and Daniel Faris, *Grindhouse: The Forbidden World of "Adults Only" Cinema* (New York: St Martin's Press, 1996), 143.

40. Luke Ford, *A History of X* (Amherst, NY: Prometheus, 1999), 91–92; Ford uses the phrase "generally regarded by critics as the best porn movie ever," yet clearly this is his personal opinion.

41. "Building a Blockbuster," *XBIZ* Feature, Dec 8, 2007, www.xbiz.com/articles/87522.

42. Carol Queen, "Good Vibrations, Women, and Porn: A History," in Lynn Comella and Shira Tarrant, eds. *New Views on Pornography, Sexuality, Politics, and the Law* (Santa Barbara: Praeger, 2015), 179–190.

43. Luke Ford, *A History of X* (Amherst, NY: Prometheus, 1999), 35–37.

44. http://www.imdb.com/title/tt0073682.

45. "Charting the Adult Industry," *AVN Adult Entertainment Guide, 1995,* 67–68.

46. Rodger Jacobs, "Where Are They Now?" *XBIZ* Feature, Aug 1, 2005, www.xbixz.com/articles/80070.

47. Erik Jay, "In the Director's Chair: Zander," *XBIZ* Feature, Oct 15, 2009, www.xbiz.com/articles/113751.

48. Tod Hunter, "New Market for Classic Porn," *XBIZ* Feature, Apr 2, 2007, www.xbiz.com/articles/80450.

49. Mike South, "Why Can't We In Porn Make Good Movies," Nov 22, 2013, www.mikesouth.com.

50. Robert Rosen, *Beaver Street: A History of Modern Pornography* (London: Headpress, 2012), 124–125.

51. Frederick Wasser, *Veni, Vidi, Video: The Hollywood Empire and the VCR* (Austin: University of Texas Press, 2001), 3.

52. William Serrin, "Sex Is a Growing Multibillion Business," *NYT*, Feb 9, 1981, B1, B6.

53. Lawrence G. Walters, "'Throat' in Court," *XBIZ* Feature, Feb 2, 2007, www.xbiz.com/articles/19431; Academic authority Frederick Wasser states, "The concurrence of the Betamax [VCR] and the new, more plot-driven erotica led to adult titles becoming the first big genre for prerecorded cassettes." *Veni, Vidi, Video: The Hollywood Empire and the VCR* (Austin: University of Texas Press, 2001), 94.

54. *AVN Adult Entertainment Guide, 1993*, 28.

55. *AVN*, 19 (1) (Jan 2003), 35.

56. Paul Fishbein, "The Decade in Review, part 1," *AVN*, 4 (7) (Dec 1989), 49–53, see p. 52.

57. Matt O'Connor, "Original Roy Karch," *XBIZ* Feature, Apr 18, 2006, www.xbiz.com/articles/80582.

58. Roy Karch, "Is This the End of Deeper, Harder, Faster?" *XBIZ* Feature, Feb 17, 2011, www.xbiz.com/articles/130724.

59. Patchen Barss, *The Erotic Engine: How Pornography Has Powered Mass Communication from Gutenberg to Google* (Toronto: Anchor Canada, 2010), 103–108.

60. Tony Schwartz, "The TV Pornography Boom," *NYT*, Sept 13, 1981, SM 111.

61. Erik Jay, "In the Director's Chair: David Lord," *XBIZ* Feature, Oct 19, 2010, www.xbiz.com/articles/126464.

62. June 18, 2003, http://business.avn.com/articles/video/DVD-Rentals-Surpass-VHS-Rentals-For-First-Time-31608.html.

63. Aug. 20, 2004, http://business.avn.com/articles/video/Private-U-S-A-To-Discontinue-VHS-40014.html.

64. "New Horizons," *XBIZ* Feature, Mar 10, 2007, www.xbiz.com/articles/80447.

65. Henri Pachard, quoted in Legs McNeil and Jennifer Osborne, *The Other Hollywood* (New York: HarperCollins, 2005), 366.

66. Robert J. Stoller, *Porn: Myths for the Twentieth Century* (New Haven: Yale University Press, 1991), 126.

67. David Jennings, *Skinflicks* (Bloomington, IN: 1rst Books, 2000), 166.

68. http://www.ynot.com/adult-loses-true-pioneer-rip-candida-royalle/.

69. http://candidaroyalle.com/femme-catatlogue/.

70. Catherine Pearson, "Meet the Powerful Women Directors Working in Porn," http://www.huffingtonpost.com/entry/meet-the-powerful-women-directors-working-in-porn_55ca50a7e4b0f1cbf1e68c13.

71. Acme Anderson, "It Takes a Woman's Touch," *XBIZ* Feature, July 27, 2007, www.xbiz.com/articles/82439; Katy Terrega, "Candida Royalle," *XBIZ* Feature, Feb 11, 2006, www.xbiz.com/articles/13422; Maya Gallus, "I Remember: Candida Royalle," [Toronto] *Globe and Mail*, Sept 30, 2015, S6.

72. Denise LaFrance, "Candida Royalle Interview," 2004, http://deniselafrancethepainter.blogspot.ca/2015/09never-before-seen-my-candida-royalle.html.

73. "Vivid Video to Start Up Women Director's Series," *AVN*, 6 (9) (Sept 1991), 29.

74. See the Holliday interview in Robert J. Stoller, *Porn: Myths for the Twentieth Century* (New Haven, Yale UP, 1991), 170.

75. Joanne Cachapero and Gram Ponante, "A Jim Holliday Box Set," *XBIZ* Feature, Sept 21, 2007, www.xbiz.com/articles/84414.

Ch. 4: Is Porn Bad?

1. Melissa Santana, "Industry Pays Tribute to Bill 'Papa Bear' Margold," *XBIZ Premiere*, March 2017, 10.

2. https://www.usmagazine.com/celebrity-news/news/jessica-drake-accuses-donald-trump-of-sexual-misconduct-w446294/.

3. Dan Miller, "Porn Panel Talks Mainstreaming of Erotica at USC," *XBIZ* News, Oct 15, 2015, www.xbiz.com/news/200183.

4. Alvin Shuster, "...Nor Gloom of Censorship," *NYT*, Aug 2, 1959, SM11.

5. "Midwest Leaders Ask Curbs on Smut," *NYT*, Nov 19, 1959.

6. "F.B.I. Chief Urges Drive to Bar Smut," *NYT*, Jan 2, 1960.

7. On successive court decisions, see Chauntelle Anne Tibbals, "When Law Moves Quicker Than Culture: Key Jurisprudential Regulations Shaping the U.S. Adult Content Production Industry," *The Scholar,* 15 (2013), 213–259.

8. https://supreme.justia.com/cases/federal/us/354/476/case.html.

9. Alex Henderson, "50 Years After 'Roth'," *XBIZ* Feature, June 20, 2007, www.xbiz.com/articles/23698.

10. United States Commission on Obscenity and Pornography. *Report of the Commission on Obscenity and Pornography* (New York: Bantam Books, 1970) .

11. Jim Holliday, *Only the Best* (Van Nuys, CA: Cal Vista Direct, 1986), 28.

12. For a summary of *Memoirs* and for Burger's opinion in 1973, see "Excerpts From Pornography Opinions," *NYT*, June 22, 1973, 42.

13. Alex Henderson, "Miller Turns 33," *XBIZ* Feature, Apr 7, 2006, www.xbiz.com/articles/14269.

14. "Sex Week Is Quiet at U. of Alabama," *NYT*, Mar 24, 1974, 48.

15. James Sterba, "Pornography Fight Lags Across Nation," *NYT*, Nov 26, 1974, 1.

16. "*AVN* Presents Adult Panel at CES, SRO Crowd Sees 'Women of the Industry,'" *AVN*, 3 (3) (Feb 1988), 12.

17. "Charting the Adult Industry," *AVN Adult Entertainment Guide, 1995*, 68.

18. See David Jennings, *Skinflicks* (Bloomington, IN: 1st Books, 2000), 339–368

19. "The Nation's Hot Spots," *AVN*, 7 (21) (Feb 1992), 15.

20. See Benjamin Edelman, "Red Light States: Who Buys Online Adult Entertainment?" *Journal of Economic Perspectives*, 23 (2009), 209-220. See also Cara C. MacInnis et al., "Do American States with More Religious or Conservative Populations Search More for Sexual Content on Google?" *Archives of Sexual Behavior*, 3 Oct 2014; DOI 10.1007/s10508-014-0361-8.

21. Alex Henderson, "Harvey Helps Others," *XBIZ* Feature, Oct 31, 2006, www.xbiz.com/articles/17893.

22. Whitney Strub, *Perversion for Profit: The Politics of Pornography and the Rise of the New Right* (New York: Columbia University Press, 2010), 210.

23. Lawrence G. Walters, "Sex, Lies & Children," *XBIZ* Feature, Sept 9, 2009, www.xbiz.com/articles/112520.

24. https://en.wikipedia.org/wiki/People_v._Freeman; Acme Anderson, "The Genesis of Gonzo," *XBIZ* Feature, Aug 8, 2007, www.xbiz.com/articles/82784.

25. Kimberly A. Harchuck, "Pornography and the First Amendment Right to Free Speech," in Lynn Comella and Shira Tarrant, eds., *New Views on Pornography, Sexuality, Politics, and the Law* (Santa Barbara: Praeger, 2015), 9–24. For an interview with Harchuck that captures the thrill of First Amendment work, see "WIA Profile: Kimberly A. Harchuck," *XBIZ* Feature, Dec 15, 2015, www.xbiz.com/articles/201682.

26. Quoted in, https://en.wikipedia.org/wiki/Stormy_Daniels, ref no. 5.

27. For an appraisal of the evidence base of the antiporn academics and activists, see Ronald Weitzer, "Interpreting the Data: Assessing Competing Claims in Pornography Research," in Lynn Comella and Shira Tarrant, eds., *New Views on Pornography: Sexuality, Politics, and the Law* (Santa Barbara: Praeger, 2015), 257–275.

28. Linda Williams, *Hard Core: Power, Pleasure, and the "Frenzy of the Visible,"* expanded ed. (Berkeley: University of California Press, 1999), 4–5.

29. "Obscenity Fought by Women's Clubs," *NYT*, May 2, 1959, 48.

30. Arnold H. Lubasch, "Hearing Assails the Smut 'Flood,'" *NYT*, Feb 19, 1970, 44.

31. On the origins of the women-against-porn movement see Carolyn Bronstein, "Clashing at Barnard's Gates: Understanding the Origins of the Pornography Problem in the Modern American Women's Movement," in Lynn Comella and Shira Tarrant, eds., *New Views on Pornography, Sexuality, Politics, and the Law* (Santa Barbara: Praeger, 2015), 57–76. The main antiporn feminist texts are Gail Dines et al., *Pornography: The Production and Consumption of Inequality* (New York: Routledge, 1998); Andrea Dworkin and Catharine A. MacKinnon, *Pornography and Civil Rights: A New Day for Women's Equality* (Minneapolis: Organizing against Pornography, 1988); and Catharine A. MacKinnon, *Only Words* (Cambridge: Harvard UP, 1993).

32. Richard Neville, "Has the First Amendment Met Its Match?" *NYT*, Mar 6, 1977, 193.

33. Andrea Dworkin, *Pornography: Men Possessing Women* (New York: Perigee, 1981).

34. Judy Klemesrud, "Women, Pornography, Free Speech: A Fierce Debate at N.Y.U.," *NYT*, Dec 4, 1978, D10.

35. On the origins of sex-negative radical feminism see John Heidenry, *What Wild Ecstasy: The Rise and Fall of the Sexual Revolution* (New York: Simon & Schuster, 1997), 110–115.

36. Georgina Voss, "Trade Associations, Industry Legitimacy, and Corporate Responsibility in Pornography," in Lynn Comella and Shira Tarrant, eds., *New Views on Pornography, Sexuality, Politics, and the Law* (Santa Barbara: Praeger, 2015), 191–216.

37. Chauntelle Tibbals, *Exposure: A Sociologist Explores Sex, Society, and Adult Entertainment* (Austin, Texas: Greenleaf, 2015), 13. For a counter-attack on the sex-negative feminists see Lisa Duggan and Nan D. Hunter, *Sex Wars: Sexual Dissent and Political Culture* (New York: Routledge, 1995).

38. Lindsey Lovehands, "Today's Lesson: Don't Judge a SLUT by Her Cover," Apr 6, 2010, www.mikesouth.com.

39. *XBIZ* board, thread "Normal friends," Dee Severe post of Feb 28, 2015. www.xbiz.net/index.php?c=discussion.view_thread&id=14400.

40. "WIA Profile: Sabrina Miller," *XBIZ* Feature, Dec 14, 2011, www.xbiz.com/articles/141937.

41. Barefootsies post of Aug 12, 2014, thread "He stopped watching porn," www.xbiz.net/index.php?c=discussion.view_thread&id=12734.

42. Matt Purple, "Rare Under-40 Poll: Porn Is Ruining Our Sex Lives?" Sept 18, 2014, http://rare.us/story/one-third-of-young-people-say-porn-is-ruining-their-sex-lives/.

43. BDF/Toby Ross post of June 10, 2013, on thread "Watched Porn Hub last night and I understand why this is the road to nowhere," www.xbiz.net/index.php?c=discussion.view_thread&id=8920. BDF stands for the company Big Dik Factory.

44. Mar 1, 2001, http://business.avn.com/articles/video/Why-E-PORN-Hasn-t-Wooed-Or-Wowed-WOMEN-and-Ways-To-Win-FEMALE-TRAFFIC-40105.html.

45. Nichi Hodgson, "The Intimate Confessions of a Female Porn Fan," *Telegraph*, Aug 7, 2014, www.telegraph.co.uk/women/sex/11019232/Porn-Why-us-women-love-watching-sex-play-out-online.html.

46. Steve Lick, "Adult Entertainment: The Unsung Employer," Nov 21, 2008, www.mikesouth.com.

47. Zachary Goode interview, *XBIZ* Feature, May 24, 2015.

48. Kayden Kross, "Dear Grant," June 28, 2008, www.mikesouth.com.

49. Denise LaFrance, "Candida Royalle Interview," 2004, http://deniselafrancethepainter.blogspot.ca/2015/09never-before-seen-my-candida-royalle.html.

50. James D. Griffith et al., "Pornography Actresses: An Assessment of the Damaged Goods Hypothesis," *Journal of Sex Research*, 50 (2013), 621–632; doi: 10.1080/00224499.2012.719168.

51. Cited on "Porn in the USA," CBS News, http://www.cbsnews.com/news/porn-in-the-usa-21-11-2003.

52. http://jonmillward.com/blog/studies/deep-inside-a-study-of-10000-porn-stars/9.

53. Tod Hunter, "The Comeback Trail: Brittany O'Connell," *XBIZ* Features, July 18, 2009, www.xbiz.com/articles/125327.

54. Christine Schoenwald, Mar 2015, www.bustle.com/articles/70091-i-met-porn-star-keisha-and-it-completely-changed-everything.

55. L.R. Goldman, "Interview: Annette Haven," *AVN*, 2 (1) (Mar 1987), 22, 70.

56. Paul L. Montgomery, "'Throat' Obscene, Judge Rules Here," *NYT*, Mar 2, 1973, 1.

57. http://reason.com/blog/2008/07/24/the-porn-loving-people-vs-noam.

58. See the review by Dan Gutierrez, https://twitter.com/badoinkofficial/status/611398119385919489.

59. "The 2003 XRCO Awards," *AVN*, 19 (6), (June, 2003), 75.

60. See on this Whitney Strub, *Perversion for Profit: The Politics of Pornography and the Rise of the New Right* (New York: Columbia University Press, 2011), 240. Strub argues that porn became a mobilizing theme for the entire New Right.

61. Edwin Meese III, *Final Report of the Attorney General's Commission on Pornography* (Nashville: Rutledge Hill Press, 1986).

62. On the membership of the Meese Commission see Goldstein, *My Screwed Life*, 263–264.

63. See Jim Holliday, "Only the Best" column, *AVN*, 6 (1) (Jan 1991), 56, 61.

64. Philip Shenon, "A Second Opinion on Pornography's Impact," *NYT*, May 18, 1986, E8.

65. For a critique, see Andy Ruddock, "Pornography and Effects Studies: What Does the Research Actually Say?" in Lynn Comella and Shira Tarrant, eds., *New Views on Pornography: Sexuality, Politics, and the Law* (Santa Barbara: Praeger, 2015), 297–317.

66. Allison Vivas, *Making Peace with Porn* (Alameda, CA: Hunter House, 2013), 68.

67. Anthony D'Amato, "Porn Up, Rape Down," *Northwestern University School of Law: Public Law and Legal Theory Research Paper Series*, http://anthonydamato.law.northwestern.edu/.

68. George C. Thomas III, "A Critique of the Anti-Pornography Syllogism," *Maryland Law Review*, 52 (1993), 122–161, 124.

69. Quoted in Barry Reay et al., *Sex Addiction: A Critical History* (Cambridge: Polity Press, 2015), 157.

70. Helen Lewis, "10 Years on Twitter," *Financial Times*, Mar 5–6, 2016, 18.

71. William Robbins, "Beachhead in a War on Pornography, *NYT*, Nov 2, 1987, A16.

72. Academic writing on porn "addiction" tends to be highly judgmental. One big study found that "spending more than 11 hours a week on-line for sex" was "problematic." That works out to about 1.6 hours a day. Significant, to be sure, but pathological by whose standards? Alvin Cooper et al., "Sexuality on the Internet: From Sexual Exploration to Pathological Expression," *Professional Psychology Research and Practice*, 30 (1999), http://www.sex-centre.com/Internetsex_Folder/MSNBC_Study_pp.htm.

73. Barry Reay et al., *Sex Addiction: A Critical History* (Cambridge: Polity Press, 2015), 163.

74. Julie M. Albright, "Sex in America Online: An Exploration of Sex, Marital Status, and Sexual Identity in Internet Sex Seeking and Its impacts," *Journal of Sex Research*, 45 (2008), 175–186.

75. OldJeff post of Mar 1, 2016, on thread, "Is 'porn addiction' a real thing?" www.xbiz.net/index.php?c=discussion.view_thread&id=17652.

76. Nicole Prause et al., "Modulation of Late Positive Potentials by Sexual Images in Problem Users and Controls Inconsistent with 'Porn Addiction,'" *Biological Psychiatry*, 109 (2015), 192–199, 197. In related research, Prause reported that viewing porn increased sexual responsiveness rather than the opposite, as others had hypothesized. Prause et al., "Viewing Sexual Stimuli Associated with Greater Sexual Responsiveness, Not Erectile Dysfunction," *Sexual Medicine*, http://onlinelibrary.wiley.com/doi/10.1002/sm2.58/full.

77. "This porn star wants to help you have better sex," *Philadelphia City Paper*, Apr 23, 2015, http://citypaper.net/blogs/this-porn-star-who-wants-to-teach-you-how-to-have-better-sex/.

78. Dee Severe post of July 14, 2012, on thread "Do you ever defend what you do in the industry?" www.xbiz.net/index.php?c=discussion.view_thread&id=6748.

79. On the sex-positive views of women in the industry, see the interviews of Stormy Daniels, Michelle Freridge , Nina Hartley, Joy King, and Sharon Mitchell in Clay Calvert and Robert D. Richards, "Porn in Their Words: Female Leaders in the Adult Entertainment Industry Address Free Speech, Censorship, Feminism, Culture and the Mainstreaming of Adult Content," *Vanderbilt Journal of Entertainment and Technology Law*, 9 (2006), 255–299.

80. https://www.shelleylubben.com/shelleys-blog/02-21-11/shelley-lubben-calls-porn-modern-day-slavery-cambridge-university. In January 2016 Lubben's "Pink Cross Foundation," established in 2008 to educate about the evils of pornography, closed its doors. "After 11 years of doing this, I am porn'd out," said Lubben. See "Shelley Lubben's Pink Cross Foundation Shuts Down," *XBIZ* News, Jan 25, 2016, www.xbiz.com/news/203605.

81. "Jacklyn Lick Takes on Shelley Lubben," Feb 25, 2008, www.mikesouth.com.

82. Diane Duke, "How – and Why – I Became a Porn Industry Advocate," *Cosmopolitan*, Mar 24, 2015, www.cosmopolitan.com/sex-love/news/a38155/how-i-a-feminist-became-a-porn-industry-advocate, 5.

83. Adult Blog Writer post of June 1, 2013, on thread "*XBIZ World* talk back question," www.xbiz.net/index.php?c=discussion.view_thread&id=8759.

84. Erik Jay, "The Journey of Nica Noelle," *XBIZ* Feature, Dec 15, 2009, www.xbiz.com/articles/122864.

85. E.J. Dickson, "Porn Star Asa Akira Takes Us Inside Her New Book, 'Insatiable,'" May 20, 2014, www.dailydot.com/lifestyle/asa-akira-memoir-qanda/.

86. Dec 9, 2005, http://business.avn.com/articles/gay/Innerview-Unzipped-Video-s-Caryn-Goldberg-46827.html.

87. Ellen Willis, "Feminism, Moralism, and Pornography." This article was published originally in 1979. Ellen Willis, *Village Voice*, Oct. 15, 1979, Nov. 12, 1979, and reprinted in Ellen Willis, *Beginning to See the Light: Sex, Hope, and Rock-and-Roll*, 2nd ed. (Middletown, CT: Wesleyan University Press, 1992).

88. Ellen Willis, "Lust Horizons: Is the Women's Movement Pro-Sex?" reprinted in *No More Nice Girls: Countercultural Essays* (Hanover: University Press of New England [for] Wesleyan University Press, 1992).

89. Iris Blocks, "Forever Nina," *AVN*, 30 (1) (Jan 2014), 80.

90. Gayle Rubin, "Thinking Sex: Notes for a Radical Theory of the Politics of Sexuality," in Carole S. Vance, ed., *Pleasure and Danger: Exploring Female Sexuality* (London: Routledge, 1984), 267–319.

91. "Paul Cambria: 1," *XBIZ* Feature, Feb 15, 2007, www.xbiz.com/articles/19660/Sturman.

92. "The Cambria List," https://en.wikipedia.org/wiki/Paul_Cambria.

93. Emma Jacobs, "Porn's New Marketing Tactics," *Financial Times*, June 24, 2015.

94. Josh Israel, "This Is the Way the War on Pornography Ends," http://thinkprogress.org/justice/2014/10/08/3577238/failed-war-on-pornography-2/. In 2008, however, the British government enacted in the Criminal Justice and Immigration Act, provisions against the viewing of "extreme pornography," which included practices that were actually not extreme (in the world of adult, rather normal in fact) but were apparently included because various drafters found them distasteful. For a critique of this legislation, and citation of the relevant scientific literature undermining its assumptions, see Clarissa Smith, et al., "Why Do People Watch Porn?" in Lynn Comella and Shira Tarrant, eds., *New Views on Pornography: Sexuality, Politics, and the Law* (Santa Barbara: Praeger, 2015), 277–296, 294, fn. 21.

95. Stephen Yagielowicz, "The Reclamation of Feminist Porn?" *XBIZ* Newswire, Feb 9, 2017.

Ch. 5: Porn stars

1. Jim Gunn post of May 12, 2012, on thread "Porn star vs actor porn," www.xbiz.net/index.php?cdiscussion.view_thread&id=6387.

2. John Hubner, "Essays 1966–74, Scandinavian Porn," www.lukeisback.com/essays/essays/1966.htm. In New Orleans, once a porn center, around 1950 the models were said to be mainly prostitutes. Steven V. Roberts, "Pornography in U.S.: A Big Business," *NYT*, Feb 22, 1970, 1, 66.

3. This population has been poorly studied by scholars, partly because it is difficult to access, partly because of academic distaste for "porn." But see James D. Griffith et al., "Sexual Behaviors and Attitudes, Quality of Life, and Drug Use: A Comparison Between Bisexual and Heterosexual Pornography Actresses," *Journal of Bisexuality*, 13 (2013), 4–20; doi: 10.1080/15299716.2013.755729.

4. Tod Hunter, "WIA Profile: Kristin of Evil Angel Cash," *XBIZ* Feature, Sept 30, 2008, www.xbiz.com/articles/99709.

5. Jimmycooper post of Nov 20, 2011, on thread "What leads some of the hottest women anywhere to do porn?" www.xbiz.net/index.php?c=discussion.view_thread&id=5070.

6. David Houston, "The Birth of Porn Valley: 2," *XBIZ* Feature, June 16, 2005, www.xbiz.com/articles/9149.

7. Carly Milne, "Talent Agencies: Part 1," *XBIZ* Feature, May 2, 2005, www.xbiz.com/articles/8560.

8. Gram Ponante, "Writing for the Blue Screen," *XBIZ* Feature, Jan 1, 2008, www.xbiz.com/articles/88359.

9. http://jonmillward.com/blog/studies/deep-inside-a-study-of-10000-porn-stars/.

10. Richard Pacheco/Howie Gordon, *Hindsight: True Love & Mischief in the Golden Age of Porn* (Albany, GA: BearManor Media, 2013), 338–339.

11. "Shave Tail" ad, *AVN*, 1 (20) (Dec 1984), 10; "Shaved," *AVN*, 1 (21) (Jan 1985), 13.

12. http://www.gamelink.com/naked_truth.jhtml?id=earl-miller-interview; Wolf was on the cover of *Penthouse* in June 1985; some of the inside photos show her shaved, others not.

13. "Furburgers" ad, *AVN*, 2 (4) (June 1987), 19.

14. "Caballero Announces Traci Lords Blockbuster," *AVN*, 2 (5) (July/Aug 1987), 70.

15. "Selected Young Girl Titles Stocking Guide," *AVN*, 20 (5) (May 2004), 48, a box in Mark Kernes' story, "Chronic Youth," 37f.

16. http://jonmillward.com/blog/studies/deep-inside-a-study-of-10000-porn-stars/.

17. Roald Riepen, "Celebrating 15 years of FreeOnes," http://hostones.com/temp/Roald/infograph.jpg.

18. See Robert Rosen, *Beaver Street: A History of Modern Pornography* (London: Headpress, 2012), 177–178.

19. Jenna Jameson, *How to Make Love Like a Porn Star* (New York: Harper Collins, 2004), 513.

20. Roald Riepen, "Celebrating 15 years of FreeOnes," http://hostones.com/temp/Roald/infograph.jpg. For unclear reasons, these age figures may be on the high side: The average age of female models at entry into the industry, according to London-based Jon Millward's analysis of 7,000 female porn stars in the IAFD database, 1981-2013, was 22. http://jonmillward.com/blog/studies/deep-inside-a-study-of-10000-porn-stars/. An academic study of 176 female performers who were taking routine medical tests found their average age at the time of interview (in 2006) to be 26. James D. Griffith et al., "Why Become a Pornography Actress?" *International Journal of Sexual Health*, 24 (2012), 165–180. doi: 10.1080/19317611.2012.666514.

21. Paul Markham post of Mar 2, 2012, on thread "Why is fetish so big?" www.xbiz.net/index.php?c=discussion.view_thread&id=5671.

22. "Interview: Russ Meyer" *AVN*, 1 (4) (June 1983), 1, 10.

23. For details, see "Yanks.com Releases First Promotional Infographic," *XBIZ* Company Press, Jan 26, 2016, www.xbiz.com/news/203637.

24. I am grateful to Todd S. at YanksCash.com for sharing this questionnaire.

25. Edward O. Laumann et al., *The Social Organization of Sexuality: Sexual Practices in the United States* (Chicago: University of Chicago Press, 1994), Tab 9.1, 328.

26. Saharah Eve post of June 15, 2010, on thread "Is it worth it to be a porn star in 2011?" www.xbiz.net/index.php?c=discussion.view_thread&id=1930.

27. James D. Griffith et al, "Why Become a Pornography Actress?" *International Journal of Sexual Health*, (2012), 165-180. doi: 10.1080/19317611.2012.666514.

28. Vicky Vette discussion comment, *XBIZ* meeting in Los Angeles, Jan 13, 2016.

29. https://www.lelo.com/blog/oral-sexy-survey-results/.

30. "An Impolite Interview With Danyel Cheeks," *AVN*, 8 (4), (Mar 1993), 114.

31. Jon Millward, Feb 14, 2013, http://jonmillward.com/blog/studies/deep-inside-a-study-of-10000-porn-stars/.

32. Jim Holliday, quoted in David Jennings, *Skinflicks* (Bloomington, IN: 1st Books, 2000), 268.

33. David Jennings, *Skinflicks* (Bloomington, IN: 1ˢᵗ Books, 2000), 268.

34. Rodger Jacobs, "Taylor Wane," *XBIZ* Feature, Apr 5, 2006, www.xbiz.com/14239.

35. Joanne Cachapero, "The Business of Being Brittany," *XBIZ* Feature, Feb 18, 2008, www.xbiz.com/articles/90305.

36. Bob Johnson, "Kelly Madison's 'Mom & Pop' Studio Spans 16 Years," *XBIZ* News, June 5, 2015, www.xbiz.com/news/195351.

37. Mike South, "Den's Top Ten," Oct 3, 2003, www.mikesouth.com.

38. Mike South, "Want My Help? Read This," Dec 13, 2008, www.mikesouth.com.

39. Dan Miller, "WIA Profile: Francine Amidor," *XBIZ* Feature, June 27, 2011, www.xbiz.com/articles/135620.

40. "A Company Owner Writes," Dec 30, 2004, www.mikesouth.com.

41. Kayden Kross, "Glam and Gloss," *XBIZ*, July 21, 2008, www.xbiz.com/aerticles/96872.

42. Stormy Daniels interview, mikesouth.com, July 8, 2005.

43. http://www.xbiz.com/news/235290/stormy-daniels-named-penthouse-pet-of-the-century.

44. Mike South, "Contract Girls or Concubines?" May 8, 2003, www.mikesouth.com. I have redacted the name of the company.

45. Don Houston, post of Nov 9, 2014, on thread "Richest porn stars?" www.xbiz.net/index.php?c=discussion.view_thread&id=13535.

46. Ron Jeremy, *The Hardest (Working) Man in Showbiz* (New York: Harper Collins, 2008), 3.

47. Upbeat media articles about the lives of porn stars tend to downplay the negative aspects and the excellent chances that one will not be a long-term success. For a typical example see Doug Elfman, *Las Vegas Review Journal*, Oct 29, 2015, http://www.reviewjournal.com/opinion/columns-blogs/doug-elfman/society-much-more-accepting-porn-stars-these-days.

48. Lindsey Lovehands, "Today's Lesson: Don't Judge a SLUT by Her Cover," Apr 6, 2010, www.mikesouth.com.

49. David Jennings, *Skinflicks* (Bloomington, IN: 1ˢᵗ Book, 2000), 291.

50. Erik Jay, "Gonzo: Taking a Toll," *XBIZ* Feature, Sept 10, 2007, www.xbiz.com/articles/83870.

51. Jett Lynn, "The Deal with User-Generated Content," *XBIZ* Feature, Apr 12, 2008, www.xbiz.com/articles/92416.

52. Brooke Tyler, "The Vast Majority of Porn Valley Performers Are Destined for the Industry Standard of an Extremely Short Career," Jan 9, 2014, www.mikesouth.com.

53. See Jeffrey Escoffier, "Porn Stars/Stripper/Escort: Economic and Sexual Dynamics in a Sex Work Career," http://jh.haworthpress.com; doi: 10.1300/J082v53n01_08.

54. "And Bob Writes," Feb. 9, 2005, www.mikesouth.com.

55. http://www.lukeisback.com/2016/03/bree-olsons-untold-story/.

56. Harris Gaffin, *Hollywood Blue: The Tinseltown Pornographers* (London: Batsford, 1997), 179.

57. http://jonmillward.com/blog/studies/deep-inside-a-study-of-10000-porn-stars/.

58. Mike South, email to Edward Shorter, Aug 9, 2015.

59. B.L., "The Great Porn Depression of 2006," July 1, 2006, www.mikesouth.com.

60. Jim Holliday, *Only the Best* (Van Nuys, CA: Cal Vista Direct, 1986), 22.

61. "WIA Profile Joanna Angel," *XBIZ* Feature, May 16, 2008, www.xbiz.com/articles/94049.

62. Samantha38G, post of Oct 17, 2012, on thread "Do porn stars see no value in socializing with their peers here?" www.xbiz.net/index.php?c=.discussion.view_thread&id=7297.

63. Paul Thomas, "Their Favorite Sex Scenes, Part II: The Ladies," *AVN*, 1 (34) (June 1986), 55–56.

64. Dr. X, "Lisa Ann," *AVN*, 11 (3) (Jan 1996), 94, 106.

65. Richard Pacheco/Howie Gordon, *Hindsight: True Love & Mischief in the Golden Age of Porn* (Albany, GA: BearManor Media, 2013), 344.

66. Kayden Kross, "Dear Grant," June 28, 2008, www.mikesouth.com.

67. Kayden Kross, "Ode to the Dumb Cooze," June 21, 2008, www.mikesouth.com.

68. Boss Bitch, *XBIZ Premiere*, Apr 2015, 60.

69. David Jennings, *Skinflicks* (Bloomington, IN: 1st Books, 2000), 279.

70. Lindsey Lovehands, "Today's Lesson: Don't Judge a SLUT by Her Cover," Apr 6, 2010, www.mikesouth.com.

71. July 7, 2003, http://business.avn.com/articles/video/Mike-South-8217-Continues-Hallmark-of-Fresh-Faces-for-i-Southern-Magnolias-i-31520.html.

72. Acme Anderson, "Gonzo Newbie," *XBIZ* Feature, Sept 15, 2008, www.xbiz.com/articles/127894.

73. Stefan G., post of June 15, 2010, on thread "Is it worth it to be a porn star in 2011?" www.xbiz.net/index.php?c=discussion.view_thread&id=1930.

74. Christopher Hufnail, "*AVN*, 6 (10) (Oct 1991), 56; Admin, "Taylor Wane is Not Just a Fucking Whore, but She Says [person named] Is," Jan 3, 2005, www.mikesouth.com.

75. Louis Theroux, "How the Internet Killed Porn," *The Guardian*, June 5, 2012, www.theguardian.com/culture/2012/jun/05/how-internet-killed-porn. The Theroux piece was characterized by the usual moralistic handwringing: "lives of damage and abuse," the "tawdry" business.

76. Lacey Blake, "How I Tripped and Fell into the Politics of the Adult Industry," Dec 4, 2013, www.mikesouth.com.

77. "A Decade of Beautiful Sunsets," *AVN*, 17 (1) (Jan 2001), 149–153. The "Queen" sobriquet was used in an ad in March 2002, *AVN*, 18 (3), 119.

78. "Moonlite Bunnyranch" ad, *AVN*, 17 (7) (July 2001), 93. On the Howard Stern radio show, Kendra Jade Rossi discussed quite unabashedly escorting at the Bunny Ranch for $3,000 per client. Feb 14, 2000, http://business.avn.com/articles/video/Kendra-on-Stern-Annie-Ander-Sinn-finds-Vaginal-Millionaire-last-week-34084.html.

79. Mark Kernes, "Porn Star Prostitutes," *AVN*, 18 (4) (Apr 2002), 38–46.

80. Deemented [sic] post of May 24, 2011, on thread "Pros and cons, adult vs mainstream?" www.xbiz.net/index.php?c=discussion.view_thread&id=3941.

81. E.J. Dickson, "When Porn Stars Become Escorts: Lucrative New Trend Could Also Be Risky." *Salon*, http://www.salon.com/2014/02/24/when_porn_stars_become_escorts_lucrative_new_trend_could_also_be_risky/.

82. June 21, 2004, http://business.avn.com/articles/video/EscortSupport-Launches-Pretty-Girl-Model-Search-39244.html.

83. Mike South, "Then and Now," Oct 13, 2014, www.mikesouth.com.

84. Robbie post of Dec 22, 2010, on thread, "Are porn actresses prostitutes?" www.xbiz.net/index.php?c=discussion.view+thread&i0d=2945.

85. "20th Anniversary: A Retrospective," *AVN*, 2003, 204.

86. David Jennings, *Skinflicks* (Bloomington, IN: 1ˢᵗ Books, 2000), 101.

87. Mike South post of Nov 2, 2012, on thread "Do you consider the escort biz a segment of the adult entertainment industry?" www.xbiz.net/imndex.php?c=discussion.view_thread&id=7401.

88. Mike Ramone, "Ariana Jollee," *AVN*, 20 (5) (May 2004), 112.

89. Kayden Kross, "Dear Darrah," June 14, 2008, www.mikesouth.com.

90. Free Speech Coalition, "White Paper, 2005," http://www.globalcitizen.net/data/topic/knowledge/uploads/20090531182642533.pdf.

91. David Houston, "Dance Circuit Stars: 1," *XBIZ* Feature, Aug 12, 2005, www.xbiz.com/articles/9910; Peter Smith, "Stripping for Success," *XBIZ* Feature, Dec 22, 2008, www.xbiz.com/articles/126975.

92. David Houston, "Dance Circuit Stars: 2," *XBIZ* Feature, Aug 13, 2005, www.xbiz.com/articles/9916.

Ch. 6 Pioneering Women

1. Angie Rowntree, interview Aug 18, 2015, Montreal.

2. Jim Holliday, *Only the Best* (Van Nuys, CA: Cal Vista Direct, 1986), 232.

3. Holliday, *Only the Best*, 115.

4. Denise LaFrance, "Candida Royalle Interview," 2004, http://deniselafrancethepainter.blogspot.ca/2015/09never-before-seen-my-candida-royalle.html.

5. Denise LaFrance, "Candida Royalle Interview," 2004, http://deniselafrancethepainter.blogspot.ca/2015/09never-before-seen-my-candida-royalle.html.

6. Gila Morgan, "Stacey Hirsch," *XBIZ* Feature, Oct 22, 2006, www.xbiz.com/articles/80767.

7. Jared Rutter, "In the Company of Legends," *XBIZ* Feature, May 18, 2014, www.xbiz.com/articles/179097.

8. Ava Cadell, "Naked Truth: How Playboy Magazine Can Stay on Top," *XBIZ Premiere*, Nov 2015, 74.

9. Robbie post of Feb 13, 2014, on thread "When is a MILF/GILF too old?" www.xbiz.net/index.php?c=discussion.view_thread&id=10833.

10. Rhett Pardon, "Exec Seat: Eddie Arenas, Naughty America," *XBIZ* Feature, May 3, 2013, www.xbiz.com/articles/162156.

11. Roald Riepen, "Celebrating 15 years of FreeOnes," http://hostones.com/temp/Roald/infograph.jpg. The average age of MILFs, in the IADB data base, was 33. Jon Millward, http://jonmillward.com/blog/studies/deep-inside-a-study-of-10000-porn-stars/.

12. Cheryl Wischhover, "[Nina Hartley] Why I'm Still Doing Porn in My Late 50s [NSFW]." *Cosmopolitan*, May 19, 2015. [NSFW means "Not Safe For Work"] http://www.cosmopolitan.com/sex-love/a40596/nina-hartley-porn-late-50s/ It would be fairer to say that *American Pie* popularized the term MILF, which cropped up on the internet in the mid-1990s.

13. "The Golden Age of Pornhub," Pornhub Insights, Mar 2, 2015, www.piornhub.com/insights/pornhub-age. Founded in 2007, the giant website Pornhub produced periodically statistics, some of which are cited in this book, which must be taken with a grain of salt and have a reputation within the industry of being unreliable. See Ben Suroeste, "Strange But True: Porn Existed Before Pornhub," *YNOT* News, Dec 2, 2014, www.ynot.com/content/120198-strange-true-porn-existed-pornhub.html. I cannot judge that. But nowhere does Pornhub ever give the absolute numbers on which its percentages are based,

and tests of statistical significance lack entirely. Still, the statistics probably have a ballpark veracity, and they are the only statistics that we have.

14. Legs McNeil and Jennifer Osborne, *The Other Hollywood* (New York: HarperCollins, 2005), 372.

15. Rich Moreland, *Pornography Feminism* (Winchester, UK: Zero Books, 2015), 77-79.

16. Rob Perez, "CineKink's Club 90 Reunion," XCritic [2015], http://www.xcritic.com/columns/column.php?columnID=4488. On Club 90 see also Mark Kernes, "Candida Royalle," *AVN*, 8 (4) (Mar 1993), 112.

17. Feb 10, 2004, http://business.avn.com/articles/video/Jenna-Jameson-Siren-of-the-New-York-Media-37745.html.

18. Jenna Jameson, *How To Make Love Like a Porn Star* (New York: Harper Collins, 2004), 542.

19. May 1, 2001, http://business.avn.com/articles/video/1-On-1-With-Jenna-40101.html.

20. "Vicky Vette Celebrates Turning 50 With Site Promotion," *XBIZ* News, June 12, 2015, www.xbiz.com/news/195667. On the "double ender," see "Vicky Vette 'Double Ender' Available From Doc Johnson," Feb 4, 2015, *XBIZ* News, www.xbiz.com/news/190599.

21. Joanne Cachapero, "The Business of Being Brittany," *XBIZ* Feature, Feb 18, 2008, www.xbiz.com/articles/90305.

Ch. 7: Abuse?

1. Rodger Jacobs, "Eric Edwards," *XBIZ* Feature, Feb 10, 2006, www.xbiz.com/articles/13399.

2. Mar 1, 2000, http://business.avn.com/articles/video/HAS-ADULT-VIDEO-CONTENT-GONE-TOO-FAR-33865.html.

3. Dec 3, 2003, http://business.avn.com/articles/video/Byron-and-Black-are-Back-in-AVN-37208.html.

4. Thread "Would you let your kids enter the industry? Begun Jan 27, 2014, www.xbiz.net/index.php?c=discussion.view_thread&id=10657.

5. Mike South, "Kaiser Soze Sends me a Top Ten List," Jan 28, 2011, www.mikesouth.com.

6. Halcyon, "Take the High Road," *XBIZ* Feature, Mar 23, 2007, www.xbiz.com/articles/20240.

7. Scott Fayner, "Dick Delaware," *XBIZ* Feature, Jan 4, 2007, www.xbiz.com/articles/80403.

8. Dee Severe, "Performer Consent and Safety on Set Starts With the Director," *XBIZ* Dec 11, 2015, www.xbiz.com/news/202142.

9. "TRPWL Spotlight: Alexia Vosse," www.xbiz.net/index.php?c=user.view_blog&id=10408.

10. "Janet Mason Talks About Shooting in Pro Porn and Why She Won't Be Doing It Anymore," Jan 4, 2010, www.mikesouth.com.

11. Mike South, "Diane Duke Says Pornographers Have 'A Code of Ethics', Wait! What!" mikesouth.com, Mar 23, 2011.

12. http://jonmillward.com/blog/studies/deep-inside-a-study-of-10000-porn-stars/.

13. Sophia St. James post of Dec 17, 2009, on thread "How NOT to speak to potential talent," www.xbiz.net/index.php?c=discussion.view_thread&id=915.

14. L.R. Goldman, "Interview: Marlene Willoughby," *AVN*, 1 (11) (Jan 1984), 1, 12.

15. Joanne Cachapero, "Horror Stories From the Set," *XBIZ* Feature, Oct 20, 2006, www.xbiz.com/articles/80765.

16. David Jennings, *Skinflicks* (Bloomington, IN: 1 Books, 2000), 276.

17. Papillon, "Another Scumbag Exposed," guest column, July 29, 2003, www.mikesouth.com.

18. Al Goldstein, *I, Goldstein: My Screwed Life* (New York: Thunder's Mouth Press, 2006), 255.

19. Memphis Monroe, "Branding a Star," *XBIZ* Feature, May 8, 2008, www.xbiz.com/articles/93583.

20. www.cutyvibe.com/newyork/PremiumEscorts/memphis-monroe-porn-sgtar/279601.

21. Mar 2, 2000, http://business.avn.com/articles/video/Scotty-on-Ed-33857.html.

22. [Assault story], Jan 29, 2003, www.mikesouth.com.

23. Jerome Tanner, in discussion, "*AVN* Directors' Roundtable: Old School/New School, Smackdown, part 2,"*AVN*, 19 (2) (Feb 2003), 50.

24. Veronica Hart in discussion, "*AVN* Directors' Roundtable: Old School/New School, Smackdown, part 2,"*AVN*, 19 (2) (Feb 2003), 52.

25. Paul Thomas, "Their Favorite Sex Scenes, Part II: The Ladies," *AVN*, 1 (34)) (June 1986), 55–56.

26. Feb 4, 2000, http://business.avn.com/articles/video/Vivian-Valentine-on-Rough-Sex-34169. html; an even more graphic incident is at Mar 1, 2000, http://business.avn.com/articles/video/ROUGH-SEX-PULLED-IN-WAKE-OF-CONTROVERSY-33864.html.

27. Samantha38G (Samantha Anderson), post of Oct 29, 2014, on thread "Brand new producer here," http://www.xbiz.net/index.php?c=discussion.view_thread&id=13430&offset=0&perpage=50.

28. R.S. Benedict, Dec 4, 2015, https://unicornbooty.com/the-porn-industry-handles-rape-better-than-hollywood.

29. See Edward Shorter, *Before Prozac: The Troubled History of Mood Disorders in Psychiatry* (New York: Oxford University Press, 2009).

Ch. 8: Internet

1. Gretchen Gallen, ""Exclusive Interview with Video Secrets," *XBIZ* Feature, Apr 26, 2004, www.xbiz.com/articles/3004.

2. Holly Randall, "The *XBIZ* Events," *XBIZ* Feature, May 17, 2008, www.xbiz.com/articles/94085.

3. "Ambush Interview: Shap," www.ambushinterview.com/42/interview42.html.

4. Rich, post of May 24, 2011, on thread "Pros and cons: adult vs mainstream," www.xbiz.net/index.php?c=discussion.view_thread&id=3941.

5. Patchen Barss, *The Erotic Engine: How Pornography Has Powered Mass Communication from Gutenberg to Google* (Toronto: Anchor Canada, 2010), 197.

6. On the Lensman story, see Lori Z., "An Interview With Lensman, Part 1," *XBIZ* Feature, Nov 22, 2004, www.xbiz.com/articles/2076; Slav Kandyba, "Joe Lensman Leaves Playboy's Webmaster Business," *XBIZ* News, Dec 11, 2008, www.xbiz.com/news_piece,php?id=102734&mi=all&q=Lensman [sic].

7. Robbie post of June 18, 2011, on thread "Streaming vs download," www.xbiz.net/index.php?c=discussion.view_thread&id=4096. Robbie post of Apr 10, 2011, on thread "Porn industry to flee California?" www.xbiz.net/index.php?c=discussion.view_thread&id=3638.

8. Jay Kopita to Edward Shorter, personal communication, Nov 25, 2015.

9. Joanne Cachapero, "Rick Muenyong," *XBIZ* Feature, Sept 11, 2006, www.xbiz.com/articles/17095.

10. Robert Jenkins (Khan), to Edward Shorter, personal communication, Nov 27, 2015.

11. Colin Rowntree to Edward Shorter, personal communication, Nov 25, 2015.

12. http://www.forbes.com/1998/07/10/feat_side1.html; on Mansfield see Frederick S. Lane III, *Obscene Profits: The Entrepreneurs of Pornography in the Cyber Age* (New York: Routledge, 2000), 89.

13. Rick Muenyong (Moby) to Edward Shorter, personal communication, Nov 28, 2015.

14. July 1, 2003, http://business.avn.com/articles/video/Thinking-of-the-Key-Why-Wasteland-com-s—Colin-Rowntree-is-Our-Hero-38907.html.

15. David Kushner, Jan 27, 2015, http://www.rollingstone.com/culture/features/strippers-rappers-and-vr-porn-welcome-to-internext-20150127.

16. Robert Jenkins (Khan) to Edward Shorter, personal communication, Nov 27, 2015.

17. Josh Israel, "This Is the Way the War on Pornography Ends," http://thinkprogress.org/justice/2014/10/08/3577238/failed-war-on-pornography-2/.

18. Nicolas DiDomizio, July 7, 2015, http://mic.com/articles/121846/11-unexpected-things-you-didn-t-know-about-millennials-and-porn#.PxZTmhDrK.

19. Erik Jay, "Gonzo: Taking a Toll," *XBIZ* Feature, Sept 10, 2007, www.xbiz.com/articles/83870.

20. Post of Jan 7, 2016, http://www.ynot.com/are-images-worth-anything-today/.

21. Mike South post of May, 12, 2014, on thread "Improving Porn for Modern Times?" www.xbiz.net/index.php?c=discussion.view_thread&id=11762.

22. Jonathan Coopersmith, "Does Your Mother Know What You *Really* Do? The Changing Nature and Image of Computer-Based Pornography," *History and Technology*, 22 (2006), 1–25, doi: 10.1080/07341510500508610.

23. Acme Anderson, "Old School Meets New," *XBIZ* Feature, Dec 19, 2008, www.xbiz.com/articles/126971.

24. Nov 1, 2005, http://business.avn.com/articles/video/AVNONLINE-FEATURE-200511-Bridling-the-Bandwidth-Beast-46444.html.

25. John Scura, "Karl Bernard," *XBIZ* Feature, Nov 20, 2006, www.xbiz.com/articles/18225.

26. Gila Morgan, "Steve Lightspeed," *XBIZ* Feature, Mar 19, 2007, www.xbiz.com/articles/20147. See also, Mar 1, 2005, http://business.avn.com/articles/video/PROFILE-200503-Lightspeed-Cash-Embracing-the-Rock-Star-Phenomenon-42401.html; David Kesmodel, "Keeping an Adult Biz and Family Life Separate," *Wall Street Journal*, Apr 14, 2006, http://www.wsj.com/public/article/SB114441900916020032-Ho7GX_b6DPtDWqLDdXewKIcVFl0_20070413.html.

27. Nov 1, 2002, http://business.avn.com/articles/video/Future-Shock-Trends-in-New-Adult-Technology-31137.html.

28. Arch Stanton, "John Stagliano, the Evil Angel Emperor," *XBIZ* Feature, July 15, 2009, www.xbiz.com/articles/125324.

29. Mike South, "See anybody ya know: from Lukeford.com," Aug 15, 2002, www.mikesouth.com

30. Jon Swartz, "Purveyors of Porn Scramble to Keep Up with Internet," *USA Today*, http://usatoday30.com/tech/techinvestor/industry/2007-06-05-internet-porn_N.htm.

31. This paragraph on Gamma is based on a number of announcements in *XBIZ*, most recently, Dan Miller, "On a Mission," *XBIZ Premiere*, Apr 2015, 67, 116.

32. "Porn.com Gives PimpRoll a Boost," *XBIZ*, Jan 8, 2008, www.xbiz.com/articles/88557.

33. Stephen Yagielowicz, "Adult Comes Full Circle," *XBIZ* Feature, Mar 28, 2011, www.xbiz.com/articles/132060.

34. Joe Daniels, "Jim Enright," *AVN*, 5 (12) (Dec 1990), 70–72.

35. Dan Savage, interview, *Sexual Health*, Spring, 2017. 75-76.

36. See posts by Danny Cox of Oct 25, 2011, on thread "How did you start in the 'XBiz'?" www.abiz.net/index.php?c=discussion.view_thread&id=4897; Jan 8, 2013 on the thread, "Opinions and help," www.xbiz.net/index,php?c=discussion.view_thread&id=7807; and Apr 11, 2013 on the thread, "19 Years and counting!" www.xbiz.net/index.php?c=discussion.view_thread&id=8389.

37. Blaise Cronin and Elisabeth Davenport, "E-rogenous Zones: Positioning Pornography in the Digital Economy," *The Information Society*, 17 (2001), 38–44.

38. Erik Jay, "Gonzo: Taking a Toll," *XBIZ* Feature, Sept 10, 2007, www.xbiz.com/articles/83870.

39. Holly Randall, "Pushing the Envelope," *XBIZ* Feature, Oct 25, 2008, www.xbiz.com/aerticles/100930.

40. Kris Conesa, Oct 14, 2004, http://www.miaminewtimes.com/news/the-ride-to-perdition-6367591.

41. Anna Cahnda, *YNOT*, Dec 19, 2014, www.ynot.com/content/120245-top-adult-niche-2014-take-wild-guess.html.

42. Doug Evans, "Many Flavors of Amateur: 1," *XBIZ* Feature, Mar 29, 2006, www.xbiz.com/14144.

43. Rodger Jacobs, "Homegrown Video," *XBIZ* Feature, Jan 3, 2006, www.xbiz.com/articles/80042.

44. Mike South, "Holding Up a Mirror," July 30, 2008, www.mikesouth.com.

45. Will Ryder discussion comment at *XBIZ* meeting in Los Angeles, Jan 13, 2016.

46. Jett Lynn, "The Deal with User-Generated Content," *XBIZ* Feature, Apr 12, 2008, www.xbiz.com/articles/92416.

47. Master Ryan post of July 26, 2013, on thread "People who can't get over the state of the industry," www.xbiz.net/index.php?c=discussion.view_thread&id=9288.

48. Joe D. post of Mar 15, 2012, on thread "So who gives away the most free porn?" www.xbiz.net/index.php?c=discussion.view_thread&id=5936.

49. Dee Severe blog post of Aug 26, 2014, www.xbiz.net/index.php?c=discussion.view_thread&id=12784.

50. https://en.wikipedia.org/wiki/MindGeek.

51. "Vampire Porn," http://www.slate.com/authors.david_auerbach.2.html.

52. Mike South, "No I Don't Help Girls Get Into the Business Anymore," Nov 27, 2011, www.mikesouth.com.

53. Brooke Tyler, "The Vast Majority of Porn Valley Performers Are Destined for the Industry Standard of an Extremely Short Career," Jan 9, 2014, www.mikesouth.com.

Ch. 9: New Tastes

1. Lotza Ed, "Lori Anderson Evolves," *XBIZ* Feature, www.xbiz.com/articles/17785.

2. Thread "Porn doesn't ruin sex?" Rochard (Richard Buss) post of Oct 14, 2014, www.ynot.com/adult-industry-board/84285-porn-doesn't-ruin-sex.html.

3. Nicolas DiDomizio, July 7, 2015, http://mic.com/articles/121846/11-unexpected-things-you-didn-t-know-about-millennials-and-porn#.bRog9XI7n.

4. http://www.thehollywoodgossip.com/2007/07/kelly-madison-and-chelsea-handler-discuss-celebrity-gossip/.

5. Dexter Stanley, "Producer Peter North," *XBIZ* Feature, Feb 8, 2006, www.xbiz.com/articles/80514.

6. Ivan Crozier, "Performing the Western Sexual Body after 1920," in Crozier, ed., *A Cultural History of the Human Body in the Modern Age* (Oxford: Berg, 2010), 43–70, 66.

7. July 25, 2003, http://business.avn.com/articles/video/RayVeness-Returns-to-Porn-31206.htm.

8. http://www.imdb.com/title/tt0081323/plotsummary?ref_=tt_stry_pl.

9. Interview with Kay Parker, in Robert J. Stoller, *Porn: Myths for the Twentieth Century* (New Haven: Yale University Press, 1991), 130.

10. www.adultvdempire.com/reviews/24427/barely-legal-4-porn-movies.html.

11. http://www.boobpedia.com/boobs/andrea_kurtz.

12. http://www.xvideos.com/tags/goldenshowers.

13. Rachel Hills, http://www.cosmopolitan.com/sex-love/news/a33905/sex-talk-realness-golden-showers/.

14. Rhett Pardon, "Q&A With Kink.com's Peter Acworth," *XBIZ* Feature, Oct 26, 2012, www.xbiz.com/articles/155554.

15. "Amateur BlowBang Site Debuts," July 29, 2015, http://www.ynoteurope.com/amateur-blowbang-site-debuts.

16. Gene Ross, "Starbangers I," *AVN*, 8 (8) (July 1993), 18.

17. XCritic Interviews: "Keisha Grey Is the New Gangbang Girl," XCritic, www.xcritic.com/columns/columnphp?columnID=4644.

18. Alejandro Freixes, "Fall in Lovia," *XBIZ Premiere*, Nov 2017, 61f, 121.

19. Dan Miller, "Natural High: Australian Star Angela White Discusses the Making of 'Angela 2,'" *XBIZ Premiere*, Sept 2015, 64, 114.

20. Jim Holliday, *Only the Best* (Van Nuys, CA: Cal 1986), 218–219.

21. Dec 7, 1999, http://business.avn.com/articles/video/Chloe-Fist-in-Her-Class-34688.html; Jan 20, 2000, http://business.avn.com/articles/video/This-Is-The-Fist-The-Whole-Fist-and-Nothing-But-the-Fist-34349.html.

22. Susannah Breslin, "Extreme Porn Crackdown," http://www.salon.com/2001/07/12/seymore/.

23. http://fistingday.com.

24. Steven Ziplow, *The Film Maker's Guide to Pornography* (New York: Drake, 1977), 31–32.

Ch. 10: Gonzo

1. Mike South, "What's Hot, What's Not," July 12, 2005, www.mikesouth.com.

2. May 7, 2003, http://business.avn.com/articles/video/I-The-Adventures-of-Buttman-I-Remastered-For-DVD-Release-31997.html.

3. Mar 11, 2008, http://business.avn.com/articles/video/Pure-Play-Brings-i-Homegrown-Classics-i-to-DVD-for-First-Time-26929.html.

4. Angel@XesNetwork, post of Oct 25, 2011, thread "How did you start in the 'X Biz'?" www.xbiz.net/index.php?c=discussion.view_thread&id=4897.

5. Jan 20, 2000, http://business.avn.com/articles/video/Karch-On-Seven-34350.html.

6. Jan 18, 2000, http://business.avn.com/articles/video/Bruce-Seven-Dies-34377.html.

7. Acme Anderson, "The Genesis of Gonzo," *XBIZ* Feature, Aug 8, 2007, www.xbiz.com/82784.

8. John Stuart, "The Internet and Gonzo," *XBIZ* Feature, Sept 5, 2007, www.xbiz.com/articles/83732.

9. "Elegant Angel Signs Alexis Texas," *XBIZ World*, July 2015, 75.

10. See Rich Moreland, *Pornography Feminism* (Winchester, UK: Zero Books, 2015), 239, n 41.

11. Acme Anderson, "Gonzo In Their Own Words," *XBIZ* Feature, Sept 12, 2007, www.xbiz.com/articles/83949/Sturman.

12. Steve Javors, "The Godfathers of Gonzo," *XBIZ* Feature, Sept 25, 2007, www.xbiz.com/articles/84467.

13. Gene Ross, "Ed Powers," *AVN*, 5 (10) (Sept 1990), 52–53.

14. Acme Anderson, "The Genesis of Gonzo," *XBIZ* Feature, Aug 8, 2007 , www.xbiz.com/82784.

15. "Gonzo," *AVN*, 7 (12) (Nov 1992), 67.

16. Ernest Greene (Ira Levine), "The Magic Formula," *XBIZ* Feature, Aug 31, 2007, www.xbiz.com/articles/83642.

17. Oct, 27, 1999, http://business.avn.com/articles/video/Interview-With-Rodney-Moore-35058.html.

18. John Stuart, "The Internet and Gonzo," *XBIZ* Feature, Sept 5, 2007, www.xbiz.com/articles/83732/John+Desjardins.

19. "The Powers That Be," *XBIZ* Feature, Sept 12, 2008, www.xbiz.com/articles/127902.

20. Harris Gaffin, *Hollywood Blue: The Tinseltown Pornographers* (London: Batsford, 1997), 191.

21. Tom Hymes, "In the Executive Seat: Richard Cohen," *XBIZ* Feature, Mar 9, 2009, www.xbiz.com/articles/105661.

22. Paul Fishbein, "The Decade in Review, part 1," *AVN*, 4 (7) (Dec, 1989), 49.

23. Gram Ponante, "Writing for the Blue Screen," *XBIZ* Feature, Jan 1, 2008, www.xbiz.com/articles/88359.

24. Rodger Jacobs, "Faster, Cheaper, Nastier," *XBIZ* Feature, Aug 6, 2006, www.xbiz.com/articles/80645.

25. Gram Ponante, "Writing for the Blue Screen," *XBIZ* Feature, Jan 1, 2008, www.xbiz.com/articles/88359.

26. Ernest Greene (Ira Levine), "Behind the Camera," *XBIZ* Feature, June 14, 2008, www.xbiz./articles/95341.

27. Acme Anderson, "Under the Radar: Girls," *XBIZ* Feature, Mar 13, 2008, www.xbiz.com/articles/91094.

28. On blacks in adult films see Lawrence C. Ross, Jr., *Money Shot: Wild Days and Lonely Nights Inside the Black Porn Industry* (New York: Thunder's Mouth Press, 2007).

29. Gram Ponante, "Writing for the Blue Screen," *XBIZ* Feature, Jan 1, 2008, www.xbiz.com/articles/88359.

30. Roy Karch, "Stuck in the Middle With You," *XBIZ* Feature, Aug 5, 2010, www.xbiz.com/articles/123793.

31. Joanne Cachapero, "Gonzo Facing the Curtain," *XBIZ* Feature, Jan 1, 2007, www.xbiz.com/articles/80397.

32. Robert Dante, "Marketing: Story-Driven Porn," *AVN*, 17 (2) (Feb 2001), 35.

33. Mike South, "The Great Porn Depression of 2006," July 1, 2006, www.mikesouth.com.

34. Ernest Greene (Ira Levine), "Money in the Middle," *XBIZ* Feature, May 23, 2008, www.xbiz.com/articles/94344.

35. Erika Lust, "How Virtual Reality Could Change Porn for the Better," *Fortune*, July 29, 2015. http://fortune.com/2015/07/29/virtual-reality-porn/.

36. "Goodbye to Buttman," *AVN*, 21 (2) (Feb 2005), 227.

37. "*AVN* Directors' Roundtable: Old School/New School, Smackdown, part 2," *AVN*, 19 (2) (Feb 2003), 2.

38. Feb 20, 2004, http://business.avn.com/articles/video/Suze-Randall-Returns-to-Live-Action-Porn-37839.htm.

Ch. 11: Shooting

1. Tim Case, "Day 3 in the Ongoing Saga of 'The Foxes go to Porn Valley,'" June 28, 2002, www.mikesouth.com.

2. Tim Case, "The Latest in the Ongoing Saga 'Fifi does LA,'" July 3, 2002, www.mikesouth.com.

3. Julie Meadows, "Damien Michaels, and How Porn is Not All Bad," Nov 20, 2009, www.mikesouth.com.

4. Holly Randall, "Pushing the Envelope," *XBIZ* Feature, Oct 25, 2008, www.xbiz.com/articles/100930.

5. "Director Greg Lansky Discusses Blacked.com, Career," *XBIZ* News, June 18, 2015, www.xbiz.com/news/195853.

6. Stephen Yagielowicz, "*XBIZ* Polls: About You," Feb 24, 2003, www.xbiz.com/articles/1852.

7. Nica Noelle, "Cinepornographers: Porn's Producers Get Technical," *XBIZ* Feature, Dec 29, 2010, www.xbiz.com/articles/128923.

8. Paul Markham, on thread, "Trying to produce an amateur series solo with no experience. How's my business plan?" YNOT chatboard, 2014, www.ynot.com/adult-industry-board/84786-trying-produce-amateur-series-solo-experience-hows-business-plan.html. The YNOT chatboard posts are undated.

9. Erik Jay, "Paul Thomas," *XBIZ* Feature, Nov 20, 2007, www.xbiz.com/articles/86738.

10. Harris Gaffin, *Hollywood Blue: The Tinseltown Pornographers* (London: Batsford, 1997), 24.

11. Erik Jay, "Paul Thomas," *XBIZ* Feature, Nov 20, 2007, www.xbiz.com/articles/86738.

12. Apr 24, 2003, http://business.avn.com/articles/video/Belladonna-Speaks-About-Directing-for-Evil-Angel-32122.html.

13. Luke Ford, "Essays, 1966-74," www.lukeisback.com/essays/essays/1966.htm.

14. David Jennings, *Skinflicks* (Bloomington, IN: 1st Books, 2000), 177.

15. Ron Jeremy, *The Hardest (Working) Man in Showbiz* (New York: Harper Collins, 2008), 319.

16. Matthew Garrahan, "Rude Awakening," Oct 3, 2008, http://www.ft.com/intl/cms/s/0/4d57a930-8e9b-11dd-9b46-0000779fd18c.html.

17. Joanne Cachapero, "Horror Stories From the Set," *XBIZ* Feature, Oct 20, 2006, www.xbiz.com/articles/80765/Horror+stories+from+the+set.

18. Erik Jay, "Chris Streams: Working Class Biker," *XBIZ* Feature, Aug 17, 2008, www.xbiz. com/articles/127922.

19. Quoted in Ernest Greene, "Behind Every Director Is A Hard-on," *XBIZ* Feature, Sept 19, 2008, www.xbiz.com/articles/99385.

20. Jan 18, 2000, http://business.avn.com/articles/video/Bruce-Seven-Dies-34377.html.

21. Jim Holliday, *Only the Best* (Van Nuys CA: Cal Vista Direct, 1986), 8.

22. Rob Perez, "CineKink's Club 90 Reunion," XCritic [2015], http://www.xcritic.com/columns/column.php?columnID=4488.

23. Scott St. James et al., "Vow of Passion," *AVN*, 6 (12) (Dec 1991), 56, 59.

24. Bob Johnson, "Alexander DeVoe: Devoted to Porn," *XBIZ* Feature, May 24, 2011, www.xbiz.com/articles/134242.

25. Paul Markham, "An Introduction to Shooting Content: 2," *XBIZ* Feature, Sept 6, 2003, www.xbiz.com/articles/2016.

26. Paul Markham, "An Introduction to Shooting Content: 2," *XBIZ* Feature, Sept 6, 2003, www.xbiz.com/articles/2016.

27. Stephen Yagielowicz, "*XBIZ* Polls: About You," Feb 24, 2003, www.xbiz.com/articles/1852.

28. Ayrora Temple (Dawn Yagielowicz), "How To Treat a Model," *XBIZ* Feature, Sept 7, 2001, www.xbiz.com/articles/1409.

29. Dec 6, 1999, http://business.avn.com/articles/video/Bondage-Shoot-Cause-for-Concern-34705.html.

30. "Interview: Russ Meyer," *AVN*, 1 (4) (June 1983), 1, 11.

31. Matt Writes, July 30, 2008, www.mikesouth.com.

32. Robert J. Stoller, *Porn: Myths for the Twentieth Century* (New Haven: Yale University Press, 1991), 153.

33. "Matt Writes," July 30, 2008, www.mikesouth.com.

34. Addie Juniper, "Addie Juniper Tells Us Why She Got Into Porn," Mar 12, 2015, www.mikesouth.com.

35. Angels Royale blog post, Sept 27, 2014, www.xbiz.net/index.php?c=discussion.view_thread&id=12784.

36. Holly Randall, "Let's Talk About Penis Size," *XBIZ* Feature, Dec 13, 2008, www.xbiz.com/articles/102797.

37. Jenny Kutner, Feb 4, 2016, http://mic.com/articles/124849/what-porn-stars-want-you-to-know-about-the-difference-between-porn-sex-and-real-sex#.NnTqwDxJ2.

38. Oct 27, 1999, http://business.avn.com/articles/video/Interview-With-Rodney-Moore-35058.html.

39. Joe Daniels, "Jim Enright," *AVN*, 5 (12) (Dec 1990), 70–72.

40. "Interview with Veruca James," Aug 7, 2015, XCritic, http://www.xcritic.com/columns/column.php?columnID=4620.

Ch. 12: Woodsmen

1. Harris Gaffin, *Hollywood Blue: The Tinseltown Pornographers* (London: Batsford, 1997), 51.

2. Ron Jeremy, *The Hardest (Working) Man in Showbiz* (New York: Harper Collins, 2008), 1–2.

3. Harris Gaffin, *Hollywood Blue: The Tinseltown Pornographers* (London: Batsford, 1997), 50.

4. HepMan post of Feb 25, 2013, on thread "Reasons to work on [sic] porn," www.xbiz.net/index.php?c=discussion.view_thread&id=8063.

5. Sharan Street, "Seasoned Player: Tom Byron Celebrates Three Decades in the Business," *AVN*, 28 (12), (Dec, 2012), 58.

6. Oct 27, 1999, http://business.avn.com/articles/video/Interview-With-Rodney-Moore-35058.html.

7. "Career Launching," *AVN*, 8 (5), (Apr 1993), 97.

8. David Jennings, *Skinflicks* (Bloomington, IN: 1st Books, 2000), 309–310.

9. Joanne Cachapero, "Horror Stories From the Set," *XBIZ* Feature, Oct 20, 2006, www.xbiz.com/articles/80765.

10. David Jennings, *Skinflicks* (Bloomington IN: 1st Books, 2000), 274.

11. Adrian Chen, http://gawker.com/5946695/the-king-of-porn-gossip-meet-mike-south-the-man-who-got-to-the-bottom-of-porns-syphilis-outbreak.

12. Mike South, "Why? Lemme tell you why," Oct 16, 2002, www.mikesouth.com.

13. http://jonmillward.com/blog/studies/deep-inside-a-study-of-10000-porn-stars, p.9.

14. Blog comment, Sep 15, 2014, in *XBIZ* chatboard, www.xbiz.net/index.php?c=discussion.view_thread&id=13039.

15. Erik Jay, "Evermore, Everlong, Everhard," *XBIZ* Feature, Jan 15, 2009, www.xbiz.com/articles/126960.

16. Robert J. Stoller, *Porn: Myths for the Twentieth Century* (New Haven: Yale University Press, 1991), 159.

17. Acme Anderson, May 1, 2005, http://business.avn.com/articles/ADULTVIDEONEWS-MAY-2005-ON-THE-COVER-The-Men-Of-Porn-it-s-a-Woman-s-World-Men-Just-Fuck-in-it-44619.html.

18. Ron Jeremy, *The Hardest (Working) Man in Showbiz* (New York: Harper Collins, 2008), 10.

19. Note, *AVN*, Sept 1995, 48.

20. Gene Ross, "Citizen Holmes," *AVN*, 3 (6) (May 1988), 16.

21. See the Holliday interview in Robert J. Stoller, *Porn: Myths for the Twentieth Century* (New Haven, Yale UP, 1991), 166.

22. According to Greg Dark, in Legs McNeil and Jennifer Osborne, *The Other Hollywood* (New York: HarperCollins, 2005), 380.

23. Jim Holliday, *Only the Best* (Van Nuys, CA: Cal Vista Direct, 1986), 241. According to Luke Ford, Dick Rambone led the pack, with 15 inches. *A History of X* (Amherst, NY: Prometheus, 1999), 173.

24. David Jennings, *Skinflicks* (Bloomington, IN: 1st Books, 2000), 313.

25. Debby Herbenick et al., "Erect Penile Length and Circumference Dimensions of 1,661 Sexually Active Men in the United States," *Journal of Sexual Medicine*, 11 (2014), 93–101; 5.6" to be exact.

26. Robert J. Stoller, *Porn: Myths for the Twentieth Century* (New Haven: Yale University Press, 1991), 35.

27. Ron Jeremy, *The Hardest (Working) Man in Showbiz* (New York: Harper Collins, 2008), 49–53.

28. Ron Jeremy, *The Hardest (Working) Man in Showbiz* (New York: Harper Collins, 2008), 63.

29. Alexander Poe, "Forward Progress: Directors Say Technology Shaping Future," *XBIZ* Feature, Sept 10, 2015, www.xbiz.com/articles/198598.

30. "Retail Feedback," *AVN Confidential*, 1 (4) (June 1985), 8, 18.

31. David Jennings, *Skinflicks* (Bloomington, IN: First Books, 2000), 40–41.

32. Legs McNeil and Jennifer Osborne, *The Other Hollywood* (New York: HarperCollins, 2005), 233.

33. David Jennings, *Skinflicks* (Bloomington, IN: 1st Books, 2000), 54.

34. On AIDS as a possible cause of Holmes's death, see Gene Ross, "Citizen Holmes," *AVN*, 3 (6) (May 1988), 18.

35. Al Goldstein, *I, Goldstein: My Screwed Life* (New York: Thunder's Mouth Press, 2006), 149.

36. http://www.imdb.com/name/nm0000465/bio?ref_=nm_ov_bio_sm.

37. Ron Jeremy, *The Hardest (Working) Man in Showbiz* (New York: Harper Collins, 2008), 257.

38. Legs McNeil and Jennifer Osborne, *The Other Hollywood* (New York: HarperCollins, 2005), 366.

39. May 7, 2003, http://business.avn.com/articles/video/Tom-Byron-Sets-Up-His-Own-Studio-31992.html.

40. Acme Anderson, "Under the Radar: Guys," *XBIZ* Feature, Mar 12, 2008, www.xbiz.com/articles/91051.

41. Candida Royalle post of Aug 19, 2011, on thread "Marketing male porn stars," www.xbiz.net/index.php?c=discussion.view_thread&id=4490.

Ch. 13 Dominance

1. Conversation on set at pornshoot in Montreal, Aug 19, 2015.

2. See Patricia A. Cross and Kim Matheson, "Understanding Sadomasochism: An Empirical Examination of Four Perspectives," *Journal of Homosexuality*, 50 (2006), 133–166; doi: 10.1300/J082v50n02_07.

3. LELO, 2015, https://www.lelo.com/blog/the-bondage-survey-results-BDSM-statistics/.

4. For example, see David Bain et al., "Pain, Pleasure, and Unpleasure," *Review of Philosophy and Psychology*, 5 (2014), 1–14, who seem baffled at the phenomenon of sexual masochism. http://link.springer.com/article/10.1007/s13164-014-0176-5/fulltext.html.

5. Havelock Ellis, "Love and Pain," *Studies in the Psychology of Sex*, III (1913), 2 rev ed. (Philadelphia: Davis, 1928), 66–188, 82.

6. See Edward Shorter, *Written in the Flesh: A History of Desire* (Toronto: University of Toronto Press, 2005), Ch. 9.

7. On the great number of men as submissives, see Anne McClintock, "Maid to Order: Commercial S/M and Gender Power," in Pamela Church Gibson et al., eds., *Dirty Looks: Women, Pornography, Power* (London: BFI Pub., 1993), 207–231.

8. Barbara Ehrenreich, Elizabeth Hess, and Gloria Jacobs, *Re-Making Love: The Feminization of Sex* (New York: Anchor/Doubleday, 1986), 125–126.

9. Dee Severe, post of Oct 12, 2014, on thread "Kink to Rebrand Their Extreme Sites." http://www.xbiz.net/index.php?c=discussion.view_thread&id=13251.

10. Lori Gottlieb, http://www.nytimes.com/2014/02/09/magazine/does-a-more-equal-marriage-mean-less-sex.html?r=0.

11. Toronto woman, 39 at time of interview on Aug 4, 2014.

12. Keri Pentauk, *Spanked Husbands Satisfied Wives* (Los Angeles: Retro Systems, 1998).

13. Anna Cahnda, Jan. 11, 2016, www.ynot.com/avn-to-honor-fishbein-with-visionary-award/.

14. Christian C. Joyal et al., "What Exactly Is an Unusual Sexual Fantasy?" *Journal of Sexual Medicine*, 2014, doi: 10.1111/jsm.12734.

15. Melissa E. Travis, "Assume the Position: Exploring Discipline Relationships," Georgia State University, Department of Sociology, doctoral dissertation, 2013, http://scholarworks.gsu. edu/cgi/viewcontent.cgi?article=1070&context=sociology_diss.

16. "Hub Insights: More of What Women Want," July 25, 2015, www.pornhub.com/insights/ women-gender-demographics-searches.

17. Donald R. McCreary and Nancy D. Rhodes, "On the Gender-Typed Nature of Dominant and Submissive Acts," *Sex Roles*, 44 (2001), 339–350, 349.

18. Dan Cameron, "Playing for Keeps: Future of the Fetish/BDSM Market," *XBIZ* Feature, June 22, 2014, www.xbiz.com/articles/180716.

19. See Eddie Muller and Daniel Faris, *Grindhouse: the Forbidden World of "Adults Only" Cinema* (New York: St Martin's Press, 1996), 101–103.

20. See Eddie Muller and Daniel Faris, *Grindhouse: The Forbidden World of "Adults Only" Cinema* (New York: St Martin's Press, 1996), 128.

21. Jim Holliday, *Only the Best* (Van Nuys, CA: Cal Vista Direct, 1986), 69.

22. Review of "Dominant Dames," *AVN*, 7 (11) (Oct 1992), 94.

23. Sam Masters, "Alternative Sexuality and the Video Retailer," *AVN*, 8 (12) (Nov 1993), 60.

24. July 1, 2002, http://business.avn.com/articles/video/PERVERTS-VERSUS-POSEURS-Kink-Connoisseurs-Frown-Upon-Web-Sites-Produced-by-People-Who-Don-t-Understand-the-BDSM-and-Fetish-Lifestyles-39341.html.

25. "Mistress Dee Severe Interview," XCritic, www.xcritic.com/columns/column. php?columnID=4282.

26. "WIA Profile: Isabella Sinclaire," *XBIZ* Feature, July 11, 2008, www.xbiz.com/articles/96182.

27. Saharah Eve post of Aug 19, 2010, on thread "Soft core v hard core," www.xbiz.net/index. php?c=discussion.view_thread&id=2281.

28. "2015 Femdom Awards Winners Announced," *XBIZ World*, Mar 2015, 53.

29. See Edward Shorter, *Sadomasochism and Ardent Love: A Reader's Guide to "Fifty Shades of Grey,"* (Toronto: Bev Editions, March 2012), http://www.beveditions.com.

30. Conversation on the set of a pornshoot, Montreal, Aug 19, 2015.

31. Within the BDSM community, the novel and movie were not well received. The novel depicts Christian as dominant because of pathological childhood experiences (rather than because he simply likes spanking people). And the actual content of his encounters with Ana is very much on the milquetoast side. Still, the novel has been eye-opening for millions of people, and it was not written for insiders. For BDSM-community reactions, see for example, the blog "Miss Demeanour's BDSM-Talk," post "Fifty Shades of Misconception," www. BDSM-talk.co.uk/fifty-shades-of-misconception; Jacky St. James, "If 'Fifty Shades' Teaches Anyone About BDSM, We're All in a Lot of Trouble," Feb 13, 2015, www.craveonline.com/ film/articles/823223-fifty-shades-teaches-anyone-bdsm-lot-trouble.

32. Ariana Rodriguez, "Williams Trading Preps Retailers for *Fifty Shades* DVD Release," *XBIZ* News, Apr. 30, 2015, www.xbiz.com/news/194051.

33. "50 Shades of Pornhub," Feb 18, 2015, www.pornhub.com/insights/50-shades-bdsm-searches.

34. Bob Johnson, "Nevada Brothel Reports BDSM Spike From *50 Shades* Phenom," *XBIZ* News, Aug 5, 2014, www.xbiz.com/news/182998.

35. Jared Rutter, "Diversity Drives Market Trends in Fetish Video," June 26, 2014, www.xbiz. com/articles/181050.

36. John Sanford, "Kink Announces Rebranding," *XBIZ* News, Oct 10, 2014, www.xbiz.com/news/186231.

37. Rhett Pardon, "Q&A With Kink.com's Peter Acworth," *XBIZ* Feature, Oct 26, 2012, www.xbiz.com/articles/155554.

38. https://melmagazine.com/en-us/story/kink-is-dead-long-live-kink-2.

39. Ariana Rodriguez, "Heroes of Kink: Lovehoney Plays Instrumental Role in Mainstreaming BDSM," *XBIZ*, June 10, 2015. www.xbiz,com/articles/195262.

40. Lyn Bimey, "Mainstream Media: BDSM Unshaded," *XBIZ* Feature, Sept 3, 2012, www.xbiz.com/articles/152890.

41. Anna Cahnda, Oct 16, 2015, www.ynot.com/living-a-bdsm-lifestyle-on-the-edge/.

42. Jared Rutter, "Studio Execs Discuss State of Fetish Video," *XBIZ*, June 14, 2015; www.xbiz.com/articles/195320.

43. Jill Hagara, "'Fifty Shades of Grey' Movie Inspires Kinky Lingerie Fashion Styles," *XBIZ* Feature, May 10, 2015, www.xbiz.com/articles/194186.

44. For an overview, see Alexander Poe, "Instructionals: The Rise of Educational & Instructional Sex Videos," *XBIZ* Feature, Dec 21, 2014, www.xbiz.com/articles/189181.

45. SunFunBill post of Nov 26, 2014, thread ""Bad marketing," YNOT chatboard, www.ynot.com/adult-industry-board/84706-bad-marketing.html.

46. For the English edition see Richard von Krafft-Ebing, *Psychopathia Sexualis*, English translation by Franklin S. Klaf (New York: Stein and Day, 1965), 122–123.

47. A.J. Hall, "Niche Producers Still Killing It Sales-Wise," *XBIZ World*, Nov 2015, 12, 84. Italics added.

48. Stewart Tongue, "Content That Sells," *XBIZ* Feature, Mar 25, 2013, www.xbiz.com/articles/160950.

49. March 1, 2005, http://business.avn.com/articles/video/AVN-COM-BUSINESS-PROFILE-Homegrown-Video-Both-Sides-Now-Their-Video-and-Internet-Components-Feed-Each-Other-and-Thrive-44432.html.

50. "Studio Execs Discuss State of Fetish Video," *XBIZ* Feature, June 14, 2015, www.xbiz.com/articles/195320.

51. "Studio Execs Discuss State of Fetish Video," *XBIZ* Feature, June 14, 2015, www.xbiz.com/articles/195320.

52. Harris Gaffin, *Hollywood Blue: The Tinseltown Pornographers* (London: Butler, 1997), 34.

53. Holly Randall, "So Goes My Toes," *XBIZ*, Aug 1, 2007, www.xbiz.com/articles/82585.

54. Peter Smith, "Kink on the Web," *XBIZ* Feature , Aug 1, 2008, www.xbiz.com/articles/97316.

55. Dcgohard post of June 5, 2011, on thread "Why is this about interracial?" www.xbiz.net/index.php?c=discussion.view_thread&id=4001.

56. YNOT chatboard, thread "Are there any popular fetishes..." initiated May 20, 2015. www.ynot.com/adult-industry-board/86354-popular-fetishes-just-dont-get.html.

57. Harris Gaffin, *Hollywood Blue: The Tinseltown Pornographers* (London: Batsford, 1997), 138–139.

58. http://vintagelesbian.tumblr.com/post/1684097317/queering-strap-on-c1890.

59. http://www.thatposition.com/blog/august-2014/history-of-strap-on-sex.

60. Judson Rosebush to Edward Shorter, personal communication, Dec 13, 2015.

61. See, for example, Annie Le Brun et al., eds., *Oeuvres Complètes du Marquis de Sade*, vol 8 (Paris: Pauvert, 1987), 198, 459, 475-476, 560; this is parts 1-3 of the *Histoire de Juliette*.

62. Curran Nault, "*Bend Over Boyfriend* to *Take it Like a Man*: Pegging Pornography and the Queer Representation of Straight Sex," *Jump Cut: A Review of Contemporary Media*, no. 52 (Summer, 2010); www.ejumpcut.org/archive/jc52.2010/naultPegging/text.html.

63. Curran Nault, "*Bend Over Boyfriend* to *Take it Like a Man*: Pegging Pornography and the Queer Representation of Straight Sex," *Jump Cut: A Review of Contemporary Media*, no. 52 (Summer, 2010); www.ejumpcut.org/archive/jc52.2010/naultPegging/text.html.

64. *Samantha Fox's X-Rated Cinema*, Aug 1985, 29-21, shows an image of a female nude with the (partial) caption "begging for a pegging." In this case, the recipient is a female, but the use of the term does antedate Savage. Dan Savage, "Let's Vote," *The Stranger*, May 24, 2001, www.thestranger.com/seattle/SavageLove?old=7446.

65. Dale Gordon, *Anal Eroticism: Greek Style* (Cleveland: PhD Classic Library, 1968), 98–99.

66. Mark Kernes, "Only the Very Best on Film," *AVN*, 7 (12) (Dec 1992), 66.

67. Christopher Hufnail, "Taylor Wane," *AVN*, 6 (10) (Oct 1991), 56–57.

68. "Nasstoys Presents The Boss," *AVN*, 8 (10) (Sept 1993), 103.

69. "Strap-on Sally" ad, *AVN*, 8 (13) (Dec 1993), 107.

70. July 1, 2002, http://business.avn.com/articles/video/THE-NICHE-BITCH-With-10-Successful-Websites-Brittany-Andrews-is-Dominating-the-Internet-39340.html.

71. Sept 28, 2005, http://business.avn.com/articles/video/LeWood-Debuts-Fem-Dom-Series-45867.html.

72. Jan 31, 2006, http://business.avn.com/articles/video/i-Devinn-Lane-8217-s-Guide-to-Strap-on-Sex-i-Set-for-Release-47613.html.

73. Alex Henderson, "Making The Future: Major Pleasure Product Trends for 2015," *XBIZ* Feature, Mar 16, 2015, www.xbiz/com/articles/192250.

74. Anon to Edward Shorter, personal communication, July 15, 2014.

75. Apr 1, 2003, http://business.avn.com/articles/video/The-AVN-Online-Interview-Aria-38978.html.

76. Tina Tyler, "Bi Roots," *XBIZ* Feature, Feb 22, 2008, www.xbiz.com/articles/90455.

77. Johnny J., "History of Female Domination Magazines: 1900–1970," http://elisesutton.homestead.com/fdmags2.html.

78. Reed Gilmore, *The Punishment Complex* (New York: Unique Books, 1967) see Ch. 5.

79. AngelsRoyale post of Mar 4, 2012, on thread "Why is fetish so big?" www.xbiz.net/index.php?c=discussion.view_thread&id=5671

80. Kayden Kross, "About That," Nov 1, 2008, www.mikesouth.com.

81. Jason Kidd post of Aug 12, 2011, on thread "What's with people's fascination with 'cuckold' porn?" www.xbiz.net/index.php?c=discussion.view_thread&id=4434.

82. Adult Blog Writer, post of Sept 14, 2013, thread "Are you a cuckold?" www.xbiz.net/index.php?c=discussion.view_thread&id=9652.

83. "Could You Be A Cuckold?" Pornhub Insights, Nov 5, 2013, www.pornhub.com/insights/could-you-be-a-cuckold.

84. MistressCnLA, post of Sept 16, 2013, on thread "Are you a cuckold?" www.xbiz.net/index.php?c=discussion.view_thread&id=9652.

85. "Sumiso de Ama Nadya: FemDom Polls," http://chien-de-nadya.tumblr.com/polls.

86. Lila Gray, "King Adult Broadcast Network Announces Femdom Awards Show," *XBIZ* Feature, Jan 19, 2015, www.xbiz.com/news/189999.

Ch. 14: Fetish and BDSM

1. http://paulmarkham.com/fetish-porn/.

2. Lila Gray, "Lovehoney: Well-Educated People Have Less Sex, Enjoy Bondage," *XBIZ* News, May 22, 2014, www.xbiz.com/news/179467.

3. LELO, "The Bondage Survey Results: BDSM Statistics!" *Volonté*, nr 5 (2015), https://www.lelo.com/blog/the-bondage-survey-results-bdsm-statistics/.

4. Joanne Cachapero, "Fetish Retail," *XBIZ* Feature, July 6, 2007, www.xbiz.com/articles/81593.

5. Alejandro Freixes, "Wasteland, Severe Sex Join Forces for Exile-Distributed DVD Series," *XBIZ* News, Mar 31, 2016, www.xbiz.com/news/206245.

6. Richard von Krafft-Ebing, *Psychopathia Sexualis* (1886), English translation by Franklin S. Klaf (New York: Arcade, 2011), 157.

7. See Alex Henderson, "The Evolution and Diversification of Fetish Fashion," *XBIZ* Feature, Apr 29, 2013, www.xbiz.com/articles/162136.

8. Martin Robbins, www.theguardian.com/science/the-lay-scientist/2015/apr/30/porn-data-visualizing-fetish-space.

9. Joanne Cachapero, "Fetish Retail," *XBIZ* Feature, July 6, 2007, www.xbiz.com/articles/81593.

10. Mistress Hellkitty interview, Montreal, Aug 19, 2015.

11. Barbara Ehrenreich, Elizabeth Hess, and Gloria Jacobs, *Re-Making Love: The Feminization of Sex* (New York: Anchor/Doubleday, 1986), 123.

12. Quentin Boyer, "Consumers Embracing BDSM, Fetish Products Like Never Before," *XBIZ* Feature, June 29, 2014, www.xbiz.com/articles/181054.

13. Edward Shorter, *Written in the Flesh: A History of Desire* (Toronto: University of Toronto Press, 2005), 204, 206–207.

14. Alfred Binet, "Le Fétchisme dans l'Amour," *Etudes de Psychologie Expérimentale*, no vol. number (1888), 1–85, "le grand fétichisme" and "le petit fétichisme." 4–5.

15. On BDSM writing around 1900, called then "algolagnia" or "algophilia," love of pain, see Ivan Crozier, "Philosophy in the English Boudoir: Havelock Ellis, Love and Pain, and Sexological Discourses on Algophilia," *Journal of the History of Sexuality*, 13 (2004), 275–305; doi: 10.1353/sex.2005.0007.

16. On "London Life" see Valerie Steele, *Fetish: Fashion, Sex and Power* (New York: Oxford, 1996).

17. Johnny J., "History of Female Domination Magazines: 1900–1970," http://elisesutton.homestead.com/fdmags2.html.

18. On Eric Stanton see https://www.goodreads.com/author_blog_posts/1046988-eric-stanton-aka-ernest-stanten-aka-ernest-stanzoni-aka-stan-or-in.

19. Johnny J., "History of Female Domination Magazines: 1900–1970," http://elisesutton.homestead.com/fdmags2.html.

20. Johnny J., "History of Female Domination Magazines: 1970 – Present," http://elisesutton.homestead.com/fdmags3.html.

21. See Edward Shorter, *Written in the Flesh: A History of Desire* (Toronto: University of Toronto Press, 2005), 224–236.

22. Apr 1, 2005, http://business.avn.com/articles/video/AVN-COM-BUSINESS-PROFILE-Harmony-Concepts-All-Girl-Bondage-Company-Disciplines-Itself-to-Adapt-44437.html.

23. Jan 3, 2000, http://business.avn.com/articles/video/STORMY-LEATHER-UP-FOR-SALE-34438.html.

24. Alex Henderson, "Kink's Cornerstone: Stockroom's 25th Anniversary," *XBIZ* Feature, Apr 4, 2014, www.xbiz.com/articles/177349.

25. Alex Henderson, "The Bettie Page Revival: 2," *XBIZ* Feature, May 26, 2006, www.xbiz.com/articles/15001.

26. Jim Holliday, *Only the Best* (Van Nuys, CA: Cal Vista Direct, 1986), 38.

27. Sam Masters, "Alternative Sexuality and the Video Retailer," *AVN*, 8 (12) (Nov 1993), 60.

28. Alex Henderson, "BDSM Shakes Up Vanilla Porn," *XBIZ* Feature, May 19, 2008, www.xbiz.com/articles/94154.

29. Ernest Greene (Ira Levine), "Hardcore Kink Rules," *XBIZ* Feature, Aug 2, 2008, www.xbiz.com/articles/97373.

30. Ernest Greene, "Hardcore Kink Rules," *XBIZ* Feature, Aug 2, 2008, www.xbiz.Feature, Aug 2, 2008, www.xbiz.com/articles/97373.

31. Ernest Greene, "Hardcore Kink Rules," *XBIZ* Feature, Aug 2, 2008, www.xbiz.Feature, Aug 2, 2008, www.xbiz.com/articles/97373.

32. Alex Henderson, "BDSM Shakes Up Vanilla Porn," *XBIZ* Feature, May 19, 2008, www.xbiz.com/articles/94154.

33. Ernest Greene, "Hardcore Kink Rules," *XBIZ* Feature, Aug 2, 2008, www.xbiz.com/articles/97373.

34. Apr 5, 2005, http://business.avn.com/articles/video/Adam-Eve-to-Release-Hartley-s-Guide-to-Bondage-43006.html.

35. Jared Rutter, "Diversity Drives Market Trends in Fetish Video," *XBIZ* Feature, June 26, 2014, www.xbiz.com/articles/181050.

36. http://business.avn.com/articles/video/Sex-at-350RPM-The-F-ing-Machine-Ain-t-No-Mechanical-Bull-39344.html.

37. Joanne Cachapero, "Really Kinky: 1," *XBIZ* Feature, Mar 15, 2007, www.xbiz.com/articles/20100; Tom Hymes, "Kink.com: Demystifying Alternative Sexuality," *XBIZ* Feature, Feb 12, 2009, www.xbiz.com/articles/104566.

38. See Dan Miller, "Hurts So Good," *XBIZ Premiere*, June 2015, 66-67, 114; June 1, 2005, http://business.avn.com/articles/video/PROFILE-200506-CyberNet-Bucks-Turning-fetish-into-a-fortune-43925.html.

39. Bob Johnson, "King of the Kinkdom," *XBIZ* Feature, June 25, 2012, www.xbiz.com/articles/150124.

40. Jared Rutter, "Diversity Drives Market Trends in Fetish Video," June 26, 2014, www.xbiz.com/articles/181050.

41. "Severe Society Films: Serious About Severity," *YNOT* News, Sept 9, 2014, www.ynot.com/content/120012-severe-society-films-serious-severity,html.

42. Lila Gray, "Exile Inks Distro Deal with Severe Sex," *XBIZ* Feature, Sept 29, 2014, www.xbiz.com/news/185641.

43. Judson Rosebush email to Edward Shorter, Aug 10, 2015.

44. Jared Rutter, "Fetish: More Than Meets the Eye," *XBIZ* Feature, June 17, 2013, www.xbiz.com/articles/163969.

45. Stephen Yagielowicz, "Wasteland," *XBIZ* Feature, Mar 27, 2005, www.xbiz.com/articles/80053; Colin Rowntree post of Oct 25, 2011 on thread "How did you start in the 'X Biz?'" www.xbiz.net/index.php?c=discussion.view_thread&id=4897.

46. Stephen Yagielowicz, "Wasteland," *XBIZ* Feature, Mar 27, 2005, www.xbiz.com/articles/80053.

47. Alex Henderson, "BDSM and Affiliate Marketing," *XBIZ* Feature, Oct 2, 2008, www.xbiz.com/articles/99808.

48. Alex Henderson, "BDSM: Customer Service and Customer Care," *XBIZ* Feature, Mar 30, 2009, www.xbiz.com/articles/106527.

49. Master Ryan blog post, Sept 28, 2014, www.xbiz.net/index.php?c=discussion.view_thread&id=12784.

50. https://en.wikipedia.org/wiki/Sex_(book).

51. "BDSM Shakes Up Vanilla Porn," *XBIZ* Feature, May 19, 2008, www.xbiz.com/articles/94154.

52. Dee Severe post of Feb 24, 2011, on thread "Reaching 18 to 34 year old males?" www.xbiz.net/index.php?c=discussion.view_thread&id=3315.

53. PornLaw (Michael Fattorosi) post of Oct 28, 2014, http://www.xbiz.net/index.php?c=discussion.view_thread&id=13430.

54. Judson Rosebush email to Edward Shorter, Aug 10, 2015.

55. Alex Parker, "How To Prepare for the Next Big Thing in Adult Retail," *XBIZ* Feature, Mar 26, 2015, www.xbiz.com/articles/192681.

Ch. 15: Anal

1. http://www.dailydot.com/lifestyle/asa-akira-memoir-qanda/; see also http://www.salon.com/2015/02/02/ass_is_the_new_pussy_why_anilingus_is_on_the_rise_partner/.

2. Ron Jeremy, *The Hardest (Working) Man in Showbiz* (New York: Harper Collins, 2008), 7.

3. Charlie Glickman, "Back Door Basics: Get Ready for Anal Sex Month," *XBIZ* Feature, Aug 16, 2015, www.xbiz.com/articles/197563.

4. Catherine H. Mercer et al., "Changes in Sexual Attitudes and Lifestyles in Britain Through the Life Course and Over Time: Findings From the National Surveys of Sexual Attitudes and Lifestyles (Natsal)," *Lancet*, 382 (Nov 30, 2013), 1781–1794, see tab 4, p. 1789.

5. C.E. Coppen et al., "Sexual Behavior, Sexual Attraction, and Sexual Orientation in the United States: Data From the 2011-2013 National Survey of Family Growth," *National health statistics reports*; no. 88. Hyattsville, MD: National Center for Health Statistics. 2016, tab 1.

6. Dan Cameron, "When It Comes to Sex Toys, Gay Consumers Are the Trendsetters," *XBIZ* Feature, Mar 28, 2014, www.xbiz.com/articles/177090.

7. Barb Corbett, "Retailing Adult: Cleveland," *AVN*, 8 (9) (Aug 1993), 98.

8. Coleen Singer, "The Fascination with Anal Sex in Porn and Relationships," www.eroticscribes.com/the-internets-fascination-with-anal-sex-in-porn/.

9. Nicolas DiDomizio, July 7, 2015, http://mic.com/articles/121846/11-unexpected-things-you-didn-1-know-about-millennials-and-porn.

10. Lila Gray, "Pleasure Chest to Host Anal August State Fairground," *XBIZ* Feature, Aug 7, 2014, www.xbiz.com/news/183150.

11. Frank Kobola, "7 Quick and Easy Ways to Experiment With Kink," www.cosmopolitan.com/sex-love/news/a30020/quick-and-easy-ways-to-experiment-with-kink/.

12. William Margold interview in David Hebditch and Nick Anning, *Porn Gold: Inside the Pornography Business* (London: Faber and Faber, 1988), 98.

13. Luke Ford, *A History of X* (Amherst, NY: Prometheus, 1999), 208-209.

14. John Paone, "Interview: Barbara Dare," *AVN*, 1 (45) (Nov 1986), 44.

15. http://jonmillward.com/blog/studies/deep-inside-a-study-of-10000-porn-stars/.

16. Al Goldstein, *I, Goldstein: My Screwed Life* (New York: Thunder's Mouth Press, 2006), 196.

17. Dec 10, 1999, http://business.avn.com/articles/video/Jewel-De-Nyle-on-Anal-34650.html.

18. "America Runs on Anal," Pornhub Insights, July 30, 2014, www.pornhub.com/insights/america-runs-on-anal.

19. http://blog.iafd.com/2015/08/24/tom-byron-breaks-3000-titles-on-iafd/.

20. I.L. Slifkin, "Interview: Ron Jeremy," *AVN*, 1 (10) (Dec 1983), 1, 8.

21. R.D. Writes, Apr 15, 2003, www.mikesouth.com.

22. Hardball post on "Anal in porn" thread, Aug 29, 2015, www.xbiz.net/index.php?c=discussion.view_thread&id=15943.

23. "R.D. Makes a Lot of Really Good Points," Apr 17, 2003, www.mikesouth.com.

24. www.wikiporno.org/wiki/XRCO_Award.

25. See "Rooster Alpha Advanced" ad, www.xbiz.com/ppi/206060.

26. Dan Miller, "Stepping Up: Industry Vets Eye Next Big Star," *XBIZ Premiere*, Aug 2015, 52–53.

27. Charlie Glickman, "Back Door Basics: Get Ready for Anal Sex Month," *XBIZ Premiere*, July 2015, 90.

28. After being turned down by major publishers, the book came out under the San Francisco imprint Cleis Press.

29. Michelle Lhooq, "A Rosebud by Any Other Name Would Smell Like Shit," www.vice.com/read/a-rosebud-by-any-other-name-would-smell-like-shit.

30. Michelle Lhooq, "A Rosebud by Any Other Name Would Smell Like Shit," www.vice.com/read/a-rosebud-by-any-other-name-would-smell-like-shit.

31. Colin Rowntree post on "Anal in porn" thread, Aug 29, 2015, www.xbiz.net/index.php?c=discussion.view_thread&id=15943.

32. Robbie post of May 23, 2012, on thread "Have we seen the last of the real porn star legends?" www.xbiz.net/index.php?c=discussion.view_thread&id=6434.

Ch. 16: Gays and Lesbians

1. Jeffrey Escoffier, *Bigger Than Life: The History of Gay Porn Cinema from Beefcake to Hardcore* (Philadelphia: Running Press, 2009), 6.

2. Dan Cameron, "When Worlds Collide: What Happens When Two Industry Powers Team Up?" *XBIZ Feature*, Apr 5, 2015, www.xbiz.com/articles/193069.

3. Edward Shorter, *Written in the Flesh: A History of Desire* (Toronto: University of Toronto Press, 2005), 152–153.

4. See Ian Young, *Out in Paperback: A Visual History of Gay Pulps* (Albion, NY: MLR Press, 2012), 20–25.

5. Alex Henderson, "Honoring an Icon: XR Brands Celebrates Gay Erotica Pioneer," *XBIZ Feature*, Mar 24, 2015, www.xbiz.com/articles/192547; Oct 5, 1999, http://business.avn.com/articles/video/Tom-Of-Finland-First-Local-Showing-35252.html.

6.   "Steven Toushin," *XBIZ* Feature, July 2, 2007, www.xbiz.com/articles/23909.

7.   J. C. Adams, "Gay Adult Retail," *XBIZ* Feature, Sept 21, 2009, www.xbiz.com/articles/113010.

8.   Robert Mainardi, ed., *Jim French Diaries: The Creator of Colt Studio* (np, nd [2011]), 88-89; see also, Rhett Pardon, "COLT Studio Founder Jim French Passes Away," *XBIZ* News, June 21, 2017, www.xbiz.com/news/221105.

9.   "Obituary: COLT Studio Founder Jim French Passes Away," *XBIZ World*, Aug 2017, 76, 84.

10. Bob Johnson, "Falcon Founder Chuck Holmes Documentary Premieres April 10," *XBIZ* News, Apr 9, 2015, www.xbiz.com/news/193262.

11. Dan Cameron, "Aspen Adventure," *XBIZ* Feature, Aug 10, 2011, www.xbiz.com/articles/136975.

12. Aug 5, 2006, http://business.avn.com/articles/gay/Innerview-Chris-Ward-45060.html.

13. Dan Cameron, "Crowded House: Falcon Studios Group is a Gay Porn Juggernaut," *XBIZ* Feature, Nov. 15, 2014, www.xbiz.com/articles/187726.

14. Dan Cameron, "Crowded House: Falcon Studios Group is a Gay Porn Juggernaut," *XBIZ* Feature, Nov. 15, 2014, www.xbiz.com/articles/187726.

15. Dan Cameron, "Birds of a Feather," *XBIZ* Feature, Apr 13, 2011, www.xbiz.com/articles/132784.

16. Dan Cameron, "Falcon Studios Reflects on Merger," *XBIZ* Feature, Dec. 13, 2013, www.xbiz.com/articles/171871.

17. For an overview of these developments, see "Steven Scarborough," *XBIZ* Feature, Nov. 26, 2007, www.xbiz.com/articles/86848.

18. "Buddy Profits Relaunches HotHouse.com," *XBIZ World*, July 2015, 78.

19. Dan Cameron, "Move Over Mr. T.: Falcon Studios Group's New A-Team," *XBIZ* Feature, Dec 13, 2014, www.xbiz.com/articles/188924.

20. Tod Tomorrow, "Chi Chi LaRue: Channel 1's Queen Bee, Part 2," *XBIZ* Feature, Nov. 21, 2009, www.xbiz.com/articles/123655.

21. Dan Cameron, "Vegas Baby! Hot House Looks Forward to a New Era by the Strip," *XBIZ* Feature, Dec. 15, 2014, www.xbiz.com/articles/188928/.

22. Keith Griffith, "Cruising the Community," *XBIZ* Feature, Feb., 22, 2006, www.xbiz.com/articles/13588.

23. Rhett Pardon, "Q&A With Douglas Richter, AWEmpire.com," *XBIZ* Feature, Mar 5, 2013, www.xbiz.com/articles/160143.

24. Dan Cameron, "Book of Landon: All-Time Great Eyes End of Remarkable Career," *XBIZ* Feature, July 11, 2015, www.xbiz.com/articles/196524.

25. Erik Jay, "Chi Chi LaRue," *XBIZ* Feature, Nov 14, 2007, www.xbiz.com/articles/86377.

26. C. E. Coppen et al., "Sexual Behavior, Sexual Attraction, and Sexual Orientation in the United States: Data From the 2011–2013 National Survey of Family Growth," *National Health Statistics Reports*; no 88. Hyattsville, MD: National Center for Health Statistics. 2016, tab 5.

27. Dan Cameron, "Club Inferno: Fire in the Hole," *XBIZ* Feature, Aug 12, 2014, www.xbiz.com/articles/183088.

28. Dan Cameron, "Hot Like a Foxx," *XBIZ Premiere,* Aug 2015, 94, 117.

29. J. C. Adams, "Sexalicious David Dakota," *XBIZ* Feature, Sept 24, 2008, www.xbiz.com/articles/127917.

30. PornLaw post of Feb 25, 2014, on thread "When porn stars become escorts," www.xbiz.net/index.php?c=discussion.view_thread&id=10944; on male porn star escorting see Jeffrey Escoffier, "Porn Stars/Stripper/Escort: Economic and Sexual Dynamics in a Sex Work Career," http://jh.haworthpress.com; doi: 10.1300/J082v53n01_08.

31. Rhett Pardon, "Remembering David Forest, 1948–2015," *XBIZ Premiere*, Oct. 2015, 42.

32. Harris Gaffin, *Hollywood Blue: The Tinseltown Pornographers* (London: Batsford, 1997), 140–141.

33. Brandon Baker, "Gay Content Today," *XBIZ* Feature, Nov 2, 2005, www.xbiz.com/articles/11073.

34. "Icon Male Debuts," *XBIZ World*, Sept. 2015, 79.

35. The thread was "Gays watch straight porn, straights watch gay porn, untapped market?" www.xbiz.net/index.php?c=discussion.view_thread&id=3336.

36. "Corbin Fisher: Straight Talk with a Gay Eye," *XBIZ* Feature, June 13, 2011, 1–3.

37. Shine Louise Houston, "Tricks of the Trade: Mighty Real," *XBIZ* Feature, undated, www.xbiz.com/article/188189.

38. Matt O'Connor, "Tapping Into a New Corner," *XBIZ* Feature, July 7, 2006, www.xbiz.com/articles/15864.

39. https://yougov.co.uk/news/2015/08/16/half-young-not-heterosexual/.

40. C. E. Coppen et al., "Sexual Behavior, Sexual Attraction, and Sexual Orientation in the United States: Data From the 2011–2013 National Survey of Family Growth," *National Health Statistics Reports*; no 88. Hyattsville, MD: National Center for Health Statistics. 2016, tab 2.

41. Dan Cameron, "When It Comes to Sex Toys, Gay Consumers Are the Trendsetters," *XBIZ* Feature, Mar 28, 2014, www.xbiz.com/articles/177090.

42. See thread "16 mm gay glory holes," begun May 11, 2015, http://xbiz.net/index?c=discussion.view_thread&id=15021.

43. "The Gay Fringe," *XBIZ* Feature, May 22, 2008, www.xbiz.com/articles/94304.

44. Steve Lick, "No DVD Slowdown for Harder Gay Genres," May 2, 2008, www.mikesouth.com.

45. Oct 14, 2005, http://business.avn.com/articles/gay/Company-Profile-CyberBears-LLC-46109.html.

46. Dan Cameron, ""When It Comes to Sex Toys, Gay Consumers Are the Trendsetters," *XBIZ* Feature, Mar 28, 2014, www.xbiz.com/articles/177090.

47. Steve, "Mainstreaming Gay Business: Part 2," *XBIZ* Feature, Oct 22, 2003, www.xbiz.com/articles/2055.

48. Ogi Ogas and Sai Gaddam, *A Billion Wicked Thoughts* (New York: Plume, 2011), 145.

49. Dan Cameron, "Rough & Wilde: Director Paul Wilde Has Stepped Out of the Shadows," *XBIZ* Feature, Oct 14, 2013.

50. Chris Steele, "Top Billing," *XBIZ* Feature, Feb 17, 2008, www.xbiz.com/articles/12907.

51. Victor Hoff, "Fetishism Swings Back," *XBIZ* Feature, Oct 19, 2009, www.xbiz.com/articles/123657.

52. Alex Henderson, "Gay Niches," *XBIZ* Feature, Oct 1, 2007, www.xbiz.com/articles/84523.

53. Tod Tomorrow, "Chi Chi LaRue: Channel 1's Queen Bee, Part 1," *XBIZ* Feature, Oct 18, 2009, www.xbiz.com/articles/123656.

54. Joanne Cachapero, "Gay Terms," *XBIZ* Feature, Nov 6, 2007, www.xbiz.com/articles/86020.

55. See Cherry Smyth, "The Pleasure Threshold: Looking at Lesbian Pornography on Film," *Feminist Review*, no. 34 (Spring 1990), 152–159.

56. Anne Winter, "Where Are the Real Lesbians?" *XBIZ* Feature, Oct 30, 2007, www.xbiz.com/articles/85796.

57. Whitney Strub, "Queer Smut, Queer Rights," in Lynn Comella and Shira Tarrant, eds., *New Views on Pornography, Sexuality, Politics, and the Law* (Santa Barbara: Praeger, 2015), 147–164, see 148–149.

58. Jared Rutter, "Feminist Porn Spreads Its Wings," *XBIZ* Feature, July 17, 2013, www.xbiz.com/aerticles/166148.

59. Shar Rednour and Jackie Strano, "Steamy, Hot, and Political: Creating Radical Dyke Porn," in Lynn Comella and Shira Tarrant, eds., *New Views on Pornography, Sexuality, Politics, and the Law* (Santa Barbara: Praeger, 2015), 165–177, 175.

60. The phrase is from the *AVN* review of *Suburban Dykes*, www.avn.com/movies/42719.html.

61. "San Francisco Lesbians, Part 1" ad, *AVN*, 7 (8) (July 1997), no page number.

62. Ernest Greene (Ira Levine), "The Magic Formula," *XBIZ* Feature, Aug 31, 2007, www.xbiz.com/articles/83642.

63. Jared Rutter, "Lesbian Video: The Niche That Keeps on Giving," *XBIZ* Feature, Sept 19, 2012, www.xbiz.com/articles/154161.

64. Lisa Briggs, "The Rise of Girl Power: 2," *XBIZ* Feature, Nov 23, 2006, www.xbiz.com/articles/18284.

65. Dan Miller, "Girlfriends Partner Up," *XBIZ* Feature, May 28, 2011, www.xbiz.com/articles/134432.

66. Lisa Briggs, "The Rise of Girl Power: 1," *XBIZ* Feature, Nov 22, 2006, www.xbiz.com/articles/18283.

67. Anne Winter, "Where Are the Real Lesbians?" *XBIZ* Feature, Oct 30, 2007, www.xbiz.com/articles/85796.

68. Dan Miller, "WIA Profile: Kay Brandt," *XBIZ* Feature, Feb 2, 2012, www.xbiz.com/articles/143762.

69. http://www.alligator.org/the_avenue/lifestyle/image_dab3d937-007a-51ca-bfd1-ae51e3489bd7.html.

70. Jesse FameDollars, May 26, 2015, on thread "Is softcore solo and girl/girl scenes still can be interesting?" [*sic*], begun May 25, 2015, http://xbiz.net/index?c=discussion.view_thread&id=15119.

71. Dee Severe, post of Oct 28, 2014, on thread "Brand new producer here," http://www.xbiz.net/index.php?c=discussion.view_thread&id=13430.

72. Dee Severe, post of May 26, 2015, thread "Is softcore solo and girl/girl," begun May 25, 2015, http://xbiz.net/index?c=discussion.view_thread&id=15119.

73. Dan Miller, "Tori Black Talks *True Lust*, Directing for ArchAngel," *XBIZ* Feature, Mar 9, 2015, www.xbiz.com/news/192041.

74. "Girlsway Introduces 'Lesbian Porn Noir' With *The Business of Women*," *XBIZ* News, Aug 13, 2015, www.xbiz.com/news/197861.

Ch. 17: Toys

1. Domina Doll, post of Sept 7, 2012, on thread "Fifty Shades — a quick flame or a cultural awakening?" www.xbiz.net/index.php?c=discussionview_thread&id=7088.

2. Anna North, "Women of Sex Tech, Unite," *New York Times,* Aug 20, 2017, 22-23.

3. https://vibereview.com/sex_toys/stormy_danielss_precious_private_parts; see also https://www.realdoll.com/product/stormy-daniels-wicked/.

4. Wayne Hentai, "Susan Colvin: Woman's Touch Innovates Adult Toy Market," *AVN,* 17 (7) (July 2001), 36.

5. Alex Glass, "CalExotics: Trailblazing Into the Future," *XBIZ* Feature, June 12, 2014, www.xbiz.com/articles/180237.

6. Sharan Street, "Woman's Touch," *AVN,* 30 (1) (Jan 2014), 86.

7. "WIA Profile: Susan Colvin," *XBIZ* Feature, Sept 10, 2008, www.xbiz.com/articles/98885.

8. http://news.bbc.co.uk/2/hi/science/nature/4713323.stm.

9. Marty Klein, *America's War on Sex* (Santa Barbara: Praeger, 2006), 89.

10. Lily Morrigan, "Dixie Dildos," *XBIZ* Feature, Apr 5, 2005, www.xbiz.com/articles/8195.

11. Erik Jay, "Bob Christian: Mad Hatter of Adam & Eve," *XBIZ* Feature, Nov 15, 2010, www.xbiz.com/articles/127327.

12. http://www.nytimes.com/2015/03/14/nyregion/dell-williams-founder-of-sex-boutique-dies-at-92.html?_r=0.

13. Kim Airs, "Executive Profile: Teddy Rothstein," *XBIZ* Feature, Nov 9, 2012, www.xbiz.com/156383; Kim Airs, "Doin' the Nasst(oys) Since 1975," *XBIZ* Feature, Sept 5, 2012, www.xbiz.com/articles/153309.

14. See John Heidenry, *What Wild Ecstasy: The Rise and Fall of the Sexual Revolution* (New York: Simon & Schuster, 1997), 74–77.

15. Ariana Rodriguez, "The Doc Is In," *XBIZ* Feature, Apr 20, 2011, www.xbiz.com/articles/133063/Kristina+Rose.

16. Ariana Rodriguez, "Doc Johnson Marketing Milestone," *XBIZ* Feature, Dec 7, 2011, www.xbiz.com/articles/141765.

17. Kim Airs, "Sales Manager Joanie Lee Discusses Evolution of Icon Brands," *XBIZ* Feature, Dec 27, 2014, www.xbiz.com/articles/189336.

18. Quentin Boyer, "A Man's World: Male Sex Toy Sales Continue Upward Trajectory," *XBIZ* Feature, Aug 23, 2014, www.xbiz.com/articles/183658.

19. Quentin Boyer, "Pleasure Products, Sophistication & Sales," *XBIZ* Feature, Aug 24, 2014, www.xbiz.com/articles/183659.

20. Anne Winter, "JT's Stockroom," *XBIZ* Feature, June 27, 2007, www.xbiz.com/articles/23835.

21. Ariana Rodriguez, "WIA Profile: Layla Ross," *XBIZ* Feature, July 11, 2012, www.xbiz.com/articles/150835.

22. Nov 1, 2001, http://business.avn.com/articles/video/MyPleasure-s-Principles-San-Francisco-Startup-Follows-The-Gap-in-Quest-to-Make-Sex-Toys-as-Popular-as-Khakis-40036.html.

23. Rodger Jacobs, "A Tightening Toy Market: 1," *XBIZ* Feature, May 30, 2005, www.xbiz.com/articles/8929.

24. Alex Glass, "Sticking Around: Sportsheets Looks Back on Milestones," *XBIZ* Feature, May 7, 2013, www.xbiz.com/articles/162405.

25. Brian Sofer, "Sportsheets Founder Tom Stewart Talks Brand Beginnings, Fifty Shades," *XBIZ* Feature, Feb 20, 2015, www.xbiz.com/articles/191135.

26. Jan 26, 2005, http://business.avn.com/articles/video/Sportsheets-Serves-Up-Vanilla-Bondage-41962.html.

27. Dec 2, 2003, http://business.avn.com/articles/video/Sportsheets-A-Family-Whose-Business-is-Vanilla-Bondage-Equipment-37201.html.

28. Bob Johnson, "Symphony of Fetish," *XBIZ* Feature, June 19, 2013, www.xbiz.com/articles/164000.

29. Nelson X, "The Male Masturbation Market Rises Again," *XBIZ* Feature, Aug 31, 2011, www.xbiz.com/articles/137853.

30. "Agency Is Assailed on Mail-Order Smut," *NYT*, Sept 3, 1965, 6.

31. David Jennings, *Skinflicks* (Bloomington, IN: 1st Books, 2000), 47.

32. "Teri Diver," *AVN*, 7 (12), (Nov 1992), 68.

33. "The Raquel Vagina," *AVN*, 8 (8) (July 1993), 128.

34. "The Realistic Vagina," *AVN*, 8 (12) (Nov 1993), 115.

35. www.austinchronicle.com/screens/2012-05-11/pressing-the-flesh/2/.

36. Kayden Kross, "Go Forth and Multiply," Jan 30, 2009, www.mikesouth.com.

37. Jon Millward, "Down the Rabbit-Hole: What One Million Sex Toy Sales Reveal About Our Erotic Tastes, Kinks and Desires," http://jonmillward.com/blog/studies/down-the-rabbit-hole-analysis-1-million-sex-toy-sales/.

38. Aug 27, 1999, http://business.avn.com/articles/video/TOYS-FOR-SERENITY-35496.html.

39. "Exclusive Interview: Taylor Wane," Jan 3, 2005, http://rockconfidential.com/2005/01/exclusive-interview-taylor-wane.

40. Bob Johnson, "Doc Johnson Announces Vicky Vette Vagina Mold," *XBIZ* Feature, Mar 30, 2011, http://www.xbiz.com/news/news_piece.php?id=132300&mi=all&q=Pocket+Pussy.

41. Anne Winter, "Mold Me," *XBIZ* Feature, Mar 6, 2008, www.xbiz.com/articles/90869.

42. "Doc Johnson to Create Exclusive Dani Daniels Product Line," *XBIZ Premiere*, June 2015, 22.

43. Alejandro Freixes, "Q&A: Eva Lovia Talks Stardom, Endgame," *XBIZ* News, Mar 25, 2016, www.xbiz.com/news/205863.

44. Paul Näcke, "Kritisches zum Kapitel der normalen und pathologiuschen Sexualität," *Archiv für Psychiatrie und Nervenkrankheiten*, 32 (1899), 356–386, 368 n1.

45. Edward Shorter, *Written in the Flesh: A History of Desire* (Toronto: University of Toronto Press, 2005), 171–172.

46. Lynn Brown Rosenberg, "Talking Toys: Q&A With the Pleasure Chest's Thip Nopharatana," *XBIZ* Feature, Dec 29, 2015, www.xbiz.com/articles/202404.

47. Scott Ross, "Steady Rise – Spartacus Leathers' Josh Miller," *XBIZ* Feature, June 26, 2013, www.xbiz.com/articles/165413.

48. "Fifty Shades of Grey – Pleasure and Pain Nipple Rings," *XBIZ* Product Information, Dec 2, 2014, www.xbiz.com/ppi/184847.

49. Ariana Rodriguez, "CalExotics Debuts Complete Collection of Nipple Accessories," *XBIZ* News, June 25, 2015, www.xbiz.com/news/196082.

50. Genie Davis, "Manufacturers Discuss Growing Erotic Jewelry, Accessories Market," *XBIZ* Feature, Oct 4, 2015, www.xbiz.com/articles/199533.

51. Regina Nuzzo, "Good Vibrations: U.S. Consumer Web Site Aims to Enhance Toy Safety," *Scientific American,* https://www.scientificamerican.com/article/good-vibrations-us-consumer—web-site-aims-to-enhance-sex-toy-safety/.

52. Ariana Rodriguez, "WIA Profile: Lucy Vonne," *XBIZ* Feature, Jan 13, 2015.

53. Jon Millward, "Down the Rabbit-Hole: What One Million Sex Toy Sales Reveal About Our Erotic Tastes, Kinks and Desires," http://jonmillward.com/blog/studies/down-the-rabbit-hole-analysis-1-million-sex-toy-sales/.

54. Mark Espinosa, "Pleasure Products: Rivalry Online," *XBIZ* Feature, Aug 3, 2014, www.xbiz.com/articles/182596.

55. Duncan Robinson, "Latest Buzz Puts 'Slippers and Cocoa' Image to Bed," *Financial Times Weekend*, Nov 9, 2014.

56. See Danielle J. Lindemann, "Pathology Full Circle: A History of Anti-Vibrator Legislation in the United States," *Columbia Journal of Gender and Law*, 15 (2006), 326–346.

57. http://www.marksfriggin.com/news99/1-11-99.htm.

58. "Orgasms Okay Again in Alabama," *AVN*, Mar 31, 1999, http://business.avn.com/articles/video/Orgasms-Okay-Again-In-Alabama-36187.html.

59. Rona March, "Joani Blank: A Sexual Aide," *San Francisco Chronicle*, Feb 14, 2003, http://www.webcitation.org/5wDN4hmjV.

60. Lynn Comella, *Vibrator Nation: How Feminist Sex-Toy Stores Changed the Business of Pleasure* (Durham: Duke University Press, 2017).

61. Rodger Jacobs, "A Tightening Toy Market: 2," *XBIZ* Feature, June 1, 2005, www.xbiz.com/articles/8961.

62. Jon Millward, "Down the Rabbit-Hole: What One Million Sex Toy Sales Reveal About Our Erotic Tastes, Kinks and Desires," http://jonmillward.com/blog/studies/down-the-rabbit-hole-analysis-1-million-sex-toy-sales/.

63. Brian Evans and Lori Z, "*XBIZ* Interviews Larry Flynt: Part 2," *XBIZ* Feature, Oct 28, 2004, www.xbiz.com/articles/2058.

64. Ayrora Temple (Dawn Yagielowicz), "Sex Toys for Fun and Profit," *XBIZ* Feature, June 6, 2005, www.xbiz.com/articles/8991.

65. https://en.wikipedia.org/wiki/Hitachi_Magic_Wand.

66. Conversation at a pornshoot in Montreal, Aug 19, 2015.

67. Colin Rowntree, "Penetrating Into Mainstream," *XBIZ* Feature, Mar 21, 2013, www.xbiz.com/articles/160764.

68. Lynn Brown Rosenberg, "Porn: A Good Thing or a Bad Thing?" *XBIZ Premiere*, Sept 2015, 72, 111.

69. Anna Breslaw and Michelle Ruiz, "Crazy Kink Cool," *Cosmopolitan*, 258 (2) (Feb, 2015), 145–151.

70. "Pleasure Bound," *AVN*, 18 (3) (Mar 2002), 203.

71. Neal Slateford and Richard Longhurst presentation, *XBIZ* 360 meeting, Los Angeles, Jan 14, 2016.

72. Nelson Ayala, "Lovehoney's Fifty Shades of Grey Collection," *XBIZ* Feature, May 24, 2013, www.xbiz.com/articles/163005.

73. "Lovehoney's Longhurst Talks U.K. E-tailer's Success," *XBIZ*, May 8, 2015. www.xbiz.com/news/194348; http://www.bathchronicle.co.uk/Fifty-Shades-Grey-Mot-rhead-welcome-boost-sex-toy/story-28140882-detail/story.html#1.

74. July 30, 2015, www.ynot.com/fifty=shades-of-grey-playroom-collection-bows/.

75. Kay Airs, "XR Brands: Branding Beyond the Niche," *XBIZ* Feature, Sept 28, 2014, www.xbiz.com/articles/185605.

76. Brian Sofer, "Q&A With Edward Wheeler of the Love Store," *XBIZ* Feature, Mar 22, 2015, www.xbiz.com/articles/192411.

77. Saskia Vogel, "Kinky Couples: Couples-friendly Retailing," *XBIZ* Feature, Apr 15, 2013, www.xbiz.com/articles/161611.

78. Bob Johnson, "Sportsheets Product Featured in U.K.'s Selfridges Department Stores," *XBIZ* News, Nov 12, 2014, www.xbiz.com/news/187725.

79. Jeremy Wilson, "The Weird World of Male Chastity," http://kernelmag.dailydot.com/features/report/6439/the-weird-world-of-male-chastity/.

80. http://www.tpe.com/~altarboy/survey.htm. A questionnaire of July 12, 1997, reviewed the different male devices readers might purchase.

81. Dan Cameron, "Playing for Keeps: Future of the Fetish/BDSM Market," *XBIZ* Feature, June 22, 2014, www.xbiz.com/articles/180716.

82. Mr. Feet, "Review of The Stockroom's Houdini Cock Cuff," www.tpe.com/~altarboy/not90722.htm.

83. See the ad in *XBIZ Sensuals*, Summer 2015, 19.

84. Jan 6, 2000, http://business.avn.com/articles/video/CYBERTOYS-FOR-CYBERSEX-34417.html.

85. Ariana Rodriguez, "Sexual Upgrade," *XBIZ Premiere*, Apr 2015, 49–50.

86. Joanne Cachapero, "Party Circuit," XBIZ Feature, July 3, 2006, www.xbiz.com/articles/80631.

87. Erin V, "Profit Party," *XBIZ Premiere,* Aug 2015, 68.

88. Joanne Cachapero, "Party Circuit," *XBIZ* Feature, July 3, 2006, www.xbiz.com/articles/80631.

89. Dan Cameron, "Exec Seat: Q&A With Nalpac's Glenn LeBoeuf," *XBIZ* Feature, Jan 29, 2014, www.xbiz.com/articles/173918.

90. Rebecca Adams, "The Shame-Free Guide to Buying A Sex Toy," www.huffingtonpost.com/2014/09/09/sex-toys-the-shame-free-guide_n_5759210.html.

91. Brian Sofer quote in "Talk Back," *XBIZ Premiere* July 2015, 72.

92. Jared Rutter, "Future in Focus: Toy, Novelty Market Growth," *XBIZ* Feature, Aug 18, 2013, www.xbiz/com/articles/167573.

93. May 1, 2002, http://business.avn.com/articles/video/Electrify-Me-David-Levine-Catches-a-Profitable-Buzz-Selling-Sex-Toys-Online-39350.html.

94. Gram Ponante, "Sex Toy Tech: Form Follows Function in Adult Pleasure Product Market," *XBIZ* Feature, Sept 20, 2013, www.xbiz.com/articles/169137.

Ch. 18: Camming

1. Blush Boss post of Mar 27, 2014, on thread "How does 'porn' translate into the following languages?" www.xbiz.net/index.php?c=discussion.view_thread&id=11337.

2. On Flirt4Free, available on Pornhub.

3. Quentin Boyer, "Adult Innovations," *XBIZ* Feature, Apr 16, 2008, www.xbiz.com/articles/92634.

4. See Blaise Cronin and Elisabeth Davenport, "E-Rogenous Zones: Positioning Pornography in the Digital Economy," *The Information Society*, 17 (2001), 33-48, a contribution that has not had the impact it deserves.

5. Gary Jackson, "Exec Seat: CCBill's Gary Jackson," *XBIZ* Feature, Mar 31, 2013, www.xbiz.com/articles/161113.

6. Kate Darling, "IP Without IP? A Study of the Online Adult Entertainment Industry," *Stanford Tech Law Rev*, 17 (2014), 709-771, 750-751; http://stlr.stanford.edu/pdf/ipwithoutip.pdf.

7. http://business.time.com/2012/04/04/sex-on-the-internet-sizing-up-the-online-smut-economy/.

8. For this story see Robert Rosen, *Beaver Street: A History of Modern Pornography* (London: Headpress, 2012), 12–15.

9. See Patchen Barss, *The Erotic Engine: How Pornography Has Powered Mass Communication from Gutenberg to Google* (Toronto: Anchor Canada, 2010), 175–178.

10. Gretchen Gallen, ""Exclusive Interview with Video Secrets," *XBIZ* Feature, Apr 22, 2004, www.xbiz.com/articles/2961.

11. Sources for this account include Aug 1, 2002, http://business.avn.com/articles/video/Carol-Cox-Doing-Amateur-the-Right-Way-40976.html, plus various posts of Danny Cox on the *XBIZ* chatboard.

12. Danny Cox post of Nov 9, 2012, on thread "New Cam Ring for Solo Girl Sites," www.xbiz.net/index.php?c=discussion.view_thread&id=7445.

13. Tom Hymes, "A Live Chat With VS Media," *XBIZ* Feature, May 24, 2007, www.xbiz.com/articles/23212.

14. Jesse Quinn post of Apr 11, 2013, on thread "Cam girls?" www.xbiz.net/index.php?c=discussion.view_thread&i0d=8388.

15. B.K. Boleyn post of Mar 30, 2015, on thread "Webcam models profile," www.xbiz.net/index.php?c=discussion.view_thread&id=14738&anchor_post_id=159278#p159278; on typical rates see Andy T post of Aug 15, 2010, on thread "Adult/porn girls on cam networks?" www.xbiz.net/index.php?c=discussion.view_thread&id=2225.

16. Roald post of Mar 30, 2015, on thread "What can a pretty girl earn on Chaterbate [sic]?" www.xbiz.net/index.php?c=discussion.view_thread&id=14738&anchor_post_id=159278#p159278.

17. www.wouj.com/chaturbate-performer-tips/.

18. tripleXdigital post of Oct 19, 2012, on thread "Best converting cam models," www.xbiz.net/index.php?c=discussion.view_thread&id=7302.

19. Clark and Roberts both are quoted in Stewart Tongue, "Cam Mania: What Does It Take to Succeed as a Cam Performer?" *XBIZ* Feature, June 15, 2015, www.xbiz.com/articles/195326.

20. 2Muchmark post of Mar 10, 2014, on thread "Adult industry is dead," www.xbiz.net/index.php?c=discussion.view_thread&id=11093.

21. June 1, 2004, http://business.avn.com/articles/video/The-AVN-Online-Interview-Kyla-Cole-38852.html.

22. BlushBoss post of Apr 11, 2013, on thread "Cam girls?" www.xbiz.net/index.php?c=discussion.view_thread&i0d=8388.

23. Gretchen Gallen, ""Exclusive Interview with Video Secrets," *XBIZ* Feature, Apr 22, 2004, www.xbiz.com/articles/2961.

24. Bob Johnson, "Q&A: Camming Con Founder Clinton Cox on Adult's Bright Spot," *XBIZ* News, July 10, 2014, www.xbiz.com/news/181798.

25. "Q&A With Cherry Pimps Owner Jack Avalanche," *XBIZ* Feature, June 13, 2015, www.xbiz.com/articles/195325.

26. http://www.economist.com/news/international/21666114-internet-blew-porn-industrys-business-model-apart-its-response-holds-lessons%20.

27. Rhett Pardon, "Karoly Papp: Guiding Live Jasmin," *XBIZ World,* Dec 2015, 24.

28. Desperate Amateurs post of Nov 6, 2011, on thread "Is there any money in webcamming?" www.xbiz.net/index.php?c=discussion.view_thread&id=4985.

29. Samanatha38G post of Oct 17, 2012, on thread "Do porn stars see no value in socializing with their peers here?" www.xbiz.net/index.php?c=discussion,view_thread&id=7297.

30. Aria DeLaunay post of Nov 23, 2011, on thread, "What leads some of the hottest women anywhere to do porn?" www.xbiz.net/index.php?c=discussion.view_thread&id=5070.

31. Alex Henderson, "Gearing Up: Professional Domination Comes With a Price," *XBIZ* Feature, June 28, 2013, www.xbiz.com/articles/165422.

32. Thread "Why aren't more strippers/strip clubs..." begun May 26, 2015, contributions of Daisy Destin and Extreme Bank Adam, http://www.xbiz.net/index.php?c=discussion.view_thread&id=15134.

33. Stephen Yagielowicz, "The Live Adult Webcam Sector Is Thriving," *XBIZ* Feature, June 30, 2015, www.xbiz.com/articles/195717.

34. Alex Henderson, "MyFreeCams: At the Top After 6 Years," *XBIZ* Feature, Feb 16, 2011, www.xbiz.com/articles/130493.

35. Unique post of Nov 13, 2012, on thread "Adult webcam stats," www.xbiz.net/index.php?c=discussion.view_thread&id=7446.

36. Ayrora Temple (Dawn Yagielowicz), "Girls of the Web," *XBIZ* Feature, Dec 25, 2006, www.xbiz.com/articles/18738.

37. June 17, 2004, http://business.avn.com/articles/video/A-Voyeuristic-Q-A-with-Allie-of-NaughtyAllie-com-39199.html.

38. Amanda Hess, "Who Gets to Be Sexy," *New York Times*, May 5, 2018; www.nytimes.com/2018/05/05/style/porn-women-nonbinary-queer.html.

Ch. 19: Black Porn

1. Ashley Moore interview, *AVN*, 19 (1) (Jan 2003), 126.

2. Mireille Miller-Young: *A Taste for Brown Sugar: Black Women in Pornography* (Durham: Duke University Press, 2014), 69.

3. http://www.blaxploitationpride.org/2009/01/lialeh-aka-black-lialeh-aka-black-deep.html.

4. http://jonmillward.com/blog/studies/deep-inside-a-study-of-10000-porn-stars/.

5. Gila Morgan, "The Racial Market," *XBIZ*, Jan 3, 2007, www.xbiz.com/articles/80401.

6. Joe Daniels, "Greg Dark," *AVN*, 6 (4) (Mar 1991), 18–20.

7. Susie Bright, "The Image of the Black in Adult Video," AVN, 2 (2) (Apr 1987), 56.

8. http://business.avn.com/articles/video/Black-Video-Forward-or-Back-35859.html.

9. Harris Gaffin, *Hollywood Blue: The Tinseltown Pornographers* (London: Batsford, 1997), 57.

10. Sam Williams, "Being a Stud," *XBIZ*, May 5, 2006, www.xbiz.com/articles/14781.

11. http://www.imdb.com/name/nm0546155/bio#overview.

12. http://business.avn.com/articles/video/Black-Video-Forward-or-Back-35859.html.

13. http://business.avn.com/articles/video/Black-Video-Forward-or-Back-35859.html.

14. Nov 15, 1999, http://business.avn.com/articles/video/Jenna-J-Mr-Marcus-34920.html For a list of further white porn stars who refused to have sex with blacks, see Luke Ford, *A History of X* (Amherst, NY: Prometheus, 1999), 203.

15. http://business.avn.com/articles/video/Black-Video-Forward-or-Back-35859.html.

16. Erik Jay, "Boobs, Butts and B-Sides," *XBIZ* Feature, June 17, 2009, www.xbiz.com/articles/125292. Jay was quoting an article written in 2007.

17. Steven Andrew, "Mr. Marcus," *XBIZ* Feature, Apr 4, 2007, www.xbiz.com/articles/80453.

18. http://www.bbc.co.uk/newsbeat/article/19368744/porn-actor-says-hes-to-blame-for-syphilis-outbreak.

19. Arch Stanton, "The Renaissance Will Be Televised," *XBIZ* Feature, May 17, 2009, www.xbiz.com/articles/126348/Renaissance.

20. http://business.avn.com/articles/video/Stocking-Black-Product-Key-Lines-35861.html.

21. Dan Miller, "Heather Hunter," *AVN*, 20 (1) (June 2004), 120.

22. http://business.avn.com/articles/video/Black-Video-Forward-or-Back-35859.html.

23. Steve Javors, "Crossing Over: 2," *XBIZ* Feature, Mar 13, 2007, www.xbiz.com/articles/20062.

24. John Scura, "Shane Diesel," *XBIZ* Feature, Sept 12, 2006, www.xbiz.com/articles/80758.

25. Jennifer C. Nash, "Strange Bedfellows: Black Feminism and Antipornography Feminism," in Lynn Comella and Shira Tarrant, eds., *New Views on Pornography: Sexuality, Politics, and the Law* (Santa Barbara: Praeger, 2015), 97–123.

26. Robbie post of Sept 23, 2010, on thread "Do surfers still not really trust porn sites?" www.xbiz.net/index.php?c=discussion.view_thread&id=2445.

27. "Hub Insights: More of What Women Want," July 25, 2015, www.pornhub.com/insights/women-gender-demographics-searches.

28. Nelson X., "No Boundaries: A Look At the Ethnic/Interracial Markets," *XBIZ* Feature, May 8, 2012, www.xbiz.com/articles/147875.

29. Arch Stanton, "The Renaissance Will Be Televised," *XBIZ* Feature, May 17, 2009, www.xbiz.com/articles/126348/Renaissance.

30. Casey Calvert, discussion comment at XBIZ meeting in Los Angeles, Jan 13, 2016. http://www.avn.com/movies/110491.html.

31. Nelson Ayala, "David Christopher Talks Three Decades of Filth," *XBIZ* Features, Aug 22, 2012, www.xbiz.com/articles/152546.

32. Linda Williams, "Skin Flicks on the Racial Border: Pornography, Exploitation, and Interracial Lust," in Linda Williams, ed., *Porn Studies* (Durham: Duke University Press, 2004), 271–308, 302.

33. Luke Ford, *A History of X* (Amherst, NY: Prometheus, 1999), 204-205.

34. E. J. Dickson, "Porn Star Asa Akira Takes Us Inside Her New Book, 'Insatiable,'" May 20, 2014, www.dailydot.com/lifestyle/asa-akira-memoir-qanda/.

35. Debby Herbenick et al., "Erect Penile Length and Circumference Dimensions of 1,661 Sexually Active Men in the United States," *Journal of Sexual Medicine*, 11 (2014), 93–101.

36. The most careful investigation to date concluded, "There are no indications of differences in racial variability in our present study," David Veale et al., "Am I Normal? A Systematic Review and Construction of Nomograms for Flaccid and Erect Penis Length and Circumference in Up to 15,521 Men," *British Journal of Urology International*, 115 (2015), 978–986.

37. Johnny Steele, "Dominique Simone," *AVN*, 6 (10), (Oct 1991), 57–59.

Ch. 20: Porn Today

1. See on this Edward Shorter, *Written in the Flesh: A History of Desire* (Toronto: University of Toronto Press, 2005).

2. "Kayden Kross, Manuel Ferrara Direct 'Carter Cruise Wide Open,'" *XBIZ* News, May 15, 2015.

3. Jared Rutter, "Evil Angel's Fetish Feast," *XBIZ* Feature, June 22, 2012, www.xbiz.com/articles/150122.

4. "Michael Ninn," *AVN*, 7 (11) (Oct 1992), 50.

5. Robert Dante, "Marketing Story-Driven Porn," *AVN*, 17 (2) (Feb 2001), 35–36.

6. Steve Lick, "Is That a Back Spasm or an Orgasm?" May 21, 2008, www.mikesouth.com.

7. Michael Stabile, "End of the Porn Golden Age," *Salon*, Mar 2, 2012, www.salon.com/2012/03/03/life_after_the_golden_age_of_porn/

8. Jim Edwards, Aug 8, 2011, www.cbsnews.com/why-playboy-is-getting-out-of-the-porn-business/.

9. Ben Fritz, "Tough Times in the Porn Industry," www.latimes.com/local/la-fi-ct-porn10-2009aug10-story.html#page=1.

10. "Naked Capitalism," *Economist*, http://www.economist.com/news/international/21666114-internet-blew-porn-industrys-business-model-apart-its-response-holds-lessons%20.

11. Rob Perez, "Porno Dan Leal Plots European Expansion, Live Cam Conquest," *XBIZ* Feature, Mar 25, 2016, www.xbiz.com/articles/205878.

12. Alexander Poe, "Seven Directors Focus on the Current Condition of Porn," *XBIZ* News, Aug 20, 2014, www.xbiz.com/news/183848.

13. "Naked Capitalism," Economist, http://www.economist.com/news/international/21666114-internet-blew-porn-industrys-business-model-apart-its-response-holds-lessons%20.

14. Damian post of June 1, 2013, on thread "Is the Internet killing the porn industry?" www.xbiz/net/index.php?c=discussion.view_thread&id=8843.

15. Sept 1, 2000, http://business.avn.com/articles/video/DEMOGRAPHICS-AND-MARKETING-ON-THE-ADULT-NET-40783.html.

16. http://business.avn.com/articles/video/DEMOGRAPHICS-AND-MARKETING-ON-THE-ADULT-NET-40783.html.

17. Constance Penley, "Crackers and Whackers: The White Trashing of Porn," in Linda Williams, ed., *Porn Studies* (Durham Duke University Press, 2004), 309–331.

18. www.fannyhunter.co.uk/dogma/year-porn-fannys-review-2013.

19. Bob Johnson, "Exec Seat: Rodney Moore," *XBIZ* Feature, Aug 25, 2013, www.xbiz.com/articles/167588.

20. Tripp Daniels, Aug 21, 2003, http://business.avn.com/articles/video/b-Trippin-Out-b-08-21-03-31225.html.

21. Lila Seidman, article of Sept 3, 2015, http://www.laweekly.com/arts/need-a-porn-star-for-your-tv-show-call-howard-levine-5921072.

22. Magnus Sullivan, "Hardcore Market: Fixing a Fundamentally Broken Model," *XBIZ* Feature, Dec 4, 2015, www.xbiz.com/articles/201056.

23. Mike South, "2 Days to My Birthday," Dec 24, 2004, www.mikesouth.com.

24. Alex Henderson, "Not So Private," *XBIZ* Feature, Sept 13, 2006, www.xbiz.com/articles/17136.

25. May 26, 2005, http://business.avn.com/articles/video/Private-Rocks-Cannes-43858.html.

26. Melody post of May 23, 2013, on thread "*XBIZ World* talk back question," www.xbiz.net/index.php?c=discussion.view_thread&id=8759.

27. Charlie Warzel, Sept 24, 2015, http://www.buzzfeed.com/charliewarzel/if-they-build-it-will-we-come-meet-the-tech-entrepreneurs-tr?utm_term=.ds8KRkB6m#.fl2X64og5.

28. Dan Miller, "Porn Panel Talks Mainstreaming of Erotica at USC," *XBIZ* News, Oct 15, 2015, www.xbiz.com/news/200183.

29. Alex Henderson, "Porn Gets Lots of Coverage," *XBIZ* Feature, July 27, 2006, www.xbiz.com/articles/16200; Frank Rich, http://www.nytimes.com/2001/05/20/magazine/naked-capitalists.html?pagewanted=all.

30. https://medium.com/@MissLoreleiLee/dear-new-york-times-9f64155b5e19#.da8v323p6. Thomas Fuller's article of Feb 18, 2016, in the NYT is at: http://www.nytimes.com/2016/02/19/us/actors-in-pornographic-films-fight-proposal-to-enforce-safety-regulations.html?_r=1.

31. Feb 9, 2000, http://business.avn.com/articles/video/Porn-Report-34124.html/.

32. Nichi Hodgson, "The Intimate Confessions of a Female Porn Fan," *Telegraph*, Aug 7, 2014, www.telegraph.co.uk/women/sex/11019232/Porn-Why-us-women-love-watching-sex-play-out-online.html.

33. http://3hattergrindhouse.com/tag/angie-rowntree/.

34. Tristan Taormina et al., *The Feminist Porn Book: The Politics of Producing Pleasure* (New York: Feminist Press, 2013).

35. John Sanford, "Feminism Fuels Evil Angel's Roster," *XBIZ* News, Apr 8, 2015, http://www.xbiz.com/news/news_piece.php?id=193220&mi=all&q=John+Sanford.

36. Rhett Pardon, "Kelly Holland Acquires Penthouse Entertainment," *XBIZ* News, Feb 19, 2016, www.xbiz.com/news/204647.

37. Jeremy Stone, "The Director's Corner: Anthony Spinelli," *AVN*, 2 (1) (Mar 1987), 68–70.

38. "Charting the Adult Industry," *AVN Adult Entertainment Guide,* 1995, 68.

39. http://business.avn.com/articles/video/DEMOGRAPHICS-AND-MARKETING-ON-THE-ADULT-NET-40783.html.

40. Sharon Reed, Sept 1, 1999, "What do Women Want on the Internet?" http://business.avn.com/articles/video/What-Do-Women-Want-On-The-Internet-41086.html.

41. May 26, 1999, http://business.avn.com/articles/video/Women-Surf-for-Sex-Too-35797.html. See also Sharon Reed, Sept 1, 1999, "What Do Women Want on the Internet?" http://business.avn.com/articles/video/What-Do-Women-Want-On-The-Internet-41086.html, which reported Media Matrix data that "nearly 20 percent of female internet users 18 and older visited a sex site in May of 1999, up from 15 percent in January of 1998."

42. Mireya Navarro, "Women Tailor Sex Industry to Their Eyes," *NYT*, Feb 20, 2004, A1. The words are those of the *New York Times* journalist.

43. Julie M. Albright, "Sex in America Online: An Exploration of Sex, Marital Status, and Sexual Identity in Internet Sex Seeking and Its impacts," *Journal of Sex Research*, 45 (2008), 175–186.

44. YNOT, Jan 31, 2017, Marty O'Brien, http://www.ynot.com/theres-porn-on-social-media-networks-who-knew/.

45. Ernest Greene (Ira Levine), "The Magic Formula," *XBIZ* Feature, Aug 31, 2007, www.xbiz.com/articles/83642.

46. Sam Williams, "Naughty America," *XBIZ* Feature, July 4, 2006, www.xbiz.com/articles/15812.

47. Charyn Pfeuffer, http://www.refinery29.com/2015/11/97566/avn-porn-reviewer-sex-tips?utm_source=email&utm_medium=email_share#slide.

48. Oct 20, 2005, http://business.avn.com/articles/video/Chick-Media-A-Woman-s-POV-46234.html.

49. Angie Rowntree interview, Montreal, Aug 19, 2015.

50. Jason S. Carroll et al., "Generation XXX: Pornography Acceptance and Use Among Emerging Adults," *J. Adol Res*, 23 (2008), doi: http;//jar.sagepub.com/content/23/1/6; a huge compendium of statistics and pseudo-statistics is the highly slanted antiporn tract *Covenant Eyes, Pornography Statistics* (2014 edition), www.covenanteyes.com.

51. "Studio Execs Discuss State of Fetish Video," *XBIZ* Feature, June 14, 2015, www.xbiz.com/articles/195320.

52. "Hub Insights: More of What Women Want," July 25, 2015, www.pornhub.com/insights/women-gender-demographics-searches.

53. "Coming of Age: Millennials," Pornhub Insights, July 5, 2015, www.pornhub.com/insights/millennials-demographics-statistics.

54. https://xhamster.com/blog/posts/911001.

55. I am grateful to Chris Hacker for giving me access to these proprietary, unpublished figures.

56. Amanda de Cadenet, "More Women Watch (and Enjoy) Porn Than You Ever Realized: A Marie Claire Study," Oct 19, 2015, http://www.marieclaire.com/sex-love/a16474/women-porn-habits-study/.

57. Anne Winter, "Inside the Head of an Adult Store Buyer," *XBIZ* Feature, Sept 17, 2009, www.xbiz.com/articles/124151.

58. Serena West, "Babeland Offers Workshops," *XBIZ* Feature, June 26, 2006, www.xbiz.com/articles/80617.

59. Jill Hamilton, "The 15 Best Porn Sites for Women," *Cosmopolitan*, July 22, 2015. http://www.cosmopolitan.com/sex-love/news/a43169/the-best-porn-sites-for-women/.

60. Mason, a female director, in discussion, in "*AVN* Directors' Roundtable: Old School/New School, Smackdown," *AVN*, 19 (2) (Feb 2003), 68.

61. Linda Williams, *Hard Core* expanded ed. (Berkeley: University of California Press, 1999), 267.

62. "GameLink Reveals Top 10 Adult Movies Watched by Women," YNOT [2015] www.ynot.com/announcements-spam/85985-gamelink-reveals-top-10-adult-movies-watched-women.html.

63. Sharon Reed, Sept 1, 1999, "What do Women Want on the Internet?" http://business.avn.com/articles/video/What-Do-Women-Want-On-The-Internet-41086.html.

64. Acme Anderson, "It Takes a Woman's Touch," *XBIZ* Feature, July 27, 2007, www.xbiz.com/articles/82439.

65. DWB post of Mar 11, 2014, on thread "Do you think that full scenes are overrated?" www.xbiz.net/index.php?c=discussion.view_thread&id=11123.

66. Erika Lust, *Good Porn: A Woman's Guide,* trans from Spanish (Berkeley: Seal Press, 2010), 4.

67. Catherine Pearson, "Meet the Powerful Women Directors Working in Porn," Aug 27, 2015, http://www.huffingtonpost.com/entry/meet-the-powerful-women-directors-working-in-porn_55ca50a7e4b0f1cbf1e68c13.

68. "More of What Women Want," Pornhub Insights, July 25, 2015, www.pornhub.com/insights/women-gender-demographics-searches.

69. Jodie Gummow, "What Kind of Porn Turns Women On?" AlterNet, Apr 8, 2014, www.alternet.org/gender/what-kind-of-porn-turns-women.

70. Veronica Hart discussion comment, in "Directors' Roundtable," *AVN*, 19 (1) (Jan 2003), 60.

71. Susan Dominus, "What Women Want to Watch," *NYT*, Aug 29, 2004, AR1.

72. http://www.gartner.com/newsroom/id/2996817.

73. Betsy Hauenstein, http://flipthemedia.com/2012/04/adding-value-to-paid-porn-with-quentin-boyer/.

74. http://www.porn.com/blog/porn-usage-in-the-modern-age/.

75. Alexander Poe, "Directors Say Technology Is Shaping the Future," *XBIZ Premiere*, Aug 2015, 54–55.

76. "The Golden Age of Pornhub," Pornhub Insights, Mar 2, 2015, www.pornhub.com/insights/pornhub-age.

77. Kelli Roberts post of Aug 10, 2014, on thread "700,000 Views on Hip Hop," www.xbiz.net/index.php?c=doscussion.view_thread&id=12715.

78. http://www.porn.com/blog/porn-usage-in-the-modern-age/.

79. "Porn in Your Pocket," *XBIZ* Feature, Aug 15, 2008, www.xbiz.com/articles/127920.

80. "Cell Erotica in the U.S.," *XBIZ* Feature, Mar 27, 2008, www.xbiz.com/articles/91669.

81. Charlie Warzel, Sept 24, 2015, http://www.buzzfeed.com/charliewarzel/if-they-build-it-will-we-come-meet-the-tech-entrepreneurs-tr?utm_term=.ds8KRkB6m#.fl2X64og5.

82. Master Ryan post of Mar 7, 2014, on thread "Adult industry is dead," www.xbiz.net/index.php?c=discussion.view_thread&id=11093.

83. Dan Miller, "Porn Panel Talks Mainstreaming of Erotica at USC," *XBIZ* News, Oct 15, 2015, www.xbiz.com/news/200183.

Glossary

1. Patchen Barss, *The Erotic Engine: How Pornography Has Powered Mass Communication from Gutenberg to Google* (Toronto: Anchor Canada, 2010), 171.

2. *XBIZ Premiere*, July 2015, 14.

3. Jayson Romaine, "Tina Tyler," *XBIZ* Feature, Mar 12, 2006, www.xbiz.com/80553.

4. Tom Byron, quoted in Legs McNeil and Jennifer Osborne, *The Other Hollywood* (New York: HarperCollins, 2005), 367.

5. Dan Savage, "Let's Vote," *The Stranger*, May 24, 2001, www.thestranger.com/seattle/SavageLove?old=7446.

6. Tim Case, "Bringing us to the King," Dec 18, 2002, www.mikesouth.com.

7. Andy Fair, "Straight Flash, Gay Cash?" *XBIZ* Feature, Feb 2, 2006, www.xbiz.com/articles/13230.

8. https://www.blackhatworld.com/seo/chartubate-white-label.1009954.

Index

as feminist, 89–90, 92
Femme Productions, 48–49, 90
in New York, 19–20
woodsmen, promotion of, 147–48
Rubin, Gayle, 68
Ruderman, Carl, 222
Rufus, JoJo, 107
Ruprecht, Holly, 16
Rutherford, John, 192, 193, 197
Ryder, Will, 111

Sacher-Masoch, Count von, 174
sadism, sexual, 150
Saharah Eve, 74, 155
Saint, Silvia, 107
Samantha, 144–145
Samantha38G (Samantha Anderson), 100, 226
San Fernando Valley. *See* Porn Valley
San Francisco scene, 23–25, 27, 40
Santoro, Tony, 230
Satana, Tura, 153
Saurini, Jocelyn, 209
Savage, Dan, 108, 164, 290n64
Savannah (Shannon Wilsey), 135
Sawyer, Diane, 62
Scandinavian films, 44
Scarborough, Steven, 192–193
Schaefer, Eric, 36
Schneider, Kurt, 10
Schneider, Maria (Marie Christine Gélin), 43
Seka (Dorothea Hundley Patton), 27, 90, 185
sensuality, modern emphasis on, 16, 253–254
Serenity, 211
Seven, Bruce (Bruce Behan), 121, 134
Severe Society Films, 179–180
Sex (Madonna), 181
sex addiction, 64–65
SexandSubmission.com, 179
sex-negative activism, 56–57
sex-positive pornography, 11, 19–20, 43
sex positivism, 7, 68–69
sex tech industry, 206
SexTracker, 239–240
sexual attraction, changes in, 198
sexual imagination, the, 12–13
sexuality, historical overview of, 8–11
sexuality threatening communities, 10
sexual responsiveness, 272n76
Shap, Sean, 102
Sheridan, Nicole, 109
Sheri's Ranch, 157
shooting pornography, 129–139
  as business, 133–134
  models, importance of, 132
  projecting desire, 137–139
  sets, 130–131

techniques for, 132–135
Tim Case's journal excerpt, 129–130
what not to do, 135–136, 196
Shubin, Steve, 211
Siffredi, Rocco, 31, 44, 107, 122, 144
Silvera, Joey, 144
Simone, Dominique, 235
Sin City Entertainment, 31
Sinclaire, Isabella, 155
sissification, 166–167
Sjöman, Vilgot, 41
Skow, B., 203
Slateford, Neal, 157–158, 216
Slater, J.D., 192
Slater, Ken, 199
SlutWerkz, 250
smartphones, 252–253
smoking porn, 153
social media, 251–253
societal changes, 16
Sofer, Brian, 220
South, Jim (James M. Souter, Jr.), 26, 32, 45, 71, 141
South, Mike (Mike Strothers)
  about, 76
  on abuse, 77, 96
  on escorting, 87
  on first timers, 76
  on girl/girl, 203
  on gonzo decline, 127
  on the Internet, 105, 110–111, 113
  on models, 71, 76–77, 80, 83
  on niches, 14
  on pegging, 164
  on sex in mainstream films, 241
  woodsmen, problems with, 141–142
Spallone, Rob, 141
Spangler, Larry G., 26
spanking, 162
Spears, Randy, 120
Spelvin, Georgina (Michelle Graham), 20, 42, 98
Spice Network, 30–31
Spinelli, Anthony (Sam Weinstein), 43, 97–98, 245
Sportsheets, 209–210
Sprinkle, Annie, 44, 89, 91
squirting, 115
Stabile, Michael, 157, 179
stag films, 36–37, 146
Stagliano, John. *See also* Evil Angel video company
  anal, promotion of, 121–122, 127, 187
  and features, 127
  on *Fifty Shades of Grey,* 158, 247
  and gonzo, 120, 121–122, 134
  on the Internet, 107